Introducing Windows® 7 for Developers

Yochay Kiriaty
Laurence Moroney
Sasha Goldshtein
and Alon Fliess

PUBLISHED BY
Microsoft Press
A Division of Microsoft Corporation
One Microsoft Way
Redmond, Washington 98052-6399

Library of Congress Control Number: 2009930293

Printed and bound in the United States of America.

1 2 3 4 5 6 7 8 9   WCT   4 3 2 1 0 9

Distributed in Canada by H.B. Fenn and Company Ltd.

A CIP catalogue record for this book is available from the British Library.

Microsoft Press books are available through booksellers and distributors worldwide. For further information about international editions, contact your local Microsoft Corporation office or contact Microsoft Press International directly at fax (425) 936-7329. Visit our Web site at www.microsoft.com/mspress. Send comments to mspinput@microsoft.com.

Microsoft, Microsoft Press, Access, ActiveX, Aero, ClearType, Direct3D, DirectX, Excel, Expression, Fluent, IntelliSense, Internet Explorer, MS, MSDN, Outlook, PowerPoint, Silverlight, SQL Server, Virtual Earth, Visual Basic, Visual C#, Visual C++, Visual Studio, Win32, Windows, Windows Live, Windows Media, Windows Mobile, Windows PowerShell, Windows Server and Windows Vista are either registered trademarks or trademarks of Microsoft Corporation in the United States and/or other countries. Other product and company names mentioned herein may be the trademarks of their respective owners.

The example companies, organizations, products, domain names, e-mail addresses, logos, people, places, and events depicted herein are fictitious. No association with any real company, organization, product, domain name, e-mail address, logo, person, place, or event is intended or should be inferred.

This book expresses the author's views and opinions. The information contained in this book is provided without any express, statutory, or implied warranties. Neither the authors, Microsoft Corporation, nor its resellers, or distributors will be held liable for any damages caused or alleged to be caused either directly or indirectly by this book.

Acquisitions Editor: Juliana Aldous
Developmental Editor: Maria Gargiulo
Project Editor: Lynn Finnel
Editorial Production: Christian Holdener, S4Carlisle Publishing Services
Technical Reviewer: Christophe Nasarre; Technical Review services provided by Content Master, a member of CM Group, Ltd.
Cover: Tom Draper Design

Body Part No. X15-74127

*To my lovely wife -Adi, and amazing kids -Alma and Tom, who had to "schedule" appointments
to see me and too
often had to hear "after I finish this chapter..."*

—Yochay Kiriaty, October 2009

*To Dina Zeliger, the love of my life, for her unconditional support.
To my grandfather Aaron, may you rest in peace.*

—Sasha Goldshtein, October 2009

*To my beloved wife Liat; to Yarden and Sa'ar, my cute boys; to Adva, my new girl that was born
during the writing of the book. Thank you all for your understanding and support.*

—Alon Fliess, October 2009

*To my family who put up with me while I was writing – not an easy task I'll tell you!
To Rebecca, Claudia and Christopher! Thanks guys!*

—Laurence Moroney, October 2009

Table of Contents

Foreword..xiii

Acknowledgments xv

Introduction..xvii

1   Welcome to Windows 7..1

     What Has Changed Since Windows Vista? 1

     Seven Ways to Shine on Windows 7..3

         Taskbar...4

         Libraries 6

         Touch, Multitouch, and Gestures...8

         Sensor and Location 9

         Ribbon 10

         Enhanced Graphics Platform..13

         Improved Fundamentals 15

     Summary...18

2   Integrate with the Windows 7 Taskbar: Basic Features 19

     Design Goals of the Windows 7 Taskbar..21

     A Feature Tour of the Windows 7 Taskbar 21

         Jump Lists 22

         Taskbar Overlay Icons and Progress Bars................................25

         Thumbnail Toolbars..26

         Live Window Thumbnails..27

         Backward Compatibility 29

     Integrating with the Windows 7 Taskbar...30

         Application ID...30

         Taskbar Progress Bars and Overlay Icons.................................35

     Summary...40

What do you think of this book? We want to hear from you!

Microsoft is interested in hearing your feedback so we can continually improve our books and learning resources for you. To participate in a brief online survey, please visit:

www.microsoft.com/learning/booksurvey/

**3   Integrate with the Windows 7 Taskbar:
Advanced Features**..**43**

Jump Lists 43

Anatomy of a Jump List.. 44

Recent and Frequent Destinations 45

Custom Destinations... 49

User Tasks 53

Thumbnail Toolbars.. 56

Customizing Thumbnails.. 59

Thumbnail Clipping 61

Custom Thumbnails 62

Custom Live Previews.. 65

Window Switchers.. 66

Summary 71

4   Organize My Data: Libraries in Windows 7..............................**73**

Windows Explorer 73

Changes Made to Windows Explorer in Windows 7 75

Welcome to Libraries 77

Libraries under the Hood 79

Working with Libraries.. 84

Summary 100

**5   Touch Me Now:
An Introduction to Multitouch Programming**............................ **101**

Multitouch in Windows 7 101

Windows 7 Multitouch Programming Models...104

The Good Model: Supporting Legacy Applications 104

The Better Model: Enhancing the Touch Experience....................105

The Best Model: Experience Optimized for Multitouch 106

How Multitouch Works in Windows 7...106

Architecture Overview: Messages Data Flow 107

Supporting Legacy Applications 108

Working with Gestures 110

Handling the WM_GESTURE Message...111

Use the Pan Gesture to Move an Object 113

Use the Zoom Gesture to Scale an Object 115

Use the Rotate Gesture to Turn an Object.................................... 117

Use a Two-Finger Tap to Mimic a Mouse Click 119

Use the Press-and-Tap Gesture to Mimic a Mouse Right-Click 121

Configuring Windows 7 Gestures... 121

Summary 124

6   Touch Me Now: Advanced Multitouch Programming 127

Working with Raw Touch Messages 127

Setting Up Windows for Touch 128

Unpacking WM_TOUCH Messages 129

Using the Manipulation and Inertia Engines 135

Multitouch Architecture: The Complete Picture, Part 1 136

Using Manipulation 138

Using Inertia 144

Multitouch Architecture: The Complete Picture, Part 2 145

Summary 151

7   Building Multitouch Applications in Managed Code 153

Building Your First Touch-Sensitive Application 153

Using Windows 7 Touch to Move an Object 155

Using Windows 7 Touch to Scale an Object 158

Using Windows 7 Touch to Rotate an Object....................................... 160

Using Inertia with Gestures 161

Extending for Multiple Objects.. 164

Building a Gesture-Enabled Picture Control 165

Using the Gesture-Enabled Picture Control 168

Classes to Support Touch and Gestures 170

UIElement Additions 171

Summary 172

8   Using Windows 7 Touch with Silverlight 173

Introducing Silverlight.. 173

Creating Your First Silverlight Application 176

Building Out-of-Browser Applications in Silverlight 179

Using the Silverlight *InkPresenter* Control 183

An Example of Ink Annotation in Silverlight................................. 184

Silverlight Ink Classes for JavaScript Programmers....................... 185

Programming for Ink in Silverlight 189
Using the Touch APIs in Silverlight...195
Expanding the Application for Multitouch................................196
Summary 200

9   Introduction to the Sensor and Location Platform 201
Why Sensors?...201
A Word on Security..203
Architecture of the Sensor and Location Platform...........................204
What Is a Sensor?..205
Working with Sensors 207
Integrating Sensors into Your Application 207
Discovering Sensors 207
Requesting Sensor Permissions 213
Interacting with Sensors 218
Reading Sensor Data Using Managed Code............................227
Ambient Light Sensor Application 230
Summary 232

10   Tell Me Where I Am: Location-Aware Applications 233
Why Location Awareness Is So Important 233
Location Platform Architecture..234
Location Devices Are Regular Windows 7 Sensors....................237
Location Information Is Sensitive Information 238
Working with the Location API 239
Understanding How the Location API Works 239
Requesting Location Permissions 242
Interacting with the Location Interface 244
Putting It All Together..254
Writing a Location-Aware Application Using .NET 255
Reading Location Reports and Handling Location Events 257
Using the Enhanced Default Location Provider Tool for Testing........259
Summary 260

11   Develop with the Windows Ribbon, Part 1 263
History 263
Using the Ribbon..267
Programming with the Windows Ribbon Framework 273

Ribbon Markup 275

Summary 307

12   Develop with the Windows Ribbon, Part 2 ....**309**

Programming the Ribbon 309

The Minimal Ribbon Revisited..310

Initialization Phase 316

Handling Ribbon Callbacks..318

The Property System 320

Setting Properties Directly or Indirectly...322

Controlling Controls 325

Setting Application Mode, and Showing
Contextual Tabs and Pop-Ups 347

Summary 353

13   Rediscover the Fundamentals: It's All About Performance **355**

Instrumentation and Diagnostics 356

Performance Counters 356

Windows Management Instrumentation 362

Event Tracing for Windows 365

Windows Performance Toolkit 365

Troubleshooting Platform 369

Performance and Efficiency...371

Background Services and Trigger Start Services 372

Power Management 378

Summary 382

Index..383

What do you think of this book? We want to hear from you!

Microsoft is interested in hearing your feedback so we can continually improve our books and learning resources for you. To participate in a brief online survey, please visit:

www.microsoft.com/learning/booksurvey/

Foreword

Windows 7 is arguably the best version of Windows ever. This might sound like a generic marketing claim, and if you consider that each version of Windows has more functionality, is more scalable, and supports the latest advances in hardware, each version of Windows is better than the last and hence the best version of Windows up to that point. Windows 7, however, not only delivers things that satisfy the basic check boxes required of any new release, but does it with an end-to-end polish that surpasses previous Windows releases.

Of course, Windows 7 couldn't be the great release it is without standing on the shoulders of the major advances and innovations of its predecessor, Windows Vista, but there are some differences in how Windows 7 was developed. Windows 7 is the first release of a Windows consumer operating system that actually requires fewer resources than the previous version—something that's pretty amazing considering the addition of all the new functionality. Reducing the memory footprint, minimizing background activity, and taking advantage of the latest hardware power-management capabilities all contribute to producing a sleek, yet modern, operating system that runs more efficiently on the same hardware that ran Windows Vista.

Another change from previous releases is the way Microsoft worked with PC manufacturers and hardware vendors. Throughout the Windows 7 development cycle, it kept them apprised of coming changes, shared tools and techniques, and sent engineers onsite to help them optimize their software and hardware for the new operating system. By the time of Windows 7 general availability, most partners had over a year of deep experience with the operating system, giving them plenty of time to tune and adapt their products.

While the under-the-hood and ecosystem efforts deliver the fundamentals, Windows 7 introduces a number of features that more directly enhance a user's experience. For example, the redesigned taskbar makes it easier for users to keep track of their running applications, navigate between multiple application windows, and quickly access their frequently used applications and documents. The Windows taskbar, which hadn't changed significantly from Windows 95, had become as comfortable as an old pair of slippers; but once you've used the new interface for any length of time, you'll feel cramped if you have to sit down at an older version of Windows.

Windows 7 also unlocks PC hardware devices that are becoming increasingly common, creating a platform that empowers applications to deliver more dynamic and adaptive experiences. Mobile PCs now adjust display brightness based on ambient light and have GPS and other sensors that give Windows a view of the world immediately around it. With the infrastructure and APIs for these devices delivered in Windows 7, applications can integrate with this view to provide users with information and modes of operation specific to the local environment.

As a user of Windows and a former independent software vendor (ISV), I know how disconcerting it is when an application exhibits user-interface constructs different from the ones we've grown to consider modern by the newest operating system release or version of Office we're using. It's also frustrating when you experience the seamlessness of an application that integrates with the operating system in a way that blurs the line between it and the operating system, and then run into others that seem to flout their nonconformity or shout that they were developed for 10-year-old operating systems.

The key to great software is not to force the user to learn idiosyncratic user-interface behaviors, feel like they're in a time warp when they run it, or wish that it took advantage of their PC's capabilities like other applications do. To delight the user, you need to keep abreast of technology and user-interface trends, recognize when your application can and should take advantage of them, and deliver valued innovation to your customers. Being on the cutting edge of the platform's capabilities helps your applications stand out from the competition and conveys the message to your customers that you're hip.

This book is a great one-stop resource for learning how you can make modern applications that use new PC hardware capabilities and allow users to quickly access common functionality. From using taskbar icons that show the progress of long-running operations, to taskbar icon jump lists that provide easy access to common tasks and recently used documents; from location APIs you use to deliver the most relevant results, to library APIs that allow you to integrate with and access a user's existing document collection; from a ribbon control that exposes the extent of your application's functionality and features, to supporting a touch interface for intuitive interaction—this book is your complete guide to bringing your applications into the 2010s.

For a programming book to be worth reading in this day of instant access to online documentation and code samples, it must provide complete and coherent introductions and overviews to new concepts as well as clearly explained and straightforward code samples that are easy to reuse. Yochay, Sasha, Laurence, and Alon have delivered both in this book that's sure to become your Windows 7 programming companion whether you program to .NET or Win32 APIs. I've started adding Windows 7 functionality to the Sysinternals tools and the description and example of how to exploit the taskbar icon's progress display enabled me to enhance the Sysinternals Disk2Vhd tool literally in a matter of minutes. I know I'll be turning to this as I continue to update the tools, and I'm confident you will too, as you strive to give your applications that extra edge.

Mark Russinovich
Technical Fellow
Windows Division, Microsoft Corporation

Introduction

Introducing Windows 7 for Developers was conceived before the Windows 7 Beta was released. Seeing the massive excitement that followed the Windows 7 debut at the Microsoft PDC keynote address in October 2008, we realized that Windows 7 was going to be a huge success. We realized then that with great performance improvements, an incredibly low memory and CPU footprint, exciting new user interface technologies, and continued investment in fundamentals Windows 7 was likely going to be the operating system of choice for users and the operating system that developers would target. We realized that many of its features—such as multitouch; hardware sensors, with light and 3D sensor devices and location awareness; libraries; the Homegroup and taskbar improvements; the new graphics platform; and many other features—would be likely to light up developer interest in this operating system.

Windows 7 offers numerous technologies and features to light up your application and make it shine. In this book, we chose to focus on the features we think bring the most added value to the end user experience and that require relatively little development effort. We try to highlight the variety of new features and technologies, and provide realistic and practical samples of how they are useful when using both native (C++) and managed (C#) APIs. Still, some of the features deserve more detailed treatment—in which case, we encourage you to learn more about them using the Windows SDK, the MSDN Library, the Microsoft Channel 9 Web site, and the numerous Windows 7 blogs that are springing up like mushrooms after rainfall.

Who This Book Is For

First and foremost, this is a book about developing applications for Windows. This book is intended for enthusiastic Windows developers willing to learn about the new features of Windows 7 and how to best integrate them with existing and new applications. Regardless of whether you are a C++ or .NET developer, this book leaves no developer behind as it offers samples and inline code snippets in both C++ and .NET. Even if you haven't programmed in C++ in your life, you will still find this book very useful as its "native" sections explain in details how the new features in Windows 7 works. Nonetheless some understanding of the Win32 programming paradigm will be advantageous.

What This Book Is About

The book begins with an overview of Windows 7 and the features developers primarily will use to make sure their applications shine on Windows 7. The remainder of the book provides a detailed tour of the Windows 7 features, where each of the major fundamental features has its own chapter or two. Finally, the last chapter of the book provides a much-needed perspective about system performance and instrumentation, lest they be forgotten in the rush of implementing more high-level, user-oriented features.

Chapter 1, "Welcome to Windows 7," traces the evolution of Windows 7 and introduces its new features and the key scenarios they help to enable, as well as the new opportunities these features open up for developers.

Chapter 2, "Integrate with the Windows 7 Taskbar: Basic Features," shows how the new taskbar represents an evolution of launch surfaces and provides insight into the design goals for the taskbar and User Experience (UX) guidelines.

Chapter 3, "Integrate with the Windows 7 Taskbar: Advanced Features," shows how to integrate the new taskbar with managed and native applications and how to use taskbar previews, Jump Lists, thumbnail toolbars, and other features.

Chapter 4, "Organize My Data: Libraries in Windows 7," demonstrates how users can take advantage of libraries to organize their data and how applications should be library-aware to maintain a consistent and organized experience.

Chapter 5, "Touch Me Now: An Introduction to Multitouch Programming" explains the rationale behind multitouch support in Windows 7, the multitouch architecture, and out-of-the-box multitouch gestures.

Chapter 6, "Touch Me Now: Advanced Multitouch Programming" focuses on advanced multitouch scenarios using raw touch events and using the manipulation and inertia processors.

Chapter 7, "Building Multitouch Applications in Managed Code," shows how the next version of Windows Presentation Foundation (WPF 4) (to ship with the Microsoft .NET Framework 4.0) supports multitouch applications on Windows 7.

Chapter 8, "Using Windows 7 Touch with Silverlight," focuses on how Microsoft Silverlight 3.0 supports multitouch on Windows 7 through the Windows integration mode as an out-of-browser application.

Chapter 9, "Introduction to the Sensor and Location Platform," introduces the architecture of the Windows 7 Sensor and Location Platform. The chapter also shows you how application developers as well as sensor providers can have an easier and more consistent experience using the platform from managed and native code.

Chapter 10, "Tell Me Where I Am: Location-Aware Applications," shows how location devices work in Windows 7 and how parts of the system, as well as applications, can enhance themselves with location awareness.

Chapter 11, "Develop with the Windows Ribbon, Part 1," describes the architecture of the Windows 7 Ribbon Framework and the declarative XML syntax for building Ribbon applications.

Chapter 12, "Develop with the Windows Ribbon, Part 2," shows how to load the Ribbon markup and integrate it with a Win32 application. The chapter also explains how to take advantage of the advanced Ribbon features.

Chapter 13, "Rediscover the Fundamentals: It's All About Performance," goes back to fundamental features such as instrumentation and tracing. It also looks at the background improvements in Windows 7, specifically trigger-start services and the Troubleshooting Platform.

Prerelease Software

This book was written and tested against the Beta, RC, and RTM versions of Windows 7. Microsoft released the final version of Windows (build number 7600) only a few weeks before the publication of this book. We did review and test our examples against the Windows 7 RTM milestone. However, you might find minor differences between the production release and the examples, text, and screen shots in this book.

Most of the .NET code in this book is based on the Windows API Code Pack for the .NET Framework (which you can read about and download from: *http://code.msdn.microsoft.com/WindowsAPICodePack*). This free open source library is provided by Microsoft for .NET developers to be able to take advantage of the new features found in Windows 7. This library is the closest thing to an official .NET API for Windows, but you should consider it as free open source library.

Chapter 7, "Building Multitouch Applications in Managed Code" uses The Microsoft .NET Framework 4.0 which will be released with Visual Studio 2010. This chapter is based on Visual Studio 2010 October CTP (Beta 2)

Companion Content

This book features a companion Web site that makes available to you all the code used in the book. This code is organized by chapter, and you can download it from the companion site at this address: *http://www.microsoft.com/learning/en/us/books/13697.aspx*.

Hardware and Software Requirements

You'll need the following hardware and software to work with the companion content included with this book:

- Microsoft Windows 7 Home Premium edition, Windows 7 Business edition, Windows 7 Enterprise edition, or Windows 7 Ultimate edition.

- Microsoft Visual Studio 2008 Standard edition, Visual Studio 2008 Professional edition, or Microsoft Visual C# 2008 Express edition and Microsoft Visual C++ 2008 Express edition.

- Microsoft Visual Studio 2010, October CTP (Beta 2) in any of its editions: Standard edition, Professional edition, or Express edition.

- Microsoft Windows 7 Software Development Kit.

- Microsoft Windows API Code Pack v1.0 or later.

- 1.6-GHz Pentium III+ processor, or faster.

- 1 GB of available, physical RAM.

- Video (1024 × 768 or higher resolution) monitor with at least 16-bit colors.

- Graphics card with DirectX 10 support.

- CD-ROM or DVD-ROM drive.

- Microsoft mouse or compatible pointing device.

- For testing multitouch application – a certified Windows 7multitouch device.

Support for This Book

Every effort has been made to ensure the accuracy of this book. As corrections or changes are collected, they will be added to a Microsoft Knowledge Base article accessible via the Microsoft Help and Support site. Microsoft Press provides support for books, including instructions for finding Knowledge Base articles, at the following Web site:

http://www.microsoft.com/learning/support/books/

If you have questions regarding the book that are not answered by visiting the site above or viewing a Knowledge Base article, send them to Microsoft Press via e-mail to *mspin-put@microsoft.com*.

Please note that Microsoft software product support is not offered through these addresses.

We Want to Hear from You

We welcome your feedback about this book. Please share your comments and ideas via the following short survey:

http://www.microsoft.com/learning/booksurvey

Your participation will help Microsoft Press create books that better meet your needs and your standards.

> **Note** We hope that you will give us detailed feedback via our survey. If you have questions about our publishing program, upcoming titles, or Microsoft Press in general, we encourage you to interact with us via Twitter at *http://twitter.com/MicrosoftPress*. For support issues, use only the e-mail address shown above.

Acknowledgments

There are four coauthors for this book, but the list of people who helped put this book together is too long to fit on a single page. We apologize in advance if we have forgotten anyone—thanks!

First, special thanks to Dima Zurbalev, senior consultant at Sela Group, who provided invaluable insight and help during the writing of most of this book's chapters. Without Dima's exceptional investigatorial and debugging skills, this book would not be as complete.

Thanks to David Bassa, Sela Group CEO, who supported Alon and Sasha in their decision to write this book and accepted countless excuses related to our sleepless nights.

This book would not be as detailed and accurate without the input and support of members of the Windows 7 development team, who explained how the APIs work, answered our questions, and provided useful code samples. We thank the following people for their input to: the book:

Ben Betz	Dan Polivy
Rob Jarrett	Gavin Gear
Greg Lett	Alec Berntson
David Washington	Nicolas Brun
Reed Townsend	Shawn Van Ness
	Ryan Demopolous

Finally, thanks to the following people from Microsoft Press: Maria Gargiulo, developmental editor; Lynn Finnel, project editor; Roger LeBlanc, copy editor; and Christophe Nasarre, technical reviewer. If it weren't for their extraordinary patience with the undisciplined authors of this book, we would never have made it.

Chapter 1
Welcome to Windows 7

Welcome to Windows 7, the latest operating system from Microsoft, which features great engineering, new innovations, exciting new features, and functionality that will deliver compelling new user experiences!

Windows 7 is by far the fastest, easiest to use, and most engaging version of Windows yet it's designed to take advantage of a new generation of hardware, such as screens or devices that support touch, including those that have multiple touch points, sensors of the environment, location providers, and more. In addition, the operating system offers some great new services, such as a built-in ribbon similar to the one you find in the Microsoft Office applications, and the Windows 7 taskbar, which provides a platform that allows your users to interact with your application more easily.

Another new feature is the Troubleshooting platform (TSP) that provides a consistent automated troubleshooting experience. This platform provides a standard way to diagnose, resolve and verify problems in Windows and in your application, driving better higher user satisfaction.

Beyond some of these developer-oriented features, Windows 7 is an upgrade across the board, containing a new search system that, as hard drives get bigger and computers store more content, allows you to find your stuff more quickly and accurately. The Windows Media Center, the center of the digital home, has been fully upgraded, with a new user experience and support for more hardware and HDTV.

Ultimately, the focus of this book is a specific set of new developer features and application programming interfaces (APIs) that will allow you to build better applications that can take advantage of the new features in Windows 7. Note that this book is looking only at what is new for developers, so if you've never built a Windows application before, some of the book's content might be a little difficult for you to grasp. However, we've tried to use examples that show you full applications that take advantage of some of the new features.

What Has Changed Since Windows Vista?

You might have already upgraded your Windows application to Windows Vista, or perhaps you might be happy with what Windows XP gives you. Either way, we understand that you might be hesitant to possibly having to handle some breaking changes in the operating system.

As a developer, all you really want is to be able to build applications that meet certain requirements, while maintaining application compatibility so that the application doesn't break on the new operating system. At the same time, you want to provide end users with a work environment they understand and feel comfortable navigating.

Helping you to do this is one of the core tenets the development team at Microsoft followed when building Windows 7. Although Windows 7 is built on the foundation laid with Windows Vista, the operating system fundamentals have been improved and a rock-solid infrastructure has been created that enables you to provide compelling user experiences.

Hundreds of changes have been made to the underlying infrastructure in Windows 7. And, it's important to note that these are not breaking changes. These are changes were made to the operating system to improve its performance and reliability. Windows 7 has a much smaller disk footprint than Windows Vista, it consumes significantly less memory, it consumes less CPU resources when idle, it performs less I/O activity, and—above all—the system consumes less power. At the same time, Windows 7 is much more responsive to user input and delivers better performance. There are no disturbances in the user interface, and user interactions with the system—whether it is handling input or showing the Start menu or taskbar—are immediate.

Windows 7 loads faster than ever, and it can scale up to 256 processors. This might sound like a large number, but keep in mind that Windows 7 needs to be in service for the next 5 to 8 years, and it's more than likely that we'll see such multicore desktop systems at some time during that period. Changes were made to the internal threading dispatchers, removing locks from critical resources to enable much faster context switching. All of that (and much more) was done while minimizing breaking changes and keeping a focus on stability, reliability, and performance. And most importantly, you will not be disturbed with changes that force you to spend time and money on nonfunctional features.

Microsoft also understands that for you to be a successful Windows developer, the operating system needs to support your efforts and include built-in tools and technologies that will help boost your productivity. Windows 7 ships with a large number of development tools and frameworks to assist with your development efforts and increase ease of deployment. Technologies such as .NET 3.5 Service Pack 1 (SP1), Windows PowerShell 2, MSI 5.0, Native Web Services API, and a new Ribbon Framework are just some examples of Windows 7 built-in technologies.

This is your opportunity to create new and exciting user experiences using all the great features that Windows 7 has to offer developers.

Seven Ways to Shine on Windows 7

Windows 7 offers numerous technologies and features to light up your application and make it shine. In this book, we chose to focus on the features we think bring the most added value to the end user experience and that require relatively little development effort. Think of these features as giving you the best overall user experience value for your time, effort, and money.

There is no single, silver bullet Windows 7 feature that transforms your application into the best Windows application. The built-in Windows features help you create amazing applications, but it's up to you to make the right decision about which features best fit your application scenarios. You can pick and choose any combination of Windows 7 features that will all play together, and thus create a solid application that uses the right features at the right time. From nonfunctional features such as Restart and Recovery or Kernel Transaction Manager, to more user-based features such as the new taskbar, Windows 7 Libraries, or multitouch. In this book, we'll focus on a few of the most important features and the ones that you are most likely to want to use while lighting up your application with Windows 7, such as the following:

- Taskbar

- Libraries

- Multitouch

- Sensor and location

- Ribbon

- Improved fundamentals

- Enhanced graphics platform

You can mix and match any of these seven features or any other Windows 7 features. All the features in the preceding list are independent of each other. There is no one single feature that you need to implement, but it make sense to make your application feel like a Windows 7 application by optimizing its taskbar behavior and making it properly work with Windows 7 Libraries. Next, you can start differentiating your application from others by creating next-generation user experiences that involve multitouch, sensors, location, the new ribbon, and the new graphics stack.

The rest of this chapter provides a short overview of the various technologies this book focuses on.

Taskbar

So you've got Windows 7 installed and you log on for the first time, eagerly waiting for the "Preparing your desktop . . ." prompt to go away. The first user-interface change you'll notice with Windows 7 is the new, reworked Windows taskbar.

Over the years, the Windows taskbar evolved into the somewhat cluttered form that you might be familiar with from Windows Vista. The abundance of launch surfaces made it more difficult for users to navigate to their favorite programs, switch between applications, and access frequent destinations. The new taskbar reflects many years of user-interface design and usability testing, and it represents a revolution in the design of launch surfaces. It has never been so easy to navigate Windows and windows—the new user interface is simple, intuitive, fresh, and clean. Users will find it easier to launch their favorite applications, to switch between windows, to control applications that do not currently have focus, and to reach their recent documents—all of which are just a mouse click away. The following illustration shows the sleek, clean look of the Windows 7 taskbar and Start menu:

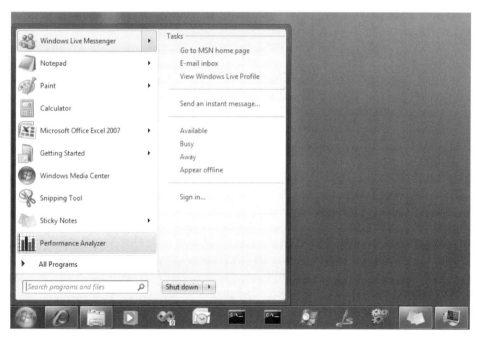

This book will show you the new features of the Windows 7 taskbar, as well as explain how to ensure your application takes advantage of every relevant piece of functionality. In Chapter 2, "Integrate with the Windows 7 Taskbar: Basic Features," we show you how to use the new taskbar features that require relatively little effort on your part—providing a progress indicator through a taskbar button, showing an overlay icon that gives additional status information, and distinguishing windows and applications by assigning them separate taskbar buttons. In Chapter 3, "Integrate with the Windows 7 Taskbar: Advanced Features," we discuss the more sophisticated features that users will come to expect from your application—thumbnail toolbars for remotely controlling a window from its taskbar thumbnail, jump lists for quickly accessing recent documents and frequent tasks, tools for completely customizing taskbar thumbnails, and tools for creating live window previews. All of these features combine to deliver a compelling experience to users of your applications.

In these two chapters, you'll learn how Internet Explorer presents live previews of its internal Web page tabs, how Windows Media Player enables you to play music from its application thumbnail, how Windows Live Messenger allows you to change your online availability and navigate to your e-mail inbox from its jump list, and how Sticky Notes shows you a thumbnail of a stack of notes and allows you to create another note with a single click of the mouse. The following screen shot shows Internet Explorer 8 tabs as taskbar button thumbnails:

Throughout these chapters, we'll look at the native Windows APIs that make this magic possible, including the underlying COM interfaces, window messages, and Win32 functions. We'll also use the Windows API Code Pack for Microsoft .NET Framework to interact with Windows 7 from managed code. We'll do this by using a well-designed layer of abstraction for organizing taskbar features that will be immediately familiar to you if you're writing code with the .NET Framework.

Almost every application needs the new taskbar to truly shine on Windows 7. If you're writing a document-oriented application, you can give your users immediate access to their recent and frequent documents. If you're developing an application rich with media, you can give your users a thumbnail toolbar for quick access to media-oriented operations and live, vivid previews of your application from the taskbar button. If you're programming a utility that lurks in the background and pops up only once in a while, you might find that the best place for your application is on the Windows taskbar, where it can give users a live progress indicator and a status icon. Even if you're programming for the browser, one day you'll find that your users are eager to have your application out of the browser because they're enjoying the rich world of the Windows 7 taskbar.

Libraries

Since Windows XP, you've had the option to store your content (documents, videos, pictures, or any other files) in a set of special dedicated folders such as My Documents and My Pictures. These folders are unique for each user, and in Windows Vista they were automatically indexed to provide a superior search experience. But didn't you wish you were able to extend these special folders and include additional folders on your local hard drive or on remote shares? Libraries in Windows 7 allow you to do just that!

With Windows 7 Libraries, you are in control of your data. Using Windows 7 Libraries enables you to manage your own set of folders for various purposes, or add more folders to the My Images library. Libraries are user-defined collections of folders aggregated into a single unified view. By including folders in Libraries, the user is telling Windows (and you the developer) where his important data is located.

Windows 7 Libraries are the users' new entry point for accessing their data. Users will go to Libraries to manage their documents, music, pictures, and other files. And users will expect your application to work with Libraries because they are an integral part of the Windows Shell and play a dominant role within Windows Explorer and other parts of the operating system, such as the Common File dialog.

In some ways, a library is similar to a folder. From a user's point of view, a library looks and behaves just like a regular folder. However, unlike a folder, a library gathers files that are stored in several locations into a unified view. This is a subtle but important difference between a library and a folder. Libraries don't actually store users' items, they only monitor folders that contain items and let users access and arrange these items in different ways. Nonetheless, let's perform a little experiment. Go ahead and launch Notepad and try to save the file to the Documents library. The save operation will complete successfully. However, we just said that libraries are not regular folders that contain files, so what's going on here?

In Chapter 4, "Organize My Data: Libraries in Windows 7," you will read all about Windows 7 Libraries. By reading this chapter, you'll gain an understanding of the underlying architecture of the Libraries feature and see why saving files to the Documents (or any other) library works in Windows 7. The chapter also explains in detail the API needed to work and manage Windows 7 Libraries. You might find that your application already supports Libraries, but even if your application does not, you'll see that it doesn't take a lot of effort to turn your application into a library-aware application that can work and consume Windows 7 Libraries content. As we do in most chapters of this book, we address both the native C++ (mostly COM) APIs and, where possible, the managed code APIs. We explain the architecture and concepts using the native API and dive into specific examples of how to use the new Libraries API using the managed code API.

Almost any Windows application that enables user to load and save files from the local hard drive will want to seamlessly integrate with Windows 7 Libraries to enable users to enjoy the rich search and visual experience offered by Windows Explorer and to have a friction-free experience while running on Windows 7.

Touch, Multitouch, and Gestures

Whenever you see a demonstration of Windows 7, touch, multitouch, and gestures are likely the most prominent features in the demonstration. Since Microsoft first demonstrated the Surface platform, interest in applications and scenarios that allow the user to touch the screen in multiple places to interact with user interfaces has reached an all-time high! Windows 7 fully supports touch interfaces, and it's flexible enough to handle many different touch types. You might be familiar with building applications for touch with Tablet PCs using the inking subsystem, but that's just the beginning.

Because of the importance and popularity of these features, we spend a lot of time in this book talking about the new multitouch APIs. We first go into detail about how the underlying system works and how the operating system manages the vastly diverse touch hardware. In the past, the only touch hardware was either a Tablet PC containing a single input via a pen or specialized hardware having specialized drivers that a developer would have to learn. With Windows 7, hardware vendors can now build screens or external devices and hook them up to the new touch driver system, and you as a developer can take advantage of this.

In Chapter 5, "Touch Me Now: An Introduction to Multitouch Programming," we cover the basic concepts of Windows multitouch programming and provide a detailed architecture review as well as a thorough review of the native C++ (COM) APIs. This chapter mainly focuses on the Windows 7 built-in gesture engine, which enables developers to enhance their application with multitouch support with very little effort.

In Chapter 6, "Touch Me Now: Advanced Multitouch Programming" we'll move up the stack a little bit and look at the .NET Framework and in particular the Windows Presentation Foundation. If you're not familiar with these, the .NET Framework is a set of classes built for you by Microsoft that provide a friendlier programming interface that can be used with languages such as Microsoft Visual Basic or C#. One part of the .NET Framework is the Windows Presentation Foundation, which is designed to provide access to everything you need to build the visual layer of a rich UI application. Of course, the touch system falls under this domain, and version 4.0 of WPF provides not just access to the touch system but also to a group of APIs that tell you about user gestures.

A gesture is a fixed action that can happen in a multitouch environment. To understand this, think about how you would interact with a photograph in a multitouch environment. Typically, a photograph is rendered as a rectangle oriented vertically. You can zoom in and out usually with a mouse wheel or a slider. But what about when you can touch the screen? Wouldn't it be nice if you could put your thumb on one corner and your index finger on the opposite corner and then bring your fingers together to make the picture get smaller as the corners follow your fingers? In a similar vein, you can make the picture bigger by moving your fingers apart, rotate it by twisting your wrist, or move it to another part of the screen by moving your hand and having the picture follow it. These are the concepts in Windows 7 that are called *gestures*. In Chapter 6, you'll see how you can easily add gesture support to your application.

In Chapter 7, "Building Multitouch Applications in Managed Code," we deepen our discussion and dive into more powerful and more complex multitouch APIs. This chapter covers Windows 7 raw-touch support and the native manipulation and inertia engines.

In these two chapters, you'll get a full tour of the multitouch features, and after finishing them you'll have a good understanding of how the touch system works in Windows 7. These two chapters are not required for the two chapters that follow them, which deal with Windows Presentation Foundation (WPF) and Silverlight multitouch. However, they'll provide you with a solid understanding of the relevant parts of the architecture, making it easier for you to understand the .NET multitouch abstraction layers.

Microsoft released a technology called Silverlight in 2007. Silverlight is a browser plug-in that provides a rich programming interface and a miniature version of the .NET Framework that allows you to build and easily deploy applications that can take advantage of features of the operating system. A feature of Silverlight that makes it compelling is the ability for it to be run out-of-browser, whereby a user can choose to remove the dependency of the application on the browser and install it to her desktop. In Chapter 8, Using Windows 7 Touch with Silverlight," we'll look at Silverlight—what it is and what it does. You'll see how easy it is to build an application in .NET that is delivered across the Internet using Silverlight. You'll then see how to add touch to your Silverlight application in Windows 7 by using the inking capabilities for Tablet PCs as well as the raw touch objects that allow you to process multitouch messages.

By the end of Chapter 8, you'll know all you need to know about touch and a whole lot more—from the underlying touch system to the .NET APIs for gesturing provided by WPF, all the way up to adding touch functionality to rich Web applications.

Sensor and Location

The Sensor and Location Platform is among the coolest and most useful new technologies offered in Windows 7, for both users and developers. The Windows 7 Sensor and Location Platform enables developers to create adaptive applications that can change the way the application looks and behaves according to different environmental conditions. You might wonder why even bother with this type of functionality, but take a quick look around you. You see mobile devices that change their display orientation based on the relative position of the device. More and more computers include an ambient light sensor that allows your computer to automatically adjust your screen's brightness based on the current lighting conditions, so when you use your computer in a dark environment, you don't have to strain your eyes.

Ambient light sensors also enable applications to optimize their content for readability, making your computer more useful and user friendly in a wider range of operating environments than ever before.

The Sensor and Location Platform provides a standard way to integrate sensor and location devices into Windows, as well as a standard programming interface for applications to take advantage of these devices. Lack of such functionality has been a long-standing problem, because previously Windows developers had to choose specific sensor hardware and sets of APIs to work with in their applications. Switching between different vendors was extremely expensive because of the lack of standardization. And with Windows 7, applications have a uniform, standard interface to use the sensors on data, and the user has control over how data from these sensors is exposed to applications.

In this book, we dedicated two chapters to the Windows 7 Sensor and Location Platform. Chapter 9, "Introduction to the Sensor and Location Platform," provides an introduction to the Sensor and Location Platform. The chapter focuses on the core architecture of the platform and explains the role of the different components. Next, the chapter describes the way developers can integrate sensory inputs into their applications by discovering sensors and programmatically accessing data that the sensors provide. By the end of Chapter 9, you'll know how to program both the native C++ (COM) APIs as well as the .NET-managed APIs.

Chapter 10, "Tell Me Where I Am: Location-Aware Applications," explains in detail the location part of the platform. The Windows Location APIs, which are a dedicated set of higher-level abstraction APIs, are built on top of the Windows 7 Sensor platform. The Location APIs exist to answer one simple question: "Where am I, or what is my current location?" The answer is simple because it is stated as a set of values representing longitude, latitude, and an error radius. There is so much you can do with accurate real-time location information—you can have location-based services that can optimize a search for your current location or a mapping application that focuses on your current position and keeps track of it as you travel and change your location. After reading Chapter 10, you'll know everything that you need to know for integrating location into your application and see how easy it is to integrate the location APIs with your application.

Ribbon

When you start the Microsoft Paint program in Windows 7, what is the first thing you notice? What has changed since Windows Vista (or should we say, "Since Windows XP")? Now start WordPad. What do you see? In Windows 7, there are new versions of the popular Paint and WordPad applications (See Figure 1-1).

Both applications include new features such as the ability to paint with all your fingers (on a multitouch machine) or open a Word 2007 .docx document without having Microsoft Office

Word 2007 installed on your computer. But the most noticeable change is the new Ribbon user interface.

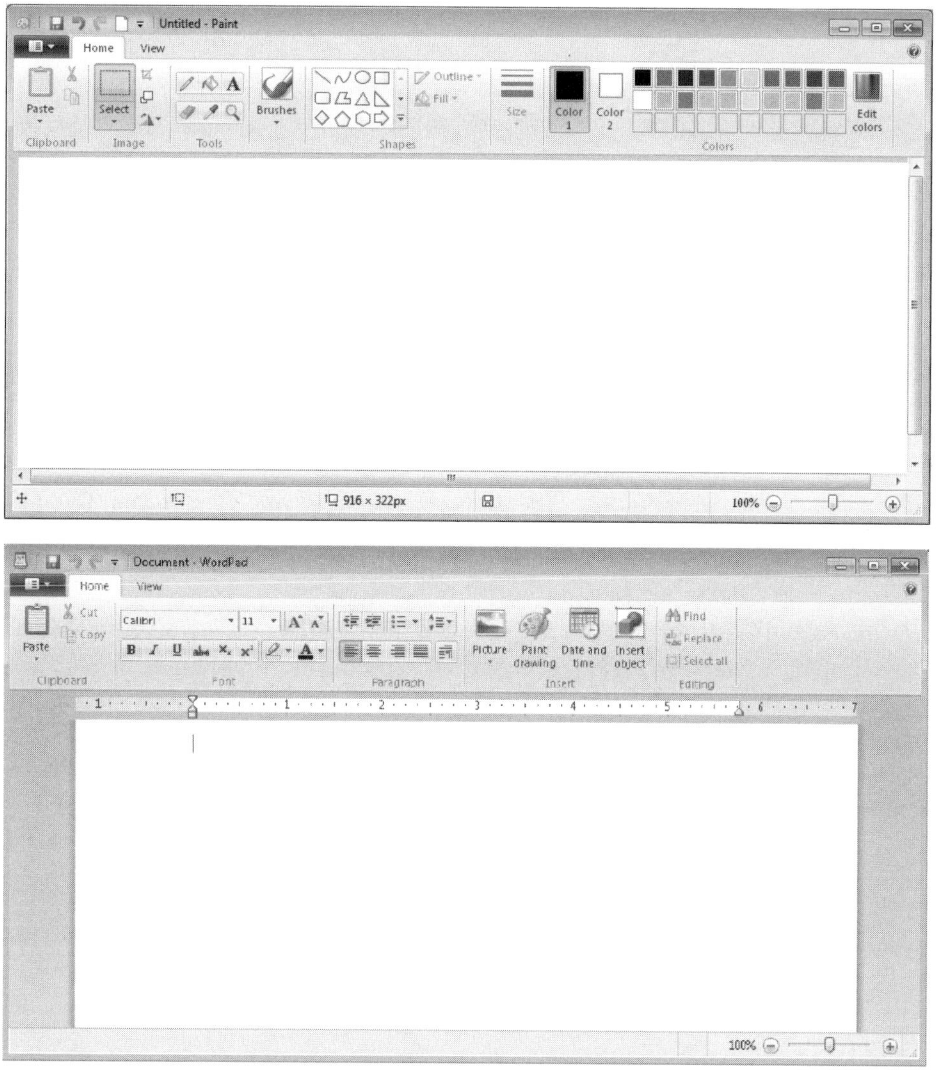

Figure 1-1   The new look of Paint (in the top screen shot) and WordPad (in the bottom screen shot)

We are living in an era in which software is everywhere and used by everyone. Alon's 3-year-old son watches TV using Windows Media Center. His mother sends e-mail to her friends, and his home automation system is programmed to control the TV and to send timed e-mail messages—and it also wakes him up every morning by raising the shutters on his bedroom windows. Nowadays software is much more complicated than it used to be. There are many more features, we can do much more with it, and we can use it to help realize our potential. However, the user interface and, more importantly, the user experience provided by most Windows applications has not changed much to support all these new features and uses of software. It's a bit like using a car's steering wheel and pedals to fly an airplane!

The first group within Microsoft to understand that the traditional user interface based on menus and toolbars was failing the user was the Office development team. With each new release of Office, new features were added, but no one found or used them. The product became more and more complicated. The user interface became bloated. People felt that they could do more, but they didn't know how.

In Office 2007, the Office team took another, refreshing, user interface (UI) design approach— instead of thinking about commands, they thought about features. They call it result-oriented design. The Ribbon was born and, with it, a new user experience. Using the power of the modern CPUs combined with visual galleries, the Ribbon can show the outcome of an action whenever the mouse cursor is hovering over the command icons. If you want to set a style, just hover the cursor over each of the style icons in the style gallery. Any style that gets the focus shows you a preview of how the document would change to reflect it. The user just needs to pick the style that makes the document look best. The feature-based design makes Office 2007 much more productive than any older version of Office.

As always, the Office team is the user-interface pioneer. We can find many followers of their fine example by looking at the UI elements in other Microsoft products, such as the new Ribbon support in Visual Studio 2008 SP1 Microsoft Foundation Classes (MFC) or the Ribbon toolkit for WPF and Windows 7 introduces the Windows Ribbon Framework. It has never been so easy to have a rich user interface and provide a positive user experience in Win32-based applications.

In many modern user-interface frameworks, the UI part is separated from the code that handles UI events and controls the business logic. In the case of the Windows Ribbon Framework, the UI is written using XML-based markup language that is similar to the WPF XAML in many ways, whereas the code-behind compilation unit uses COM as its interfacing technology.

Chapter 11, "Develop with the Windows Ribbon, Part 1," lays the foundation for understanding and using the Windows Ribbon Framework. This chapter deals with the Ribbon building blocks. You'll see how to create the Ribbon using its markup language and how to set its sizing behavior; you'll become familiar with the various Ribbon controls. As a side benefit, you'll even become a better user of the Ribbon!

In Chapter 12, "Develop with the Windiws Ribbon, Part 2," you'll see how to program with the Windows Ribbon Framework, how to initialize and load the Ribbon, how to interact with it, how to reflect the application state in the UI, and how to support the Office Fluent UI approach.

Even if you are a .NET developer who will not use the Windows Ribbon Framework, we encourage you to read the chapters related to it to get a better understanding of this new user-interface concept. Then, based on the technology you are using (Web, WPF, or Windows Forms), pick the most suitable Ribbon control suite. Native developers can take their old applications and make them shine on Windows 7!

Enhanced Graphics Platform

This book doesn't include any chapters on the new graphics stack available in Windows 7. It looked like there was going to be too much information to fit into one, two, or even three chapters, and we didn't want to turn a substantial part of this book into a "Developing Windows 7 Graphics" course. With that said, the new DirectX graphics stack in Windows 7 offers innovations and great tools for developers to easily create hardware-accelerated 2D and text applications, on top of the DirectX APIs. So we decided to write a little bit about the enhancements to the graphics platform in Windows 7 to at least provide a high-level overview.

Before Windows 7

The Microsoft Windows graphics device interface (GDI) enables applications to use graphics and formatted text on both the video display and the printer. Windows-based applications do not access the graphics hardware directly. Instead, GDI interacts with device drivers on behalf of applications. Since Windows 3.0, developers have been using GDI, and since the release of Windows XP a lot of applications have been exploiting GDI+, which is a completely new set of APIs. Even higher abstraction layers, such as the .NET WinForms rendering, are based on GDI+. With that said, Windows application developers have long used DirectX to provide high-quality, hardware-accelerated, 3D graphics. When the technology debuted in 1995, developers could provide high-quality 3D graphics for games and engineering applications for gamers and professionals willing to pay extra for a 3D-graphics board. Now, even the most inexpensive PCs include capable 3D-graphics hardware. The WPF rendering engine uses DirectX and allows managed code developers to write cutting-edge graphical applications that are hardware accelerated.

In Windows Vista, the Windows Display Driver Model (WDDM) was introduced. The WDDM infrastructure for DirectX enabled multiple applications and services to share the resources of the Graphical Processing Unit (GPU). The Desktop Window Manager (DWM) uses this technology to animate task switching in 3D, to provide dynamic thumbnail images of application windows, and to provide Windows Aero glass effects for desktop applications.

New in Windows 7

In Windows 7, Microsoft introduced a more modern set of APIs, which we hope will eventually help replace GDI+. Windows 7 places more graphics capabilities into the hands of application developers. Through a new set of DirectX APIs, Win32, and managed code, developers can take advantage of the latest innovations in GPUs to add to their applications fast, scalable, high-quality, 2D and 3D graphics; text; and images. All these new technologies were designed to interoperate with GDI and GDI+, ensuring that developers can easily preserve their existing investment and providing a clear migration path.

These enhanced graphics capabilities are provided by the following COM-based APIs (and some are also available in managed code through the Windows API Code Pack):

- Direct2D for drawing 2D graphics

- DirectWrite for arranging and rendering text

- Windows Imaging Component (WIC) for processing and displaying images

- Direct3D 10 for drawing 3D graphics

- Direct3D 11 for drawing 3D graphics and providing access to next-generation GPU technologies, such as tessellation, limited support for texture streaming, and general-purpose computing

- DirectX Graphics Infrastructure (DXGI) for managing devices and GPU resources and providing interoperability between DirectX and GDI

Direct2D   Built on Direct3D, Direct2D offers Win32 developers immediate-mode, resolution-independent, 2D APIs that use the power of the graphics hardware. Direct2D provides high-quality 2D rendering with performance superior to GDI and GDI+ even when using full-software rendering without hardware acceleration. It provides Win32 and managed-code developers finer control over resources and their management and a higher abstraction of the complex DirectX APIs.

DirectWrite   A great deal of Windows applications target worldwide users, which often means using multiple languages. This calls for a technology that supports high-quality text rendering, resolution independence, and Unicode text and layout. GDI and GDI+ do not provide these features, but DirectWrite, a new DirectX component, provides these features and more. DirectWrite provides the following capabilities:

- High-quality, sub-pixel, ClearType text rendering that can use GDI, Direct2D, or application-specific rendering technologies

- Hardware-accelerated text, when used with Direct2D

- A device-independent text layout system that improves text readability in documents and in the UI

- Support for multiformat text

- GDI-compatible layout and rendering

- Support for advanced typography features

The DirectWrite font system enables "any font, anywhere" font usage, where users don't have to perform a separate installation step just to use a font. It also has an improved structural hierarchy for font groupings to help with manual or programmatic font discovery. The APIs support measuring, drawing, and hit-testing of multiformat text, as shown in Figure 1-2.

Figure 1-2   An example of text drawn using DirectWrite

The new graphics API in Windows 7 offer many existing GDI+-based applications clear and developer-friendly integration path to the newer APIs.

Improved Fundamentals

The features described in the previous sections might tempt you to doubt the performance of Windows 7. After all, how is it possible to integrate so much additional functionality into the operating system without hurting performance even a little bit? Surely, every additional feature requires another upgrade of your computer's RAM, a faster CPU, and a larger hard drive.

In fact, Windows 7 has the same hardware requirements as Windows Vista, and it runs faster on any hardware. As I write this, I'm running the RTM build of Windows 7 on my 9-inch netbook, which "features" a single, low-end 900-MHz CPU and 1 GB of physical memory. It's equipped with an extremely slow 16-GB, solid-state hard drive, which made even Internet browsing nearly impossible when I had Windows XP installed. This particular netbook has been running Windows 7 since the Release Candidate, and I've never been happier about its performance.

This represents a great effort by the Windows developers to improve the system's performance and reliability with regard to nearly every feature of the operating system. Windows 7 boots faster, enters standby mode faster, hibernates faster, and shuts down faster than ever before. Windows 7 runs for hours with 0% CPU utilization and barely noticeable memory usage, it consumes less power, and it conserves more system resources than its predecessors.

But wait, there's more! Windows 7 supports 256 cores, which gives you quite some time before you need to start worrying about seeing hardware that can't be used to its full capacity by the operating system. Windows 7 takes advantage of the latest advances in CPU and memory architecture—the Non-Uniform Memory Access (NUMA) paradigm—and it features scalability improvements across the board. Windows 7 also has additional improvements to power management and energy consumption so that your mobile PC lasts an entire day in the field. You'll also find fewer background services running at any given time, and you'll see that some tasks will trigger-start only when you really need them—for example, when connecting to a network or when adding an external digitizer device, a Bluetooth component, or a USB dongle to your system.

Indeed, two of the major requirements of Windows users for the past few years have been for the system to run faster and consume fewer resources. This is impossible to achieve from the operating system end alone—it requires cooperation and hard work from you, developers writing software for Windows 7. Other than the amazing effort put into the Windows kernel to improve performance, there are some things you need to know about to make sure your users enjoy the same experience with your applications as they do with an out-of-the-box installation of Windows 7.

Windows 7 does not leave you alone with this daunting task. There are great tools, which we'll explore in the closing chapter of this book, that will assist you in profiling, troubleshooting, and monitoring the performance of your applications. Windows 7 works great with the Windows Performance Toolkit, which serves as a profiler and performance analyzer. Windows 7 builds on the foundation laid by Windows Vista with improvements to the Performance Monitor and the Reliability Monitor. Windows 7 supports production debugging techniques that will make it easier to troubleshoot your applications in the field. Windows 7 even features a Troubleshooting Platform to ensure that your users will be able to solve problems on their own—and if they don't, the Problem Steps Recorder will always be there to assist them with reproducing the problem and sending it to you to analyze. Some of these Windows 7 tools are depicted in the following screen shots:

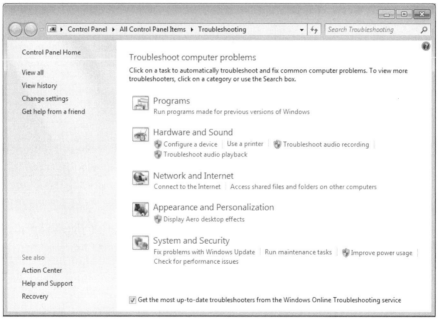

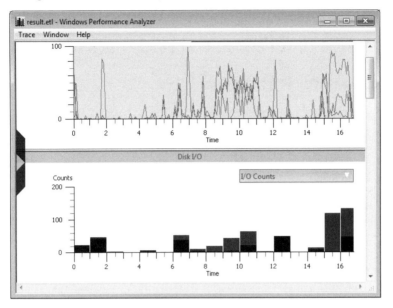

And finally, if you stumble across a legacy application that doesn't work quite right on Windows 7, you can always use the built-in Windows XP virtual machine that is integrated into the operating system. You can have a Windows XP application running on your Windows 7 desktop, with the familiar, working Windows XP look and feel.

Summary

Welcome to Windows 7! The book that you have in your hands is the result of hundreds of hours of work by the authors cutting through the mystery of the new APIs to put together specific, tangible, and actionable solutions to help you quickly master the use of the new features in Windows 7.

We hope this chapter whetted your appetite to learn more about the major new features of Windows 7. Now that the overview is done, let's get into more detail, starting with the new Windows 7 taskbar, and how you can use it to light up your Windows 7 applications!

Chapter 2
Integrate with the Windows 7 Taskbar: Basic Features

Excitement and anticipation were with me everywhere I went at the Microsoft Professional Developers Conference (PDC) in October 2008. New technologies were being announced at every corner; you couldn't find your way from one session to another without seeing another lab, another ad, another brochure on yet another Microsoft technology. And yet the most exciting attraction of all, for me, was the unveiling of Windows 7, Microsoft's new operating system. With eyes glued to the screen, thousands of attendees waited as Steven Sinofsky showed us around the M3 (6801) build of Windows 7.

The first feature that had everyone nodding with approval was the new Windows 7 taskbar. It was like a breath of fresh air in the conditioned air of the keynote hall, and it contributes to the sleek, light look of Windows 7.

Why is the Windows 7 taskbar so different from previous versions of Windows? What happened to the slow, methodical evolution of features being added with every release? Previous versions of Windows gave us the Quick Launch bar, desktop icons, the system tray, the Start menu, the Search text box, the Run dialog, and many other launch surfaces— consolidating them all into square taskbar buttons seemed like a bold move. Some might say it was returning to the roots of the Windows user interface, the taskbar of Windows 1.0:

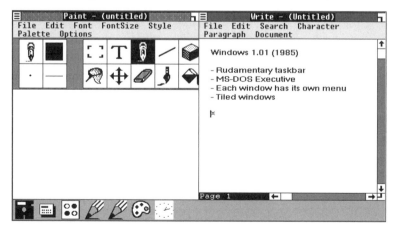

Compare the preceding screen shot to the initial user interface of the Windows Vista desktop:

If I were a user of Windows 1.0 who saw the Windows Vista desktop for the first time and was asked how to open Outlook, I would be confused—I see multiple Outlook icons!

Apparently, as indicated by telemetry information collected at Microsoft over several years and by usability studies conducted with thousands of users, quantity does not always translate to quality. When user interface design is concerned, it's often advisable to have only one way of accomplishing a given task. Again, a multitude of ways to do something can be more confusing than liberating. When most users work with fewer than 10 open windows during their session and most "advanced" features offered by the existing taskbar are not used, there is no choice but to radically redesign the state of affairs. This redesign gives us the new Windows 7 taskbar. It is a *revolution* in the design of launch surfaces.

> **Note** An analysis of user sessions, open windows, and taskbar customizations performed by Microsoft and discussed at the PDC 2008 reveals that 90 percent of user sessions involve fewer than 15 open windows, 70 percent of user sessions involve fewer than 10 windows, and nondefault taskbar options (such as auto-hide, docking the taskbar at the top of the screen, and so forth) are used by fewer than 10 percent of users. Some other options are used by fewer than 1 percent of users.
>
> A good bit of the Windows UI was designed and implemented for complicated scenarios and affected the user's ability to easily switch between windows and to launch applications. This was not acceptable and led to the revolutionary changes seen in the Windows 7 taskbar.

Running applications, multiple instances of running applications, pinned programs—these concepts are all consolidated into the new taskbar. The Quick Launch toolbar is deprecated, the notification area (system tray) is considered out of bounds for applications, and large taskbar buttons dominate the user experience after the first logon to Windows 7.

This chapter takes you through the design goals of the Windows 7 taskbar and on a whirlwind tour of its new features. We explore in depth the governing principle of the application ID and see how to light up applications with taskbar overlay icons and progress bars. In the next chapter, we'll take a look at the taskbar's more advanced features.

Design Goals of the Windows 7 Taskbar

The Windows 7 taskbar was engineered with several design goals in mind, resulting from a series of usability studies and requirements processing. These design goals are as follows:

- **Single launch surface for frequently used programs and favorite destinations** Applications and data that you use all the time should be at your fingertips—no more scouring through the Start menu to find your favorite photo album application. Recent documents, frequently visited Web sites, and favorite photos should all be a click away via the new taskbar.

- **Easily controllable**   Windows and running applications should be easily controllable and reachable for the user. Switching between applications, controlling the activity of another window, and obtaining a live preview of another window should all be performed without loss of productivity.

- **Clean, noise-free, simple**   Plagued with features creeping into new releases of Windows, the "old" taskbar was crippled with desk bands, toolbars, notification icons, context menus—each customized for yet another application. The Windows 7 taskbar has a sleek, clean appearance because it's the first UI element to greet the user after the logon screen.

- **Revolution**   The Windows 7 taskbar offers new extensibility opportunities as well as differentiating opportunities for applications willing to take advantage of the new user experience design guidelines. Adhering to the design guidelines of the Windows 7 taskbar is almost guaranteed to improve your application's usability and your users' productivity.

A Feature Tour of the Windows 7 Taskbar

Large, animated taskbar buttons greet you at the gate of the Windows 7 desktop. Highlighted as you hover over them with your cursor and slightly morphing when you click them or touch them with your finger, taskbar buttons are a vivid representation of running programs and of shortcuts for launching applications. Running applications are always visible in the taskbar;

applications can be pinned to the taskbar by the user (and by the user *only*) for quick-access launching.

Four visual effects are used to distinguish between taskbar button states, all of which are shown here:

The Internet Explorer icon (the first one after the Start button at the far left) is enclosed in a rectangle, meaning that it's currently running. The stacked taskbar buttons that appear behind it (which you can see behind the right edge of the Internet Explorer icon) indicate that multiple Internet Explorer windows are currently running on the system. Clicking the stack brings up an array of thumbnails that represent the various windows of Internet Explorer and allow you to effortlessly bring to the front a specific window.

Next from the left, the new Windows Explorer icon is enclosed in a rectangle without any stacked buttons behind it, meaning that only one Explorer window is currently open. It's followed by the Windows Media Player and Microsoft Visual Studio buttons, neither of which is enclosed by a rectangle, meaning that both are currently not running. Clicking one of these buttons launches the associated application.

The second button from the right is the Microsoft Office Outlook taskbar button, which has a light-colored background, indicating that it's the currently active application. Finally, the icon on the far right is a command prompt, and it's highlighted because the mouse pointer is currently hovering over it. This feature is called *Color Hot-Tracking*, and it uses a blend of colors from the application's icon to determine the dynamic ambience of the button.

Taskbar buttons are the clean façade of the Windows 7 taskbar, and behind them is an abundance of new functionality for us to explore.

Jump Lists

Right-click any taskbar button, and there's a menu of choices sliding from the bottom of the screen (or from another side if you repositioned your taskbar), giving you access to frequent tasks and destinations for your application. (*Destinations* are files your application can open and handle and that can be grouped into categories.)

The Start menu has been the canonical location for application tasks and documents for all applications installed on the system. To launch an application, you would wearily navigate the Start menu until you reached its program group. To take a quick look at your recent Microsoft Office Excel spreadsheets in this paradigm, you have to manually filter out recent documents from all other programs—programs that you're not interested in seeing at that moment.

The jump list is your application's opportunity to have its very own mini Start menu—an area where you can group popular tasks and destinations to enhance your users' productivity. Two types of items can be placed in a jump list—*destinations*, which are the groupable files your application can open and handle (as mentioned earlier in this section), and *tasks*, which are launchers for common functionality your users frequently need. It's easy to envision destinations as your recent Microsoft Office Word documents or your Internet Explorer browsing history; it takes a little more imagination to come up with useful tasks. The Windows Live Messenger jump list goes to great lengths to provide useful tasks and to make them accessible without even opening the application window—you can change your online presence status or go to your Live Mail inbox from the taskbar jump list.

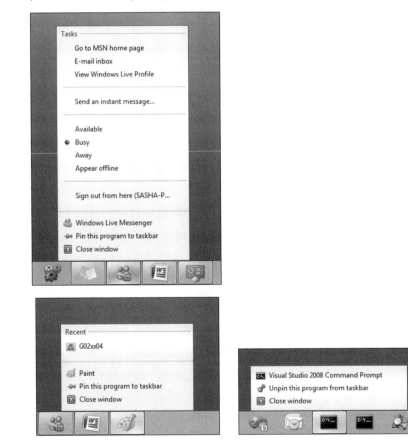

Even if an application does nothing to enhance its jump list (which is precisely what Windows Paint does), Windows automatically populates the jump list with recent documents of the application's registered file type, as well as a set of three predefined system tasks (launch the application, pin the application to the taskbar or unpin it from the taskbar, and close the application's window). However, well-behaved applications are expected to use this opportunity to provide a convenient, one-click-away mechanism for launching and interacting with programs and data. Showing absolutely nothing in the jump list (such as the Visual Studio Command Prompt button just shown) is frowned upon because users are becoming more and more accustomed to using the jump list for interacting with programs and data.

Even though the most natural place to find the jump list is right next to the taskbar button, the jump list can also appear within the Start menu, the same Start menu that it is destined to replace. If an application is currently visible in the Start menu area devoted to frequently used applications, a small arrow exposes the presence of the same jump list you would see if you clicked the application's taskbar button:

Properly interacting with jump lists, as well as designing and implementing applications that use them, is the subject of the next chapter. For now, it will suffice to say that almost any application has a justification to customize its jump list for the benefit of its users. If you're writing a document-oriented application, you'll immediately reap the benefits of the Recent and Frequent categories of destinations. Even if it seems you have no well-defined file type, and you need to consider which useful tasks and destinations will be beneficial for your users, you'll quickly become addicted to the ease of use and productivity gains the jump list brings to your application.

Taskbar Overlay Icons and Progress Bars

The typical way to convey status information in previous versions of Windows was through the system notification area (affectionately known as the system tray). Ranging from the relatively unobtrusive balloon tips to taskbar buttons flashing multiple times, all the way to focus-stealing, system-wide, modal pop-up dialogs, there hasn't been a single consolidated mechanism for conveying status information from an application that is not in the foreground. Windows 7 ensures that the notification area stays uncluttered by letting only the user decide which applications are allowed to show notifications and be visible in the system notification area.

We've already seen how a traditional approach to launching applications and accessing frequently used data is abstracted away and tied to the consolidated launch surface—the taskbar buttons. In a similar way, status information can be exposed from a Windows 7 taskbar button by using overlay icons—small icons that appear on the lower right of the taskbar button and provide immediate feedback to the user without switching to the application or even previewing its state.

Windows Live Messenger is a great demonstration of this functionality's usefulness. Your online status (Away, Busy, and so forth) is always present in the application's taskbar button:

However, overlay icons are not always enough, especially if the status information is dynamic. This is often the case when you need to expose progress information from your application. Fortunately, you can also light up the taskbar button with progress information, making it a mini–progress bar for your application. In fact, if you use some of the default Windows APIs for manipulating files (specifically, the *SHFileOperation* function or the *IFileOperation* interface that superseded it in Windows Vista), you get the file operation's progress automatically reflected in your taskbar button. Otherwise, you have to work a little harder, but the result is aesthetically pleasing. Consider the following transitions in the appearance of the Internet Explorer taskbar button when downloading a relatively large file:

The biggest benefit of taskbar overlay icons and progress bars is that the user can focus on one task at a time without status information distracting him and interrupting his work flow. To immediately know the status of the most recent download or file copy operation, all the user has to do is look at the relevant taskbar button. It might take only a fraction of a second less than switching to or previewing the target window, but when these fractions accumulate, without even realizing it, we're up to an immense productivity gain.

Thumbnail Toolbars

Much as the jump list is a mini Start menu for your application, regardless of whether it's running or not, a thumbnail toolbar provides a remote control for an individual window in an active application. Thumbnail toolbars let you control the state of another application without switching to its window, thus maximizing performance (because you do not perform a full switch to the application, which requires drawing code to run and possibly paging) and productivity (because you do not have to completely lose focus on what you are currently working on).

The classic example of a thumbnail toolbar is the Windows Media Player. Like every media player, it offers the user the ability to switch to the next and previous items, as well as to pause and resume media playback. Considering that Media Player used to install a *taskbar toolbar* (also known as a desk band) for the same purpose that consumed valuable screen real estate and confused users, the simplicity and elegance of the new Media Player's thumbnail toolbar are highly attractive.

Note that there is a significant difference between jump list tasks and items that belong on a thumbnail toolbar. Jump list tasks are fairly static and do not depend on having an active instance of the application running—for example, Media Player tasks include Resume Last Playlist and Play All Music Shuffled. On the other hand, thumbnail toolbars are present and visible only when the application is running, and each window can have its own thumbnail toolbar buttons to control the state of that window.

Live Window Thumbnails

The productivity features discussed earlier in this section minimize the need to switch to another application's windows. However, this is still a very acute need, and the success at delivering a live, vivid preview of another window is crucial for the following two key scenarios:

- Working in one application and quickly previewing the status of another application or the data presented by another application.

- Determining which window to switch to by examining the previews of multiple windows. (Prior to Windows 7, this was usually accomplished by using Flip-3D, a three-dimensional stack of window previews that was relatively difficult to navigate.)

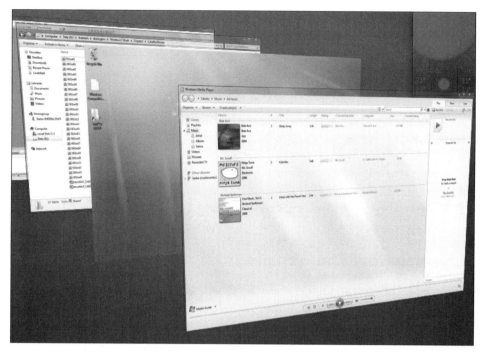

Flip-3D is still available in Windows 7, but window switching and previewing is another subset of the functionality consolidated into the new taskbar. The Windows Vista thumbnails were the first live window representations on the taskbar; the Windows 7 taskbar introduces several significant enhancements to these thumbnails, including the following:

- Multiple thumbnails for tabbed-document interface (TDI) applications, such as Internet Explorer, including switching support to a specific tab

- Live preview of the window (in full size) when hovering the cursor over the thumbnail

- A quick-access Close button on the thumbnail itself

This makes window navigation and switching so aesthetically pleasing that you might find yourself or your users playing with the live preview features (also known as *Aero Peek*) without any intent to switch between windows!

TDI applications or applications willing to expose a custom window preview can take advantage of these new features to plug into the Desktop Window Manager's (DWM) pipeline for thumbnail and preview generation.

Backward Compatibility

Although the Windows 7 taskbar is fully compatible with Windows XP and Windows Vista applications, considering compatibility up front in your porting process ensures that your applications seamlessly integrate with the experience expected by Windows 7 users. Among the topics you should be considering are the following:

- The quick launch area of the taskbar is deprecated and not shown by default; although it's possible to enable it, most users are likely to never do so. Installation programs should refrain from asking the user whether she wants to install a quick-launch icon.

- The system notification area (the *system tray*) belongs to the user and should be kept clean; applications should not attempt to pop up messages or otherwise escape the notification area boundaries. Overlay icons and taskbar progress bars should replace the need for notification area icons.

- Proper file associations are required for integration with taskbar jump lists (the subject of the next chapter). The Recent and Frequent destination categories cannot be populated by the system if your application does not have a properly registered file type.

- Users will expect destinations and tasks to be surfaced in the jump list, as a replacement for Start menu navigation. Presenting an empty or default jump list is likely to leave users confused.

- Child windows that represent an important part of an application (for example, MDI child windows or Web browser tabs) should be represented as separate thumbnails, similar to the way it happens in Internet Explorer 8.

Integrating with the Windows 7 Taskbar

We hope you've enjoyed the whirlwind tour of the Windows 7 taskbar features. It's time to focus in depth on the various features so that you can light up your application in Windows 7.

When designing your application for the Windows 7 taskbar, your first and foremost concern should be your taskbar button. A beautiful taskbar button with a clear, properly sized icon with a reasonable color balance will whet the user's appetite for interacting with your application. Remember that only users can pin applications to the taskbar, and if you miss your chance to convince the user to do this with your application because you've provided an ugly taskbar button, there's no way for you to force your application on the user.

This might sound trivial, but you must test your taskbar button with various Windows color themes and glass colors—some of the billions of Windows users are using the pink theme with almost transparent glass, others use the Windows Basic theme without Aero Peek support, and yet others require high-contrast themes for accessibility reasons. The same applies for high dots-per-inch (DPI) designs, which are discussed in depth later in this book and might mutate your icon beyond comprehension if you do not ship it in various sizes.

If you've got your taskbar button right, you're already halfway to a stunning Windows 7 application.

Application ID

During our discussion of the Windows 7 taskbar buttons, one thing might have struck you as odd: How does the shell determine which windows are associated with a specific taskbar button? Somehow, as if by magic, all Internet Explorer tabs are grouped under the Internet Explorer button, all Word documents are stacked behind the Word taskbar button, and so on. It might appear as if the only control you can exercise over this grouping is to launch another window or another process, which will be associated with the same taskbar button as all other windows or processes belonging to the same application.

However, the truth is slightly more subtle than that. Some applications might require a behavior that is more sophisticated than just associating all windows with the same taskbar button as the process. For example, assume that you have a host process that runs all kinds of office-productivity applications (e.g., a word processor, a spreadsheet, a finance manager). The host process in this case does not want a taskbar button *at all*, whereas the plug-ins require separate taskbar buttons for each application type.

Various Combinations of Windows and Taskbar Buttons

To better demonstrate the various combinations of windows and taskbar buttons— which complicate the requirements analysis for associating processes, windows, and their taskbar representation—this sidebar shows you a collection of screen shots that illustrate the different possibilities.

The following screen shot is an example of a single process that creates multiple windows, all grouped on the same taskbar button.

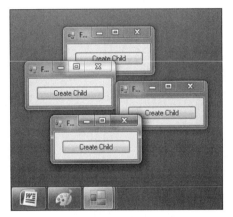

The following screen shot is an example of multiple processes, each creating a single window and all grouped on the same taskbar button. Note that the previous screen shot and the next one are virtually indistinguishable.

Next, the following screen shot shows that multiple windows belonging to the *same process* can have different taskbar buttons—if you use the same icon for all taskbar buttons or different icons for some of them.

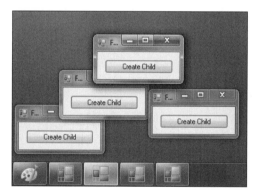

It would be impossible for the system to automatically come up with a heuristic that joins windows from different processes together and separates windows from the same process onto different taskbar buttons. This is why application IDs were born.

This variety of scenarios is addressed by assigning each window an identifier called the *application ID*, which determines the taskbar button to which the window belongs. The default application ID for a window is a default application ID generated for the process to which the window belongs, which is in turn a default application ID generated for the executable file that the process runs. These defaults explain very well the default behavior for windows within multiple processes of the same executable. (Try running Notepad several times.) However, customizing these defaults to suit your productivity application host involves setting an explicit application ID for the process (which affects all windows within that process) or even setting a different value for each individual window so that each plug-in application type can get its own taskbar button.

The various scenarios for multiplexing processes, windows, and application IDs are summarized in Table 2-1.

Table 2-1 Scenarios for Process, Window, and Application ID Combinations

Scenario	Number of Processes	Number of Windows	Number of Application IDs
Application host	One	Multiple	Multiple
Simple application	One	One	One
Document application	One	Multiple	One
Multi-instance application	Multiple	Multiple	One

Figure 2-1 demonstrates exactly how the application ID (AppID) is determined for a specific window. The dashed arrows represent fall-back scopes—if the window does not have an explicit app ID, the process application ID is checked; if the process does not have an explicit application ID, the shortcut is checked; finally, the executable itself is used to compute the application ID.

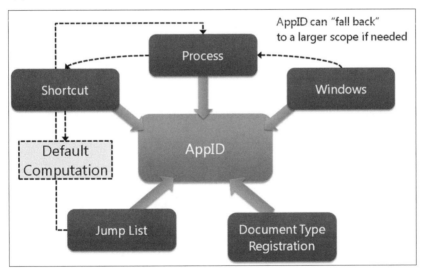

Figure 2-1 The process of determining the application ID for a window

Setting the explicit application ID for a process involves a single call to the *SetCurrentProcessExplicitAppUserModelID* function from *shell32.dll*. In the Windows API Code Pack, this is exposed by the *Instance.ApplicationId* static property, which can be set to a string and which sets the application ID. Note that the process application ID must be set during application initialization, before displaying any user interface elements or creating a jump list. Subsequent changes to the process application ID do not have any effect.

Setting the application ID for a window is slightly less straightforward—it requires calling the *SHGetPropertyStoreForWindow* function and then manipulating the resulting *IPropertyStore* object to retrieve the requested property. Although this isn't exactly rocket science, the managed wrapper is more user friendly because it exposes the *TaskbarManager.Instance.SetApplicationIdForSpecificWindow* static method and an overload method that accepts a *System.Windows.Window* object.

The nature of these APIs makes it possible to change the application ID of a window dynamically, at run time. The following code demonstrates how by pressing a button, an application switches its main window to a different application ID, which makes it "jump" across the taskbar to a different taskbar button:

```
string currentAppID = "AppID0";

void ToggleAppID_Click (object sender, EventArgs e)
{
    if (currentAppID == "AppID0")
    {
        currentAppID = "AppID1";
    }
    else
    {
        currentAppID = "AppID0";
    }
    TaskbarManager.Instance.SetApplicationIdForSpecificWindow(Handle, currentAppID);

}
```

This behavior has interesting side effects because the taskbar button is associated with additional resources, such as the application jump list (which is also dependent on the application ID) and the taskbar overlay icon. Switching application IDs at run time, however, has great potential to confuse users, so the recommended best practice is to set the application ID for your process or window during startup (or before startup, when configuring an *IShellLink* object or a shell association for your file type) and not to change it at run time.

> **Note** If terms such as *IShellLink* and *IShellItem* seem confusing to you, make sure you've read the section titled "Introduction to the Windows Shell" in Chapter 1, "Welcome to Windows 7." The following sections assume you're familiar with fundamental shell concepts and interfaces, and they use the *ITaskbarList3* interface extensively for interacting with the Windows 7 taskbar.

Because it's less straightforward to work with the unmanaged interface for changing a specific window's application ID, the following partial code listing should make it easier for you:

```
PROPVARIANT pv;
InitPropVariantFromString(L"MyAppID", &pv);

IPropertyStore *pps;
HRESULT hr = SHGetPropertyStoreForWindow(hwnd, IID_PPV_ARGS(&pps));
hr = pps->SetValue(PKEY_AppUserModel_ID, pv);
hr = pps->Commit();
```

Be sure to keep in mind that once you begin using explicit application IDs (overriding the default shell algorithm for determining the application ID for your windows, which groups windows according to their process), you must stick to the same consistent and deterministic approach. For example, if you forget to specify the application ID explicitly when populating a jump list, you'll likely encounter an exception or undefined behavior if your window is associated with an explicit application ID.

One last thing to note is that only top-level windows can be associated with an application ID. Although it might seem useful to associate a child window, an individual MDI document, or a TDI tab with a taskbar button, this can be accomplished through the use of custom window switchers, without using the explicit application ID mechanism. Custom window switchers are the subject of the next chapter.

Taskbar Progress Bars and Overlay Icons

Earlier in this chapter, you saw how taskbar overlay icons and progress bars give your application an effective way to convey status information even if the application's window is not currently in the foreground or is not even shown. In this section, you'll see the Win32 and managed APIs that your application must call to take advantage of this feature.

Setting a taskbar overlay icon is an extremely simple process. The *ITaskbarList3* shell interface provides the *SetOverlayIcon* method, which you call by passing your window handle and another two parameters: an icon handle (*HICON*) and an accessibility description string. The managed equivalent is the *Taskbar. Manager.Instance.SetOverlayIcon* method. Setting the icon to null removes the overlay altogether, giving the taskbar button its original appearance.

Unfortunately, there is no simple process that doesn't involve using some kind of a trick. If you're tempted to toggle the overlay icon during your application's startup process, you must be aware of a potential subtlety. Attempting to set an overlay icon before the taskbar button is created can result in an exception (when creating the *ITaskbarList3* object). Therefore, you must wait for the notification that the taskbar button has been created, which is delivered to your window procedure as a window message. This message does not have a predefined code, so you must use the *RegisterWindowMessage* function (passing the

"TaskbarButtonCreated" string as a parameter) to obtain the message number used by the Shell to notify your window.

When using the managed wrapper, the application passes the window handle for its main window to the *TaskbarManager.Instance.SetOverlayIcon* method. When using the taskbar APIs directly, the window handle is provided as a parameter to the *ITaskbarList3::SetOverlayIcon* method.

> **Note** To obtain a window handle in a Windows Forms application, use the *Handle* property of the *Form* class inherited by your form. In a Windows Presentation Foundation (WPF) application, instantiate a *WindowInteropHelper* instance with your WPF *Window* instance, and then use the resulting object's *Handle* property to obtain the window handle.

The following code snippet shows how an instant messaging application (such as Windows Live Messenger) changes the overlay icon on its taskbar button after the user updates his online presence status. Providing an icon description for accessibility reasons is highly encouraged.

```
//C#
void OnlinePresenceChanged(PresenceStatus newStatus)
{
    Icon theIcon = _overlayIcons[(int)newStatus];
    TaskbarManager.Instance.SetOverlayIcon(Handle, theIcon, newStatus.ToString());
}
```

```
//C++
ITaskbarList3* ptl;
CoCreateInstance(CLSID_TaskbarList, NULL, CLSCTX_ALL, IID_ITaskbarList3, (LPVOID*)&ptl);
ptl->SetOverlayIcon(hwnd, hicon, L"Accessible Description");
```

Controlling the taskbar progress bar is also the responsibility of the *ITaskbarList3* interface— this time through its *SetProgressState* and *SetProgressValue* methods. The former method accepts an enumeration value that can have any of four values (discussed later), and the latter method accepts a current and a maximum value, expressed as unsigned long parameters.

The managed wrapper contains the same functionality in the *Taskbar.Manager.Instance.SetProgressValue* and method, and the maximum value is provided to this method call as well.

> **Note** It is also easy to write a progress bar control that, in addition to updating its own visual state in the form user interface, automatically exposes progress information to the window's taskbar button, if one is present.

Taskbar-Integrated Progress Bar Control

A taskbar-integrated progress bar control reports to the taskbar any changes in the progress control value. This is a highly useful pattern to use for an application that has a single progress bar displayed at a time because the progress bar's status is automatically reflected to the taskbar.

This is a classic example of the decorator design pattern—the *TaskbarProgressBarControl* class contains a *ProgressBar* and acts as one, but it also reports progress to the Windows 7 taskbar when its value is updated:

```
public sealed class TaskbarProgressBarControl : UserControl
{
    //Windows forms control code omitted for clarity

    ProgressBar progressBar;

    public TaskbarProgressBarControl()
    {
        progressBar = new ProgressBar();
    }

    public int Value
    {
        get
        {
            return progressBar.Value;
        }
        set
        {
            progressBar.Value = value;
            TaskbarManager.Instance.SetProgressValue(value, MaxValue);
        }
    }

    public int MaxValue
    {
        get
        {
            return progressBar.Maximum;
        }
        set
        {
            progressBar.Maximum = value;
        }
    }

    public int MinValue
    {
        get
        {
            return progressBar.Minimum;
```

```
        }
        set
        {
            progressBar.Minimum = value;
        }
    }
}
```

This is a Windows Forms implementation of the control; it's quite straightforward to produce a similar implementation for WPF.

The taskbar progress bar is quite sophisticated, and besides displaying progress values it can also be set to four different states (indeterminate, normal, paused, and error). Here are the appearances of those taskbar progress states:

Indeterminate	Normal	Paused	Error
A green marquee	A green bar	A yellow bar	A red bar

The following code shows how to change the progress bar's value and state when performing work in an application using the Background Worker pattern of Windows Forms:

```
BackgroundWorker worker = new BackgroundWorker();

private void btnStart_Click(object sender, EventArgs e)
{
    TaskbarManager.Instance.SetProgressState(TaskbarProgressBarState.Normal);
    worker.DoWork += new DoWorkEventHandler(worker_DoWork);
    worker.ProgressChanged += new ProgressChangedEventHandler(worker_ProgressChanged);
    worker.WorkerReportsProgress = true;
    worker.WorkerSupportsCancellation = true;
    worker.RunWorkerAsync();
}


void worker_ProgressChanged(object sender, ProgressChangedEventArgs e)
{
    TaskbarManager.Instance.SetProgressValue(e.ProgressPercentage, 100);
}


void worker_DoWork(object sender, DoWorkEventArgs e)
{
    for (int i = 0; i < 100; ++i)
```

```
    {
        //Do some work
        worker.ReportProgress(i);
        if (worker.CancellationPending)
        {
            return;
        }
    }
}


private void btnCancel_Click(object sender, EventArgs e)
{
    TaskbarManager.Instance.SetProgressState(TaskbarProgressBarState.Error);
    worker.CancelAsync();
}
```

Note that the creation time limitation applies to this API as well—you can modify the taskbar progress state or value only after the taskbar button has been created. See the instructions mentioned earlier for how to intercept this notification and ensure that you do not perform undefined operations.

As mentioned before, applications taking advantage of the Windows shell's built-in file operations (the *SHFileOperation* function and *IFileOperation* interface) get the taskbar progress behavior by default. Interacting with these APIs is simple, and using them provides a cancelable user interface for file operations that is the same as that used by Windows Explorer. Using these APIs ensures that your file operations behave consistently with what the user expects, and as a bonus you get the taskbar progress for free while the operation takes place. Even a console application can take advantage of this API.

Using *IFileOperation* from managed code can be tricky. Aside from the fact that you have to interact with COM interfaces, the advanced capabilities of this feature require that you register a COM sink (the COM event-handler equivalent), which is not quite straightforward in managed code. Fortunately, Stephen Toub's *MSDN Magazine* article ".NET Matters: IFileOperation in Windows Vista," published in December 2007, provides an elegant framework for performing shell I/O operations using the *IFileOperation* interface.

To design and develop your own applications that take advantage of *IFileOperation*, download the code from Stephen's article from *http://msdn.microsoft.com/en-us/magazine/cc163304.aspx* and make the *FileOperation* class public. You're ready to go. First, you feed the *FileOperation* object a list of operations that you want to perform (copy, new item, delete, rename), and then you call the *PerformOperations* method to batch all operations together.

> **Note** Despite its appearance, the *IFileOperation* interface does *not* provide transactional semantics for file operations. The transactional file system introduced in Windows Vista is accessible through a completely different set of APIs. A good place to start is the documentation for the Win32 *CreateFileTransacted* function.

The following code shows how to use the file operation APIs to copy files from one location to another:

```
static void Main(string[] args)
{
    string file = CreateLargeFile();
    FileOperation operation = new FileOperation();
    for (int i = 0; i < 100; ++i)
    {
        operation.CopyItem(file, Path.GetDirectoryName(file),
            Path.ChangeExtension(Path.GetFileName(file), ".bak" + i));
    }
    operation.PerformOperations();
}
```

The progress dialog and taskbar icon's progress display are shown here:

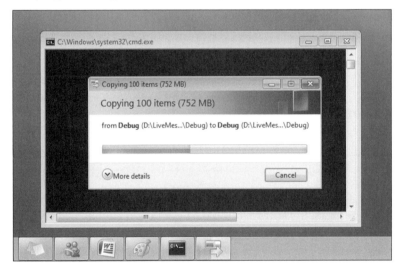

Summary

In this chapter, you saw why the Windows 7 taskbar has been designed as a revolutionary change of launch surfaces. It's now a consolidated area of the Windows shell that contains facilities for launching applications, switching windows, and obtaining status information, all of which improve user productivity.

The Windows 7 taskbar is a collection of new features for application developers, giving you a differentiating opportunity to make your applications shine on the Windows 7 platform and giving your users an unforgettable experience from their very first logon. These features include jump lists, thumbnail toolbars, progress bars, overlay icons, live previews, and tab thumbnails.

We also explored the details of assigning an application ID to a process or a window to exercise fine-grained control over the allocation of taskbar buttons to active windows. You saw how to use the Win32 and the managed APIs to set an overlay icon for a taskbar button and to modify a taskbar button's progress state and value.

In Chapter 3, "Integrate with the Windows 7 Taskbar: Advanced Features," we'll continue to experiment with the new Windows 7 taskbar APIs, and we'll take a detailed look at the implementation of jump lists, thumbnail toolbars, custom window switchers, and thumbnail customization.

Chapter 3
Integrate with the Windows 7 Taskbar: Advanced Features

In Chapter 2, "Integrate with the Windows 7 Taskbar: Basic Features" we gave you a whirlwind tour of the new Windows 7 operating system taskbar. We also discussed in depth the design considerations and application programming interfaces (APIs) for programming application IDs, taskbar overlay icons, and progress bars.

In this chapter, we'll examine the more advanced features of the Windows 7 taskbar:

- Jump Lists   These are mini Start menus that every Windows 7 application has. They provide fast access to frequent destinations (documents) and tasks.

- Thumbnail toolbars   This feature customizes the application's taskbar thumbnail with remote control of the application window.

- Taskbar thumbnails   These render a live preview of all the application's windows from the taskbar button.

- Live preview (also known as *Aero Peek*)   This is a full-size desktop preview of the target application's windows.

- Custom switchers   This advanced functionality is required by multiple-document interface (MDI) and tabbed-document interface (TDI) applications for providing thumbnail previews and live previews.

In our discussion of these features, we'll again look at the design considerations pertinent to integrating an application with the Windows 7 taskbar and the Windows 7 user experience guidelines, and we'll look at the native and managed APIs that make this integration possible.

Jump Lists

The Windows Vista Start menu revolutionized the accessibility of applications and documents by giving us the amazing search box, which can enhance productivity in countless ways. However, in spite of these improvements, the Start menu—which is a global, system-wide location—can't provide us with access to tasks and documents that are specific to a single application. When the application is running, the Start menu can display a menu or surface common tasks in its notification area icon—but when the application is not running, the only thing the user can do is start the application up.

With the consolidation and revolution of launch surfaces that is integral to the Windows 7 desktop, every application now has a Start menu. This Start menu, known as the *Jump List*, gives every application a place for categorized *destinations* and *tasks* that are specific to that application. As we saw in the previous chapter, the Windows 7 desktop has two manifestations of the Jump List: one is part of the traditional Start menu, and another is a popup menu from the application's taskbar button.

Anatomy of a Jump List

The following screen shot depicts the typical Jump List of a Windows 7 application, shown after right-clicking the application's taskbar button. It's divided into three functionally different areas, which we'll review from the bottom of the screen shot to the top:

- **Taskbar tasks** The three items on the bottom of the menu are the *taskbar tasks*, which are present in the Jump List of every application, even if it has absolutely no integration with the Windows 7 taskbar. The first task (from the top) allows you to launch the application or launch another instance of it if it's already running. The second task allows you to pin the application to the taskbar (which means its taskbar button will be shown even if the application isn't running) or unpin it from the taskbar if it is already pinned. Finally, the third task allows you to close the application's window (but only if it is already running).

- **User tasks** The section above the taskbar tasks in the menu contains *user tasks*, which might contain additional separators to group related tasks together. Despite their name, it is the application—not the user—that populates the Jump List with these tasks. Typical tasks are shortcuts to additional functionality that is related to the application and that can be used even if the application is not currently running (in contrast to thumbnail toolbars, which are displayed only when the application is running). For example, Windows Media Player provides the Resume Previous List and Play All Music user tasks. The application in the screen shot provides the Launch Notepad and Launch Calculator user tasks. User tasks are phrased as verbs that are related to the application.

- **Categorized destinations**   The topmost section in the menu contains categorized *destinations*, which are usually documents the application can handle and open. Destinations are nouns, and users usually expect them to open in the same application. (Even if the application does not have a well-defined file type or is not the primary handler for a specific file type, *virtual* destinations in the application's Jump List might still redirect the user to specific functionality.) The system provides applications with the Recent and Frequent categories—although it usually makes sense to include only one of them in the Jump List. However, applications might add more categories of destinations to the Jump List—for example, an e-mail application might have Inbox and Follow-up categories, a Web browser might have a Favorites category, and so on. Finally, the system also provides a Pinned category, which contains items explicitly pinned by the user. These items cannot be programmatically controlled, and it's up to the user's discretion what gets pinned here. (Users can pin an item by right-clicking on the destination once the jump list is open.)

Applications control the contents of the Jump List using the COM *ITaskbarList3* interface (implemented by the Windows 7 taskbar and obtained by co-creating the *CLSID_TaskbarList* COM object), which can be used as soon as the application's taskbar button is created. The managed equivalent of *ITaskbarList3* is the *TaskbarManager* class in the Windows API Code Pack.

> **More Info** The Windows API Code Pack is an open-source managed library for interacting with the new Windows 7 features. It is not an official part of the .NET Framework, but it will give you a head start with your managed applications on Windows 7. It can be downloaded for free from *http://code.msdn.microsoft.com/WindowsAPICodePack*, where you'll always find the latest version. The Windows API Code Pack was still under development while this book was written; this means that some APIs covered in the book might have changed in the final release of the library.

Recent and Frequent Destinations

The Windows Shell populates and manages the Recent and Frequent destination categories. Simple mechanisms govern the definition of what a recent or frequent item might be—and performing integration tasks with these mechanisms does not require any interaction with taskbar-specific APIs.

If your application has a well-defined file type, your application's installer should register this file type to associate it with your application. This association is recorded in the Windows registry, under the *HKEY_CLASSES_ROOT* registry hive. Even if your application is not the primary handler for the file type (for example, Microsoft Visual Studio can open XML documents, but it's not necessarily the primary handler for *.xml* files), you should still associate it with file types that it can open.

Associating Your Application with a File Type

To associate your application with a file type, you need to fill the registry entries under the *HKEY_CLASSES_ROOT* registry hive. Specifically, you need to create a key with your file extension (for example, *.xml*) and a subkey called *OpenWithProgIds*. Within the subkey, create a string value with your ProgID in the standard ProgID format (for example, *VisualStudio.9.0*).

> **Note** The following MSDN page offers a detailed walkthrough of this process: *http://msdn.microsoft.com/en-us/library/cc144148(VS.85).aspx*. Additionally, you might find useful the *Windows7.DesktopIntegration.RegistrationHelper* utility, which performs the necessary steps to register a file type association in the Windows registry. (The utility is available as part of the Windows 7 Taskbar Sample Library at *http://code.msdn.microsoft.com/Windows7Taskbar*.)

Next, create another key under the *HKEY_CLASSES_ROOT* registry hive with the name of the ProgID used in the previous steps. Under that key, add subkeys to form the following path: *shell\Open\Command*. Within the *Command* subkey, add a default string value with the full path to your executable and additional command-line parameters if desired. Within the command-line string, you can use the *%1* placeholder, which the Windows Shell replaces with the name of the document being opened. The following screen shot is an example of a registry association for the .ascx file extension with the Visual Studio ProgID.

If you successfully followed these steps, the Windows Shell recognizes your application as a handler for the specified file type. Successful completion of these steps enables users to launch your application by double-clicking items with your file extension in Windows Explorer, and it enables you to embed destinations in your application's Jump List.

The Windows Shell adds items to the Recent and Frequent lists for your application when one of the following actions occurs:

- The item is used to launch your application directly—for example, when you double-click a file or a shortcut in Windows Explorer.

- The item is selected by a user in a common file dialog (Open or Save).

- The item is passed as a parameter to the *SHAddToRecentDocs* function, which is part of the Windows Shell API.

Note Common file dialogs provide a standard look and feel as well as additional functionality to Open and Save operations throughout the Windows Shell. Applications that use the common file dialogs will always benefit from the latest version of the user interface provided by the underlying operating system (regardless of the version of Windows they were compiled on). Taking advantage of Windows Shell Libraries and of Recent and Frequent categories is greatly simplified if you use common file dialogs in your application. For more information about common file dialogs, consult the MSDN documentation at *http://msdn.microsoft.com/en-us/library/bb776913(VS.85).aspx*. (Also see Chapter 4, "Organize My Data: Libraries in Windows 7," to learn how common file dialogs can interact with Shell Libraries in Windows 7.)

The first two actions do not require any interaction on your application's behalf—the Windows Shell automatically maintains the Recent and Frequent item lists for your application. Therefore, if your Jump List contains the Recent or Frequent destination category and your application is registered as a handler for some file type, the application's Jump List automatically contains recently or frequently accessed items.

If you choose to notify the Windows Shell directly, you can use the *SHAddToRecentDocs* Win32 API or the managed equivalent—the *JumpList.AddToRecent* method—which is part of the Windows API Code Pack. This has the same effect as populating the Jump List with the recently or frequently accessed items.

The only thing left to do, then, is to let the taskbar know that your application requires a Jump List with one of the system destination categories—Recent or Frequent. Remember that to display the Jump List correctly and associate it with the appropriate taskbar button, you need to set the window application ID (or the process application ID) to the same consistent value you use throughout your application. (See Chapter 2, "Integrate with Windows 7 Taskbar: Basic Features," for more details.)

If you decide to use the Recent destination category, you don't need to do anything else to get the Jump List to work. However, if you want to use the Frequent destination category, you need to follow through with a list-building transaction. The following code sample, which displays both the native and managed APIs, shows how to create a Jump List for an application, add to it the Frequent destination category, and ensure that it's populated with one recently used item:

```
//C++:

ICustomDestinationList* pJumpList = NULL;
if (FAILED(CoCreateInstance(
        CLSID_DestinationList, NULL, CLSCTX_INPROC_SERVER, IID_PPV_ARGS(&pJumpList))))
    goto Cleanup;

if (FAILED(pJumpList->SetAppID(L"Microsoft.Samples.MyApplication")))
    goto Cleanup;

UINT uMaxSlots;
IObjectArray* pRemoved;
if (FAILED(pJumpList->BeginList(&uMaxSlots, IID_PPV_ARGS(&pRemoved))))
    goto Cleanup;
if (FAILED(pJumpList->AppendKnownCategory(KDC_FREQUENT)))
    goto Cleanup;
if (FAILED(pJumpList->CommitList()))
    goto Cleanup;

Cleanup:
if (pJumpList != NULL)
    pJumpList->Release();
```

```
SHAddToRecentDocs(SHARD_PATHW, L"MyFile.ext");
```

```
//C#:
```

```
JumpList jumpList = JumpList.CreateJumpList();
jumpList.KnownCategoryToDisplay = JumpListKnownCategoryType.Frequent;
jumpList.AddToRecent("MyFile.ext");
jumpList.Refresh();
```

After completing these steps, your application will have a Jump List with the Recent or Frequent category enabled. If your users are using Windows Explorer to launch your application from individual items, and if you're using the common file dialogs for Open and Save functionality, there's nothing else you need to do to manage the Recent and Frequent categories.

> **Note** It usually doesn't make sense to include both the Recent and Frequent categories in the same Jump List. It is recommended that you choose one or the other.

Custom Destinations

If the default Recent and Frequent destination categories provided by the Windows Shell are not enough for your application, you'll want to create custom categories and store your destinations within them. As we saw before, an e-mail application might want to use Inbox and Follow-up categories, a Web browser might want to use a Favorites category, and so on.

Most destinations are nouns, and in the Windows Shell world nouns are usually represented by *IShellItem* objects, although *IShellLink* objects can be used as well. Therefore, to create custom destination categories, you first need to create custom destinations—namely, their *IShellItem* or *IShellLink* representations. If you place shell items in the Jump List, clicking them opens your application (as a registered file handler for these shell items). If you place shell links in the Jump List, they can point to arbitrary locations and arbitrary applications might be used to open them. However, users will expect your application to be launched as a result of clicking on an item in your application's Jump List.

> **More Info** For more information on the Windows Shell object hierarchy, including *IShellItem* and *IShellLink*, see Chapter 4, "Organize Your Data: Libraries in Windows 7". In native code, obtaining a shell item usually involves calls to APIs such as *SHCreateItemFromParsingName*, whereas creating a shell link involves co-creating *CLSID_ShellLink* and then setting the properties of the resulting object. In managed code, the Windows API Code Pack provides the *JumpListItem* and *JumpListLink* classes for working with shell items and shell links.

Before populating your Jump List with custom destinations, there are two things to bear in mind:

- There is a limited amount of screen state for your custom categories and items. You can retrieve the maximum amount of items that can be placed in the Jump List by using the *pcMaxSlots* parameter of the *ICustomDestinationList::BeginList* method or its managed equivalent, *JumpList.MaxSlotsInList*, from the Windows API Code Pack. Placing more items on the screen than is allowed will not result in an error—extraneous items will be truncated, top to bottom.

- The Jump List belongs to the user and not to the application, which means the user can choose to remove items from the Jump List even if you carefully placed them in specific destination categories. When your application re-populates the Jump List for any reason, it must remember the user's choices and refrain from re-adding items that the user removed earlier. Attempting to add an item that the user removed after the last list-building transaction causes an exception.

Items Removed by the User

If your application displays Jump List items that are of no interest to the user, the user can choose to remove them from the list. Your application cannot add items that were previously removed by the user back to the Jump List—doing so causes an exception when the Jump List is constructed. The following screen shot shows how the user can remove an item from a custom destination category displayed in an application's jump list:

The *ICustomDestinationList::BeginList* method provides you with an opportunity to discover that the user removed items from the Jump List. The *ppv* parameter of this method will contain a collection (typically *IObjectArray*) of removed items—*IShellItem* and *IShellLink* objects. It's also possible to call the *ICustomDestinationList::GetRemovedDestinations* method directly to retrieve the list of removed items without initiating a list-building transaction.

The managed equivalent for determining that items were removed from the Jump List is the *JumpList.RemovedDestinations* property of the Windows API Code Pack, which proactively discovers removed items. Fortunately, the Windows API Code Pack automatically deletes removed items from the custom categories provided by the application to ensure that items removed by the user are not re-added to the application's Jump List.

Working with custom destinations requires the *ICustomDestinationList* interface, which is obtained by co-creating the *CLSID_DestinationList* COM object. If your application uses an explicit application ID, you must use the *ICustomDestinationList::SetAppID* method before using the resulting object. As always, the managed Windows API Code Pack streamlines this work for you—custom categories can be added using the *JumpList.AddCustomCategories* method, and the application ID is automatically propagated from the *TaskbarManager.Instance.ApplicationID* property.

A list-building transaction begins with a call to the *ICustomDestinationList::BeginList* method. Subsequent method calls will not be applied to the actual Jump List until the *CommitList* method is called to commit the changes, or until the *AbortList* method is called to roll back the work. The managed wrapper does not require multiple steps—it refreshes the Jump List when changes are made to the underlying model and the JumpList.Refresh method is called.

To construct the Jump List categories, a two-step approach is required. First, you construct a collection (usually *IObjectCollection*) of custom destinations (*IShellItem* or *IShellLink* objects) that belong to a category—or, in managed code, create a *JumpListCustomCategory* object and add *JumpListItem* and *JumpListLink* objects to it. Next, you call the *ICustomDestinationList::AppendCategory* method to append the entire category to the list— or, in managed code, pass the *JumpListCustomCategory* object to the *JumpList.AddCustomCategories* method.

The following code snippet, which displays both the native and managed code, shows how to construct a Jump List with one custom category:

```
//C++:

ICustomDestinationList* pJumpList = NULL;
if (FAILED(CoCreateInstance(
```

```
            CLSID_DestinationList, NULL, CLSCTX_INPROC_SERVER, IID_PPV_ARGS(&pJumpList))))
        goto Cleanup;

    if (FAILED(pJumpList->SetAppID(L"Microsoft.Samples.MyApplication")))
        goto Cleanup;

    UINT uMaxSlots;
    IObjectArray* pRemoved;
    if (FAILED(pJumpList->BeginList(&uMaxSlots, IID_PPV_ARGS(&pRemoved))))
        goto Cleanup;

    IObjectCollection* pContents = NULL;
    if (FAILED(CoCreateInstance(
        CLSID_EnumerableObjectCollection, NULL, CLSCTX_INPROC_SERVER, IID_PPV_ARGS(&pContents))))
        goto Cleanup;

    IShellItem* pItem = NULL;
    if (FAILED(SHCreateItemInKnownFolder(
            FOLDERID_Documents, KF_FLAG_DEFAULT, L"MyFile.txt", IID_PPV_ARGS(&pItem))))
        goto Cleanup;

    if (FAILED(pContents->AddObject(pItem)))
        goto Cleanup;

    IObjectArray* pContentsArr = NULL;
    if (FAILED(pContents->QueryInterface(IID_PPV_ARGS(&pContentsArr))))
        goto Cleanup;

    if (FAILED(pJumpList->AppendCategory(L"My Category", pContentsArr)))
        goto Cleanup;

    pJumpList->CommitList();

Cleanup:
    if (pContentsArr != NULL)
        pContentsArr->Release();
    if (pItem != NULL)
        pItem->Release();
    if (pContents != NULL)
        pContents->Release();
    if (pJumpList != NULL)
        pJumpList->Release();

    //C#:

    JumpList jumpList = JumpList.CreateJumpList();
    JumpListCustomCategory category = new JumpListCustomCategory("My Category");
    category.AddJumpListItems(new JumpListItem(Path.Combine(
        Environment.GetFolderPath(Environment.SpecialFolder.MyDocuments), "MyFile.ext")));
    jumpList.AddCustomCategories (category);
    jumpList.Refresh();
```

Clearing the Jump List

If at any time you want to clear the Jump List, you can use the *DeleteList* method of the *ICustomDestinationList* interface. In managed code, you can create an empty *JumpList* instance and then call its *Refresh* method.

You should not clear the application Jump List when your application starts—or worse, during normal application execution. Users rely on the contents of the Jump List to remain stable and like to retain the same categorized destinations and tasks across multiple uses of an application. The reasonable use case for clearing the application's Jump List is when your application is uninstalled, or when the user explicitly asks to do so—for example, using a Clear History command in a Web browser.

User Tasks

User tasks—despite their name—are additional tasks that can be placed in your application's Jump List. These are verbs that can invoke your application or any other application, and they're usually represented by *IShellLink* objects. After you've mastered the intricate details of adding categorized destinations to the Jump List, user tasks are much easier to grasp.

> **Note** Because user tasks are not connected to an existing application instance, it makes sense to set them up during application installation. To do this, you can either ensure that your installer has the same AppID as the application itself, or you can launch an auxiliary application from within the installer that claims the same AppID and creates the user tasks. (This auxiliary application could also be your main application with a "quiet-mode" switch that creates the tasks and exits without displaying UI.)

You need the *ICustomDestinationList* interface if you're working from native code. After beginning a list-building transaction (with *BeginList*), you can use the *AddUserTasks* method to add a collection of tasks—usually represented by an *IObjectCollection* containing *IShellLink* objects.

As you might remember, the task list can contain separators that group related tasks. To add a separator, create an *IShellLink* object and use the *IPropertyStore* interface to set its *System.AppUserModel.IsDestListSeparator* property to *TRUE*. This object can then be added to the Jump List along with the rest of the tasks.

The managed equivalent for adding user tasks is the *JumpList.AddUserTasks* method, which accepts *JumpListLink*, *JumpListItem*, and *JumpListSeparator* objects and adds them to the underlying tasks collection. The following code snippet, which displays both the native and managed code, demonstrates how to add a few user tasks to the application's Jump List:

```
//C++:

ICustomDestinationList* pJumpList = NULL;
if (FAILED(CoCreateInstance(
        CLSID_DestinationList, NULL, CLSCTX_INPROC_SERVER, IID_PPV_ARGS(&pJumpList))))
    goto Cleanup;

if (FAILED(pJumpList->SetAppID(L"Microsoft.Samples.MyApplication")))
    goto Cleanup;

UINT uMaxSlots;
IObjectArray* pRemoved = NULL;
if (FAILED(pJumpList->BeginList(&uMaxSlots, IID_PPV_ARGS(&pRemoved))))
    goto Cleanup;

IObjectCollection* pContents = NULL;
if (FAILED(CoCreateInstance(
    CLSID_EnumerableObjectCollection, NULL, CLSCTX_INPROC_SERVER, IID_PPV_ARGS(&pContents))))
    goto Cleanup;

IShellLink* pLink = NULL;
IPropertyStore* pStore = NULL;
PROPVARIANT var;

//Create a simple link to calc.exe:
if (FAILED(CoCreateInstance(CLSID_ShellLink, NULL,
        CLSCTX_INPROC_SERVER, IID_PPV_ARGS(&pLink))))
    goto Cleanup;
if (FAILED(pLink->SetPath(L"C:\\Windows\\System32\\calc.exe")))
    goto Cleanup;
if (FAILED(pLink->QueryInterface(IID_PPV_ARGS(&pStore))))
    goto Cleanup;
InitPropVariantFromString(L"Launch Calculator", &var);
if (FAILED(pStore->SetValue(PKEY_Title, var)))
    goto Cleanup;
if (FAILED(pStore->Commit()))
    goto Cleanup;
if (FAILED(pContents->AddObject(pLink)))
    goto Cleanup;
pStore->Release(); pStore = NULL;
pLink->Release(); pLink = NULL;

//Create a separator link:
if (FAILED(CoCreateInstance(CLSID_ShellLink, NULL,
        CLSCTX_INPROC_SERVER, IID_PPV_ARGS(&pLink))))
    goto Cleanup;
if (FAILED(pLink->QueryInterface(IID_PPV_ARGS(&pStore))))
    goto Cleanup;
InitPropVariantFromBoolean(TRUE, &var);
if (FAILED(pStore->SetValue(PKEY_AppUserModel_IsDestListSeparator, var)))
    goto Cleanup;
```

```
if (FAILED(pStore->Commit()))
    goto Cleanup;
if (FAILED(pContents->AddObject(pLink)))
    goto Cleanup;

//Create a simple link to notepad.exe:
if (FAILED(CoCreateInstance(CLSID_ShellLink, NULL,
        CLSCTX_INPROC_SERVER, IID_PPV_ARGS(&pLink))))
    goto Cleanup;
if (FAILED(pLink->SetPath(L"C:\\Windows\\System32\\notepad.exe")))
    goto Cleanup;
if (FAILED(pLink->QueryInterface(IID_PPV_ARGS(&pStore))))
    goto Cleanup;
InitPropVariantFromString(L"Launch Notepad", &var);
if (FAILED(pStore->SetValue(PKEY_Title, var)))
    goto Cleanup;
if (FAILED(pStore->Commit()))
    goto Cleanup;
if (FAILED(pContents->AddObject(pLink)))
    goto Cleanup;

IObjectArray* pContentsArr = NULL;
if (FAILED(pContents->QueryInterface(IID_PPV_ARGS(&pContentsArr))))
    goto Cleanup;
if (FAILED(pJumpList->AddUserTasks(pContentsArr)))
    goto Cleanup;
pJumpList->CommitList();

Cleanup:
if (pLink != NULL)
    pLink->Release();
if (pStore != NULL)
    pStore->Release();
if (pContentsArr != NULL)
    pContentsArr->Release();
if (pContents != NULL)
    pContents->Release();
if (pRemoved != NULL)
    pRemoved->Release();
if (pJumpList != NULL)
    pJumpList->Release();

//C#:

JumpList jumpList = JumpList.CreateJumpList();
jumpList.AddUserTasks(
    new JumpListLink(@"C:\Windows\System32\Calc.exe", "Launch Calculator"),
    new JumpListSeparator(),
    new JumpListLink(@"C:\Windows\System32\Notepad.exe", "Launch Notepad"));
jumpList.Refresh();
```

Unlike custom destinations, tasks cannot be removed from the Jump List by the user, nor can they be pinned to the list. Tasks receive an additional preference when there's not enough room in the Jump List—they are trimmed last so that only the space that remains after displaying all user tasks can be used by the rest of the Jump List categories.

> **Note** Users expect the user tasks area of the Jump List to remain static. The state of the application should not affect the list of user tasks, especially because the application might shut down unexpectedly, leaving the Jump List in an undesired state. Nonetheless, there are some applications—including Windows Live Messenger—that use contextual user tasks, such as Sign In and Sign Out, with great success.

Thumbnail Toolbars

Thumbnail toolbars are an exceptional productivity feature that gives users the ability to do more with the application's thumbnail without switching to the application's window and interrupting their work. A thumbnail toolbar is essentially a remote control for the application, which is displayed beneath the application's thumbnail. For example, the Windows Media Player thumbnail toolbar shown in the following screen shot features the Play, Previous, and Next toolbar buttons—with the standard icons for these operations.

> **Note** Unlike user tasks in a Jump List, thumbnail toolbar contents should be contextual—after all, the toolbar is displayed only if the application is running. As you'll see in this section, you can disable and hide buttons from the thumbnail toolbar if they are irrelevant. For example, when there is no playlist, Windows Media Player's toolbar buttons are disabled.

Although a thumbnail toolbar might be extremely handy, take extra care to ensure that you are not abusing it. Many applications do not need a remote control for their window and require the user to fully switch to the application before interacting with it. This behavior is still encouraged under the Windows 7 user experience guidelines.

The thumbnail toolbar is limited to seven toolbar buttons at most. Additionally, although it's possible to hide or disable toolbar buttons after the toolbar is constructed, you cannot remove or add toolbar buttons. This means that you must decide—when constructing the toolbar—which thumbnail buttons your application will require throughout its entire lifetime. Later on, you can enable, disable, hide, and show some of the buttons—but you can't change the initial set of toolbar buttons without re-creating the window itself.

> **Note** In low-resolution scenarios or when you have a large number of thumbnails to display, the system might trim the thumbnail toolbar from right to left as needed. Prioritize your commands so that the most important ones appear on the left part of the thumbnail toolbar.

Adding toolbar buttons to the thumbnail toolbar requires the *ITaskbarList3* interface—specifically, the three methods *ThumbBarAddButtons*, *ThumbBarSetImageList*, and *ThumbBarUpdateButtons*. The *ThumbBarAddButtons* method adds an array of up to seven toolbar buttons to the thumbnail toolbar. This method uses a structure called *THUMBBUTTON*, which contains all the necessary information to create the button, including its ID, text, ToolTip text, and other parameters.

When a thumbnail toolbar button is clicked, the system sends a *WM_COMMAND* message to the window associated with the thumbnail—the handle to this window is passed to the *ThumbBarAddButtons* method. The higher word of the *wParam* message parameter is set to *THBN_CLICKED*, and the lower word is set to the button ID provided when the toolbar was created.

Passing Taskbar Messages Through User Interface Privilege Isolation

The Windows 7 taskbar runs within the context of the *Explorer.exe* process, which has standard user privileges. However, elevated applications, enjoying administrative privileges, can also take advantage of the taskbar functionality.

Therein lies the problem—a process running with standard user privileges (more specifically, a Medium integrity-level process) is not allowed to send window messages to a process running with administrative privileges (a High integrity-level process). The mechanism that governs message filtering is called User Interface Privilege Isolation (UIPI), and it clearly presents an obstacle for every scenario that requires the taskbar to send window messages to an application.

> **More Info** For more information about the Windows Integrity Mechanism (WIM) and UIPI, consult the MSDN documentation at *http://msdn.microsoft.com/en-us/library/bb625963.aspx*.

To ensure that the taskbar can communicate with the high-privileged application, the *ChangeWindowMessageFilter* function should be called by the high-privileged process, specifying the messages that are allowed to pass through. The first parameter to the function is the window message, and the second parameter should be set to *MSGFLT_ADD*, indicating that this message is allowed through. (The Windows API Code Pack calls the appropriate method on your behalf for some of the window messages— only if you're using the Win32 APIs directly do you need to use this method.)

The relevant messages used in this and subsequent sections are the following:

- RegisterWindowMessage("TaskbarButtonCreated")

- WM_COMMAND

- WM_DWMSENDICONICTHUMBNAIL

- WM_DWMSENDICONICLIVEPREVIEWBITMAP

- WM_SYSCOMMAND

- WM_ACTIVATE

There is no need to explicitly allow these messages through if your process is not running with administrative privileges.

After the thumbnail toolbar has been created, your application can still update the toolbar. For example, you can hide or disable toolbar buttons, or even change the text or icon associated with a specific button. This is done by calling the *ThumbBarUpdateButtons* method for only the buttons that were updated.

The following code demonstrates how to add a thumbnail toolbar to an application and how to intercept the window messages that the system sends when a toolbar button is clicked:

```
//During application initialization:
UINT wmTaskbarButtonCreated = RegisterWindowMessage(L"TaskbarButtonCreated");
ITaskbarList3* pTaskbar = NULL;
HIMAGELIST hImageList;     //Initialized elsewhere
THUMBBUTTON buttons[2];

//Within the window procedure:
if (msg == wmTaskbarButtonCreated) {
    if (FAILED(CoCreateInstance(
            CLSID_TaskbarList, NULL, CLSCTX_ALL, IID_PPV_ARGS(&pTaskbar))))
        return 0;

    buttons[0].dwMask = THB_BITMAP | THB_TOOLTIP;
    buttons[0].iId = 0;
```

```
    buttons[0].iBitmap = 0;
    wcscpy(buttons[0].szTip, L"Play");

    buttons[1].dwMask = THB_BITMAP | THB_TOOLTIP;
    buttons[1].iId = 1;
    buttons[1].iBitmap = 1;
    wcscpy(buttons[1].szTip, L"Next");

    pTaskbar->ThumbBarSetImageList(hwnd, hImageList)
    pTaskbar->ThumbBarAddButtons(hwnd, 2, &buttons[0]);
}

if (msg == WM_COMMAND && HIWORD(wParam) == THBN_CLICKED) {
    DWORD id = LOWORD(wParam);
    MessageBox(hwnd, buttons[id].szTip, L"Button Clicked!", MB_OK);
}
```

The managed equivalent for creating a thumbnail toolbar is the
TaskbarManager.Instance.ThumbnailToolbars property of the Windows API Code Pack. Create
your thumbnail toolbar buttons using the *ThumbnailToolbarButton* class constructor, set their
properties as necessary, register for the *Click* event, and then add them to the toolbar using
the *AddButtons* method.

> **Note** The underlying implementation of the Windows API Code Pack creates a proxy window for
> your window. This proxy window routes the window messages originating at the thumbnail
> toolbar and processes them appropriately so that the thumbnail button click handlers are invoked
> automatically. There is no need for you to do anything in your form's window procedure.

The following code shows how the managed *TaskbarManager.Instance.ThumbnailToolbars*
property can be used to achieve the same effect as the native equivalent shown earlier:

```
ThumbnailToolbarButton tb1 = new ThumbnailToolbarButton(SystemIcons.Warning, "Play");
tb1.Click += delegate { MessageBox.Show("clicked Play"); };

ThumbnailToolbarButton tb2 = new ThumbnailToolbarButton(SystemIcons.Information, "Next");
tb2.Click += delegate { MessageBox.Show("clicked Next"); };

TaskbarManager.Instance.ThumbnailToolbars.AddButtons(Handle, tb1, tb2);
```

Customizing Thumbnails

One of the most visually stunning features of the Windows 7 desktop is the multiple live
thumbnails shown for each taskbar button (as shown in the following screen shot). The new
taskbar thumbnails are much smarter than their Windows Vista counterparts, enabling you to
preview a live rendering of the underlying window—a feature known as *Aero Peek*—and to
close the window without even switching to it. (And, of course, thumbnail toolbars extend the
productivity story even further.)

Useful as they are, taskbar thumbnails do not always allow users to see past the thumbnail without switching to the application's window. Often, the text is unreadable or the thumbnail region is too small—these are just examples of problems that might prevent thumbnails from achieving their full potential.

Customizing Thumbnail ToolTips

Although this is not much of a customization, the tooltip displayed for the thumbnail itself can also be customized using the *SetThumbnailTooltip* method of the *ITaskbarList3* interface.

However, the Windows 7 taskbar thumbnails are not just more useful—they're also significantly more extensible. In this section, you'll see how to customize taskbar thumbnails, in part or in whole, to provide a richer user experience.

> **Note** Taskbar thumbnails and live previews are rendered by a system component called the Desktop Window Manager (DWM), introduced in Windows Vista. New DWM interfaces introduced in Windows 7 are the key to extending taskbar thumbnails and live previews, which explains why the APIs and window messages in this chapter all have the *Dwm* or *WM_DWM* prefix.

Thumbnail Clipping

Jack, a college student, is writing a term paper in Microsoft Office Word. In the background, he's using a Web encyclopedia in Internet Explorer to aid with his research. After reading the Web article for a while, Jack switches back to Word but struggles to remember the precise wording of the Web article. Jack switches back to Internet Explorer. If this sounds familiar to you, perhaps you can identify the problem.

The problem is that a typical thumbnail toolbar for an Internet Explorer tab looks like the following screen shot:

It's hardly a surprise that the text is unreadable and that switching (or at least using Aero Peek) is the only way to read the full text. The key to solving this problem is noticing that the user is not always interested in the visual rendering of the *entire* window—in this case, a few lines around the current cursor position might be more than enough.

Thumbnail clipping is all about specifying a particular region of the target window that the thumbnail will display. This specificity allows applications such as text editors or games to focus on a small part of the window, making it appear bigger in the thumbnail and making the thumbnail more useful.

To clip a window's thumbnail, you use the *ITaskbarList3* interface—specifically, the *SetThumbnailClip* method. It takes a window handle as the first parameter—this is the window whose thumbnail you are clipping—and as the second parameter a pointer to a *RECT* structure, which describes the clipping region relative to the coordinates of the window (for example, {0, 0, 10, 10} describes a 10-by-10 rectangle at the upper-left corner of the window). To cancel the clipping, pass *NULL* for this second parameter.

> **Note** Try providing a clip rectangle with 119 pixels of height and 200 pixels of width. Because these are the default thumbnail dimensions on some Windows 7 installations, the resulting thumbnail will be an exact rendering of that part of the window, with no resizing required at all!

The following code demonstrates how an application can set the thumbnail clip to the top left part of the window with a width of 200 pixels and a height of 119 pixels:

```
ITaskbarList3* pTaskbar;    //Obtained elsewhere
RECT clipRect = { 0, 0, 200, 119 };
pTaskbar->SetThumbnailClip(hwnd, &clipRect);
```

The managed equivalent of thumbnail clipping can be found in the wrapper method *TaskbarManager.Instance.TabbedThumbnail.SetThumbnailClip* in the Windows API Code Pack. This method takes a window handle and a *Rectangle* structure that describes the clip region. The following code is the managed equivalent of the previous native code sample, showing how an application hosting a Rich Text Format (RTF) control can set the thumbnail clip region to a few lines around the current cursor position:

```
int index = richTextBox.GetFirstCharIndexOfCurrentLine();
Point point = richTextBox.GetPositionFromCharIndex(index);
TaskbarManager.Instance.TabbedThumbnail.SetThumbnailClip(
    Handle, new Rectangle(point, new Size(200, 119)));
```

In the following screen shots, you can see the thumbnail behavior before and after toggling the window clipping, side by side. There's hardly any doubt that the clipped thumbnail is more useful than its default counterpart.

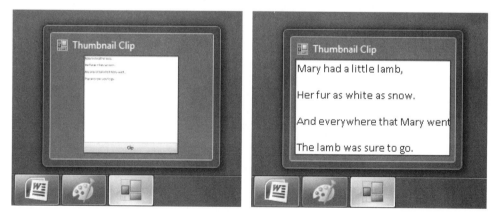

Custom Thumbnails

In the previous section, you saw how to customize the taskbar thumbnails by specifying a clip region that makes the thumbnail zoom in on the window. Naturally, this does not suffice for some applications—and the need arises to customize the thumbnail completely. For example, a picture viewer application (such as Windows Photo Gallery) can provide a thumbnail consisting of a mosaic of pictures from the current directory. Another idea is for Visual Studio to display compilation or test run status and summaries instead of an illegible preview of the source editor.

Achieving this behavior is slightly more difficult than what you did before. If you push thumbnail previews to the DWM when they are not needed (most of the time, users are not looking at any thumbnails), you are wasting CPU and system resources. On the other hand, if you provide a static preview that the DWM grabs when necessary, there is no way to update it when the underlying window changes. The proper solution involves two-way interaction between the application and the DWM:

- The application tells the DWM that it wants to customize thumbnail previews by calling the *DwmSetWindowAttribute* function and passing the *DWMWA_HAS_ICONIC_BITMAP* attribute, and again passing the *DWMWA_FORCE_ICONIC_REPRESENTATION* attribute. Both calls require a Boolean value of *TRUE* to be passed as the last parameter.

- The DWM sends the application the *WM_DWMSENDICONICTHUMBNAIL* window message when a thumbnail needs to be rendered.

- The application responds to the message by calling the *DwmSetIconicThumbnail* function and passing the thumbnail bitmap as a parameter.

- The application can invalidate the current thumbnail cached with the DWM by calling the *DwmInvalidateIconicBitmaps* function.

- When the application is no longer interested in customizing the thumbnail bitmaps, it repeats the first step, passing the Boolean value of *FALSE* as the last parameter. This step is rather unusual because most applications should customize the thumbnail preview consistently and refrain from changing this behavior at runtime.

The following code shows how an application can customize its thumbnail preview to show a randomly selected bitmap instead of the actual contents of the window:

```
//During initialization, for example, in WM_CREATE:
BOOL truth = TRUE;
DwmSetWindowAttribute(hwnd, DWMWA_HAS_ICONIC_BITMAP, &truth, sizeof(truth));
DwmSetWindowAttribute(hwnd, DWMWA_FORCE_ICONIC_REPRESENTATION, &truth, sizeof(truth));

//In the window procedure:
if (msg == WM_DWMSENDICONICTHUMBNAIL) {
    int width = HIWORD(lParam);
    int height = LOWORD(lParam);
    HBITMAP hbmp = GetRandomBitmap(width, height);
    DwmSetIconicThumbnail(hwnd, hbmp, 0);
    DeleteObject(hbmp);
}
```

Thumbnail Dimensions

The *lParam* parameter received by the window procedure for the WM_DWMSETICONICTHUMBNAIL message specifies the width and height of the requested thumbnail—the width is the high-order word, and the height is the low-order word. Providing a thumbnail that does not have the specified dimensions might result in an error.

The managed equivalent of the thumbnail customization APIs is the *TaskbarManager.Instance.TabbedThumbnail* property, part of the Windows API Code Pack. The application needs to create an instance of the *TabbedThumbnail* class and provide the handle to the window as the constructor parameter. Next, the application needs to call the *TaskbarManager.Instance.TabbedThumbnail.AddThumbnailPreview* method and pass the previously created *TabbedThumbnail* instance as the parameter. To customize the thumbnail preview bitmap, the application needs to use the *TabbedThumbnail.SetImage* method whenever the thumbnail preview should change. Alternatively, the application can register for the *TabbedThumbnail.TabbedThumbnailBitmapRequested* event, which is invoked whenever a thumbnail preview bitmap is requested, and call the *SetImage* method on demand.

> **Note** The *TabbedThumbnail* constructor expects a handle to a window and a handle to its parent window. As you'll see in the subsequent sections, this class was intended to handle the standard thumbnail preview scenario, as well as the scenario where the taskbar thumbnail should be generated from a child window (non-top-level window). If you want to customize the thumbnail of a top-level window, as we do in this section, pass the same handle twice to the *TabbedThumbnail* constructor.

There is no need to dispatch the various DWM window messages to the managed library—it creates a proxy window on your behalf that receives the DWM notifications and acts accordingly. At any time, the application can request to invalidate the thumbnail previews currently cached by the DWM by calling the *TaskbarManager.Instance.TabbedThumbnail.InvalidateThumbnails* method. Finally, the application can request to stop displaying a custom thumbnail preview by using the *TaskbarManager.Instance.TabbedThumbnail.RemoveThumbnailPreview* method, passing the window handle or the previously created *TabbedThumbnail* instance as a parameter.

> **Note** The Windows API Code Pack can work with window handles in *IntPtr* form, but most of its thumbnail-related methods also accept Windows Forms *Control* objects and Windows Presentation Foundation (WPF) *UIElement* objects. This makes the library flexible and suitable for a variety of GUI applications, but it also means that your Windows Forms application must reference WPF assemblies (specifically *WindowsBase*, *PresentationFramework*, and *PresentationCore*) to use some features of the Windows API Code Pack.

The following code demonstrates how an application can provide custom text in place of its thumbnail when the thumbnail is requested:

```
TabbedThumbnail preview = new TabbedThumbnail(Handle, Handle);
Bitmap bitmap = new Bitmap(200, 200);
using (Graphics gr = Graphics.FromImage(bitmap))
{
    int index = richTextBox1.GetFirstCharIndexOfCurrentLine();
    gr.DrawString(richTextBox1.Text.Substring(index, richTextBox1.Text.Length - index),
        new Font("Tahoma", 9),
        new SolidBrush(Color.Black),
        new PointF(0.0f, 0.0f));
}
TaskbarManager.Instance.TabbedThumbnail.AddThumbnailPreview(preview);
preview.SetImage(bitmap);
```

> **Note** In Windows 7 Beta, bitmaps provided to the DWM were displayed upside-down because of what was probably a bug. This was fixed in the Release Candidate (RC) timeframe. You might have seen on the Internet some custom code that flips the thumbnail upside-down—so that the second flip performed by the DWM shows it appropriately. (Beta versions of the Windows 7 Taskbar Sample Library used this technique.) This hack is no longer necessary.

Custom Live Previews

If your application takes advantage of custom thumbnails, you'll probably want to customize the live preview (Aero Peek) of your application's windows as well.

The process for doing so is similar to what was necessary to customize thumbnails—two-way interaction with the DWM using window messages and APIs. The process is repeated here in brief—note that only the function and constant names are different:

- The application tells the DWM that it wants to customize live previews by calling the *DwmSetWindowAttribute* function and passing the *DWMWA_HAS_ICONIC_BITMAP* attribute, and again passing the *DWMWA_FORCE_ICONIC_REPRESENTATION* attribute. Both calls require a Boolean value of *TRUE* to be passed as the last parameter.

- The DWM sends the application the *WM_DWMSENDICONICLIVEPREVIEWBITMAP* window message when a live preview needs to be rendered.

- The application responds to the message by calling the *DwmSetIconicLivePreviewBitmap* function and passing the live preview bitmap as a parameter.

- The application can invalidate the current live preview cached with the DWM by calling the *DwmInvalidateIconicBitmaps* function.

- When the application is no longer interested in customizing the live preview bitmaps, it repeats the first step, passing the Boolean value of *FALSE* as the last parameter.

The managed equivalent in the Windows API Code Pack is also similar—if you already have a *TabbedThumbnail* instance and you provided a live preview bitmap when asked, there is nothing else to be done.

There are two minor subtleties with regard to live preview customization that can be used to further tweak the user experience. The *DwmSetIconicLivePreviewBitmap* function takes two additional parameters:

- The *offset* parameter is a *POINT* structure (*Point* in managed code) that determines the offset within the client area of the original window at which the live preview bitmap should be displayed. This makes it possible to customize the live preview of some part of the window, allowing the rest of the window frame to reap the fruits of the default DWM live preview. (It becomes handy in the subsequent section regarding window switchers, where only child windows require live preview customization.)

- The *dwSITFlags* parameter determines whether a standard window frame should be drawn around the provided live bitmap. This parameter is useful if you are not capturing the window frame area and want the DWM to draw this part of the bitmap for you. (Because of its usefulness, this is also the managed wrapper's default behavior.)

> **Note** In the Windows API Code Pack, the latter parameter is exposed through the *TabbedThumbnail.DisplayFrameAroundBitmap* property. The former parameter is exposed through the *TabbedThumbnail.PeekOffset* property, and it's calculated automatically when possible (but for hidden controls it's often impossible to retrieve implicitly).

Window Switchers

In the previous section, you learned how an application can provide custom thumbnails and custom live previews to make these user-interface features more useful and productive. However, we focused on top-level windows only; these are the windows recognized by the DWM. Some other windows, such as child windows in an MDI or TDI application, are not top-level windows and nonetheless require separate window thumbnails for each document or tab. The ability to create thumbnails and live previews for child windows (or tabs) is the subject of this section.

Internet Explorer 8 is a TDI application that takes advantage of this customization functionality. Although it has only one top-level window, when the user opens multiple tabs multiple thumbnails are spawned from the taskbar button. Hovering over each produces a live preview of the individual tab within the Internet Explorer frame, as shown in the following screen shot:

Note This is clearly more user-friendly than allowing the DWM to exercise its default behavior and provide a single thumbnail of the Internet Explorer window with *all* tabs visible in one thumbnail. Some other tabbed Web browsers have not yet adapted to the Windows 7 taskbar environment and offer an inferior visual experience in this area.

To provide thumbnails and live previews for child windows, extra work is required to circumvent the following DWM limitation: the current version of the DWM is incapable of communicating with non-top-level windows. This means that for each child window, a proxy top-level window must be created—this proxy receives DWM window messages on the child window's behalf so that an appropriate thumbnail and live preview can be rendered. Here is the process for doing so using the native DWM interfaces:

- In the *WM_CREATE* message handler, the window procedure of the child window creates a proxy window (usually an invisible top-level window with a 1-by-1 size) and passes the handle to the proxy window to the *ITaskbarList3::RegisterTab* function. The main window handle also needs to be passed as the second parameter so that the taskbar knows where to group the new tab. Next, the *ITaskbarList3::SetTabOrder* function is called to let the taskbar know where the tab belongs in the thumbnail group. (Passing *NULL* for the last *hwndInsertBefore* parameter places it at the end of the list.)

- The application then repeats the steps from the previous sections (Custom Thumbnails and Custom Live Previews) to let the DWM know that it's interested in customizing the thumbnail and live preview for the proxy window. Note that the handle to the top-level proxy window must be passed to the relevant APIs because the DWM will not communicate with non-top-level windows.

- In the *WM_DWMSENDICONICTHUMBNAIL* and *WM_DWMSENDICONLIVEPREVIEWBITMAP* message handlers of the proxy window procedure, render the thumbnail or live preview, respectively, of the child window that corresponds to this proxy window, and then pass it to the DWM using the *DwmSetIconicThumbnail* and *DwmSetIconicLivePreviewBitmap* APIs, as described in the previous section.

- In the *WM_ACTIVATE* message handler of the proxy window procedure, activate the child window within the context of the application. In the case of a Web browser tab, this means switching to the tab—making it active and visible. (Remember to ensure that the *wParam* parameter of the window message is *WA_ACTIVE* or *WA_CLICKACTIVE*.)

- In the *WM_CLOSE* message handler of the proxy window procedure, close the child window within the context of the application and call the *ITaskbarList3::UnregisterTab* function with the proxy window as a parameter to let the taskbar know that the proxy window is no longer relevant. At this time, the proxy window itself can also be destroyed.

The following code shows a skeletal implementation of a proxy window that can be used to delegate DWM thumbnail and live preview requests as described earlier:

```
ITaskbarList3* pTaskbar;     //Initialized elsewhere
HWND hMainWnd;

//Child window procedure:
if (msg == WM_CREATE) {
    HWND hPrx = CreateWindow(...);
    pTaskbar->RegisterTab(hPrx, hMainWnd);
    pTaskbar->SetTabOrder(hPrx, NULL);

    BOOL truth = TRUE;
    DwmSetWindowAttribute(hPrx, DWMWA_HAS_ICONIC_BITMAP, &truth, sizeof(truth));
    DwmSetWindowAttribute(hPrx, DWMWA_FORCE_ICONIC_REPRESENTATION, &truth, sizeof(truth));
}

HWND hChildWnd;

//Proxy window procedure:
if (msg == WM_DWMSENDICONICTHUMBNAIL) {
    HBITMAP hbmp = GrabThumbnailOf(hChildWnd);
    DwmSetIconicThumbnail(hwnd, hbmp, 0);
}
if (msg == WM_DWMSENDICONICLIVEPREVIEWBITMAP) {
    HBITMAP hbmp = GrabScreenShotOf(hChildWnd);
    DwmSetIconicLivePreviewBitmap(hwnd, hbmp, NULL, 0);
}
```

```
if (msg == WM_ACTIVATE && (wParam == WA_ACTIVE || wParam == WA_CLICKACTIVE)) {
    ActivateTheChildWindow(hChildWnd);
}
if (msg == WM_CLOSE) {
    CloseTheChildWindow(hChildWnd);
    DestroyWindow(hProxyWnd);
}
```

This difficult process is significantly simplified in the managed equivalent, the already-familiar *TaskbarManager.Instance.TabbedThumbnail* property from the Windows API Code Pack. (We used this property in the previous sections.) This time, when creating the *TabbedThumbnailPreview* instance, pass the main (parent) window handle as the first parameter and the child window handle as the second parameter. The underlying library code automatically creates a proxy window for you, so you can continue using the *SetImage* method to provide a preview when necessary, or you can let the library attempt to generate a thumbnail and live preview for you.

> **Note** In this case, relying on the default behavior, which automatically generates a screen shot of the child window, is even riskier than before—it's not always possible to render a screen shot of any child window. For example, a tab page in a tab control that is not currently visible does not draw—so there is no way of obtaining its screen shot without intimate familiarity with its rendering code. In fact, it might be the case that the child window is not even rendered before it is made visible!

The following code is an excerpt from the implementation of a simple Web browser—a demonstration of the custom window switchers discussed in this section:

```
TabPage newTab = new TabPage(txtAddress.Text);
WebBrowser browser = new WebBrowser();
browser.Dock = DockStyle.Fill;
newTab.Controls.Add(browser);
browser.Navigate(txtAddress.Text);
tabs.TabPages.Add(newTab);

browser.Navigated += delegate
{
    TabbedThumbnail preview = new TabbedThumbnail(Handle, newTab);
    preview.Title = txtAddress.Text;
    TaskbarManager.Instance.TabbedThumbnail.AddThumbnailPreview(preview);
};
```

The Windows 7 Training Kit for Developers contains an excellent example of window switchers in native code. Specifically, it has the infrastructure for setting up a thumbnail preview and live preview for tab pages in a standard Win32 tab control. This infrastructure can be easily reused in your applications. To read more, see

http://blogs.microsoft.co.il/blogs/sasha/archive/2009/08/12/windows-7-taskbar-tabbed-thumbnails-and-previews-in-native-code.aspx and

http://blogs.microsoft.co.il/blogs/sasha/archive/2009/09/07/c-wrapper-for-windows-7-taskbar-tabbed-thumbnails.aspx.

The resulting Web browser has custom thumbnails and live previews for each tab, providing a visual experience that is quite similar to that of Internet Explorer 8:

Summary

In this chapter, you saw how to use the advanced Windows 7 taskbar features to increase your users' productivity and provide a compelling visual experience.

You learned how to customize application Jump Lists to contain the Recent and Frequent categories, user tasks, and categorized destinations. You added remote-control functionality to your taskbar thumbnails by providing a thumbnail toolbar. Finally, you customized thumbnails and live previews for top-level windows, as well as for child windows, to deliver the most appropriate representation of your applications.

In the next chapter, you'll see how to use Windows 7 Libraries to synchronize your application with the standard Windows 7 data organization paradigm.

Chapter 4

Organize My Data: Libraries in Windows 7

This chapter details the new functionality offered by Windows 7 Libraries. We'll review the Windows Explorer changes that promote the new user experience that Libraries offer; then we'll explore the underlying architecture supporting Libraries.

First, we'll look at the Windows Shell and Windows Explorer to better understand the important role that Libraries play in the new user experience. Then we'll dive deep into the new concept of Libraries and review how Libraries work and integrate with Windows Explorer. We'll also take a look at the native Library API and learn how to use it to work with Libraries, as well as review a few managed code samples.

Windows Explorer

To better understand the concept of Libraries in Windows 7, we need to look back to the time before Windows 7. Since the early days of Windows, Windows Explorer has been recognized by users as the main entry point into Windows. It's the main user interface through which users can manage their files, navigate the folder hierarchy, and work with their content. Windows Explorer also enables users to manage their computers, with shortcuts such as Control Panel and My Computer provided directly from Windows Explorer.

The last major update to Windows Explorer was introduced in the Windows Vista timeframe to reflect changes in the user profile storage system that were required to handle large volumes of users' files. However, that update was simply not enough because in the last couple of years we have witnessed a massive explosion of digital information, and with the ever-growing availability of cheap storage space, users tend to accumulate a lot of "stuff" on their computers. What we refer to as "stuff" is generally files such as digital images, video files, and all sorts of documents.

Prior to Windows 7, users had to store and organize their files within a hierarchical folder structure. To help manifest that approach, earlier versions of Windows, such as Windows XP, used the Constant Special Item ID List (CSIDL). The CSIDL values provide a system-independent way to identify special folders used frequently by applications. Windows Vista introduced a new storage scenario and a new user profile namespace called the "Known Folders ID system" that replaced CSIDL values with Known Folder IDs, where a *KNOWNFOLDERID* constant identifies a special folder.

The user's Known Folders are part of his profile and therefore are protected from other users. A user profile (or simply *profile* when used in this context) is a collection of data associated with a specific user. It is a digital representation of a person's identity and data, including that user's Known Folders. For example, the My Music folder can be found under *%USERPROFILE%*\My Documents\My Music, where *%USERPROFILE%* translates to the physical location of the user profile on the computer's hard drive. The default location is c:\users*UserName*\My Documents\, where *UserName* is the user login ID, also known as the *user account ID*. Later, we'll discuss how Windows 7 Libraries interact with Windows Vista Known Folders, because Windows 7 contains both the My Music folder as well as the Music Library. (The Known Folders introduced in Windows Vista still exist and are in use in Windows 7.)

Windows Vista automatically indexes the user's entire Known Folders content to achieve better search optimization. Even so, users commonly store their data files in their Known Folders as well as all over the PC, in various locations such as *c:\temp*, *d:\my work* folder, or even on a network share. Storing data outside the user's profile storage space affects the indexing and therefore the entire search experience, making files less discoverable. When a user stores data files all over the PC, it's harder for her to find that one document she needs to work on at any given time, because she might have forgotten the specific folder in which the document is stored. Windows Search might not find that file, or it might take a while to do so if the folder in which that content is stored is not automatically indexed. And when you think about all the shared network folders—an integral part of where users store data—the story really gets complicated.

Known Folder ID

To support the Known Folders system, Windows Vista includes a set of *KNOWNFOLDERID* constants, a list of GUIDs that identify standard folders registered with the system as Known Folders. Among them, you can find the expected standard user profile folders, such as Pictures, represented by the *FOLDERID_Pictures* constant, and Music, represented by the *FOLDERID_Music* constant. But there are additional Known Folders where users can store data, such as Video, Downloads, and Favorites. There are even Known Folders that users might not acknowledge as being part of their profiles—such as Desktop, Links, and Start Menu. The list of Known Folders is long and includes Program Files, Quick Launch, and Recent Items Desktop. However, these are part of the system's, rather than the user's, Known Folders. Standard users, without administrative rights, don't have write permission to any of the system Known Folders.

Let's review the structure of one *KNOWNFOLDERID* constant. Each constant includes properties, such as GUID, display name, folder type, and default path, as shown in the following table.

Property	Value
GUID	{33E28130-4E1E-4676-835A-98395C3BC3BB}
Display Name	Pictures
Folder Type	PERUSER
Default Path	%USERPROFILE%\Pictures
CSIDL Equivalent	CSIDL_MYPICTURES
Legacy Display Name	My Pictures
Legacy Default Path	%USERPROFILE%\My Documents\My Pictures

Windows 7 introduces several new FOLDERIDs. Among them you can find the Libraries Known Folder IDs, represented by *FOLDERID_Libraries*, which facilitate the new Libraries' functionality. For example, the *FOLDERID_PicturesLibrary* is the new FOLDERID supporting the Pictures library. The PicturesLibrary FOLDERID contains only a GUID property, whereas the rest of the properties are empty. This demonstrates that libraries are not regular folders and are just abstract definition.

The KNOWNFOLDERID constants for the default libraries include the following:

- FOLDERID_DocumentsLibrary
- FOLDERID_PicturesLibrary
- FOLDERID_MusicLibrary
- FOLDERID_RecordedTVLibrary
- FOLDERID_VideosLibrary

All FOLDERID values are defined in Knownfolders.h and can be found in the Windows 7 Software Development Kit at *http://msdn.microsoft.com/en-us/library/dd378457.aspx*.

Changes Made to Windows Explorer in Windows 7

In Windows 7, Libraries address the problem of users' data being stored all over the PC by allowing users to have full control over their Documents Library folder structure. This means that in Windows 7, users can define which folders to include in the Documents library. This is true for every library in Windows 7. But before we dive into the definition of a library in Windows 7, let's look at the Libraries' role in the experience of a user using Windows Explorer.

Windows 7 introduces several changes to Windows Explorer: both in the user interface and in the way users interact with Windows Explorer. The changes were made to simplify browsing as well as to provide better search capabilities so that you can quickly locate that one file you're looking for, wherever it might be stored on the local computer or remote server.

Windows Explorer in Windows 7 offers a familiar user experience to users of Windows XP and Windows Vista. Using Libraries should feel just as natural as using any other folder. With that said, Windows Explorer in Windows 7 provides a cleaner user experience around everyday tasks like navigation; viewing common files such as documents, images, and music; removing a lot of the clutter in the Navigation pane; and making it easy to preview documents in the Preview pane. Another improvement in Windows 7 is the integrated search function, which makes it easier to perform a customized search on a given library directly from Windows Explorer by adding to the existing search box specific search filters such as Authors, Modified Date, File Type, Date Taken, and others. These filters are based on metadata associated with each file and are quickly accessible to Windows Explorer because the files in a given library are indexed in advance.

For example, the following screen shot displays the view of the Pictures library, including an image preview and the search filters as shown in the gray box in the top right corner. The search filters enable the user to fine-tune a given search and therefore narrow the search results.

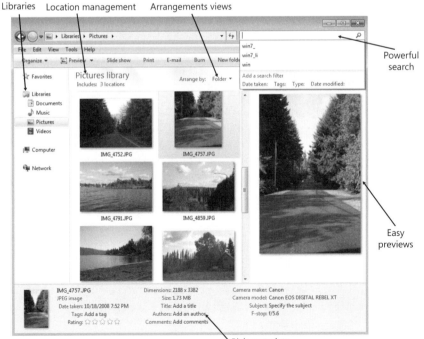

This rich and high-performance user experience is powered by Libraries and the way they integrate into the Windows Shell.

Welcome to Libraries

After presenting this brief preview, we can now say that a *library* is a logical representation of the user's data that is independent of the folder hierarchy. Users can unify and flatten the folder hierarchy by aggregating any number of folders, located at different physical locations on their local machine or, in some cases, on remote machines, into a single view represented as a library. At the same time, a library can be viewed as a collection of user folders; it's the new entry point to user data in Windows 7. Usually, libraries are used to view all files of the same type or files that share a common characteristic, such as pictures or music. By allowing users to define and add new locations to a library, Windows 7 eliminates the problem of a user's data existing outside the user's Known Folders. Now, users can simply add any number of folders, making them an integral part of a library and thus virtually including these files in the user profile Known Folders. This means you don't have to search multiple locations to find the files you're looking for. Remember, these folders are automatically indexed by Windows Search; therefore, libraries can also be viewed as locations where users can quickly and easily find and organize their data as collections of items spanning multiple locations. And the nice thing about libraries in Windows 7 is that they are just another part of Windows Explorer, so users will find that they look and behave much like regular folders do.

Note that Libraries don't actually store the files of the folders it aggregates: it provides a unified view of all the files that are present in the aggregated folders and subfolders. Libraries simply display the aggregates files as a set and enable users to access and arrange the files in different views. For instance, if a user has picture files in folders on his local hard disk or on another Windows 7 network share, the user can add these locations to his Pictures library and have a unified view of all his pictures using the Pictures library. When viewing the contents of a library, the user can choose the way files are arranged and displayed. The user can choose the way pictures are arranged and displayed in the Pictures library from the drop-down menu in the top right corner of Windows Explorer. For example, users can choose to arrange their pictures into groups by the month the picture was taken. This results in a unified view of all the pictures in the Pictures library grouped by month.

The following image illustrates the result of grouping by the *Tag* value associated with each picture.

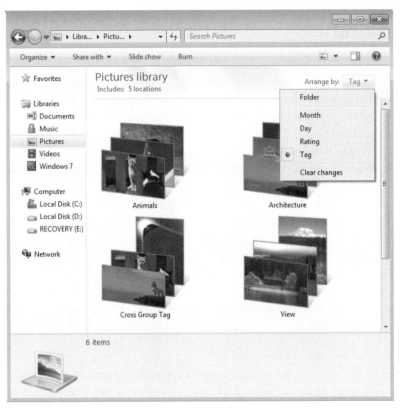

Different arrangements are available per Library type. For example, the Videos library allows you to arrange videos by their length, and the Pictures library provides arrangements by tag or the month the picture was taken. Libraries can provide this rich user experience and functionality because the folders are being indexed; therefore, the contents of the library item's metadata are highly accessible.

Having a unified view of all pictures in the Pictures library can be convenient for end users, but this is also useful for developers. Libraries promote consistency among applications. Before Windows 7, a music application—for example, Windows Media Player—had to maintain its own database that contained metadata about the location of each song. Usually, this database was not synchronized with the contents of the user's Music folder. If the user moved a song from one folder to another, that change was not reflected in the music application database, resulting in a conflict that had a negative impact on the user experience. With the unified view of the user's music files presented by the user Music library, an application such as Windows Media Player can use the Music library as its music repository.

Now applications can take advantage of the fact that there is a single location where all of the user's data is represented and accessible. Applications that rely on libraries are not required to maintain their own databases because the Windows Shell does it for them, ensuring that the application is always in sync with the user content. For example, the version of Windows Media Player that ships with Windows 7 maintains a limited database; it relies on the user's Music library and is fully synchronized with it. Any change a user makes to a song's location within the library boundaries in Windows Explorer is automatically reflected in Windows Media Player, and any change to a song location made in Windows Media Player is reflected in Windows Explorer.

In Windows 7, Windows Explorer has a dedicated user interface, allowing users to directly manipulate the contents of a library by adding or removing folders. Users can add any supported folder they want, even a library! For a folder to be supported in libraries, it must be indexable on the local machine, indexed on a remote Windows machine, or located on a server whose files are indexed by Windows Search. Libraries can contain network folders, but users won't be able to access the contents of such folders unless the network is accessible. Using the Libraries API, developers can perform all the tasks that users can perform through the UI, plus additional tasks such as adding unsupported folders to a library or changing the library icon. Later in the chapter, we'll review interfaces provided by this API.

Libraries under the Hood

Now that we have a better understanding of what libraries represent and how users as well as developers can benefit from them, let's examine how libraries work and how they integrate into the Windows Shell.

In some ways, a library is similar to a folder. From a user's point of view, a library looks and behaves just like a regular folder. For example, when you open a library, one or more files are shown. However, unlike a folder, a library gathers files stored in several locations—a subtle but important difference. Libraries monitor folders that contain files and enable users to access and arrange these files in different ways, but libraries don't really store users' files. A user can save an image directly to the Pictures library, but as we already mentioned, the Pictures library, or any other given library, is not a real folder—so where will this picture be saved? The default save location is the user's pictures folder, also known as My Pictures, which is part of the user profile. The user has full control over the default save location as well as the other locations that are part of a library.

As shown in the following screen shot, the Pictures Library Locations management dialog, accessible directly from the Windows Explorer UI, contains several locations on the local hard drive. One of the folders is designated as the default save location.

Note that the Pictures library didn't replace the My Pictures folder from Windows Vista; it simply includes that folder as one of many locations. The Pictures library is now the primary way to access pictures and the default location to which your pictures are saved. However, there is still a folder called My Pictures, which is the default save location for the Pictures library, and users can access it directly. But it's highly recommended that both users and developers use the Pictures library.

Windows 7 ships with a few libraries, including Documents, Music, Pictures, and Videos. By default, each library includes two libraries. For example, by default the Music library includes the "Public Music" folder that contains public content accessible to all users on the local machine. The second folder included in the Music library is the "My Music" folder that contains "my" music files, which are specific per user. (This is the same old My Pictures folder from Windows Vista; in Windows 7, it's just included in the Pictures library.)

A library in Windows 7 is represented by a Library definition file, an XML file with the extension .library-ms. The file name is the actual library's name. For example, the Pictures library is represented by an XML file called Pictures.library-ms. Library files in Windows 7 can be found in a Known Folder designated as *FOLDERID_Libraries*. By default, that translates to *%USERPROFILE%*\AppData\Roaming\Microsoft\Windows\Libraries, where *%USERPROFILE%* is the location of the user profile—by default, c:\users\<*USER NAME*>. Any new library created, either by the user using the Windows Explorer UI or by developers programmatically using the Windows Shell APIs, will be represented by a library file in the Libraries folder.

A newly created library is an empty library (with no folder associated with it). The contents of the library definition file are listed in the following XML snippet:

```
<?xml version="1.0" encoding="UTF-8"?>
<libraryDescription xmlns="http://schemas.microsoft.com/windows/2009/library">
    <ownerSID>S-1-5-21-2127521184-1604012920-1887927527-4897363</ownerSID>
    <version>1</version>
    <isLibraryPinned>true</isLibraryPinned>
</libraryDescription>
```

The root XML element is *libraryDescription*, which contains child elements that define the library.

Here is a summary of the code elements:

- The *ownerSID* element defines the Security ID of the user who created the library to isolated libraries and protect user data from other users.

- The *isLibraryPinned* element is a Boolean element that defines whether the library is pinned to the left navigation pane in Windows Explorer.

- The *version* element defines the content version of this library: the number of times the library definition file has been changed. We just created this library definition file, so the version number is 1.

After a user adds a folder to a library, a few more lines are added to the file, and now the library definition file looks like this:

```
<libraryDescription xmlns="http://schemas.microsoft.com/windows/2009/library">
    <ownerSID>S-1-5-21-2127521184-1604012920-1887927527-4897363</ownerSID>
    <version>6</version>
    <isLibraryPinned>true</isLibraryPinned>
    <iconReference>C:\Windows\system32\imageres.dll,-65</iconReference>
    <templateInfo>
        <folderType>{5C4F28B5-F869-4E84-8E60-F11DB97C5CC7}</folderType>
    </templateInfo>
    <propertyStore>
        <property name="HasModifiedLocations" type="boolean"><![CDATA[true]]></property>
    </propertyStore>
    <searchConnectorDescriptionList>
        <searchConnectorDescription>
            <isDefaultSaveLocation>true</isDefaultSaveLocation>
            <isSupported>true</isSupported>
            <simpleLocation>
                <url>D:\Work\Windows 7</url>
                <serialized>MBAA ... Ak43LBz</serialized>
            </simpleLocation>
        </searchConnectorDescription>
```

```
        </searchConnectorDescriptionList>
    </libraryDescription>
```

A few new XML elements were added to the original XML listing, such as *templateInfo*, *propertyStore*, and a big *searchConnectorDescriptionList* element. Here are the details of some of these elements:

- The *templateInfo* element, an optional container element, lets the author specify the folder type to control the available views and file arrangements when they are viewed in Windows Explorer. This element has no attributes and only one mandatory child that defines the *folderType*—a GUID representation of this folder type that can be documents, videos, pictures, images, or any of the special folder types.

- The *searchConnectorDescriptionList* element contains one or more search connectors that map to physical locations included in this library. Each search connector is represented by a *searchConnectorDescription* element.

- The *searchConnectorDescription* element contains a *simpleLocation* element that describes one location included in the library.

- The *url* element defines a URL for this location. This URL is provided only for human readability and should not be used by developers. Developers should use the *serialized* element to retrieve the real folder location. This value can be a regular file:// URL (as defined in RFC 1738 at *http://www.ietf.org/rfc/rfc1738.txt*).

- The *serialized* element contains a base64 encoded ShellLink that points to the location defined by the *url* element. The Windows Shell automatically creates the ShellLink from the value of the *url* element.

  If you take a closer look at one of the default libraries, such as Pictures, you'll notice that the Pictures library definition file is a bit more complex and contains a few more elements.

- The *iconReference* element defines an icon resource using the standard Windows resource style—for example, <iconReference> C:\Windows\system32\imageres.dll,-65 </iconReference>. This icon presents the library in Windows Explorer.

  Some of you might wonder what does the "–65" number represent. Well, this is the standard syntax for accessing resources in a compiled binary resource file. A resource file can be a .dll file or embedded in executable. In both cases this index number points to the relevant resource elements in the list of resources. Resources enumeration starts from the number zero and grows in a sequential way up to the total number of resource elements. The minus sign represent the relevant offset of the resource file.

With Visual Studio you can open any form of resource file that you want. You can file resources files - .rc files, or dll files or even an executable. Simply choose to open a file from Visual Studio.

For example, using Visual Studio to open the imageres.dll, found in C:\Windows\System32, results in the following image. As you can see, the dll file includes a list of icons with index number that you can view. These are the exact numbers used in the XML of any other resource reverence.

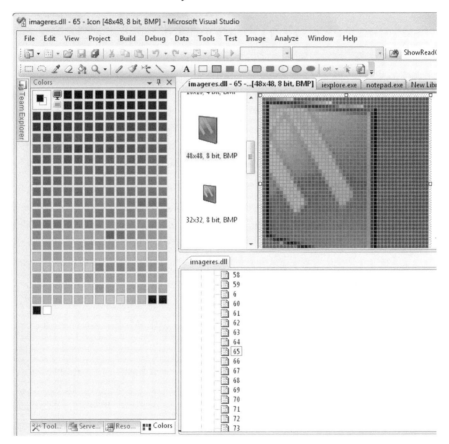

Important: It's highly recommended that you use the Shell API or the new Windows 7 Libraries API, described in detail later in this chapter, rather than directly accessing and working with a library definition file, despite the fact that Microsoft doesn't conceal the location or format of the library files.

Working with Libraries

As we've seen so far, libraries are the new entry points for user data in Windows 7. Libraries are also an integral part of the Windows Shell and are promoted across Windows 7 in Windows Explorer, the Start menu, and the Common File Dialog. Windows 7 users will use libraries in their day-to-day activities; they'll expect applications running on Windows 7 to work properly with libraries and to have the same user experience. Therefore, as developers, you need to know how to work with libraries to make your applications library aware.

Make Your Application Library Aware

Let's start by examining what happens if a given application doesn't properly support Windows 7 libraries. Let's assume an application needs to save a file to the local hard drive and prompts the user to select a location there. As part of her Windows 7 experience, the user can select the Documents library as her save destination because this is where she stores all her documents. But if the application fails to recognize that the Documents library is not a real folder and tries to perform a save operation to the Documents library location, the application will most likely fail to perform the task, because libraries are a non–file system location.

A library-aware application should be aware that users might choose a library as a save location and understand that a library is not a real folder, and it should act accordingly. Furthermore, most applications allow users to interact with the file system in their experience. An application should provide users with the same familiar entry points offered by libraries. By including folder locations in a library, a user designates where her important data lives, and thus applications should promote these locations by enabling library browsing.

As developers, we have several integration points with Windows 7 that can help applications become library aware:

- **Use the Common File Dialog.** The most basic integration option, and probably the easiest to implement, is the Common File Dialog (CFD) for picking files and folders when performing save or load operations. In the next section, "Using the Right Common File Dialog to Work with Libraries," we describe in great detail which CFD is best to use and the specific API, but for now CFD will do. Suppose that in your application you are using the CFD to prompt the user to choose a location, pick a folder, and save the file, and the user selects the Documents library. The CFD returns the default save location, which is a valid file system path that you can work with and to which you can save the file. If you are using the CFD to open files, the user can choose a file from a library, and the system returns the fully qualified file system path to your application to work with.

- **Select and consume library content.**   The second integration option is to enable applications to select and consume library content. Imagine the case of a slideshow application that presents pictures. By using libraries, the user essentially tells the system that his important pictures are stored in the Pictures library. Therefore, the application can simply be pointed directly to the Pictures library to show the user's entire pictures collection. From the development point of view, such an application will not need to maintain a separate configuration file or database of pictures, because it can rely on the Pictures library, which simplifies development efforts.

- **Manipulate Libraries.**   The last and most advanced integration option is the new *IShellLibrary* API, which you can use to stay in sync with the contents of a given library's contents and to directly manipulate libraries. The *IShellLibrary* API gives you full control over libraries, including enabling you to create new libraries and control the different properties discussed earlier in this chapter. By integrating directly with libraries, applications can drive consistency with the Windows Explorer UI in Windows 7 and provide the best user experience.

Using the Right Common File Dialog to Work with Libraries

Windows always offered the CFD that developers use in their applications to prompt users to open and save files. The CFD displays a dialog box from which the user can select a file or folder by navigating through the local machine folder hierarchy as well as that of remote servers. The CFD is widely known and used by the majority of Microsoft software products as well as by a large number of third-party software applications. Windows 7 libraries are "first-class citizens" in the CFD, a status that allows users to browse through libraries, search libraries, and even pick an actual library—rather than a specific folder in the library—as a save location.

Take, for example, Notepad. Notepad uses the CFD that was introduced in Windows Vista and upgraded in Windows 7 for working with libraries. When a user wants to save a text file, Notepad prompts the user with CFD to pick a location to save the new text file. The user can choose the Documents library as his save location, and the text file will be saved to the default save location of the Documents library. Behind the scenes, the CFD automatically detects that the Documents library is not a regular folder and returns the default save location file system path. Then Notepad saves the file to the default save location.

This behavior is the out-of-the-box experience for users and applications using the new CFD. It's highly recommended that you use the right version of Windows CFD rather than a custom proprietary dialog to stay consistent with Windows 7 Libraries.

There are two versions of the CFD, so even if a given application is using a CFD, it still needs to use the proper version. The most recent version was introduced in Windows Vista and updated in Windows 7 to support Libraries natively. Note that to support backward compatibility, the APIs for using the CFD have not changed since Windows Vista, and therefore applications that are already using the CFD will enjoy library integration in Windows 7. However, the legacy version of the CFD, shown in the next image, doesn't support libraries.

Even if libraries are present, as indicated by the Libraries icon in the left navigation pane, a user can't choose a library, such as the Documents library, as the location to save a file. Note that the Documents library is highlighted but the right bottom button caption is Open and not Save. The user will have to drill into the Documents library to choose a specific folder to save the file. The legacy CFD doesn't expose the search and sort functionalities that libraries offer. The legacy CFD also doesn't support selection across several folders, the basic functionality promoted in libraries.

It's important to use the proper APIs to show the correct version of CFD. There is a great article on MSDN that explains in details the new API's introduced in Windows Vista (*http://msdn.microsoft.com/en-us/library/bb776913.aspx*). You do this by using the family of *IFileDialog* native APIs that were introduced with Windows Vista and work perfectly in Windows7: *IFileDialog, IFileOpenDialog, IFileSaveDialog, IFileDialogCustomize, IFileDialogEvents*, and *IFileDialogControlEvents*. These APIs replace the legacy *GetOpenFileName* and *GetSaveFileName* APIs from earlier Windows versions and provide a more flexible mechanism for picking and interacting with items in the Shell namespace. By using the new *IFileDialog* APIs, your application can work directly within the Shell namespace instead of using file system paths. This is crucial when interacting with libraries, which do not return a file system path. Native applications should use the *IFileDialog* COM interface, and Microsoft .NET Framework applications should use the *System.Windows.Forms.FileDialog*–derived classes *System.Windows.Forms.OpenFileDialog* and *System.Windows.Forms.SaveFileDialog*.

Using *IFileDialog* to select libraries   The *IFileDialog* interface is the base interface for both *IFileOpenDialog* and *IFileSaveDialog*. The Shell native API is COM based; therefore, before using any COM object, you must remember to initialize the COM object by calling *CoCreateInstance*. As an example, the following code snippet prompts the user to choose a library or folder by showing the common save file dialog.

```
IShellItem *ppsi = NULL;
IFileSaveDialog *pfod;
HRESULT hr = CoCreateInstance(
    CLSID_FileSaveDialog,
    NULL,
    CLSCTX_INPROC,
    IID_PPV_ARGS(&pfod));
if (SUCCEEDED(hr))
{
    hr = pfod->SetOptions(FOS_PICKFOLDERS);
    if (SUCCEEDED(hr))
    {
        hr = pfod->Show(hWndParent);
        if (SUCCEEDED(hr))
        {
            hr = pfod->GetResult(&ppsi);
            // use the returned IShellItem
            ppsi->Release();
        }
    }
    pfod->Release();
}
```

Here you can see we're using the *IFileSaveDialog* interface, but the details and principles shown here also apply to the rest of the *IFileDialog* family. After initializing the **pfod IFileSaveDialog* variable, we set the dialog options to pick folders by passing the *FOS_PICKFOLDERS* flag to the *IFileOpenDialog.SetOptions()*. This code presents the Open dialog with the choice of folders rather than files and allows the user to choose a library. The CFD returns the default save location folder associated with the chosen library.

> **Important**   One of the flags that can be passed to the *SetOptions* function is *FOS_FORCEFILESYSTEM*, which ensures that returned items are only system items that are real file system locations. Libraries are not system items and therefore do not represent a real file system location. To make sure the CFD can choose libraries, developers must not set the *FOS_FORCEFILESYSTEM* flag.

Displaying the CFD using .NET   When it comes to showing a CFD using .NET, developers should use the *System.Windows.Forms.FileDialog*–derived classes *System.Windows.Forms.OpenFileDialog* and *System.Windows.Forms.SaveFileDialog*. Please note that the *Microsoft.Win32.FileDialog*–derived classes for WPF applications use the legacy version of the CFD and therefore .NET developers should always use the CFD from the

WinForms namespace, even WPF developers. The following code snippet prompts the user to choose a save location by showing the common save file dialog:

```
System.Windows.Forms.SaveFileDialog _fd = new System.Windows.Forms.SaveFileDialog();
_fd.Title = "Please choose a location to save your file";
_fd.FileName = "[Get Folder…]";
_fd.Filter = "Library|no.files";
if (_fd.ShowDialog() == System.Windows.Forms.DialogResult.OK)
{
    string dir_path = System.IO.Path.GetDirectoryName(_fd.FileName);
    if (dir_path != null && dir_path.Length > 0)
    {
        lblResult.Content = dir_path;
    }
}
```

Here you can see that we're setting a few properties of the *SaveFileDialog* to allow users to choose a library. We're setting the *FileName* property to *[Get Folder]* and the *Filter* property to *Library|no.files*. This combination ensures that the user can choose only a library or a folder. When the user chooses a library, the path that returns from the CFD will be the default save location of the chosen library. Running the preceding code snippet shows the correct version of the common save file dialog that allows a user to search and use different pivotal views, as shown in the following screen shot.

Working with the Shell Namespace

Before we dive into the Shell Libraries programming model, we need to understand how the Windows Shell works. The Windows Shell is the main area of user interaction in Windows. The Shell includes user-facing Windows feature such as the Taskbar, the Start Menu, Windows Explorer windows, search results, and even less obvious windows such as the Control Panel. The shell is hosted in a process called explorer.exe, and most users recognize it as Windows Explorer.

The Windows Shell enables users to accomplish a variety of tasks, including launching applications and managing the operating system by performing operations on shell objects. The most common shell objects are folders and files, followed by virtual objects such as the Recycle Bin, Printers, or the Control Panel.

Shell objects are organized into a hierarchical namespace that encompasses the file system namespace. The shell namespace includes folders and files; folders that are not part of the physical file system are also called *virtual folders*. The root of the shell namespace hierarchy is the user's Desktop, followed by virtual folders such as My Computer and Recycle Bin, and of course "regular" folders and files' shell objects. To navigate the shell namespace, programmers use item ID lists, which contain a path to a shell object. These lists can be absolute (begin at the root of the namespace) or relative, just like file system paths.

My Computer		C:\		My Docs		MyFile.htm		
Cb	abID	Cb	abID	Cb	abID	Cb	abID	2-byte NULL

Figure 4-1 A simple Shell Item ID list

Windows applications interact with and extend the Windows Shell using COM interfaces and structures, which are accessible from most Windows programming languages. Specifically, C++ and .NET applications have paved the road for direct access to the shell, which is implemented in shell32.dll. Some examples include the following:

- An application can query the search application (Windows Search by default) to retrieve information from the same index used by the rest of Windows.

- An application can register a thumbnail handler for its file type, so once a user views such an item in the Windows Explorer, a proper thumbnail is displayed.

- An application can register a preview handler for its file type so that when the user views files in Windows Explorer, a preview of the file can be displayed in the preview pane. For example, Windows Media Player files in Windows use this functionality to display a live stream of media in the preview pane.

- An application can register a namespace extension so that when the user navigates to a specific location, a virtual hierarchy of files and folders is displayed. The .NET Framework registers a namespace extension for the Global Assembly Cache store, which is navigated like a standard directory.

Other examples for shell integration include Search Providers, Desktop Gadgets, Synchronization Center handlers, Control Panel items, custom Windows Explorer toolbars, Taskbar desk bands, and many others.

In the rest of this section, we'll review some of the most important shell interfaces to provide a common understanding of these for the discussion of them in the rest of this book. Often, you will not need intimate knowledge and understanding of how a specific shell interface works; however, being aware of its existence and possibilities increases your ability to successfully integrate an application into the Windows 7 experience.

IShellFolder   The *IShellFolder* interface represents shell folder objects from the shell namespace. Its methods enable the user to determine the contents of a folder, to retrieve the display name of an item in a folder, and to parse a display name relative to the folder and obtain an item ID list. Objects implementing this interface are usually created by other Shell folder objects.

You typically begin browsing with shell folders by using the *SHGetDesktopFolder* function to retrieve the desktop folder; you then proceed from there to request a specific shell folder in the hierarchy. Known Folders, represented by the *KNOWNFOLDER* enumeration, can be accessed at any time without you having prior knowledge of their specific file system path using the *SHGetKnownFolderItem* method. Shell folder objects can be added to Windows 7 shell libraries. Note that a library is also represented by a shell folder object, which is not surprising because it appears in the shell namespace.

IShellItem   The *IShellItem* interface represents an item in the shell, typically a file. A shell item is an absolute item ID list. Items are individual, self-contained content sources. The Windows Vista extension of this interface is called *IShellItem2*, and it provides the ability to query the property store associated with a shell item. Property store represents a generic way to address different object properties. Since each shell object can have any number of properties and a wide verity of properties types, there is a need for a way to set and get any COM's object properties. The *PROPVARIANT* structure is used in the *ReadMultiple* and *WriteMultiple* methods of *IPropertyStorage* to define the type tag and the value of a property in a property set.

IPropertyStore   The *IPropertyStore* interface can be used to manage the property store associated with various shell objects. For example, a shell link is associated with a property store that specifies the application user model ID (also known as the AppID) of its target. Dozens of other properties are provided by the Windows Shell and can be set and queried programmatically by applications using the *GetValue* and *SetValue* methods.

Applications do not implement the shell item interfaces. To create a shell item, programmers use the *SHCreateItemFromIDList* and *SHCreateItemFromParsingName*, or *CoCreateInstance* with *CLSID_ShellItem*. Shell items are the currency of the Shell UI and its programming model, and they are used throughout this book—in shell libraries, Jump Lists, and elsewhere.

IShellLink   The *IShellLink* interface represents a link in the shell, typically a link to a file or a program. A shell link is associated with a path to an item (for example, a program), command-line arguments that are passed to it, an icon location and index for the shell link, the working directory for the shell link target, and a keyboard shortcut and other properties. Shell link objects can be used to resolve their target, even if it has been moved or renamed, through the *Resolve* method.

Shell links can be created using *CoCreateInstance* with *CLSID_ShellLink*. Shell links are frequently used as Windows 7 jump list tasks and destinations.

IShellLibrary   The *IShellLibrary* interface represents a Windows 7 shell library, which provides an abstraction to a collection of locations with a common trait. Using the shell library object, applications can add, modify, and remove folders from the library; enumerate folders in the library; retrieve the default save location for the library; and resolve the target location of a library folder.

Programs interact with the *IShellLibrary* interface by calling the *SHLoadLibraryFromItem*, *SHLoadLibraryFromKnownFolder*, or *SHLoadLibraryFromParsingName* function. New libraries can be created using the *SHCreateLibrary* method. Other helper functions can be found in ShObjIdl.h and ShellAPI.h, which are part of the SDK, for resolving folder paths in libraries and for adding folders to a library.

ITaskbarList   *ITaskbarList* is part of the Windows Shell programming model. However, it belongs to the Taskbar interface and not to the Libraries interface. Because we provide an overview of the Windows Shell, it makes sense to mention this interface. We describe *ITaskbarList* in great detail in Chapter 2, "Integrate with the Windows 7 Taskbar, Basic Features." The *ITaskbarList* interface (or more specifically, the *ITaskbarList3* and *ITaskbarList4* interfaces) represents the Windows taskbar functionality, which is part of the Windows Shell. Windows 7 introduces unified launching and switching taskbar button functionality, including rich thumbnail representations and previews, thumbnail toolbars, progress and status overlays, switch targets based on individual tabs, and other features that are covered in other chapters in this book.

Consuming Library Content

Libraries fit into the existing shell programming model. From the shell programming model perspective, libraries are storage backed, meaning they are just shell containers like any other file system folder. This is because libraries simply list *IShellItem* objects, which are really folders. The *IShellLibrary* API allows a developer to manipulate libraries, but internally the *IShellLibrary* is working with *IShellItem,* as explained in detail in this chapter. Therefore, a library can be viewed as an extension of a Shell folder, as shown in Figure 4-2.

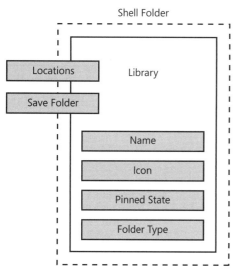

Figure 4-2 Shell Folder

Developers can use the *IShellItem* and *IShellFolder* interfaces and a bunch of helper functions such as *INamespaceWalk::Walk* to enumerate the contents of libraries just as if they were regular folders. Applications can use this behavior to consume the contents of a given library; imagine a slideshow application that can consume the entire contents of the Pictures library by enumerating through all the folders associated with the Pictures library, enumerating for each folder all the pictures in it, and then displaying these images. This means that applications can consume library content without using the new Libraries API and with little change to their existing code base.

The following code snippet shows how to use the *IShellFolder* interface to enumerate through the entire contents of the Picture library:

```
IShellItem *psi;
HRESULT hr = SHGetKnownFolderItem(
                    FOLDERID_PicturesLibrary,
                    KF_FLAG_CREATE,
                    NULL,IID_PPV_ARGS(&psi));
if(SUCCEEDED(hr)){
    IShellFolder *psf;
    hr = psi->BindToHandler(
                    NULL,
```

```
                BHID_SFObject,
                IID_PPV_ARGS(&psf));
    if(SUCCEEDED(hr))
    {
        IEnumIDList *penumIDList;
        psf->EnumObjects(
                NULL,
                SHCONTF_FOLDERS | SHCONTF_NONFOLDERS,
                IID_PPV_ARGS(&penumIDList));
        //use penumIDList to enumerate the content of the folder
    }
}
```

Here you can see that by using the helper function *SHGetKnownFolderItem* we can retrieve the library's correct location by passing the *FOLDERID_PicturesLibrary*, which is a GUID representing the known folder—in our case, the Picture library. *SHGetKnownFolderItem* is a Shell Helper function and is part of a larger group of helper functions that can be found in the *Shlobj.h* header file in the Windows 7 SDK. You want to pay attention to the third parameter of *SHGetKnownFolderItem*, an access token that is used to represent a specific user. In our sample, it is set to null, indicating the current user. However, you can also pass a different access token to impersonate a different user, but you need to make sure you have the correct security privileges. You need to remember that a known folder can be any public folder that the current user might not have access to. A successful call fills the *IShellItem *psi* interface with the correct information about the library represented as a shell item. From this point, the rest of the code is standard shell programming, where we use *BindToHandler* to bind the previously obtained shell item to a shell folder. Next, we enumerate through the different items in the shell folder, which in the case of a library can be either files or folders.

Note the *SHCONTF_FOLDERS* and *SHCONTF_NONFOLDERS* flags that we are passing. They are telling the shell folder that we want to return all the files and folders in a library. We could pass *SHCONTF_NAVIGATION_ENUM* to just get the library folders instead of the entire library contents. The Library Management Window dialog displays the list of folders in the library by passing *SHCONTF_NAVIGATION_ENUM* just to get the folders.

Using the New Libraries API

So far we've covered how libraries work in Windows 7, what effect they might have on applications, and how they fit into the existing shell programming model. But with new functionality comes a new set of APIs to use. Let's start by reviewing the equivalent code for

consuming the contents of a library using the new Windows 7 Libraries API. The following code doesn't contain the required error-handling code that must be used in production code:

```
IShellLibrary *pslLibrary;
HRESULT hr = SHLoadLibraryFromKnownFolder(
                    FOLDERID_PicturesLibrary,
                    STGM_READ,
                    IID_PPV_ARGS(&pslLibrary));
if(SUCCEEDED(hr))
{
    IShellItemArray *psiaFolders;
    hr = pslLibrary->GetFolders(
                    LFF_STORAGEITEMS,
                    IID_PPV_ARGS(&psiaFolders));

    IEnumShellItems *penumShellItems;
    psiaFolders->EnumItems(&penumShellItems);
    //work with penumShellItem to enumerate the library locations.


    penumShellItems->Release();
    psiaFolders->Release();
}
pslLibrary->Release();
```

Here you can see that we use another helper function, *SHLoadLibraryFromKnownFolder*, to create the *IShellLibrary* object. From the *IShellLibrary* object, we can call the *GetFolders* method to return an *IShellItemArray* that later is used to obtain an enumerator to traverse through the entire library contents.

In the example shown earlier, we used another helper function, *SHLoadLibraryFromKnownFolder*. This helper function and others related to Windows 7 Libraries can be found in the *Shlobj.h* header file in the Windows 7 SDK. Here's a list of the important library helper functions:

- **SHAddFolderPathToLibrary** Adds a folder to a library.

- **SHCreateLibrary** Creates an IShellLibrary object.

- **SHLoadLibraryFromItem** Creates and loads an *IShellLibrary* object from a specified library definition file.

- **SHLoadLibraryFromKnownFolder** Creates and loads an IShellLibrary object for a specified KNOWNFOLDERID.

- **SHLoadLibraryFromParsingName** Creates and loads an *IShellLibrary* object for a specified absolute path that can change based on localization. Therefore, it is best to use the *SHLoadLibraryFromKnownFolder*, which is agnostic to localization.

- **SHRemoveFolderPathFromLibrary** Removes a folder from a library.

- **SHResolveFolderPathInLibrary**   Attempts to resolve the target location of a library folder that has been moved or renamed. If you were working on a shared library and someone else (human or software) changed or removed one of the folders in the library without your knowledge, you can try and locate the folder by calling this function. This function will try to look in the history of the library files and figure out what have happened with the required library file. If the library file was deleted, it could be found in the Recycle Bin and therefore can be retrieved if needed.

- **SHSaveLibraryInFolderPath**   Saves an *IShellLibrary* object to disk, which creates an XML library definition file, as mentioned earlier in the chapter, in the desired path. Usually, it makes sense to store library definition files in the default Libraries folder using the SaveInKnownFolder passing the libraries known folder as input parameter, but you can save such a file in any valid location on your disk.

Because all these helper methods are inline functions, you can find their code in the *Shobjidl.h* header file. By reviewing their code, you can get a better understanding of how the library APIs work and how to use the low-level *IShellLibrary* methods. For example, let's review the code for creating a new library. The following code snippet is copied from the *Shobjidl.h* header file:

```
__inline HRESULT SHCreateLibrary(__in REFIID riid, __deref_out void **ppv)


{


    return CoCreateInstance(CLSID_ShellLibrary,NULL, CLSCTX_INPROC_SERVER, riid, ppv);


}
```

Here you can see that under the covers, this helper function simply takes care of calling the COM *CoCreateInstance* function for us.

Let's review another example, adding a new folder to an existing library by using *SHAddFolderPathToLibrary*:

```
__inline HRESULT SHAddFolderPathToLibrary(
    __in IShellLibrary *plib,
    __in PCWSTR pszFolderPath)
{
  IShellItem *psiFolder;
  hr = SHCreateItemFromParsingName(
    pszFolderPath,
    NULL,
    IID_PPV_ARGS(&psiFolder));
```

```
    if (SUCCEEDED(hr))
    {
        hr = plib->AddFolder(psiFolder);
        psiFolder->Release();
    }
    return hr;
}
```

Here you can see that even a helper function is using another helper function to perform its operations. However, the importance of the helper functions lies in how you use them. Let's examine the following code snippet, which creates a new library and adds a folder to it:

```
IShellLibrary *pIShellLibrary;
HRESULT hr = SHCreateLibrary(IID_PPV_ARGS(&pIShellLibrary));
if (SUCCEEDED(hr))
{
    IShellItem *pIShellItem;
    SHAddFolderPathToLibrary(
            pIShellLibrary,
            L"C:\\Users\\Public\\Documents");

    hr = pIShellLibrary->SaveInKnownFolder(
            FOLDERID_Libraries,
            L"My New Library",
            LSF_MAKEUNIQUENAME,
            &pIShellItem);

    pIShellItem->Release();
    pIShellLibrary->Release();
}
```

Here you can see that we create a new *IShellLibrary* object using the *SHCreateLibrary* method. Next, we add the public Documents folder to the library object, save the new library in the Libraries folder with the rest of the libraries, and name the new library My New Library. Behind the scenes, this code creates a new My New Library.library-ms library definition file, which includes a single folder.

In the previous sample, we used the *SaveInKnownFolder* method of the *IShellLibrary* interface to save the new library we created. The *IShellLibrary* interface exposed most of the shell library operations. Most of the methods in the *IShellLibrary* interface are self-explanatory; however, let's review some that require our attention:

- The *Commit* method commits library changes to an existing library file. This means that whenever you programmatically change a library, you need to call the *commit* method to save the changes.

- The *SetIcon* method sets the library icon and takes a string as a parameter that concatenates a resource dynamic-link library (DLL) name and Icon index, separated by a comma.

- The *SetOption* method currently has only one option: to pin the library to the libraries shown in the Windows Explorer navigation pane (the left panel). You need to set the *LOF_PINNEDTONAVPANE* flag in the LIBRARYOPTIONFLAGS structure that is passed as a parameter to the SetOption method.

- The *SetFolderType* method receives a GUID of known folder type templates as an input parameter. This GUID defines the type of library, which can be Generic, Pictures, Music, Videos, Documents, or any other type defined by *FOLDERTYPEID*. Setting the folder type template changes the Windows Explorer view of the library and enables the search options and pivotal view that are specific to the library's type.

Using the Managed Code API

So far, we've seen how to create a new library using the native *IShellLibrary* API; it is time to review a similar example using the managed code API. The following code snippet is based on the Windows API Code Pack. To work with the Code Pack, you need to include a reference in your application to *Microsoft.WindowsAPICodePack.Shell*. The following code snippet creates a new library, adds a few folders, and sets a new default save location. Next, we enumerate through the library's folders.

```
string folder1 = @"c:\temp\pic demo folder1";
string folder2 = @"c:\temp\pic demo folder2";
string folder3 = @"c:\temp\pic demo new default save location";

ShellLibrary lib = new ShellLibrary("My Pictures Demo Lib", true);
lib.Add(folder1);
lib.Add(folder2);
lib.Add(folder3);
lib.LibraryType = LibraryFolderType.Pictures;
lib.DefaultSaveFolder = folder3;

IEnumerator<FileSystemFolder> enumerator = lib.GetEnumerator();
while (enumerator.MoveNext() )
{
    // traverse through the library contents
    FileSystemFolder folder = enumerator.Current;
    Debug.WriteLine(folder.Name);
}
```

Here we're creating a new library by creating a new *ShellLibrary* object. The second parameter is a Boolean indicating whether to override an existing library, which is useful for debugging. After adding a few existing folders using the *ShellLibrary.Add("string")* method, we change the library's folder type to *FolderType.Pictures*, which affects the arrangement options and when viewing My Pictures Demo Lib in Windows Explorer promoting the picture properties. Note that if you try to add a folder that doesn't exist, a *DirectoryNotFoundException* is thrown. Next, we change the default save location—again, make sure you set the default location to a valid folder. For customized libraries, such as our My Pictures Demo Lib, the default save location is the first folder added to the library, and here we demonstrate how to change it using the *ShellLibrary.DefaultSaveFolder* property. Last, we get an enumerator to traverse through the library contents using *ShellLibrary.GetEnumerator()*. Note that *ShellLibrary* is an *IEnumerable<FileSystemFolder>* object that represents a collection of shell folders.

Another very cool feature allows you to control the library icon. This is one of those features that end users don't have access to. It's easy to use, as shown in the following code snippet:

```
library.IconResourceId = new IconReference(icon);
```

You have to obtain an *IconReference* object, but after doing so you get to change the library's icon and set your own special icons. This is a really fun feature to play with, as you can see from the following picture:

Deleting a Library

The last thing left to talk about is how you can delete a library. The *ShellLibrary* object doesn't have a self-destruct mechanism, and therefore you can't delete a library using the *ShellLibrary* object. To delete a library, you need to delete the library XML definition file. The following code snippet receives a string representing the library name, *TESTLIBNAME*, that correlates to the same library definition file we explained earlier in this chapter:

```
string librariesPath =

        System.IO.Path.Combine(

                    Environment.GetFolderPath(

                    Environment.SpecialFolder.ApplicationData),

                    ShellLibrary.LibrariesKnownFolder.RelativePath);

string libraryPath =

        System.IO.Path.Combine(librariesPath, TESTLIBNAME);

string libraryFullPath =

        System.IO.Path.ChangeExtension(libraryPath, "library-ms");

System.IO.File.Delete(libraryFullPath);
```

Here you can see how we create the path to the library definition file. We use that path to the library detention file to delete the file. Deleting the library definition file doesn't delete any of the files in the library, it just deletes the library itself.

Staying in Sync with the User Data

Many existing applications define a set of folders from which to pull data, whether these folders are added to the collection by the user or automatically by the application. If an application currently manages a set of folders, it should consider integrating these folders into one of the existing libraries, or it can create a new library and use the new Libraries APIs to manage them. Doing so establishes consistency between applications and Windows when the user is managing libraries. And users need to manage only a single list of locations instead of a new list of locations for each application. To achieve this, applications can leverage the library management dialog to provide a consistent user experience with management of Windows Explorer libraries. This dialog lets users add and remove folders from the library as well as set the default save location. Applications can simply call the native *SHShowManageLibraryUI* method to invoke this dialog or call *ShowManageLibraryUI* from managed code, as demonstrated by the following code snippet:

```
ShellLibrary lib = ShellLibrary.Load("Pictures", false);
lib.ShowManageLibraryUI( IntPtr.Zero,
    "Title here",
    "Instruction here",
    true);
```

Here we can see that after loading the Pictures library using the *ShellLibrary.Load()* method with write permissions, we invoke the libraries management dialog and allow the users to control their Pictures library from any application, again promoting consistency. If you choose to use the management dialog, changes made by the user to the library are automatically saved to the corresponding library definition file. Note that this dialog does not return any information to the application. If a given application is relying on the contents of a library or currently showing a view of a library, the application needs to receive notifications directly from the shell or file system when modifications are made to the library definition file. You can detect changes to the library definition file by using the native *SHChangeNotifyRegister* shell helper function or by using the managed *FileSystemWatcher* found in the *System.IO* namespace. Using these interfaces is well documented and therefore not covered in this book. By paying attention to changes to the library definition file, applications can detect changes to the library and act upon them by reflecting the changes in the application's user interface.

Summary

This chapter introduced you to Windows 7 Libraries and its associated programming model. First, we took a quick look at the Windows Shell and Windows Explorer to better understand the important role libraries play as part of the Windows 7 user experience. Then we took a deep dive into Windows 7 Libraries to understand what they are and learn about their underlying architecture. We also covered the different opportunities developers have to make their applications library aware. Finally, we reviewed the different available programming models and the related APIs.

Chapter 5
Touch Me Now: An Introduction to Multitouch Programming

This is the first chapter in the book that deals with multitouch. In this chapter, you'll get answers for questions such as "What is the multitouch platform in Windows 7?", "How does multitouch work in Windows 7?", and "What is its underlying architecture?" You'll also learn about the various programming models that are available, and then dive into the native API and learn what gestures are and how to work with them. This chapter will provide you with a solid understanding of multitouch capabilities in Windows 7 and help you better understand the material in the upcoming chapters, which talk about advanced, native multitouch programming and describe in detail how to fully exploit multitouch functionality in Windows Presentation Foundation (WPF).

Multitouch in Windows 7

In Windows 7, the Windows experience has been enriched with touch, establishing touch as a first-class citizen among the various ways to interact with your PC (in addition to the mouse and keyboard). Windows touch support can be dated back to the Windows XP era, a period in which you could use a stylus on a tablet laptop to work with a single touch point. Additionally, Windows XP provided you with support for ink and handwriting text-recognition technologies. However, lately we have witnessed the appearance of a range of multitouch devices that have generated extremely positive user experiences, so it's only natural for Microsoft to introduce multitouch support in Windows 7 to enable a range of new user experiences as well as enhance common activities.

With the Windows 7 multitouch platform, you'll have the freedom to directly interact with your computer. For example, you can reach out your hand and slowly scroll through your pictures directly in Windows Explorer or quickly move through them by flicking your finger. As a developer, you have the capability to add multitouch support to your application and create a highly optimized multitouch experience in Windows 7.

Before we explore the Windows 7 multitouch programming models, architecture, and APIs, let's take a look at how Windows 7 multitouch delivers an optimized touch interface for the operating system. Keep in mind that Microsoft didn't create a special Windows 7 multitouch shell—there is no special Windows Explorer version or taskbar that is available only on multitouch-capable devices. Most applications that ship with Windows 7 are touch enabled, as are the shells for these applications. They work fine using standard keyboard and mouse input, but they also support multitouch input. By supporting multitouch or recognizing touch input, these elements deliver an optimal multitouch user experience.

The simplest example involves the Windows 7 taskbar jump lists, which you can read about in Chapter 1, "Welcome to Windows 7," and Chapter 2, "Integrate with the Windows 7 Taskbar: Basic Features." In Windows 7, when you right-click on any icon that is pinned to the taskbar, you see its corresponding jump list. For example, right-clicking on the Microsoft Office Word 2007 taskbar icon shows the Office application jump list. But how can you right-click using multitouch? Although there is a right-click gesture available in Windows 7 (press and tap), you can also touch the Word icon (marked by the number "1" in the following illustration) and drag your finger (illustrated by the arrow moving toward number "2" in the following illustration)—assuming the taskbar is at its default location at the bottom of the screen.

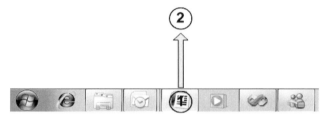

Performing that drag gesture shows the jump lists for Word. As you can see from the following image, the touch-triggered jump list (shown on the right side of the next screen shot) displays the same content as the standard jump list triggered by a mouse right-click (shown on the left side), but in a slightly different way.

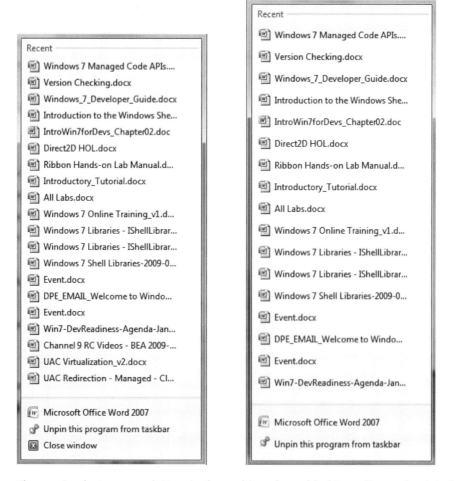

The spacing between each item in the multitouch-enabled jump list on the right is larger than the spacing between each item on the left. The reason for this difference in appearance is simple: the taskbar is optimized for a multitouch experience. Therefore, it displays the items in a way that makes it easier for you to select them by hand (provide you with a larger hit surface and thus decrease the chance you'll hit the wrong item with your fingers). Enlarging the hit surface area of an item to be touched is a standard practice when programming a touch-enabled application, and you'll find this approach used throughout Windows 7.

The taskbar is just one example of how Windows 7 doesn't create a new set of user interfaces just for touch scenarios and instead blends the new functionality into the existing infrastructure. Aero Peek, the Windows 7 feature that shows thumbnails of open applications, also uses this approach; it enables you to use a two-finger touch gesture instead of mouse hover and accommodates this functionality by providing you with larger hot spots for rearranging windows on your screen. Again, the taskbar is only one example of many multitouch-optimized experiences that ship with Windows 7. Others include the XPS viewer, Windows Photo Viewer, and Internet Explorer 8.

Another important aspect of multitouch in Windows 7 is the "No Touch Left Behind" concept. The system will not let you touch the screen and feel like nothing happened or that touch didn't work. For every touch, the system generates some sort of feedback, either a flick icon for quick-flicking gestures or, if you place your finger in the same place for longer than a few seconds, you'll see a round circle indicating a right-click context menu is available. Another touch concept is boundaries. *Boundaries* are set for user panning gestures to create the effect of bouncing the entire window when the user reaches the top or bottom of a scrollable area.

Windows 7 Multitouch Programming Models

The Windows 7 multitouch platform enables you to build touch-aware applications. Keep in mind that with time, the amount and types of hardware available for supporting multitouch will increase, more computers will support multitouch, and end users will come to expect applications to respond to touch input. To provide well-rounded Windows multitouch solutions for all kinds of application, Windows 7 has various levels of touch support. There are several scenarios you can use to enhance applications using the features of the Windows multitouch platform. Before you adopt a specific approach, you should consider what you want to do with your application.

The Windows 7 multitouch platform provides several programming models that we describe collectively as the "Good, Better, and Best" model.

The Good Model: Supporting Legacy Applications

Let's assume you have an existing (legacy) application that has a large install base, but it was not designed to support Windows 7 multitouch. We refer to these applications as *legacy applications* only in relation to multitouch support. You might ask yourself what the multitouch experience of my users will be when running such an application on a Windows 7 multitouch-enabled computer. You would expect your application to simply behave as it did in previous versions of the Windows operating system as far as handling keyboard and mouse input is concerned. But at the same time, you would also want your application to have some response to multitouch input to satisfy the end user, who is expecting some reaction when using its touch-sensitive capabilities, even if the response is limited to the application's existing functionality.

The good news is that the Windows 7 multitouch platform provides free, out-of-the-box support for legacy applications that are touch unaware and were not designed to support touch or multitouch—that is, out-of-the-box support for a few basic gestures. You can expect basic gestures to work and have the desired effect in your application. Basic gestures include a single-finger click on a menu item or button, single-finger or two-finger panning, two-finger zoom, and flick gestures that were introduced in the Windows Vista era.

You can find a range of existing touch-unaware applications, such as Microsoft Office Word 2007 or Adobe PDF Reader, that surprisingly behave as expected when confronted with single-finger or two-finger panning gestures as well as zoom gestures. All these applications benefit from the Windows 7 multitouch platform and enjoy this free, out-of-the-box touch support.

The Better Model: Enhancing the Touch Experience

The Better model addresses the need to make your application touch aware and provide better touch and multitouch support to your application than the default legacy support that was explained in the previous section. The Better model is focused on adding gestures support, as well as making other behavior and user interface (UI) changes so that applications are more touch friendly and go beyond simple gesture support.

The example we mentioned at the beginning of this chapter is the touch-optimized taskbar jump lists. In this case, the taskbar is responding to single-finger gestures (flicks) and not multiple-finger gestures (touch), but still we get a touch-optimized experience. In fact the taskbar is not using any Windows 7 multitouch APIs.

To trace the origin of the input message, identify it as a touch-related message, and respond accordingly, the taskbar uses the *GetMessageExtraInfo* function. When your application receives a mouse message (such as WM_LBUTTONDOWN), it might call the Win32 API *GetMessageExtraInfo* function to evaluate whether the message originated from a pen or a mouse device. The value returned from *GetMessageExtraInfo* needs to be mask-checked against 0xFFFFFF0 and then compared with 0xFF515700. If the comparison is *true*, this mouse message was generated by a touch-sensitive device.

However, the most common scenario in the Better model is gesture support. You can use gestures to enhance your application and provide better touch and multitouch support. Applications that respond to gestures directly have full control over how they behave when users are touching the touch-enabled device. For example, Windows 7 ships with a photo viewer, the Windows Photo Viewer. One of the nice things about using the gestures' APIs, rather than relying on the legacy support that the operating system provides, is that you can get extra information about the performed gesture. In the Photo Viewer application, you can get specific information about the location where the zoom gesture occurred in the image. That is, the zoom gesture contains information about the center point—specific X, Y coordinates—of the zoom gesture. Photo Viewer can therefore focus on the center of the gesture; whereas with the legacy support the center of the zoom is, by default, the center of the control. The Windows Photo Viewer application also uses panning and rotation gestures to deliver an excellent overall image-viewing experience with relatively little effort.

With gestures, you can also override the default panning behavior. For example, the default touch scrolling is designed to work in text-centric windows that scroll primarily vertically, such as with Web pages or documents, where dragging horizontally selects text rather than scrolling the page. In most applications, this works just fine. But what if your application needs to support horizontal scrolling? Also, for some applications the default scroll can appear chunky, going too fast or too slow. With gesture support, you can override the default panning behavior and optimize it for your application's needs.

The Best Model: Experience Optimized for Multitouch

Applications or features that fall into the Best model are designed from the ground up to support multitouch and provide amazing touch experiences. These applications build on top of the Windows touch messages, which are identified as WM_TOUCH. This message type provides raw touch data to the application, and you can consume these messages and handle multiple touch points. Most of the gestures we mentioned earlier are two-finger gestures; however, with WM_TOUCH messages you can receive as many simultaneous touch points as the underlying touch-sensitive hardware supports. Developers can use this to go beyond the core system gestures and build custom gesture support for their applications.

The Windows 7 Multitouch platform also provides a manipulation and inertia processor to help you interpolate the touch messages (that correlate to touch points on the screen) of any number of touch points on an object. Think of the manipulation processor as a black box that receives as input the object that is being touched plus all the related touch messages—the result is a simple two-dimensional (2D) affine transform matrix representing the transformation that happened as a result of the finger movement. For instance, if you were writing a photo-editing application, you could grab two photos at the same time using however many fingers you wanted and rotate, resize, and translate the photos; the manipulation process would provide the changes you need to reflect on the object. Inertia provides a basic physics model for applications that continues the smooth transition of an object even after the user has picked up her fingers from the touch-sensitive device and touch points are no longer detected. This functionality creates a simple transition effect for the object rather than stopping the object on the spot.

How Multitouch Works in Windows 7

New hardware and API elements in the Windows 7 operating system provide applications the ability to receive and handle touch and multitouch input. This capability enables applications to detect and respond to multiple simultaneous touch points. Multitouch is defined as two or more touch points. The reason we also address single touch is that there are some single-finger (single-touch-point) gestures that the multitouch API surfaces. Multitouch functionality in Windows 7 is provided by a new set of dedicated Windows messages. Let's review how these messages are generated and what you need to do to consume and work with multitouch messages.

Architecture Overview: Messages Data Flow

It all starts with touch-sensitive hardware that can detect touch input. We usually refer to such hardware as a *touch screen*, which can be either embedded in the computer screen itself or mounted as an overlay on top of the screen. There are several technologies that can detect multiple touch points: cameras on the top of the screen, an array of Infrared (IR) emitting units and an array of IR receiving units, and capacity touch digitizers that change the electromagnetic field in response to touch. Regardless of the technology employed, the touch-sensitive hardware needs to support the Windows 7 multitouch platform, which usually means it needs to have a Windows 7–compatible multitouch driver.

Figure 5-1 shows the data flows from the touch hardware to the underlying Windows 7 multitouch infrastructure, all the way to your application.

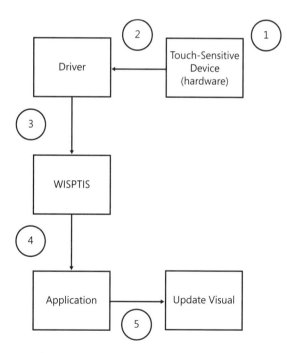

Figure 5-1 Data flow from touch hardware to the Windows 7 multitouch infrastructure to your application

In response to user input, shown in point 1 in the diagram, the touch-sensitive hardware generates a proprietary stream of data that is communicated to the driver, shown in point 2 in the diagram. The driver transforms the proprietary stream of data into proper Windows 7 touch constructs that are passed to the Tablet platform's Windows Ink Services Platform Table Input Subsystem (WISPTIS) process, shown in point 3 in the diagram. The Tablet WISPTIS process then generates Windows messages that are sent to the application, shown in point 4. The application can choose to handle or ignore these messages. Assuming the application handles the touch message, it will update the application's display.

The Tablet WISPTIS process is the heart of the Windows 7 multitouch platform, receiving as input the data from the driver and then generating Windows messages in response. It can generate either raw touch input messages in the form of WM_TOUCH messages or gesture messages in the form of WM_GESTURE. This means that the Tablet WISPTIS processes the input from the driver and recognizes when the user performs specific gestures, such as zooming, panning, or rotating. The Tablet WISPTIS is the Microsoft gesture-recognition engine.

> **Note** Keep in mind that applications receive multitouch gesture messages by default. This means Tablet WISPTIS sends gesture messages to the application whenever it detects a gesture unless you specifically request to receive raw touch messages (as described in Chapter 6, "Touch Me Now: Advance Multitouch Programming"). Raw touch messages (WM_TOUCH) and gesture messages (WM_GESTURE) are mutually exclusive, and an application can't receive both at the same time.

Dedicated API functions encapsulate the details for the creation and consumption of WM_GESTURE messages. This is done because the information associated with the message can change in the future without breaking applications that already consume this message, and it is always a good practice to use the API. There are several ways you can handle the touch messages that are sent to your application. If you're using Win32, you can check for the WM_GESTURE message in your application's *WndProc* function. WPF developers don't have to worry about handling such low-level Windows messages because the .NET Framework takes good care of that for them. We'll cover the WPF multitouch programming model in the following chapters and the native programming model in both this chapter and the next one.

But before we start addressing the new APIs, let's talk about the Good model, which is the default multitouch support you can expect from Windows 7 for legacy applications.

Supporting Legacy Applications

In the development of Windows 7, the Multitouch product team had to take into account the simple fact that the vast majority of existing applications are not touch aware and were not designed to support either touch or multitouch input. Therefore, the team had to provide a solid model for supporting multitouch in existing applications, even if it was just limited touch support. Again, we refer to these applications as *legacy applications* only in relation to multitouch support. As we mentioned before, by default, the Windows 7 multitouch platform provides a free, out-of-the-box multitouch experience for legacy applications that were not designed to support touch or multitouch.

First, we need to talk a little about how Windows communicate with your "windows-based" application. You can handle the multitouch messages from applications in Windows operating systems in many ways. If you are programming a Win32 program, you add code within the *WndProc* function to handle the messages of interest. If you are programming a Microsoft Foundation Class (MFC) or managed application, you add handlers for the messages of interest. Generally, Windows sends a bunch of messages to your application, and you decide which messages to handle. For a Win32 program, *WndProc* is the function you need to write to receive all the messages Windows sends to your application windows. Here is the function prototype:

```
LRESULT CALLBACK WndProc(HWND hWnd, UINT message, WPARAM wParam, LPARAM lParam)
```

Another part of the architecture we should mention in our overview is that Tablet WISPTIS generates WM_GESTURE messages that are sent to your application's window by default. As a developer, you can choose which messages to handle and which to ignore. Often, you use a switch-case construct to handle each message differently. If you don't want to handle a specific message, it is highly recommended that you pass that message back to Windows to ensure the message will be handled by the Windows default handling process. If you choose to ignore the WM_GESTURE messages, these messages fall through your *WndProc* switch-case construct and are sent back to the operating system as the default behavior by calling *DefWindowProc*. (It is highly recommended in Win32 that you call *DefWindowsProc* for WM messages that your application doesn't handle.) At this stage, Tablet WISPTIS once again goes into action by consuming these messages and resending alternative Windows messages to your application, as shown in Figure 5-2.

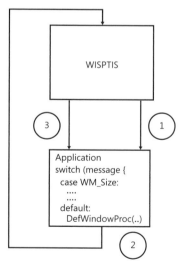

Figure 5-2 Consuming and resending of WM_GESTURE messages

For example, with single-finger panning, the platform needs to determine whether you are panning, usually a vertical gesture, or selecting text, usually a horizontal gesture. The platform checks whether your finger is performing any type of pan gesture within the boundaries of what is defined as a *pannable area*. A pannable area is any user control that displays content with a scrollbar that supports the basic vertical or horizontal scroll Windows messages: WM_VSCROLL and WM_HSCROLL. All the default user controls that support scrollbar functionality in Microsoft Foundation Classes (MFC), Win 32, and .NET WinForm also support the previously mentioned Windows messages and therefore support single-finger panning.

Two-finger panning is also supported in legacy applications; however, with two-finger panning, you can perform only panning gestures and text-selection gestures. Assuming your user control supports panning, the platform then checks to see which direction the user is performing the panning gesture. Vertical panning in a scrollable area usually results in vertical scrolling messages, WM_VSCROLL, whereas horizontal panning usually results in a WM_HSCROLL message.

Windows 7 multitouch support for legacy applications also includes support for the zoom gesture. The zoom gesture is usually described as pinching movements performed on two touch points. Any zoom gesture that is not handled by your application returns to the system, as mentioned earlier, and is re-sent to the application as Ctrl+Mouse wheel Windows messages.

Working with Gestures

Whenever the user touches a touch-sensitive device that is connected to the computer and that touch activity translates to a gesture, the Windows 7 multitouch platform sends gesture messages (WM_GESTURE) to your application by default. This is the free, out-of-the-box behavior. But if you're reading this, it is safe to assume that you want to learn how to work with gestures.

Gestures are one-finger or two-finger input that translates into some kind of action that the user wants to perform. When the gesture is detected (by the operating system, which is doing all the work for you), the operating system sends gesture messages to your application. Windows 7 supports the following gestures:

- Zoom
- Single-finger and two-finger pan
- Rotate
- Two-finger tap
- Press and tap

Handling the WM_GESTURE Message

To work with gestures, you'll need to handle the WM_GESTURE messages that are sent to your application. If you are a Win32 programmer, you can check for WM_GESTURE messages in your application's *WndProc* functions. The following code shows how gesture messages can be handled in Win32 applications:

```
LRESULT CALLBACK WndProc(HWND hWnd, UINT message, WPARAM wParam, LPARAM lParam)
{
    int wmId, wmEvent;
    PAINTSTRUCT ps;
    HDC hdc;
    switch (message){
        case WM_GESTURE:
            /* insert handler code here to interpret the gesture */
            break;
        ...
    default:
        return DefWindowProc(hWnd, message, wParam, lParam);
    }
    return 0;
}

..
```

WM_GESTURE is the generic message used for all gestures. Therefore, to determine which gesture you need to handle, first you need to decode the gesture message. The information about the gesture is found in the *lParam* parameter, and you need to use a special function—*GetGestureInfo*—to decode the gesture message. This function receives a pointer to a GESTUREINFO structure and *lParam*; if it's successful, the function fills the gesture information structure with all the information about the gesture:

```
GESTUREINFO gi;
ZeroMemory(&gi, sizeof(GESTUREINFO));
gi.cbSize = sizeof(gi);
BOOL bResult = GetGestureInfo((HGESTUREINFO)lParam, &gi);
```

Here you can see that you prepare the GESTUREINFO, *gi*, structure by clearing its content with zeros except for its size and then passing its pointer to the function to fill it with the gesture message information.

After obtaining a GESTUREINFO structure, you can check *dwID*, one of the structure members, to identify which gesture was performed. However, *dwID* is just one of the structure members. There are several other important members:

- **dwFlags**   The state of the gesture, such as begin, inertia, or end.

- **dwID**   The identifier of the gesture command. This member indicates the gesture type.

- **cbSize**   The size of the structure, in bytes; to be set before the function call.

- **ptsLocation**   A POINTS structure containing the coordinates associated with the gesture. These coordinates are always relative to the origin of the screen.

- **dwInstanceID** and **dwSequenceID**   These are internally used identifiers for the structure, and they should not be used or handled.

- **ullArguments**   This is a 64-bit unsigned integer that contains the arguments for gestures that fit into 8 bytes. This is the extra information that is unique for each gesture type.

- **cbExtraArgs**   The size, in bytes, of extra *ullArguments* that accompany this gesture.

Now you can complete the switch-case clause to handle all the different Windows 7 gestures, as shown in the following code snippet:

```
void CMTTestDlg::DecodeGesture(WPARAM wParam, LPARAM lParam)
{
    // create a structure to populate and retrieve the extra message info
    GESTUREINFO gi;
    gi.cbSize = sizeof(GESTUREINFO);
    ZeroMemory(&gi, sizeof(GESTUREINFO));
    GetGestureInfo((HGESTUREINFO)lParam, &gi);
    // now interpret the gesture
    switch (gi.dwID){
        case GID_ZOOM:
            // Code for zooming goes here
            break;
        case GID_PAN:
            // Code for panning goes here
            break;
        case GID_ROTATE:
            // Code for rotation goes here
            break;
        case GID_TWOFINGERTAP:
            // Code for two-finger tap goes here
            break;
        case GID_PRESSANDTAP:
            // Code for roll over goes here
            break;
        default:
            // You have encountered an unknown gesture
            break;
        CloseGestureInfoHandle((HGESTUREINFO)lParam);
}
```

Note In the preceding code segment, you can see how we set the stage for handling each gesture separately, as the *dwID* flag indicates the type of gesture. Also note that at the end of the function we call the *CloseGestureInfoHandle* function, which closes resources associated with the gesture information handle. If you handle the WM_GESTURE message, it is your responsibility to close the handle using this function. Failure to do so can result in memory leaks.

Note In production code, you are expected to check the return value of functions to make sure the function succeeds. For simplicity, we do not include such checks in our code snippets.

If you look carefully in the Windows 7 Software Development Kit (SDK), you'll find that the *dwID* member can also have values indicating when a gesture is starting (GID_BEGIN), which is essentially when the user places his fingers on the screen. The SDK also defines the GID_END flag, which indicates when a gesture ends. Gestures are exclusive, meaning you can't achieve the effect of zooming and rotating at the same time as using gestures. Your application can receive at a given time either a zoom or rotate gesture, but not both. But gestures can be compound, because the user can perform several gestures during one long touch episode. GID_BEGIN and GID_END are the start and end markers for such gesture sequences. To achieve the effect of zooming and rotating at the same time, you need to handle raw touch events and use the manipulation process as described in the next chapter.

Most applications should ignore the GID_BEGIN and GID_END messages and pass them to *DefWindowProc*. These messages are used by the default gesture handler; the operating system cannot provide any touch support for legacy applications without seeing these messages. The *dwFlags* member contains the information needed to handle the beginning and ending of a particular gesture.

By now, you can see that handling gesture messages is not that difficult. Handling gesture messages has a fixed process that includes configuration (which we will describe later in the chapter), decoding the gesture message, and handling each specific gesture according to your application's needs. Next, you'll learn what unique information each gesture includes and how to handle it.

Use the Pan Gesture to Move an Object

With the pan gesture, you can control the scrolling of content in a scrollable area. Or you can apply the pan gesture to a specific object, moving it in any direction by simply touching it with one or two fingers and moving it. This is also known as *transformation* because you are partially transforming the object from being located in one location to being located in another. The following figure illustrates how panning works:

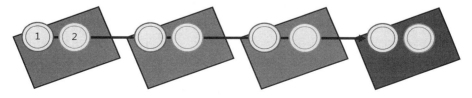

In the illustration, you can see two touch points, marked with the numbers 1 and 2. By default, the pan gesture supports both single-finger and two-finger panning. You'll see how to configure pan gestures and other gestures later in this chapter.

Now let's see what code you need to implement in your GID_PAN switch to achieve this panning effect. Our application is simple; it displays a single rectangle. We show only the parts of the code that are required to handle gesture messages. Because this is part of a larger example that is written in C++, we do not describe in detail any of the other elements, such as painting the rectangle.

The gesture info structure includes the *dwFlags* member, which is used to determine the state of the gesture and can include any of the following values:

- **GF_BEGIN**   Indicates that the gesture is starting

- **GF_INERTIA**   Indicates that the gesture has triggered inertia

- **GF_END**   Indicates that the gesture is ending

We'll use the GF_BEGIN flag to save the initial start coordinates of the touch point as a variable as a reference for the following steps. The gesture information includes the *ptsLocation* member that contains the X and Y coordinates of the touch point. Then for each consecutive pan message, we'll extract the new coordinates of the touch point. By using the initial start position that we saved before and the new coordinates, we can calculate the new position and apply the move operation to the object. Finally, we'll repaint the object in its new position. The following code snippet shows the entire GID_PAN switch:

```
case GID_PAN:
    switch(gi.dwFlags)
    {
    case GF_BEGIN:
        _ptFirst.x = gi.ptsLocation.x;
        _ptFirst.y = gi.ptsLocation.y;
        ScreenToClient(hWnd,&_ptFirst);
        break;

    default:
        // We read the second point of this gesture. It is a middle point
        // between fingers in this new position
        _ptSecond.x = gi.ptsLocation.x;
        _ptSecond.y = gi.ptsLocation.y;
        ScreenToClient(hWnd,&_ptSecond);
        // We apply the move operation of the object
        ProcessMove(_ptSecond.x-_ptFirst.x,_ptSecond.y-_ptFirst.y);
        InvalidateRect(hWnd,NULL,TRUE);
        // We have to copy the second point into the first one to prepare
        // for the next step of this gesture.
        _ptFirst = _ptSecond;
        break;
    }
    break;
```

Here you can see that in the case of GF_BEGIN flag, we use _ptFirst, a simple POINT structure, to save the initial starting touch coordinates from the gesture information in *ptsLocation*. We call the *ScreenToClient* function to convert the screen coordinates of a given point on the display to the window of our application, because the coordinates in the gesture information are always relative to the origin of the screen.

The next pan message that arrives is handled by the default case. Now we save the coordinates in the _ptSecond variable and again calculate the coordinates relative to our application window. Then we simply subtract the first touch point from the second touch point to find the new location and call *ProcessMove*, which is a helper function, to update the new coordinates of the rectangle. We call *InvalidateRect* to repaint the whole window to show the rectangle at the new coordinates. Finally, we save the latest touch point in the _ptFirst for reference for the next gesture message. When a two-finger pan gesture is used, the coordinates of the touch point in the gesture information structure, *ptsLocation*, represent the current position of the pan that is the center of the gesture. The *ullArgument* member indicates the distance between the two touch points.

The Windows 7 pan gesture also includes support for inertia. Inertia is used to create some sort of continuation to the movement that was generated by the gesture. After you take your finger off the touch-sensitive device, the system calculates the trajectory based on the velocity and angle of motion and continues to send WM_GESTURE messages of type GID_PAN that are flagged with GF_INERTIA, but it reduces the speed of the movement up to a complete stop of the motion. The inertia-flagged messages continue to include updated coordinates, but with each message the delta between the previous coordinates decreases to the point of a complete stop. You're given the option to distinguish between normal pan gestures and inertia to enable you to opt for special behavior for inertia if needed.

Use the Zoom Gesture to Scale an Object

In the previous section, you learned how to move an object using the pan gesture. The pan gesture is widely used for document reading as well as for more graphical purposes such as picture viewing and manipulation. For all these cases, the zoom gesture is also widely used by both developers and users.

The zoom gesture is usually implemented by users as a pinch movement involving two touch points, where the user moves her fingers closer together to zoom out and moves them farther apart to zoom in. For simplicity, we'll refer to zoom in as *zoom* and explicitly say zoom out for the opposite gesture. The zoom gesture allows you to scale the size of your objects.

The following figure illustrates how the zoom gesture works, with the circles labeled as 1 and 2 indicating the touch points and the arrows indicating the direction the fingers move in to produce the effect:

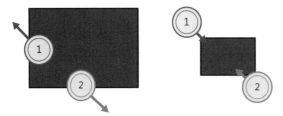

Now let's see what code you need to implement in your GID_ZOOM switch to achieve the desired zooming effect. As with the previous gesture example, we'll focus only on the parts of the code that are required to handle the gesture messages.

As before, we'll use GF_BEGIN to store a few parameters that will come handy when the next zoom gesture message arrives. Again, we'll save *ptsLocation* in *_ptFirst*. For a zoom gesture, *ptsLocation* indicates the center of the zoom. As we did previously, we call the *ScreenToClient* function to convert the screen coordinates of a given point on the display to the window of our application. In addition to saving the center location of the zoom gesture, we also save the distance between the two touch points, which can be found in the *ullArgument GestureInfo* structure. Later, the distance between the fingers allows us to calculate the zoom ratio.

The next zoom message that arrives is handled by the default case. Again, we save the coordinates in the *_ptSecond* variable and call the *ScreenToClient* function. Next, we calculate the zoom center point and the zoom ratio. Finally, we update the window to reflect the zoom center point and zooming ratio of the rectangle. Here is a short snippet showcasing these arguments:

```
case GID_ZOOM:
switch(gi.dwFlags)
{
case GF_BEGIN:
    _dwArguments = LODWORD(gi.ullArguments);
    _ptFirst.x = gi.ptsLocation.x;
    _ptFirst.y = gi.ptsLocation.y;
    ScreenToClient(hWnd,&_ptFirst);
    break;
default:
    // We read here the second point of the gesture. This is the middle point between
fingers.
    _ptSecond.x = gi.ptsLocation.x;
    _ptSecond.y = gi.ptsLocation.y;
    ScreenToClient(hWnd,&_ptSecond);

    // We have to calculate the zoom center point
    ptZoomCenter.x = (_ptFirst.x + _ptSecond.x)/2;
```

```
    ptZoomCenter.y = (_ptFirst.y + _ptSecond.y)/2;

    // The zoom factor is the ratio between the new and old distances.
    k = (double)(LODWORD(gi.ullArguments))/(double)(_dwArguments);

    // Now we process zooming in/out of the object
    ProcessZoom(k,ptZoomCenter.x,ptZoomCenter.y);
    InvalidateRect(hWnd,NULL,TRUE);

    // Now we have to store new information as starting information for the next step
    _ptFirst = _ptSecond;
    _dwArguments = LODWORD(gi.ullArguments);
    break;
}
break;
```

Here you can see that in addition to saving the location of the zoom gesture in the GF_BEGIN switch, we also extract from *gi.ullArgument* the distance between the two touch points using the *LODWORD* macro. The *ullArgument* is 8 bytes long, and the extra information about the gesture is stored in the first 4 bytes.

The next zoom message that arrives is handled by the default case. Again, we save the location of the gesture, and from the two sets of touch points we calculate the zoom center point and store it in *ptZoomCenter*. Now we need to calculate the zoom factor. This is done by calculating the ratio between the new distance and the old distance. Then we call the *ProcessZoom* helper function, which updates the new coordinates to reflect the zoom factor and center point. After that, we call *InvalidateRect* to force the window to repaint the rectangle. Finally, we save the latest touch point in *_ptFirst* and the latest distance between the two touch points in *_dwArguments* for reference for the next zoom message.

The main difference between the default legacy zoom gesture support and the zoom support just described is the knowledge about the center of the zoom gesture. In the legacy zoom gesture support, the operating system always zooms to the center of the control or to the current cursor location. However, using the zoom gesture to handle zooming on your own allows you to use knowledge about the center of the zoom gesture to zoom in and zoom out around that point, providing the user with a richer, more accurate zooming experience.

Use the Rotate Gesture to Turn an Object

Zoom and pan gestures are the most commonly used gestures. It is safe to assume that most users will naturally perform the right-handed gestures—panning and pinching to get the desired effect. This is one of the main reasons for providing the legacy support for these gestures. In the previous section, you saw how you can customize the handlers for these gestures. In this section, we'll address the rotate gesture, which after the pan and zoom gestures is probably the most widely used gesture in applications that use surfaces to display content, such as photo viewing and editing or mapping applications.

Imagine there is a real picture placed flat on your desk. It is a picture of a landscape, and it's turned upside down. To turn the picture right side up, you need to place your hand (or just two fingers) on it and move your hand in a circular motion to rotate the picture to the desired position. This is the same gesture that you can perform in Windows 7. The rotate gesture is performed by creating two touch points on an object and moving the touch points in a circular motion, as shown in the following illustration, with the numbers 1 and 2 representing the two touch points and the arrows representing the direction of movement from those points. As in the previous examples, we'll examine what kind of coding effort it takes to rotate our rectangle.

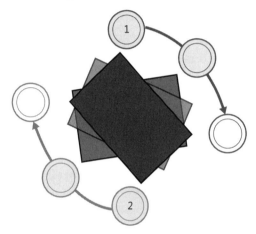

We use the GID_ROTATE value to identify the rotate gesture. As with the previous gesture handlers, we use the GF_BEGIN flag to save the initial state of the gesture. In our case, we store 0 (zero) in _dwArguments, which is used as the variable holding the rotation angle.

In the default case, we again save the location of the gesture. The *ptsLocation* member represents the center between the two touch points, and it can be considered as the center of rotation. As with all gesture messages, the *ullArguments* member holds the extra information about the gesture. In the rotate gesture, this is the cumulative rotation angle. This cumulative rotation angle is relative to the initial angle that was formed between the first two touch points, and the initial touch points are considered the "zero" angle for the current rotate gesture. That is the reason we don't need to save the initial angle in the GF_BEGIN case—we consider that angle to be zero degrees. This makes sense because you want to capture the user motion and project that relative to the object position on the screen rather than using fixed angle positions, which will force you to do a lot of calculation in the initial state.

```
case GID_ROTATE:
    switch(gi.dwFlags)
    {
    case GF_BEGIN:
        _dwArguments = 0;
        break;
```

```
default:
    _ptFirst.x = gi.ptsLocation.x;
    _ptFirst.y = gi.ptsLocation.y;
    ScreenToClient(hWnd,&_ptFirst);
    // Gesture handler returns cumulative rotation angle. However, we
    // have to pass the delta angle to our function responsible
    // for processing the rotation gesture.
    ProcessRotate(
        GID_ROTATE_ANGLE_FROM_ARGUMENT(LODWORD(gi.ullArguments))
        - GID_ROTATE_ANGLE_FROM_ARGUMENT(_dwArguments),
        _ptFirst.x,_ptFirst.y
    );
    InvalidateRect(hWnd,NULL,TRUE);
    _dwArguments = LODWORD(gi.ullArguments);
    break;
}
break;
```

Here you can see that, as with all gestures, we save the location of the gesture and convert the point to reflect the relative coordinates to our window. Next, we extract the rotation angle from the *ullArgument* using the LODWORD macro. The angle is represented in radians, and we use the GID_ROTATE_ANGLE_FROM_ARGUMENT macro to convert it to degrees. As mentioned earlier, the rotate gesture handlers return the cumulative rotation angle, but we need to use the difference between the two angles to create the rotation motion. Now we pass the delta angle and the center of the rotation to the *ProcessRotate* helper function that updates the X and Y coordinates of the object to reflect the rotation motion. We invalidate the window to repaint the rectangle. Finally, we save the current cumulative angle in *_dwArguments* to be able to subtract between the angles when the next rotate gesture message arrives.

As with the zoom gesture, *ptsLocation* holds the center of rotation, which allows you to have fine control over how you rotate the object. Instead of rotating the object around the center point of the object, you can do so around a specific rotation point to achieve higher fidelity to the user gesture and to provide a better user experience.

Use a Two-Finger Tap to Mimic a Mouse Click

So far, we have covered pan, zoom, and rotate gestures that are following a natural finger gesture, and we expect these gestures to behave as their names suggest. But there are other forms of input we use in our day-to-day work with computers, such as the mouse click, double-click, and right-click. These mouse events are used by almost every Windows application, and the Windows 7 multitouch platform needs to provide a way to mimic these behaviors. Two-finger tap gestures and press-and-tap gestures can be used as the equivalent touch gestures for clicking and right-clicking, respectively.

A two-finger tap is a simple gesture—just tap once with two fingers on the object you want to manipulate. When you handle the two-finger tap gesture, it's easy to see how you can use a double two-finger tap to mimic a mouse double-click. But because there is a difference between single-finger touch (usually used to pan) and a two-finger tap, you might consider just using a two-finger tap as a mouse double-click. The following figure illustrates a two-finger tap, with the numbers 1 and 2 indicating touch points that are touched simultaneously. In this case, we've used a two-finger tap to add two diagonals lines to the rectangle, as you can see in the image on the right.

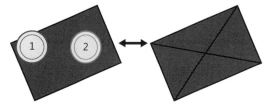

We use the GID_TWOFINGERTAP value to identify the two-finger tap gesture. As with the previous gesture handlers, *ullArguments* contains extra information about the gesture. In the case of the two-finger tap gesture, *ullArguments* contains the distance between both fingers and *pstLocation* indicates the center of the two-finger tap. In the following code snippet, we don't need to save or use the distance between the two touch points or the center of the gesture. We are going to set a flag and a timer that expires after 200 milliseconds, and we'll reset the flag we just set, unless a consecutive second two-finger tap gesture message arrives before the timer expires. If the second gesture message arrives within 200 milliseconds, we call the *ProcessTwoFingerTap* function, which paints an X on the rectangle. The code looks like this:

```
case GID_TWOFINGERTAP:
    if( _intFlag == 0)
    {
        _ bWaitForSecondFingerTap = 1;
        setTimer();
    }
    else if( _intFlag == 1)
    {
        //handle double-click
        ProcessTwoFingerTap();
        InvalidateRect(hWnd,NULL,TRUE);
        _intFlag = 0;
    }
break;
```

Here you can see that we're handling only a basic case of the message and do not inspect the message flags for the GF_BEGIN message as in the previous gesture. We just execute all the logic in the switch case of GID_TWOFINGERTAP. You might want to consider removing the flag and timer from the code just shown and handle only a single two-finger tap, mainly because we shouldn't confuse the user by trying to distinguish between single-finger panning and a two-finger tap, and there is no single tap. Therefore, you can consider a single-finger tap to be the equivalent of a mouse click and, if needed, a two-finger tap can be considered to be the equivalent of a double-click.

Use the Press-and-Tap Gesture to Mimic a Mouse Right-Click

In the previous section, we showed you how to handle the two-finger tap gesture which, among other usages, can mimic a mouse click or double-click. But what about mouse right-clicks? What hand gesture can simulate that? Well, the goal is to simulate a mouse right-click, which is actually clicking on the second mouse button. This translates into putting down one finger to create the first touch point and then tapping with the second finger—that is, form a second touch point for a short period of time. The following figure illustrates that operation by showing, left to right, the sequence of touch points.

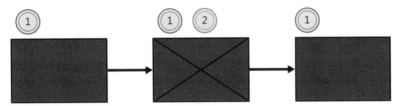

We use the GID_PRESS_AND_TAP value to identify this gesture. As with the previous gesture handlers, *ullArguments* contains extra information about the gesture. In the case of the press-and-tap gesture, *ullArguments* contains the distance between both fingers and *pstLocation* indicates the position that the first finger touched. You can use this information to customize the graphical representation of the first finger or any other similar highlighting effect. For our simple demonstration, we will not store any information for this gesture handler, nor will we use the GF_BEGIN flag. Simply, we are going to handle the *ProcessPressAndTap* function to randomly recolor the boarders of the rectangle, as the following code snippet shows:

```
case GID_PRESSANDTAP:
    ProcessPressAndTap();
    InvalidateRect(hWnd,NULL,TRUE);
break;
```

Configuring Windows 7 Gestures

As we mentioned before, gesture messages (WM_GESTURE) are sent to your application by default. Well, most of them are. All gesture types except the single-finger pan and rotate are sent to your application by default. With that said, you can choose and configure which gesture messages you want to support in your application at any given time. To determine which gesture messages you want to receive, you'll need to call *SetGestureConfig* and pass to it as an argument an array of gesture configuration structures. With the GESTURECONFIG structure, you can set and get the configuration for enabling gesture messages.

The GESTURECONFIG structure has the following members:

- **dwID**   The identifier for the type of configuration that will have messages enabled or disabled. It can be any one of the "GID_" gesture messages (zoom, pan, rotate, two-finger tap, or press and tap).

- **dwWant**   Indicates which messages to enable in relation to the gesture defined in *dwID*

- **dwBlocks**   Indicates which messages to disable in relation to the gesture defined in *dwID*

You can use the following code snippet to enable all the gestures using the special GC_AllGESTURES flag:

```
GESTURECONFIG gc = {0,GC_ALLGESTURES,0};
SetGestureConfig(hWnd, 0, 1, &gc,
                sizeof(GESTURECONFIG));
```

If you want to have finer control over the gestures you want to receive messages for, you can use the gesture configuration structure and specify which gesture message you want to get and which you want to block. For example, the following code shows how you can disable all gestures:

```
GESTURECONFIG gc[] = {{ GID_ZOOM, 0, GC_ZOOM },
                      { GID_ROTATE, 0, GC_ROTATE},
                      { GID_PAN, 0, GC_PAN},
                      { GID_TWOFINGERTAP, 0, GC_TWOFINGERTAP},
                      { GID_PRESSANDTAP, 0 , GC_PRESSANDTAP}
                     };

UINT uiGcs = 5;
bResult = SetGestureConfig(hWnd, 0, uiGcs, gc, sizeof(GESTURECONFIG));
```

This code sets five different gesture configuration structures; one for each gesture. As you can see, the first parameter of each structure is the "GID_" touch gesture message. And in each one of these structures the second parameter is set to zero, indicating we chose not to handle any message, as is the last parameter, indicating we want to block the specific gesture message.

The right time to call *SetGestureConfig* is during the execution of the WM_GESTURENOTIFY handler. WM_GESTURENOTIFY is a message sent to the application just before the operating system starts sending WM_GESTURE to your application's window. Basically, the operating system is telling you, "Hi, I am going to start sending you gesture messages real soon." In fact, this message is sent after the user has already placed his fingers on the touch-sensitive device and started performing a certain gesture. And it is the right place to define the list of gestures that your application will support. By populating the right GESTURECONFIG structures to reflect the gestures you wish to handle and calling the *SetGestureConfig* function, you can choose gestures that you want to handle in your application.

Advance Gesture Configuration

Except for the pan gesture, all gestures only can be turned on or off. Because the pan gesture is probably the most popular gesture, the Windows 7 multitouch platform allows you to set extra configuration parameters for it. If you remember, early in this chapter we mentioned the horizontal and vertical pan gestures, as well as inertia in regard to panning. It turns out you can be very specific when it comes to pan gesture configuration. You can set the *dwWant* member of the configuration structure to any of the following flag values:

- GC_PAN

- GC_PAN_WITH_SINGLE_FINGER_VERTICALLY

- GC_PAN_WITH_SINGLE_FINGER_HORIZENTALLY

- GC_PAN_WITH_GUTTER

- GC_PAN_WITH_INERTIA

Most values are self-explanatory. GC_PAN is used to enable all gestures. The next flag that requires some explanation is GC_PAN_WITH_GUTTER. A *gutter* defines the boundaries to the pannable area within which your pan gesture still works. The gutter boundary limits the perpendicular movement of the primary direction, either a vertical pan or a horizontal pan. When a certain threshold is reached, the current sequence of pan gestures is stopped. So if you are panning vertically, you don't have to pan in a perfectly straight line. You can perform somewhat diagonal vertical pan gestures. You can deviate about 30 degrees from the main perpendicular and still have the touch movement considered as a pan gesture, as shown in Figure 5-3, where the left and right gutter boundaries define a sort of a funnel. Within that area, a pan gesture still works. After putting down the first touch point, shown at number 1, you can perform the pan gesture anywhere in the area defined by the funnel. If during the gesture you pan out of the gutter, shown at number 3, the pan gesture is discontinued and the operating system stops sending you WM_GESTURE pan messages.

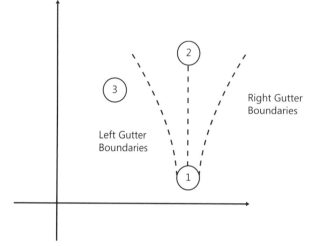

Figure 5-3 Using gutters for panning gestures

By turning the gutter off, you allow the pan gesture to enter *free-style mode*, enabling the operating system to send pan messages for every panning gesture performed on the pannable area with no regard to vertical or horizontal panning. This can make for a good experience when moving objects such as pictures on a particular surface or when panning a map. Imagine a mapping application in which you want to provide a full 2D panning experience. The following code snippet shows how you can configure the Windows 7 Multitouch platform to allow zoom, rotate, and panning gestures vertically and horizontally with gutters turned off. This is a useful configuration for a mapping application in which you want to allow the user to pan, zoom, and rotate the point of view of the map.

```
DWORD dwPanWant  = GC_PAN | GC_PAN_WITH_SINGLE_FINGER_VERTICALLY |
GC_PAN_WITH_SINGLE_FINGER_HORIZONTALLY;
DWORD dwPanBlock = GC_PAN_WITH_GUTTER;
    GESTURECONFIG gc[] = {{ GID_ZOOM, GC_ZOOM, 0 },
                          { GID_ROTATE, GC_ROTATE, 0},
                          { GID_PAN, dwPanWant , dwPanBlock}
                         };
    UINT uiGcs = 3;
SetGestureConfig(hWnd, 0, uiGcs, gc, sizeof(GESTURECONFIG));
```

A good example of this functionality is the Photo Viewer application that ships with Windows 7, which already has support for zoom and rotate functionality specified via mouse input. Now this functionality is also backed by multitouch gesture support with a relatively small amount of effort.

Summary

In this chapter, you were introduced to the wonderful world of Windows 7 multitouch. First, we defined the different programming models and described the platform capabilities. Next, we walked through the internal implementation layers of multitouch and detailed the roles of the different components.

We then dove into the support provided for gestures. As you saw, there is a lot you can do with gestures; even the basic, out-of-the-box support Windows 7 provides for legacy applications gives the end user the feeling that the application is responding to touch. You also saw how easy it is to add specific gesture handlers to your application and provide a solid and exciting multitouch user experience. We went through the steps needed to handle gestures from the first message received by using the begin flags, as well as how to clean up after the last message. Finally, we saw how you can configure specific behaviors for gestures, mainly for panning.

In the next chapter, we'll advance to examining in detail the Best Windows 7 multitouch programming model, describing how to handle raw touch events and how you can create your own gesture handlers.

For managed code developers, Chapter 6, "Touch Me Now: Advanced Multitouch Programming," gives an overview of the WPF multitouch programming model in Windows 7. And Chapter 8, "Using Windows 7 Touch with Silverlight," briefly covers how Silverlight 3 can run out-of-browser on a Windows 7 machine and deliver the multitouch experience.

Chapter 6
Touch Me Now: Advanced Multitouch Programming

In the previous chapter, you were introduced to multitouch in Windows 7 and to the various programming models offered for using it. By now, you have a solid understanding of how multitouch works in Windows 7, what the underlying architecture is, and the different programming models Windows 7 multitouch offers developers. The previous chapter focused on working with multitouch gestures, which we identified as the "better" programming option in the "Good, Better, Best" model. At this point, you know everything that is required to start working with multitouch gestures in Windows 7.

Now that you've read all about the "good" and "better" options in Chapter 5, "Touch Me Now: An Introduction to Multitouch Programming," let's dive deep into the best programming option. This is the most powerful programming model Windows 7 has to offer developers. In this chapter, we describe how to build multitouch applications that provide amazing touch experiences, as well as how to handle raw touch messages and build your own simple version of a paint program using your fingers as pens. Also, we explain what the Manipulation and Inertia processors (included as part of Windows 7) are and how to use them to make your life a little easier.

Working with Raw Touch Messages

Windows 7 gesture support offers an easy-to-use yet powerful technology that allows you to enhance your applications, creating compelling multitouch experiences. However, the supported Windows 7 multitouch gestures, described in the previous chapter, have their limitation. For example, the Windows 7 multitouch gestures that ship in box have a limitation on the total number of supported touch points: All gestures support a maximum of only two simultaneous touch points. Another limitation is the inability to combine gestures, meaning you can't perform rotate and zoom gestures on a given object at the same time. There is no way to receive both GID_ROTATE and GID_ZOOM messages to handle a combined event. Therefore, when you want to provide richer multitouch experiences in your application, you need to choose the richer multitouch API. Using this API you need to handle touch messages and interpret the performed gestures yourself rather than relying on the default gestures engine provided in Windows 7. The default gestures engine—the Windows Ink Services Platform Table Input Subsystem (WISPTIS) described in the previous chapter—is the engine that sends the default gesture messages.

To start receiving touch messages (messages designated as WM_TOUCH), first you need to ask Windows 7 to start sending touch messages to your application and stop sending the default gesture messages (messages designated as WM_GESTURE). Next, after you start receiving touch messages, you need to decode each message and unpack individual touch-point information before handling it. After the decoding is done, you have enough information about each touch point to handle and track it over time. It's your responsibility to track each touch point and detect the gestures performed by all touch points. Let's start by configuring the Windows 7 multitouch platform.

Setting Up Windows for Touch

To request Windows 7 to start sending WM_TOUCH messages to your application, you need to call the *RegisterTouchWindow(HWND hWnd, ULONG uFlags)* function. Calling this function registers a single window, defined by its HWND parameter, as being touch-capable. If you call *RegisterTouchWindow*, you'll stop receiving the default WM_GESTURE messages because WM_TOUCH and WM_GESTURE messages are mutually exclusive. The following single code line shows how easy it is to register a window to start receiving touch messages:

```
RegisterTouchWindow(hWnd, 0);
```

hWnd is the handle for the specific window you are registering to start receiving touch messages. The second parameter is a set of bit flags that specify optional modifications to the default operating system touch behavior. Zero indicates that the default behavior should be used, and it is highly recommended that you use it. All other values represent more advanced scenarios.

For example, the flags can be set to TWF_FINETOUCH, which notifies the operating system that this *hWnd* object doesn't want to receive coalesced touch messages. By default, the operating system coalesces touch messages received from the touch-sensitive device, because the volume of touch messages can be large, ranging from one hundred per second to thousands per second. By coalescing, Windows 7 "drops" several touch messages that it received from the touch driver. This effectively reduces the total number of messages sent to your application while at the same losing very little, if any, relevant information, thereby keeping the touch messages accurate enough for most applications. However, there are some scenarios, such as handwriting-recognition applications, that require a high volume of messages to be processed to drive a higher recognition accuracy rate. Most applications do not and should not use the default touch messages coalescing. We are going to use message coalescing in our examples because by using it the operating system ensures that our application always receives accurate, up-to-date touch information, representing the latest touch location.

Before asking the system to start sending touch messages to your application, you should verify that the current computer configuration supports multitouch. Assuming it does, you need to check how many simultaneous touch points the system can handle. Note that the limitation on the number of simultaneous touch points is a limit related to the touch-sensitive hardware, usually known as the *digitizer*, not a Windows 7 multitouch platform limitation. To check the current computer's configuration for multitouch support, you need to use the *GetSystemMetrics(int nIndex)* function, passing SM_DIGITIZER as the *nIndex* input parameter, to retrieve specific information about the system's touch support capabilities. The *GetSystemMetrics* function returns a 64-bit field that, when passing SM_DIGITIZER, can return one or a combination of the following bitwise values:

- **NID_INTEGRATED_TOUCH** Indicates the computer has a touch-sensitive device integrated into its enclosure—probably a touch screen

- **NID_EXTERNAL_TOUCH** Indicates that the touch-sensitive device is an external one, such as a mountable device that you place on top of your screen

- **NID_INTEGRATED_PEN** Indicates that the computer has an integrated touch-sensitive device that supports a touch pen

- **NID_EXTERNAL_PEN** Indicates that the touch-sensitive device that supports a touch pen is external—usually, a touchpad

- **NID_MULTI_INPUT** Indicates that the touch-sensitive devices (either integrated or external) supports multitouch

- **NID_READY** Indicates that the touch-sensitive device is ready for use

The following code snippet illustrates how to test for multitouch capabilities and register the windows for touch messages:

```
int value = GetSystemMetrics(SM_DIGITIZER);
if (((value  & NID_MULTI_INPUT) == NID_MULTI_INPUT))
{
  RegisterTouchWindow(hWnd, 0);
}
```

Here you can see that we call *GetSystemMetrics*, passing SM_DIGITIZER as an input parameter. Then we test the return value by comparing it to the NID_MULTI_INPUT constant to validate that the digitizer (the touch device) supports multitouch input.

Unpacking WM_TOUCH Messages

Assuming you successfully registered for multitouch support, your application starts receiving multitouch messages. Just like with gestures, you handle WM_TOUCH messages in your window *WndProc* function. After a WM_TOUCH message is received, the first step you need to perform is to decode it and unpack the message content into different touch-point elements. A single WM_TOUCH message can contain several touch-point events that need to be unpacked into an array of touch input structures. The window procedure's *wParam* parameter holds the information regarding the number of actual touch points that are in the current WM_TOUCH message. This number correlates to the number of touch points the touch-sensitive device recognizes. As a standard practice, you should unpack the WM_TOUCH message into an array of TOUCHINPUT structures, where each structure in that array represents an event from a single touch point. Unpacking is performed by calling the *GetTouchInputInfo(HTOUCHINPUT hTouchInput, UINT cInputs, PTOUCHINPUT pInputs, int cbSize)* function and passing it as the first parameter the *lParam* of the WM_TOUCH message and a newly created touch-point array as the third parameter. The following code snippet shows how you can unpack a WM_TOUCH message:

```
case WM_TOUCH:
{
    // Number of actual per-contact messages
    UINT numInputs = (UINT) wParam;

    TOUCHINPUT* pTIArray = new TOUCHINPUT[numInputs];
    if(NULL == pTIArray)
    {
        CloseTouchInputHandle((HTOUCHINPUT)lParam);
        break;
    }
    // Unpack message parameters into the array of TOUCHINPUT structures, each
    // representing an event for one single contact.
    if(GetTouchInputInfo((HTOUCHINPUT)lParam, numInputs, pTIArray, sizeof(TOUCHINPUT)))
    {
        /* handlepTIArray + custom logic */
    }
    CloseTouchInputHandle((HTOUCHINPUT)lParam);
    delete [] pTIArray;
}
break;

default:
    return DefWindowProc(hWnd, message, wParam, lParam);
```

Here you can see how we create a new TOUCHINPUT array, *pTIArray*, and that its size in terms of the number of touch points is indicated by *wParam*. Then we pass the newly created array, its size, number of touch points, and original *lParam* that holds the touch events information into the *GetTouchInputInfo* function. This function unpacks the touch-point message and fills the array with TOUCHINPUT structures. Next, we iterate through the touch-point array, applying our logic to each touch point. Finally, we clean the touch handle by calling *CloseTouchInputHandle(HTOUCHINPUT hTouchInput)*, passing the *lParam* of the original window procedure. Failing to do so will result in memory leaks. Please note that you need to close the touch handle by calling *CloseTouchInputHandle* for all code paths, including your error handling code.

This code sample doesn't do much besides unpacking WM_TOUCH messages. In the next section, "Tracking Touch-Point IDs," we provide a more complex example. However, this is the first step in handling WM_TOUCH messages. Remember, these touch points contain raw data that you need to handle, and you must figure out for yourself what gesture the user is performing. A single touch-input structure, TOUCHINPUT defined in WinUser.h, contains all the necessary information about a single touch point that you need to work with, including the following information:

- *x* and *y* coordinates of the touch point (basically the location of each touch point).

- *dwID*, which is the touch-point identifier that distinguishes a particular touch input. This value stays consistent in a touch contact sequence from the point in time the touch point contacts the surface of the screen until it is lifted up.

- *dwFlags*, which is a set of bit flags that specify the state of the touch point, such as TOUCHEVENTF_DOWN, TOUCHEVENTF_UP, or TOUCHEVENTF_MOVE, which correspond to touch-point down (making contact), touch-point up (ending contact), and touch-point move (maintaining contact but changing position), respectively. TOUCHEVENTF_PRIMARY indicates that this touch point is the primary touch point, which is the first touch point in the current sequence of WM_TOUCH messages.

- *dwTime*, which is the time stamp for the event, in milliseconds.

- *dwMask*There are additional members of the TOUCHINPUT structure—such as *dwExtraInfo*, *cxContact*, and *cxContact*—that are used for advanced multitouch scenarios and are beyond the scope of this book. This flag is a set of bit flags that specify which of the optional fields in the structure contain valid values.

Note that the x and y coordinates are in hundredths of a pixel of physical screen coordinates (that is, centa-pixels). This extra-fine resolution promotes high precision and accurate handwriting recognition, as well as aiding the performance of other applications that require fine resolution. But for most scenarios, you need to divide the touch-point x and y coordinates by a hundred to translate the touch-point coordinates to usable screen coordinates before you start using them, as you will see in the upcoming samples.

By now, you know how to handle touch messages and you have all the information you need to add real logic to your WM_TOUCH handler, such as the one described earlier in this section. Let's use this knowledge and build a multitouch paint application named Scratch Pad.

Tracking Touch-Point IDs

To create the Scratch Pad application, you need to track each touch-point movement and the path that it forms, and then paint a line along that path. To distinguish between the different touch points and to make sure you handle each touch point correctly, you assign a different color to each touch point. The first touch point, also called the *primary touch point*, always receives the color black, and the other touch points get randomized colors other than black.

In the previous code sample, you saw how to unpack touch messages. After unpacking the touch message into an array of touch input structures, *pTIArray*, you need to check each touch-point state and apply different logic for each one. In the Scratch Pad implementation, for new touch points, which are identified by the down state (TOUCHEVENTF_DOWN), you register the new touch-point ID and assign it a color. After a touch point is removed (indicated by TOUCHEVENTF_UP), you finish by painting the last point and unregister the touch point ID. In between down and up events, you most likely will get a lot of move messages (indicated by TOUCHEVENTF_MOVE). For each move message, you add a new point to the existing line and paint the new segment of the line. The following code snippet shows the entire WM_TOUCH handler that is required for the Scratch Pad application to support multitouch:

```
case WM_TOUCH:
{
    UINT numInputs = (UINT) wParam; // Number of actual per-contact messages
    // Allocate the storage for the parameters of the per-contact messages TOUCHINPUT*
    pTIArray = new TOUCHINPUT[numInputs];
    if(NULL == pTIArray)
    {
        break;
    }
    // Unpack message parameters into the array of TOUCHINPUT structures, each
    // representing an event for one single contact.
    if(GetTouchInputInfo((HTOUCHINPUT)lParam, numInputs, pTIArray, sizeof(TOUCHINPUT)))
    {
        // For each contact, dispatch the message to the appropriate message
        // handler.
        for(UINT i=0; i<numInputs; ++i)
        {
            if(TOUCHEVENTF_DOWN == (pTIArray[i].dwFlags & TOUCHEVENTF_DOWN))
            {
                OnTouchDownHandler(hWnd, pTIArray[i]);
            }
            else if(TOUCHEVENTF_MOVE == (pTIArray[i].dwFlags & TOUCHEVENTF_MOVE))
            {
                OnTouchMoveHandler(hWnd, pTIArray[i]);
```

```
                }
                else if(TOUCHEVENTF_UP == (pTIArray[i].dwFlags & TOUCHEVENTF_UP))
                {
                    OnTouchUpHandler(hWnd, pTIArray[i]);
                }
            }
        }
        CloseTouchInputHandle((HTOUCHINPUT)lParam);
        delete [] pTIArray;
    }
    break;
```

Here you can see that after unpacking the touch message into the TOUCHINPUT array, you check each touch-point state by checking the *dwFlags* value and dispatching the event to the appropriate helper function.

The key for tracking individual touch points is using the *dwID*, which remains the same throughout the duration of the specific touch stroke—that is, from the first message (WM_TOUCHDOWN) through all the move messages (WM_TOUCHMOVE) until the last up message (WM_TOUCHUP), the *dwID* stays the same for each touch point. In the *OnTouchDownHandler* helper function, you assign this ID to a *CStroke* object that is basically an array of points that represents a line. This line is the path that the user drags her finger across the touch-sensitive device. This *CStroke* object is then added to a collection of stroke objects. The following is the code snippet for the *OnTouchDownHandler* helper function:

```
 void OnTouchDownHandler(HWND hWnd, const TOUCHINPUT& ti)
{
    // Extract contact info: point of contact and ID
    POINT pt = GetTouchPoint(hWnd, ti);
    int iCursorId = GetTouchContactID(ti);

    // We have just started a new stroke, which must have an ID value unique
    // among all the strokes currently being drawn. Check if there is a stroke
    // with the same ID in the collection of the strokes in drawing.
    ASSERT(g_StrkColDrawing.FindStrokeById(iCursorId) == -1);

    // Create new stroke, add point and assign a color to it.
    CStroke* pStrkNew = new CStroke;
    pStrkNew->Add(pt);
    pStrkNew->SetColor(GetTouchColor((ti.dwFlags & TOUCHEVENTF_PRIMARY) != 0));
    pStrkNew->SetId(iCursorId);

    // Add new stroke to the collection of strokes in drawing.
    g_StrkColDrawing.Add(pStrkNew);
```

}Here you can see how you recover the new touch point location by calling yet another helper function, *GetTouchPoint(HWND hWnd, TOUCHINPUT* ti)*, which extracts the x and y coordinates from the TOUCHINPUT structure. These x and y coordinates are relative to the current window position that is the reason for passing the *hWnd* param. Then you create a new *CStroke* object, setting its *ID*, by using the TOUCHINPUT structure *dwID* member that we just described. You also assign its color—that is, the color the entire line will be painted. To assign the color, you call the *SetColor* method. You use the *GetTouchColor* helper function that returns the color black if the input parameter is *true*, which is the case for the first, or primary, touch point. Finally, you add the new *CStroke* object to the stroke collection that you'll use to paint the line.

For the move event, you simply look for the corresponding *CStroke* object that matches the touch-point ID, identified by the TOUCHINPUT *dwID* field. Then you add the location of the new touch point as a new point into the already existing line. Finally, you repaint the new segment of the line. The following is the code snippet for the *OnTouchMoveHandler* helper function:

```
void OnTouchMoveHandler(HWND hWnd, const TOUCHINPUT& ti)
{
    // Extract contact info: contact ID
    int iCursorId = GetTouchContactID(ti);

    // Find the stroke in the collection of the strokes in drawing.
    int iStrk = g_StrkColDrawing.FindStrokeById(iCursorId);
    ASSERT(iStrk >= 0 && iStrk < g_StrkColDrawing.Count());

    // Extract contact info: contact point
    POINT pt;
    pt = GetTouchPoint(hWnd, ti);

    // Add contact point to the stroke
    g_StrkColDrawing[iStrk]->Add(pt);

    // Partial redraw: only the last line segment
    HDC hDC = GetDC(hWnd);
    g_StrkColDrawing[iStrk]->DrawLast(hDC);
    ReleaseDC(hWnd, hDC);
}
```

Here you can see that you are searching for a particular *CStroke* object by calling the *FindStrokeByID(int ID)* function that received the touch-point ID found in *iCursorId*, after extracting the *dwID* from the TOUCHINPUT structure, and returned the index of the *CStroke* object in the line's collection. Next, you can get the touch- point screen coordinates by calling *GetTouchPoint;*, then you can add the new point to this line and ask for this new segment to be repainted.

Finally, you need to handle the up event that occurs when the touch point is removed. This is the last message in the sequence of down and move messages with the same touch-point ID, *dwID*. So all that is left to do is finish the stroke and unregister the ID. Again we extract the touch- point ID from the TOUCHINPUT structure and store it in *iCursorId*. Next, we find the relevant *cStorke* object, add the last point , and paint the last segment.The following is the code snippet for the *OnTouchUpHandler* helper function:

```
void OnTouchUpHandler(HWND hWnd, const TOUCHINPUT& ti)
{
    // Extract contact info: contact ID
    int iCursorId = GetTouchContactID(ti);

    // Find the stroke in the collection of the strokes in drawing.
    int iStrk = g_StrkColDrawing.FindStrokeById(iCursorId);
    ASSERT(iStrk >= 0 && iStrk < g_StrkColDrawing.Count());

    // Add this stroke to the collection of finished strokes.
    g_StrkColFinished.Add(g_StrkColDrawing[iStrk]);

    // Remove this stroke from the collection of strokes in drawing.
    g_StrkColDrawing.Remove(iStrk);

    // Request full redraw.
    InvalidateRect(hWnd, NULL, FALSE);
}
```

As you can see, creating a multitouch Scratch Pad application is not that difficult. It all comes down to a simple WM_TOUCH handler and three helper functions. All you need to do is paint a line for each touch-point path, while tracking each touch point using the *dwID* field to identify a specific touch point.

Next, we describe a slightly more complex implementation of a touch application, in which the full power of the touch platform will surface.

Using the Manipulation and Inertia Engines

In the previous section, you saw the power of handling raw touch messages rather than using the default, out-of-the-box support for gestures that we described in great detail in the previous chapter. Unlike the default gesture support, handling raw touch points lets you do whatever your heart desires.

In our example, the Scratch Pad application is not performing any sophisticated calculation on the touch points, except keeping tabs on the path each touch point forms. Much more sophisticated calculations are required to figure out which gestures the user is performing. Supporting raw touch inputs gives you the opportunity to detect custom gestures that can be far more complex than the gestures described in the previous chapter.

A complex gesture can include any number of touch points and combine multiple different gestures at the same time. For example, a complex gesture can include zooming, scaling, and translating gestures that are all happing at the same time on any number of different objects. However, the great flexibility of being able to handle such complex gestures comes with a price. Windows 7 does not provide any customizable template gesture engine for complex gestures. To detect such complex gestures, you need to do a lot of complex mathematical computation. Remember, Windows 7 has a gesture engine, which you used in the previous chapter, but Microsoft doesn't provide you the code or any way to extend that engine. If you want to detect a complex gesture using touch events, you need to build your own custom logic.

Because of the complexity of recognizing complex gestures, the Windows 7 multitouch platform provides a higher level of application programming interfaces (APIs) in the form of the Manipulation and Inertia processors. Manipulations are similar to gestures in a lot of ways, but they are a lot more powerful. Manipulations are used to simplify transformation operations on any given number of objects. You can perform a combination of specific component gestures—such as rotate, zoom, and scale—on a specific object at the same time, and the Manipulation processor yields a two-dimensional *transformation matrix* that represents the transformations in x and y coordinates, the scale of the change, and the rotation that occurred to the object over time as a result of the movement of the touch points. After the last touch point is pulled up, you might want to apply simple physics to the object so that it smoothly comes to a halt rather than abruptly stopping on the spot. To support that smooth motion, the Windows 7 multitouch platform provides the Inertia API. The rest of this chapter describes in detail what the Manipulation and Inertia processors are and how to use them.

Multitouch Architecture: The Complete Picture, Part 1

Let's return to Figure 5.1, data - Data flow from touch hardware to the Windows 7 multitouch infrastructure to your application, in Chapter 5 and update it to reflect handling raw touch data using Windows 7 Manipulation and Inertia processes.

First, you must understand that a single Manipulation processor instance works on a single object, the target object, and it needs to be attached to the target object you want to manipulate. To support the manipulation of multiple objects at the same time, you need to attach a Manipulation processor instance to each target object. In return, to touch events, a Manipulation processor instance provides a two-dimensional transform matrix for each target object, so you can manipulate multiple objects at any given time. Therefore, from now on, we'll refer to the Manipulation processor in the context of a single target object. Figure 6-1 illustrates the Manipulation processor architecture.

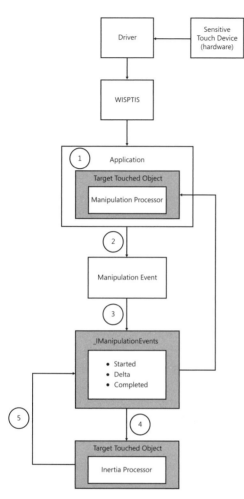

Figure 6-1 Windows 7 Multitouch Platform Manipulation Processor Dataflow

During the initialization phase of the application (which is not depicted in Figure 6-1), you attach the Manipulation processor and manipulation event sink to the target object. You fast-forward Windows 7 touch messages up to the point that Windows Ink Services Platform Table Input Subsystem (WISPTIS), which was described in the previous chapter, sends a WM_TOUCH message to the application (shown as number 1 in Figure 6-1). This message contains one or more touch-point events.

Now the application needs to find out which one of the touch points actually touches the target object. This process is called *hit testing* (which occurs at number 2 in the illustration) because you are checking which touch point "hits" the desired target object you want to manipulate. Then you pass the touch event data associated with the touch point to the object's manipulation processor, which in turn generates manipulation events, shown as number 3. These events are handled by your implementation of the event sink _IManipulationEvents interface that acts as a listener, shown at number 4.

During the initialization phase, when you attach the Manipulation process to your object, you also attach your implementation of the _IManipulationEvents interface, which we'll describe in the "Setting Up Manipulation" section later in this chapter. IManipulationEvents is responsible for updating the values of our target object so that they reflect the transformations, shown at number 5.

Using Manipulation

In the preceding section, we presented the different players that are required when using the Manipulation processor. Let's review in detail the different elements and how they interact with each other.

To successfully add manipulation support to your application, you need a manipulation process object, *ManipulationProcessor*, which is a COM object that you initialize for each target object that you want to manipulate. Refer back to Figure 6-1, where you wanted to handle manipulation for each target touch object. You need to write an event sink class that implements the _IManipulationEvents interface, which will be attached to the corresponding connection point of the Manipulation processor. This event sink acts as a listener that handles specific manipulation events that are sent by the Manipulation processor. These events include all the information mentioned in the previous section regarding the two-dimensional transformation matrix, and that is the place in your application to write custom touch-handling logic. Finally, you need to bind the target object you want to manipulate, the manipulation process, and your _IManipulationEvents interface implementation.

To summarize, you need to do the following to add manipulation support:

- Implement an event sink for _IManipulationEvents.

- Instantiate a COM object that implements the *IManipulationProcessor* interface.

- Instantiate your event sink implementation, and set up touch events by binding the Manipulation processor, the event sink implementation, and the object you want to manipulate.

- Send the touch event data to the Manipulation processor that in return raises the manipulation events. These events are handled by your event sink object.

Setting Up Manipulation

In practice, you have an object that implements an event sink for the _IManipulationEvents interface. Let's refer to this object as your *manipulation event sink*. This object also contains a pointer to an instance of a Manipulation processor object that implements the *IManipulationProcessor* interface that acts as your event provider. This Manipulation processor notifies events through the *_IManipulationEvents* interface in response to touch messages. These events are handled by your manipulation event sink object.

Your *_IManipulationEvents* implementation includes the three functions of the interface: *ManipulationStarted, ManipulationDelta,* and *ManipulationCompleted.* The *Start* event is sent when a manipulation is detected by the operating system, and it indicates the beginning of the manipulation events sequence. The *Delta* event handler is the main function that handles the manipulation during the movement of the user's fingers. The *Completed* event is sent when the manipulation ends, and this is where you will want to plug in the beginning of your inertia code.

The *ManipulationStarted* function provides the x and y coordinates of the initial starting point of the manipulation. The *ManipulationCompleted* function in addition to the location coordinates includes additional information such as *cumulativeRotation* and *cumulativeExpansion* that we use after we initiate the Inertia processor.

The most useful information is part of the *ManipulationDelta* function. This function includes parameters that represent the two-dimensional transformation that took place on the object. Here is an example of some of the information you'll find there:

- *x* and *y* coordinates in hundreds of pixels that indicate the origin of the manipulation.

- *translationDeltaX* and *translationDeltaY*, which indicate the translation change regarding the X axis and Y axis, respectively, since the last event. This is the delta of the *x* and *y* coordinates with respect to the previous event location.

- *scaleDelta*, which indicates the change in the scaling factor since the last event.

- *rotationDelta*, which indicates the change in the rotation angle since the last event. Units are measured in radians.

- *expansionDelta*, which indicates the change in the rate of the expansion.

- For all of these parameters, there is a *cumulative* counterpart that indicates the total change to the relevant scalar value since the beginning of the manipulation—for example, *cumulativeTranslationY* or *cumulativeRotation*.

The following code snippet describes our manipulation event sink implementation prototype, and it can be found in the CManipulationEventSink.h file in the Ch06_Multitouch_ManipulationAndInertia example:

```
class CManipulationEventSink : _IManipulationEvents
{
public:
    //CTOR receives a Manipulation Processor (IManipulationProcessor) and the object to
manipulate
    CManipulationEventSink(
        IManipulationProcessor *manip,
        IInertiaProcessor* inertiap,
        CDrawingObject* pcDrawingObject,
        HWND hWnd);


    //DCtor
    ~CManipulationEventSink();

    //////////////////////////////////////////////////////////
    // IManipulationEvents methods
    //////////////////////////////////////////////////////////
    virtual HRESULT STDMETHODCALLTYPE ManipulationStarted(
        /* [in] */ FLOAT x,
        /* [in] */ FLOAT y);

    virtual HRESULT STDMETHODCALLTYPE ManipulationDelta(
        /* [in] */ FLOAT x,
        /* [in] */ FLOAT y,
        /* [in] */ FLOAT translationDeltaX,
        /* [in] */ FLOAT translationDeltaY,
        /* [in] */ FLOAT scaleDelta,
        /* [in] */ FLOAT expansionDelta,
        /* [in] */ FLOAT rotationDelta,
        /* [in] */ FLOAT cumulativeTranslationX,
        /* [in] */ FLOAT cumulativeTranslationY,
        /* [in] */ FLOAT cumulativeScale,
        /* [in] */ FLOAT cumulativeExpansion,
        /* [in] */ FLOAT cumulativeRotation);

    virtual HRESULT STDMETHODCALLTYPE ManipulationCompleted(
        /* [in] */ FLOAT x,
        /* [in] */ FLOAT y,
        /* [in] */ FLOAT cumulativeTranslationX,
        /* [in] */ FLOAT cumulativeTranslationY,
```

```
        /* [in] */ FLOAT cumulativeScale,
        /* [in] */ FLOAT cumulativeExpansion,
        /* [in] */ FLOAT cumulativeRotation);


    //////////////////////////////////////////////////////////
    // IUnknown methods
    //////////////////////////////////////////////////////////
    STDMETHOD_(ULONG, AddRef)(void);
    STDMETHOD_(ULONG, Release)(void);
    STDMETHOD(QueryInterface)(REFIID riid, LPVOID *ppvObj);

private:
    void SetInertia();
    void SetElasticBoundaries();

    int m_cRefCount;

    // The IConnectionPoint interface supports connection points for connectable objects.
    CComPtr<IConnectionPoint> m_spConnection;

    // The IConnectionPoint interface supports connection points for connectable objects for
inertia.
    CComPtr<IConnectionPoint> m_spConnection2;



    // Manipulation and Inertia processors
    IManipulationProcessor* m_manipulationProc;
    IInertiaProcessor* m_inertiaProc;

    // This flag is set by the manipulation event sink
    // when the ManipulationCompleted method is invoked
    BOOL m_bIsInertiaActive;

    // Pointer to the CDrawingObject (contains the rectangle information)
    CDrawingObject* m_pcDrawingObject;

    HWND m_hWnd;};
```

Here you can see that the object constructor includes a pointer to a Manipulation processor, *IManipulationProcessor *m_manipulationProc*, and a pointer to the target object that you want to manipulate, *CDrawingObject* m_pcDrawingObject*. Note that you keep a local member of the rectangular *CDrawingObject, m_pcDrawingObject*, to manipulate it after the events are sent from the Manipulation processor.

In our examples, we handle only the *ManipulationDelta* function, by simply passing a parameter that represents the two-dimensional transformation to the *m_pcDrawingObject*, as shown by the following code snippet, which is part of the CManipulationEventSink.cpp file:

```
HRESULT STDMETHODCALLTYPE
    CManipulationEventSink::ManipulationDelta(x, y, translationDeltaX, .... )
{
    m_pcDrawingObject->ApplyManipulationDelta
        (translationDeltaX,
         translationDeltaY,
         scaleDelta,
         rotationDelta);
    return S_OK;
}
```

Here you can see that you pass to the *ApplyManipulationDelta* function the relevant changes in the x and y coordinates and changes to the scale and rotation to update these parameters in your drawing object.

Working with Manipulation

Now we take all the different elements we described so far and make them work together. As you might recall, you need to initiate a Manipulation processor for each object. In our application, we have only one target object; therefore, we initialize just one Manipulation processor. A good place to do this is in the application's *WinMain* entry point, as shown in the following code snippet:

```
//instanciate the system object that implements the IManipulationProcess interface interface
hr = g_spIManipProc.CoCreateInstance(
        __uuidof(ManipulationProcessor), NULL, CLSCTX_ALL);
if(FAILED(hr))
{
    /* Error Handling */
}
```

Next, initialize the event sink implementation, *CManipulationEventSink*, as shown in the following code snippet:

```
// Instantiate the event sink with the Manipulation processor and pointer to the rectangle
// object.
// This is the binding point between the Manipulation processor and our rect object...
g_pManipulationEventSink = new CManipulationEventSink(g_spIManipProc, g_spIinertisProc,
&g_cRect,hWnd);
if(NULL == g_pManipulationEventSink)
```

```
{
    ASSERT(g_pManipulationEventSink && L"InitInstance: failed to instantiate the
CManipulationEventSink class");
    return FALSE;
}
```

Here you can see that we create a new *CManipulationEventSink* object by passing the previously created Manipulation processor and a pointer to our *CDrawingObject*.

The last thing on our to-do list is to pass each relevant touch-point touch event data to the Manipulation processor in the WM_TOUCH event handler, as shown in the following code snippet:

```
case WM_TOUCH:
{
    UINT iNumContacts = LOWORD(wParam); // This is the number of actual
        per-contact messages
    TOUCHINPUT* pInputs = NULL;
    pInputs = new TOUCHINPUT[iNumContacts];

    if(pInputs == NULL)
    {
        //Error handling
        break;
    }
    // Unpack message parameters into the array of TOUCHINPUT structures, each
    // representing a message for one single contact.
    if(GetTouchInputInfo((HTOUCHINPUT)lParam, iNumContacts , pInputs, sizeof(TOUCHINPUT)))
    {
        // For each contact, dispatch the message to the appropriate message handler.
        for(UINT i=0; i<iNumContacts; i++)
        {
            if(TOUCHEVENTF_DOWN == (pInputs[i].dwFlags & TOUCHEVENTF_DOWN))
            {
                g_spIManipProc->ProcessDown(pInputs[i].dwID, (FLOAT)pInputs[i].x,
(FLOAT)pInputs[i].y);
            }
            else if(TOUCHEVENTF_MOVE == (pInputs[i].dwFlags & TOUCHEVENTF_MOVE))
            {
                g_spIManipProc->ProcessMove(pInputs[i].dwID, (FLOAT)pInputs[i].x,
(FLOAT)pInputs[i].y);
            }
            else if(TOUCHEVENTF_UP == (pInputs[i].dwFlags & TOUCHEVENTF_UP))
            {
                g_spIManipProc->ProcessUp(pInputs[i].dwID, (FLOAT)pInputs[i].x,
(FLOAT)pInputs[i].y);
            }
        }
    }
    else
    {
```

```
            // error handling, presumably out of memory
            ASSERT(L"Error: failed to execute GetTouchInputInfo" && 0);
            break;
    }
    if(!CloseTouchInputHandle((HTOUCHINPUT)lParam))
    {
            // error handling, presumably out of memory
            ASSERT(L"Error: failed to execute CloseTouchInputHandle" && 0);
            break;
    }
    delete [] pInputs;

    // Force redraw of the window
    InvalidateRect(hWnd,NULL,TRUE);
}
break;
```

Earlier in this chapter, we described similar code for the Scratch Pad example. Just like in that example, for each touch point, indicated by the *dwID* flag, we verify its state and pass the coordinates and touch ID to the relevant manipulation functions, as shown in the preceding code. The Manipulation processor exposes a set of functions. *ProcessDown*, *ProcessMove*, and *ProcessUp* are probably the most often used function because they are used to feed touch-point event data to the Manipulation processor. All functions receive the same three parameters: the touch point ID and the x and y coordinates.

As we mentioned before, after you call the Manipulation processor *Process** functions (such as *ProcessMove*), the Manipulation processor sends events that are handled by your event sink (in our example, *CManipulationEventSink*) listener object.

There is another set of "process" functions that in addition to the location and ID parameters also receive an exact timestamp. These functions are used for precision manipulation processing. The functions are *ProcessDownWithTime*, *ProcessMoveWithTime*, and *ProcessUpWithTime*. There are additional functions, such as *GetVelocityX* and *GetAngularVelocity*, that the Manipulation processor exposes that we'll cover in the "Using Inertia" section later in this chapter.

Because this is neither a C++ nor a COM programming book, we chose to skip a detailed description of the COM programming model except for the minimum necessities required to explain Windows 7 multitouch APIs. We encourage you to read the full source code of the examples to fully understand the details of using the multitouch COM interfaces.

Using Inertia

You might want to use inertia to incorporate some physics into the target object so that it smoothly comes to a stop, rather than abruptly stopping when the last touch point stops touching the target object. The Windows 7 multitouch API provides the Inertia processor to perform the physics calculations for you. The Inertia processor uses a simple physics model that incorporates a position, a deceleration value, and an initial displacement. Figure 6-2 outlines the physics model used for calculating object positions.

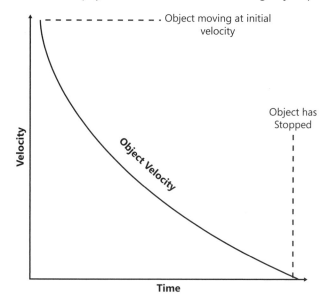

Figure 6-2 Inertia Default Deceleration Curve

You can see that the target object velocity decreases with time, allowing the object to make a smooth transition from being in motion to stopping. The Windows 7 multitouch platform allows you to override the default deceleration values to enable you to use a different deceleration model. You can even decide what the final position of the target object will be and how much time it will take the object to get there—the platform will simply do the work for you. Even more, you can completely override the default physics model and provide your own implementation. However, we'll describe a simple scenario in which we use the default values and model. But before we jump into the code, let's review the underlying architecture that supports inertia.

Multitouch Architecture: The Complete Picture, Part 2

Now we can complete our architecture overview of the Windows 7 Multitouch platform. Using Figure 6-1, which shows the Windows 7 Multitouch Platform Manipulation processor dataflow, as a starting point, let's add the Inertia processor objects and the relevant messages, as shown in Figure 6-3.

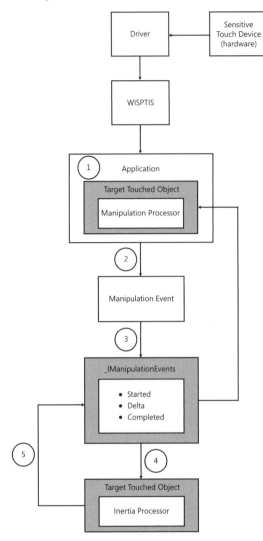

Figure 6-3 Windows 7 Multitouch platform complete dataflow

The operating system sends a WM_TOUCH message with the TOUCHEVENTF_UP flag, shown at number 1. The up event is sent after the last touch point is lifted off the target object. As we previously explained, in our WM_TOUCH handler, we call the Manipulation processor *ProcessUp* function, which generates the *ManipulationCompleted* event, as shown at number 2. Our *IManipulationEvents* implementation handles this event, shown at number 3, and this is where the difference between manipulation and inertia starts.

The *ManipulationCompleted* handler is responsible for setting the Inertia processor velocity and trajectory, and it starts the Inertia processor. To start the Inertia processor, you call the Inertia processor's *Process* or *ProcessTime* function, shown at number 4. The Inertia processor raises manipulation events that are handled by a manipulation event sink based on the _IManipulationEvents_ interface, as shown at number 5. Note that the _IManipulationEvents_ event sink class implementation from the manipulation processor is reused as an event sink for the Inertia processor. Both processors raise the same events; therefore, we use the same event sink implementation to handle both. The Inertia processor continues to raise manipulation events at a decreasing rate according to the physics model.

Setting Up Inertia

In the "Setting Up Manipulation" section earlier in the chapter, you saw the implementation of the _IManipulationEvents_ interface, _CManipulationEventSink_, that we used to handle the events raised by the Manipulation processor. However, as we just explained, the Inertia processor generates the same events as the Manipulation processor; therefore, we can use the already existing _CManipulationEventSink_ object. All we need to do is update the object constructor and the _ManipulationStarted and ManipulationCompleted_ functions to reflect that both functions handle the same events from two different sources.

The new object constructor includes a pointer to the Inertia processor in addition to the pointer to the Manipulation processor, as shown in the following code:

```
CManipulationEventSink(
    IManipulationProcessor *manip,
    IInertiaProcessor* inertiap,
    CDrawingObject* pcDrawingObject,
    HWND hWnd);
```

Here you can see that we also include a HWND handle. This handle is required for calculating the application window elastic boundaries that are described in the next section. We also include with _CManipulationEventSink_ a Boolean private field called _m_bIsInertiaActive_. It is set to _false_ in the constructor, and we will use it in the event handlers.

Next, we update the _ManipulationStarted_ function to set the _m_bIsInertiaActive_ flag to _false_, so every time a new manipulation starts it will clear the inertia flag, as shown in the following code snippet:

```
HRESULT STDMETHODCALLTYPE CManipulationEventSink::ManipulationStarted(
    FLOAT /* x */,
    FLOAT /* y */)
{
    m_bIsInertiaActive = false;
    return S_OK;
}
```

Now it's time to update the *ManipulationCompleted* function. This event is called after the last touch point is lifted off the object. Here you set up the Inertia processor with its initial velocity and angular velocity values, which represent the target object trajectory:

```
HRESULT STDMETHODCALLTYPE CManipulationEventSink::ManipulationCompleted(
    FLOAT /* x */,
    FLOAT /* y */,
    FLOAT /* cumulativeTranslationX */,
    FLOAT /* cumulativeTranslationY */,
    FLOAT /* cumulativeScale */,
    FLOAT /* cumulativeExpansion */,
    FLOAT /* cumulativeRotation */)
{
    if(false == m_bIsInertiaActive
    {
        //reset the flag
        m_bIsInertiaActive = true;
        SetInertia();
        SetElasticBoundaries();
        // Kick off the timer that handles inertia
        SetTimer(m_hWnd, 1, 10, NULL);
    }
    return S_OK;
}
```

First, check your flag. It's set to *false* because so far you have just handled manipulation events. You need to initiate the Inertia processor only once, so you reset the flag and call two helper functions, *SetInertia* and *SetElasticBoundaries*. Last and very importantly, you call *SetTimer*. The timer sends WM_TIMER messages every 10 milliseconds (msec). These events are the heartbeat of the Inertia process, and for each event you call the Inertia processor *Process* function. This function calculates the transformation of the target object according to the inertia current values and sends WM_TOUCH messages with TOUCHEVENTF_MOVE or TOUCHEVENTF_UP. These events are handled by your _IManipulationEvents implementation, as we explained before. You then call *InvalidateRect* to repaint the entire window.

```
case WM_TIMER:
    g_spIinertiaProcessor ->Process(&bInertiaComplete );
    // Force redraw of the rectangle
    InvalidateRect(hWnd,NULL,TRUE);
    break;
```

In the *setInertia* function, you set the initial value of the Inertia processor, *m_inertiaProc*, as shown in the following code snippet:

```
void CManipulationEventSink::SetInertia()
{
    // Set initial origins
    m_inertiaProc->put_InitialOriginX(m_pcDrawingObject->GetCenter().x);
    m_inertiaProc->put_InitialOriginY(m_pcDrawingObject->GetCenter().y);

    // physics settings
```

```
    // Deceleration for translations in pixel / msec^2
    m_inertiaProc->put_DesiredDeceleration(0.0003f);
    // Deceleration for rotations in radians / msec^2
    m_inertiaProc->put_DesiredAngularDeceleration(0.000015f);

    FLOAT fVX;
    FLOAT fVY;
    FLOAT fVR;

    m_manipulationProc->GetVelocityX(&fVX);
    m_manipulationProc->GetVelocityY(&fVY);
    m_manipulationProc->GetAngularVelocity(&fVR);

    //Velocities for inertia processor
    m_inertiaProc->put_InitialVelocityX(fVX);
    m_inertiaProc->put_InitialVelocityY(fVY);
    m_inertiaProc->put_InitialAngularVelocity(fVR);
}
```

First, you set the starting location of the target object to provide the Inertia processor with a reference point for the object in relation to the rest of the window. This information is critical to use with the elastic boundaries. Next, you set the horizontal, vertical, and angular velocities by using the *put_InitialVelocityX*, *put_InitialVelocityY*, and *put_InitialAngularVelocity* properties. As you can see, you extract this velocity information from the Manipulation processor because it holds the latest updated information about the target object velocity and trajectory.

Finally, you set the desired deceleration factor by calling the *put_DesiredDeceleration* property, and you set the desired angular deceleration (in case the object is rotating) factor by calling *put_DesiredAngularDeceleration*. Without setting these two parameters, the Inertia processor will not calculate the transformation at all and nothing will happen. You might want to pay close attention to the units of the input parameters passed to these functions. They are *pixel/msec^2* for velocity and *radians/msec^2* for angular velocity, and that is the reason the values are so small. I can only say that to find the deceleration model that fits your needs you need to play with and test different values.

When using inertia, you set the Inertia processor initial values with your target velocity and trajectory. Then the Inertia processor sends *ManipulationDelta* events that contain the transformation information about your target object. This information represents the continuation of your target motion. After you have an object that is moving across the screen, you will typically want it to stop before it goes outside of the user's viewpoint. The Inertia processor enables this functionality through the boundary and elastic margin properties.

Figure 6-4 illustrates the various boundary and margin properties in a typical application.

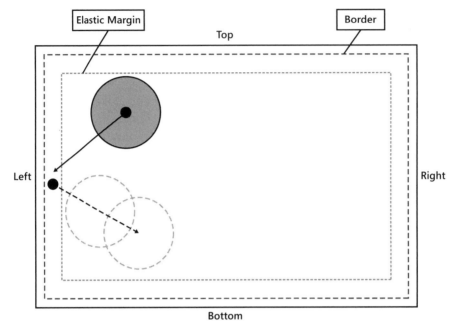

Figure 6-4 Windows 7 Window's Elastic Boundaries

Our *SetElasticBoundaries* functions look like this:

```
void CManipulationEventSink::SetElasticBoundaries()
{
    //set elastic boundaries
    RECT windowRect;
    GetClientRect(m_hWnd, &windowRect);
    inertiaProc->put_BoundaryLeft(windowRect.left);
    inertiaProc->put_BoundaryTop(windowRect.top);
    inertiaProc->put_BoundaryRight(windowRect.right);
    inertiaProc->put_BoundaryBottom(windowRect.bottom);

    inertiaProc->put_ElasticMarginLeft(windowRect.right*20);
    inertiaProc->put_ElasticMarginTop(windowRect.top*20);
    inertiaProc->put_ElasticMarginRight(windowRect.right*80);
    inertiaProc->put_ElasticMarginBottom(windowRect.bottom*80);
}
```

First, you extract the visible window dimensions, represented by the *windowRect* right and bottom fields. Then you use the boundaries properties to set all four Inertia processor boundaries with the values of the screen. Next, you set all four elastic margin properties that define the region bounding the target object.

Working with Inertia

At this point, you have updated your *CManipulationEventSink* object to use both the Manipulation and Inertia processors. Now you need to initiate an Inertia processor and a Manipulation processor. As before, a good place to do this is in the application *WinMain* entry point, as shown in the following code snippet, which includes only the additional relevant lines of code:

```
hr = g_spIinertiaProcessor.CoCreateInstance(__uuidof(InertiaProcessor), NULL, CLSCTX_ALL);
if(FAILED(hr))
{
    /* error handling */
}
```

This code is identical to initializing the *IManipulationProcessor* interface, but this time you're using the *InertiaProcessor* interface. Next, update the creation of the event sink implementation to reflect the changes we described earlier:

```
g_pManipulationEventSink = NULL;
g_pManipulationEventSink = new CManipulationEventSink(
    g_spIManipProc,
    g_spIinertisProc,
    &g_cRect,
    hWnd);
if( NULL == g_pManipulationEventSink)
{
    /* error handling */
}
```

You don't have to change the WM_TOUCH handler because the Manipulation processor and Inertia processor use the same event sink object.

By applying these changes, your target object continues to move after the last touch point is lifted because you are using the Inertia processor.

Summary

In this second multitouch chapter, you learned how to register and handle WM_TOUCH messages, register and handle raw multitouch messages, and use the Manipulation and Inertia processors. We started this chapter with an explanation of how to identify multitouch hardware and its capabilities. Then we showed you how to register a window to receive touch messages to create a simple but nice finger-painting application. Then we introduced the Manipulation and Inertia processors and showed you how to use them. In Chapter 7, "Building Multitouch Applications in Managed Code," you'll learn how easy it is to use

Windows Presentation Foundation version 4 (WPF4), which is part of Microsoft Visual Studio 2010, to create WPF multitouch applications.

This was the second multitouch chapter. We hope that by after reading both chapters you have a solid understanding of the platform capabilities and the new and exciting scenarios you can introduce into your application to create better and more intuitive user experiences for your end users.

Chapter 7
Building Multitouch Applications in Managed Code

In Chapters 5 and 6, you looked at touch-based applications—in particular, the new multitouch capabilities that are available in the Windows 7 operating system—and how to program applications to take advantage of Windows 7 multitouch features.

Perhaps you're not really that into writing in C++, or perhaps you already have applications that are written in managed code and would like to be able to use them with multitouch. This chapter will look at how you can build applications with multitouch in mind using the Microsoft .NET Framework and, in particular, the Windows Presentation Foundation (WPF) version 4.

Instead of making a dry run through the features, you're going to get hands-on experience right away and learn by doing. So fire up Microsoft Visual Studio 2010 and let's get going.

Building Your First Touch-Sensitive Application

Visual Studio 2010 supports the ability to create WPF Windows applications. You can do this from the File menu. Select New Project, and the New Project Types dialog box opens. Make sure that you've selected .NET Framework 4.0 as the target framework (on the top right side), and select WPF Application from the available templates.

Visual Studio creates a basic WPF client application for you containing a couple of XAML files: App.xaml, which contains the application definition, and MainWindow.xaml, which defines the application UI. You'll edit MainWindow.xaml in this section.

Let's take a look at the basic XAML that is created for you in Window1.xaml:

```
<Window x:Class="Chapter7_Sample1.MainWindow"
        xmlns="http://schemas.microsoft.com/winfx/2006/xaml/presentation"
        xmlns:x="http://schemas.microsoft.com/winfx/2006/xaml"
        Title="MainWindow" Height="300" Width="300">
    <Grid>

    </Grid>
</Window>
```

This example defines the window and the code that supports it. In this case, you can see that the class that implements this code is *Chapter7Sample1.Window1*. This code resides in the *code-behind* file called *MainWindow.xaml.cs*. We'll look at that in a moment.

The attributes on the Window element define the namespaces for the XAML code so that the XAML can be validated by the Visual Studio compiler. Finally, some basic properties such as *Title*, *Height*, and *Width* are set.

XAML in WPF supports a number of controls that allow you to command how the user interface is laid out. The *Grid* control is one of these; it allows you to define how your controls are laid out within defined cells. These controls can be placed anywhere within any of the cells. If the *Grid* control is used, as it is here, without cells (that is, defined using rows and columns), you should consider it a single-cell grid where only one control will be displayed.

Let's add a control to this grid. We'll add a rectangle in it, like this:

```
<Rectangle Width="100" Height="100" Fill="Red"></Rectangle>
```

This defines a 100 by 100 rectangle (also known as a square), which will appear centered within the single default cell of the grid. You can see the result in the following screen shot:

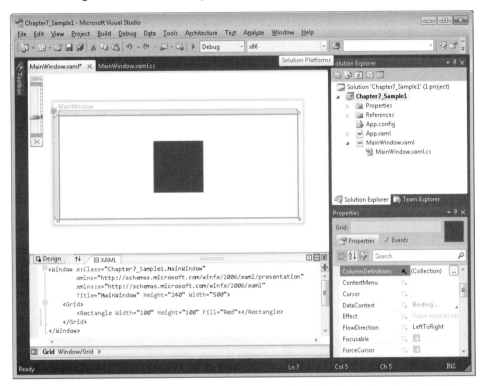

If you're thinking that this isn't very interesting, you're right. So let's make it a little more interesting by making it touch sensitive. You can manipulate an object using touch in Windows 7 in a number of ways, but we'll start with the simplest—moving it around the screen.

Using Windows 7 Touch to Move an Object

In the previous section, you built a (very) simple Windows 7 WPF application that rendered a red rectangle on the screen. Now you're going to add the first step of basic touch input by adding the code that allows you to move the rectangle around the screen using touch.

First you need to inform Windows that you want to be able to manipulate the rectangle using the touch system. You do this in XAML with the *IsManipulationEnabled* attribute. This is a Boolean value, and should be set to 'true' if you want to manipulate an object using multi touch.

```
<Rectangle Width="100" Height="100" Fill="Red" IsManipulationEnabled="True" ></Rectangle>
```

You're going to make one more change to the rectangle, and that is to add a named *Render-Transform* object that is defined by a *MatrixTransform* that does nothing. You'll see shortly that this transform can be manipulated to provide the drawing functionality that changes the shape or location of the rectangle upon user input. The *MatrixTransform* object is defined as an application resource, so if you look at your App.xaml file, you'll see a section for resources (called *Application.Resources*), where you can add the *MatrixTransform* object. Here's the code:

```
<Application.Resources>
  <MatrixTransform x:Key="InitialMatrixTransform">
    <MatrixTransform.Matrix>
      <Matrix OffsetX="0" OffsetY="0"/>
    </MatrixTransform.Matrix>
  </MatrixTransform>
</Application.Resources>
```

As you can see, this matrix transform doesn't do anything. If you apply it to the rectangle, nothing happens. However, later in the code example, you'll manipulate the transform, and it, in turn, will manipulate the rectangle.

Here's how the rectangle XAML should look with the transform applied:

```
<Rectangle Width="100" Height="100" Fill="Red" ManipulationMode="All"
RenderTransform="{StaticResource InitialMatrixTransform}"></Rectangle>
```

Now that the rectangle is configured to allow manipulation, the next step is to set up what the window needs to capture manipulation events from the operating system. These are captured using the *ManipulationDelta* event. Add this, and specify a handler to the *Window* tag at the root of the XAML for Window1.xaml.

It should look something like this:

```
<Window x:Class="Chapter7_Sample1.Window1"
  xmlns="http://schemas.microsoft.com/winfx/2006/xaml/presentation"
  xmlns:x="http://schemas.microsoft.com/winfx/2006/xaml"
  Title="Window1" Height="300" Width="300" ManipulationDelta="Window_ManipulationDelta">
```

When you created the *ManipulationDelta* event handler on the *Window* just shown, Visual Studio should have created a stub function for you. If it didn't (for example, if you cut and pasted the attribute declaration instead of typing it), you can see it here:

```
private void Window_ManipulationDelta(object sender, ManipulationDeltaEventArgs e)
{
}
```

If you're familiar with .NET programming, this code will look familiar. It's a typical event handler that takes a general object called *sender*, which refers to the object that the event was raised on, and an object containing the event arguments (that is, the metadata associated with the event).

In this case, you get a *ManipulationDeltaEventArgs* object. This object exposes a function called *GetDeltaManipulation*, which returns a *Manipulation* object that contains exactly the metadata that you need to understand *what* the user has done to the object.

Here's how you can get a handle on the manipulation that has just been performed:

```
ManipulationDelta m = e.DeltaManipulation;
```

Next, you want to get a reference to your rectangle, and to the *Matrix* that defines its *Render-Transform*. Here's the code:

```
Rectangle r = e.OriginalSource as Rectangle;
Matrix matrix = ((MatrixTransform)r.RenderTransform).Matrix;
```

The *Manipulation* object exposes a *Translation* property that returns a *Vector* object, which has member properties for the translation on *X* and *Y* that results from the user's action of moving the object. To move the object, you should call the *Translate* method on the *matrix*. (Remember from the code shown earlier, that the *matrix* here is the *RenderTransform* from the rectangle.) Here's the relevant code:

```
matrix.Translate(m.Translation.X, m.Translation.Y);
```

And now all you need to do is set the *RenderTransform* for the rectangle to be the *new* matrix (that is, the one that has been manipulated by the *Translation* function):

```
r.RenderTransform = new MatrixTransform(matrix);
```

And that's it. Now, all you have to do is implement this event handler and you can move the rectangle based on user input from the touch screen! Here's the full event handler:

```
private void Window_ManipulationDelta(object sender, ManipulationDeltaEventArgs e)
{
  Manipulation m = e.GetDeltaManipulation(this);
  Rectangle r = e.OriginalSource as Rectangle;
  Matrix matrix = ((MatrixTransform)r.RenderTransform).Matrix;
  matrix.Translate(m.Translation.X, m.Translation.Y);
  r.RenderTransform = new MatrixTransform(matrix);
}
```

Now if you run your application, you can move the rectangle around the window by touching the screen with your finger! Here's an illustration of how it works:

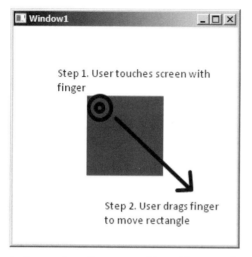

In the next section, you add to this to see how the multitouch system accepts scaling information that allows you to change the size of the object.

Using Windows 7 Touch to Scale an Object

In the previous section, you built an application that handles a single touch to move a rectangle around the screen. What's nice about this application is that it gives you everything you need to handle multitouch and gestures in your application. Now that it's in place, let's take a look at what you need to do to add scaling functionality to your application.

Scaling in a multitouch system is based on *pinch* events, where you use two touch points—usually the index finger and the thumb—and move them toward each other to shrink the object, or move them away from each other to grow the object.

The same manipulation event and transformation matrix that you used in the last section can be used for this section. All you have to do to implement the scaling is add some code to the *ManipulationDelta* event handler.

When scaling an object, you either grow it or shrink it relative to a certain point. In the case of a rectangle (or square), it's logical that the point that the object grows relative to is the center of the object. Thus when it grows, it grows evenly around this central point.

So, before continuing, let's consider the center point of the rectangle. Remember that this is the relative center point of the rectangle, so it's the point at half its width and half its height. It's not the absolute center point, which would be the center of where it is drawn on the screen.

Here's how to get it:

```
Point rectCenter = new Point(r.ActualWidth / 2, r.ActualHeight / 2);
```

Remember that a *RenderTransform* is dictating how the rectangle is drawn on the screen. To get the actual center of where the rectangle is presently drawn, you simply apply the transform with the actual center and get its result:

```
Point actualCenter = matrix.Transform(rectCenter);
```

The *Matrix* object returned by *RenderTransform* provides a *ScaleAt* function that allows you to specify how to scale an object. It takes four parameters. The first two are the amount to scale the object by on X and Y, and the next two are the point around which you should scale. The *Manipulation* retrieved from the event argument provides a *Scale* property. You can use this for each of the first two parameters, and the third and fourth parameters can be derived from the actual center:

```
matrix.ScaleAt(m.Scale, m.Scale, actualCenter.X, actualCenter.Y);
```

And that's it! In the previous section, the last line of code in the translation was to apply the matrix to the *RenderTransform* to redraw the rectangle. You keep that in place, and here's the complete event handler that provides both translation *and* scaling:

```
private void Window_ManipulationDelta(object sender, ManipulationDeltaEventArgs e)
{
  ManipulationDelta m = e.DeltaManipulation;
  Rectangle r = e.OriginalSource as Rectangle;
  Matrix matrix = ((MatrixTransform)r.RenderTransform).Matrix;
  matrix.Translate(m.Translation.X, m.Translation.Y);
  Point rectCenter = new Point(r.ActualWidth / 2, r.ActualHeight / 2);
  Point actualCenter = matrix.Transform(rectCenter);
  matrix.ScaleAt(m.Scale, m.Scale, actualCenter.X, actualCenter.Y);
  r.RenderTransform = new MatrixTransform(matrix);
}
```

Now if you run the application, you can both scale and move the rectangle. To scale the rectangle, you touch the screen with two fingers and move them away from each other, in a straight line, to make the rectangle bigger. Or you move your two fingers toward each other to make the rectangle smaller. At least one of your fingers should be on the rectangle before you move them.

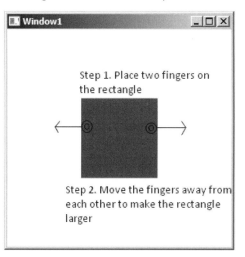

The next step is to support the gestures that allow you to rotate the rectangle. You'll see how you can add rotation support to this application in the next section.

Using Windows 7 Touch to Rotate an Object

The third gesture that is commonly used in multitouch applications is rotation. This is a dual-touch gesture where the user places two fingers on the screen and moves them in a radial motion relative to each other. WPF can capture this and raise an event that can be used to transform the rectangle and provide rotation.

Because you've been building the event handler for the manipulation up to this point, you can just continue to add on to what you have. So if you've just jumped into this section, it's advisable to go back and read the previous two sections where we first added translation gestures and then added scaling gestures. The rotation code will build on top of the code for these gestures.

You perform a rotation around a certain point. In this case, it makes sense to perform it around the center of the rectangle. You already have the *Point* object that represents this, so you can simply rotate around that.

Additionally, the *Manipulation* object that the function has been using provides feedback on how the user has applied a rotate gesture with his fingers, so all you need to do to add rotation to this application is take this rotation and apply it to your matrix around the desired center point.

You can do this with the following code:

```
matrix.RotateAt(m.Rotation, actualCenter.X, actualCenter.Y);
```

Because you've built up everything that you need in the previous sections, adding the rotation functionality requires only that one line of code.

For convenience, here is the full event handler that provides translation, scaling, and rotation functionality:

```
private void Window_ManipulationDelta(object sender, ManipulationDeltaEventArgs e)
{
  Manipulation m = e.DeltaManipulation;
  Rectangle r = e.OriginalSource as Rectangle;
  Matrix matrix = ((MatrixTransform)r.RenderTransform).Matrix;
  matrix.Translate(m.Translation.X, m.Translation.Y);
  Point rectCenter = new Point(r.ActualWidth / 2, r.ActualHeight / 2);
  Point actualCenter = matrix.Transform(rectCenter);
  matrix.ScaleAt(m.Scale, m.Scale, actualCenter.X, actualCenter.Y);
  matrix.RotateAt(m.Rotation, actualCenter.X, actualCenter.Y);
  r.RenderTransform = new MatrixTransform(matrix);
}
```

Here's an illustration of how the rotation functionality works on your rectangle:

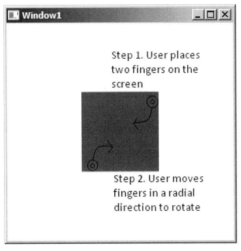

Now that you've built the code for the three basic gestures supported by WPF in Windows 7, let's try something more advanced and make your gestures more realistic by adding inertial effects.

Using Inertia with Gestures

It's all very nice to be able to move the object around and manipulate it, but for a realistic effect, you'll also want to support inertia. With inertia, once you start moving the object, WPF figures out the trajectory that you're moving it in. WPF interprets the trajectory as being one of the following three gestures:

- A translation (moving the object across the screen)

- Scaling (zooming in or out on the object)

- Rotation (turning the object around)

Each of these gestures can be associated with inertia so that when you stop the physical movement of your finger on the surface of the screen, the object will continue its movement for a short time.

To prepare your application for handling inertia, use the *ManipulationInertiaStarting* event on your window. You define this in the usual way. Here's the XAML of the *Window* that we've been looking at with this event handler added:

```
<Window x:Class="Chapter7_Sample1.MainWindow"
        xmlns="http://schemas.microsoft.com/winfx/2006/xaml/presentation"
        xmlns:x="http://schemas.microsoft.com/winfx/2006/xaml"
        Title="Window1" Height="300" Width="300"
        ManipulationDelta="Window_ManipulationDelta"
        ManipulationInertiaStarting="Window_ManipulationInertiaStarting" >
    <Grid>
        <Rectangle Width="100" Height="100" Fill="Red"
           IsManipulationEnabled="True"

           RenderTransform="{StaticResource InitialMatrixTransform}">
        </Rectangle>
    </Grid>
</Window>
```

When you catch this event, you'll get an argument of type *ManipulationInertiaStartingEventArgs*. This argument contains a method that allows you to get the initial inertia velocities as captured from the user's motion. It also allows you to *set* these velocities if you want to override them and add inertia parameters to define the inertial behavior.

Your event handler code looks like this:

```
private void Window_ManipulationInertiaStarting(object sender,
    ManipulationInertiaStartingEventArgs e)
        {}
```

When you call the *GetInitialVelocities* method of the arguments, you'll have an object of type *ManipulationVelocities* returned.

Here's the code to set this up:

```
ManipulationVelocities initial = e.InitialVelocities;
```

The *ManipulationVelocities* class exposes properties that allow you to query the velocities for linear (that is, translation), expansion (scaling), or rotational (angular) movement.

For linear motion, the value is a vector defining the acceleration/deceleration on the X and Y axes.

When defining inertia in most scenarios, you'll want the object to slow down its movement over time. To do this, you use the *DesiredDeceleration* property of the appropriate behavior and define the desired deceleration using it.

This is easier to explain in code.

```
private void Window_ManipulationInertiaStarting(object sender,

    ManipulationInertiaStartingEventArgs e)

{

        var initial = e.InitialVelocities;

        int duration = 1000;

        e.TranslationBehavior.DesiredDeceleration =

            (initial.LinearVelocity.Length / duration);

        e.RotationBehavior.DesiredDeceleration =

            (initial.AngularVelocity / duration);

        }
```

You may want to set the behavior of the object when it hits a boundary, such as the edge of the Window. This can be achieved by capturing the *ManipulationBoundaryFeedback* event. Declare the event handler in your XAML and you'll be given this stub:

```
private void Window_ManipulationBoundaryFeedback(object sender,
ManipulationBoundaryFeedbackEventArgs e)

{


}
```

The *ManipulationBoundaryFeedbackEventArgs* object exposes a property called *Boundary-Feedback* which is a *ManipulationDelta* object as you saw earlier. You can then manipulate this to define what to do in the event of hitting the boundary (such as stopping, or bouncing).

So now you've built your first multitouch WPF application that supports gestures and inertia. For the rest of this chapter, we'll take a look at the various objects and APIs that are available to you, some of which we've touched on in this chapter thus far.

Extending for Multiple Objects

The example that you've just seen demonstrated how to use a manipulation by setting the event handler to capture user manipulations on the *Window*. This approach is good for demonstrations, but when you use it in a real application it will cause some problems when you need to be able to manipulate multiple objects. In such cases, each object should handle its own *ManipulationDelta* events.

Consider this XAML, where each element has its own *RenderTransform* and the event handler is identified on it:

```xml
<Window x:Class="Chapter6_Sample1.Window1"
  xmlns="http://schemas.microsoft.com/winfx/2006/xaml/presentation"
  xmlns:x="http://schemas.microsoft.com/winfx/2006/xaml"
  Title="Window1" Height="300" Width="300">
  <Canvas>
    <Rectangle Canvas.Top="0" Canvas.Left="0" Width="100"
      Height="100" Fill="Red" IsManipulationEnabled="True"
      ManipulationDelta="Rectangle_ManipulationDelta">
    <Rectangle.RenderTransform>
      <MatrixTransform >
        <MatrixTransform.Matrix>
          <Matrix OffsetX="0" OffsetY="0"/>
        </MatrixTransform.Matrix>
      </MatrixTransform>
    </Rectangle.RenderTransform>
  </Rectangle>

    <Rectangle Canvas.Top="100" Canvas.Left="100" Width="100"
        Height="100" Fill="Red" IsManipulationEnabled="True"
        ManipulationDelta="Rectangle_ManipulationDelta_1">
    <Rectangle.RenderTransform>
      <MatrixTransform >
        <MatrixTransform.Matrix>
          <Matrix OffsetX="0" OffsetY="0"/>
        </MatrixTransform.Matrix>
      </MatrixTransform>
    </Rectangle.RenderTransform>
  </Rectangle>
</Canvas>
</Window>
```

You can see in this listing that each *Rectangle* defines its own separate *ManipulationDelta* event handler. The code for this is similar to what you saw earlier:

```csharp
private void Rectangle_ManipulationDelta(object sender, ManipulationDeltaEventArgs e)
{
  Manipulation m = e.DeltaManipulation;
  Rectangle r = e.OriginalSource as Rectangle;
  Matrix matrix = ((MatrixTransform)r.RenderTransform).Matrix;
  matrix.Translate(m.Translation.X, m.Translation.Y);
```

```
Point rectCenter = new Point(r.ActualWidth / 2, r.ActualHeight / 2);
Point actualCenter = matrix.Transform(rectCenter);
matrix.ScaleAt(m.Scale, m.Scale, actualCenter.X, actualCenter.Y);
matrix.RotateAt(m.Rotation, actualCenter.X, actualCenter.Y);
r.RenderTransform = new MatrixTransform(matrix);
}
```

This, of course, leads you to having lots of repeated code in your application, so it might be better to use control encapsulation instead. You'll see how to do that in the next section.

Building a Gesture-Enabled Picture Control

Now let's take a look at doing something a little more sensible! We'll encapsulate a lot of the repeated code from the previous example into a *Picture* control that is gesture enabled and that can be used in your WPF application.

With Visual Studio, you can create controls using the WPF User Control library. Create a new project, and select the WPF User Control Library template.

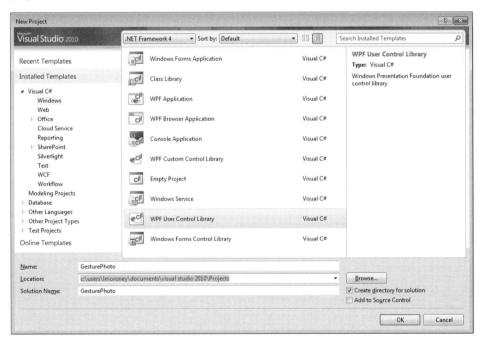

Create a new User Control called GesturePhoto, as shown in the screen shot. The template creates a default user control for you called UserControl1. Delete it, and replace it with a new one called Photo.

Visual Studio creates XAML for you. Note that it's a *UserControl* type, and its class is defined using the *x:Class* attribute in this XAML. It should be called something like Gesture-

Photo.Photo. This defines where the code that implements *UserControl* lives—and because this application is called GesturePhoto, it should contain a class definition called *Photo*. And indeed, you'll see that Visual Studio created this for you in the Photo.cs file.

Here's the XAML:

```
<UserControl x:Class="GesturePhoto.Photo"
             xmlns="http://schemas.microsoft.com/winfx/2006/xaml/presentation"
             xmlns:x="http://schemas.microsoft.com/winfx/2006/xaml"
             xmlns:mc="http://schemas.openxmlformats.org/markup-compatibility/2006"
             xmlns:d="http://schemas.microsoft.com/expression/blend/2008"
             mc:Ignorable="d"
             d:DesignHeight="300" d:DesignWidth="300">
    <Grid>
    </Grid>
</UserControl>
```

You need to add a gesture-enabled *Image* object to this, so go ahead and do so. Also, be sure that you set the *ManipulationMode* and *ManipulationDelta* attributes:

```
<Image IsManipulationEnabled="True" ManipulationDelta="Image_ManipulationDelta"
x:Name="TheImage" >
</Image>
```

Remember that you used a *RenderTransform* in the previous example to manipulate the translate, scale, and rotate movements, so go ahead and add one to this image. Here's the completed *Image* definition:

```
<Image IsManipulationEnabled="True" ManipulationDelta="Image_ManipulationDelta"
x:Name="TheImage" >
  <Image.RenderTransform>
    <MatrixTransform>
      <MatrixTransform.Matrix>
        <Matrix OffsetX="0" OffsetY="0"></Matrix>
      </MatrixTransform.Matrix>
    </MatrixTransform>
  </Image.RenderTransform>
</Image>
```

Make sure that this is within the *Grid* in your XAML, and you'll be good to go.

Now let's take a look at the code-behind C# file for this control.

First of all, this user control is a picture, so it has to allow your end users to set the picture that you're going to render. The *Image* element in XAML allows you to do this, and you are using one, so you put a property on your control that you will expose. When the user sets it, you use his setting on your *Image*.

Within Photo.cs, create a private member variable of the type *ImageSource*:

```
private ImageSource _ImageSource;
```

Now create a property of the same type that allows you to get and set this value. Remember that the image within your *UserControl* is called *TheImage*:

```
public ImageSource ImageSource
{
  get { return (ImageSource) _ImageSource; }
  set
  {
    _ImageSource = value;
    TheImage.Source = _ImageSource;
  }
}
```

The *get* function (called a *getter*) simply returns the private member variable that you created earlier, and the *set* function (called a *setter*) sets this private member variable as well as setting the source on *TheImage*. This has the effect of implementing a property called *ImageSource*, which is used to set the image.

If you look back at your XAML, you'll also see that you defined a *ManipulationDelta* attribute on the control. The event handler for this will look familiar by now—it's the same code as you saw earlier in this chapter to handle the translate, scale, and rotate gestures:

```
private void Image_ManipulationDelta(object sender, ManipulationDeltaEventArgs e)
{
  Manipulation m = e.DeltaManipulation;
  Image r = e.OriginalSource as Image;
  Matrix matrix = ((MatrixTransform)r.RenderTransform).Matrix;
  matrix.Translate(m.Translation.X, m.Translation.Y);
  Point rectCenter = new Point(r.ActualWidth / 2, r.ActualHeight / 2);
  Point actualCenter = matrix.Transform(rectCenter);
  matrix.ScaleAt(m.Scale, m.Scale, actualCenter.X, actualCenter.Y);
  matrix.RotateAt(m.Rotation, actualCenter.X, actualCenter.Y);
  r.RenderTransform = new MatrixTransform(matrix);
}
```

And that's everything you need for this custom control. When you compile this project, a dynamic-link library (DLL) assembly will be created for you. You'll see how to use this assembly in the next section.

Using the Gesture-Enabled Picture Control

In the previous section, you saw how to build a gesture-enabled picture control. Now you'll see how you can use this in a WPF application.

Create a new WPF application in the usual way. Then go to the References folder and add a reference. Browse to the location of the GesturePhoto assembly that you created in the last section and add the reference.

In the XAML for your window (likely called Window1.xaml if you're using a default application template), go to the root *Window* definition tag.

If you start typing the characters **xmlns:g=**, you'll see that autocomplete gives you a list of available references. Find one called

```
Clr-namespace:GesturePhoto;assembly=GesturePhoto
```

This reference allows you to use all classes in the assembly that you created in XAML using the *g* prefix. You can use any letter (or group of letters) —I just selected *g* for *gesture*.

When you're done, your *Window* tag will look something like this:

```
<Window x:Class="WpfApplication2.Window1"
  xmlns="http://schemas.microsoft.com/winfx/2006/xaml/presentation"
  xmlns:x="http://schemas.microsoft.com/winfx/2006/xaml"
  xmlns:g="clr-namespace:GesturePhoto;assembly=GesturePhoto"
  Title="Window1" Height="365" Width="240">
</Window>
```

Before continuing, change the default *Grid* tag for layout to a *Canvas* tag. This just makes it easier for us to directly control the layout in code.

Now, within this *Canvas* tag, type **<g:**. You'll see that autocomplete provides the *Photo* class for you, and the properties that you exposed are available. Here's the code to add three instances of the gesture-enabled *photo* control to your application:

```
    <Canvas>
        <g:Photo ImageSource="dog.jpg" Canvas.Top="0" Height="100" Width="100"></g:photo>
        <g:Photo ImageSource="donut.jpg" Canvas.Top="100" Height="100"
Width="100"></g:photo>
        <g:Photo ImageSource="flower.jpg" Canvas.Top="200" Height="100"
Width="100"></g:photo>
    </Canvas>
```

This code assumes that you have the dog, donut, and flower images in your solution. The following screen shot shows what your development environment should look like at this point:

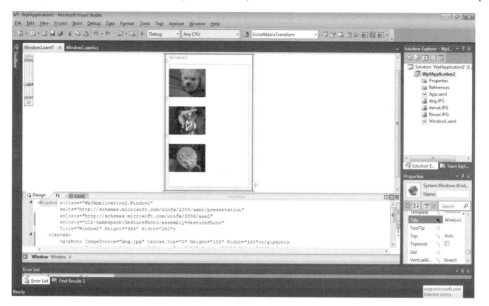

When you execute your application, you'll see something like what you can see in the following screen shot:

When you execute the application, you'll notice that the gesture functionality now works perfectly well, despite you not writing a single line of code within your application! You can see this in action in the following screen shot:

Here you saw a taste of what is possible in WPF with gestures, and how you can put together a simple application that uses this functionality very quickly. In the next section, you'll review some of the new classes in WPF that provide this functionality, before wrapping up and going to the next chapter, which deals with how you can use the touch APIs directly, without going through the gesture classes.

Classes to Support Touch and Gestures

WPF4 contains a number of API enhancements to allow you to build applications to support touch and gestures. We'll take a look at these APIs in this section, some of which you've already used, but you'll see them in a little more detail now.

UIElement Additions

To support touch and gestures, the *UIElement* has been expanded with a number of new APIs.

The *ManipulationMode* property determines *how* manipulation happens on the element. It can contain the following values, as seen earlier in this chapter:

- **None**   The shape cannot be manipulated by touch.

- **Rotate**   The shape can only be rotated using touch.

- **Scale**   The shape can only be resized using touch.

- **Translate**   The shape can only be moved using touch.

- **TranslateX**   The shape can only be moved horizontally using touch.

- **TranslateY**   The shape can only be moved vertically using touch.

- **EnableSingleContactManipulations**   Enables basic manipulation on single-touch screens, such as tablet PCs.

- **All**   Allows rotation, scaling, and translation operations.

The *ManipulationDelta* event is raised whenever the user is touching the touch contacts and moving around. It also is raised during inertial movements to keep track of them.

The *ManipulationPivot* property defines the point for single-touch rotation. If the *ManipulationMode* is for *EnableSingleContactManipulations*, and this is set, you'll be able to rotate around this point. Otherwise, single-touch rotation is disabled.

The *ManipulationStarted* event is raised when WPF first recognizes a gesture to cause a manipulation on the object.

The *ManipulationCompleted* event is raised after all the touch contacts are released and all the inertia generated by *ManipulationDelta* events is completed.

The *ManipulationInertiaStarting* event is raised alongside the *ManipulationStarted* event. It allows you to customize how inertia will work in the manipulation. The event is raised after all the touch contacts have been released, or if the developer explicitly initiates a new inertial movement using the *StartInertia* method in the event handler for the *ManipulationDelta* event.

Summary

In this chapter, you looked at the various classes that are available in WPF 4 to support multi-touch applications through gesture management, manipulations, and inertia. These are supported for *dual-touch* applications. You saw how to build an application that uses gestures and touch, and then how to build a reusable control that encapsulates this functionality. Windows 7 also supports *multitouch*, where you can have more than two fingers touching the screen at once. You'll look at how to do this in Chapter 8, "Using Windows 7 Touch with Silverlight.

Chapter 8
Using Windows 7 Touch with Silverlight

In the previous chapters, you were introduced to the Windows 7 touch and multitouch systems and saw how they can be used when building Windows-based applications using Windows Presentation Foundation (WPF). In this chapter, you'll look at Silverlight, a technology that allows you to build and deploy rich applications using the Web. These applications can be written to run outside of the browser and offline, giving you a powerful and simple API that allows you to extend your applications from the Web to the desktop.

In this chapter, we'll give you a quick look at Silverlight, what it is and does, before showing you how to build an application that runs outside the browser. Once that's done, we'll examine the touch APIs in Silverlight, starting with the Ink APIs that can be used for single-touch applications and then wrapping up with the Touch APIs that are new in Silverlight 3 and that allow you to build multitouch applications.

Introducing Silverlight

Microsoft Silverlight represents the next step toward enriching the user's experience through the technology of the Web. The goal of Silverlight is to bring to Web applications the same fidelity and quality found in the user interfaces associated with desktop applications so that Web developers and designers can build applications for their clients' specific needs. It's designed to bridge the technology gap between designers and developers by giving them a common format in which to work. This format is rendered by the browser and is based on Extensible Markup Language (XML), making it easy to template and to generate automatically. The format is XAML—Extensible Application Markup Language.

Before XAML, a Web-experience designer would use one set of tools to express a design using familiar technology. The developer would then take what the designer provided and interpret it using the technology of her choice. The design would not necessarily transfer into development properly or in a problem-free way, and the developer would need to make many alterations that could compromise the design. With Silverlight, the designer can use tools that express a design as XAML, and the developer can pick up this XAML, activate it with code, and deploy it.

Silverlight is a cross-browser, cross-platform plug-in that was developed to deliver a rich media experience and rich interactive Internet applications over the Web. It offers a full programming model that supports AJAX, the Microsoft .NET Framework, and dynamic languages such as Python and Ruby. When running on Windows 7, Silverlight gives you access to the Windows 7 touch APIs through a Touch object that you'll see later in this chapter.

Silverlight is designed to be part of a much larger ecosystem that is used to deliver the best possible end-user experience. There are a number of typical scenarios for accessing information on the Internet:

- Mobile devices

- Digital home products

- Unenhanced browsers (no plug-ins)

- Enhanced browsers (using plug-ins such as Flash, Java, or Silverlight)

- Desktop applications

- Office productivity software

Over the years, users' expectations about how these applications should work have evolved. For example, the *expectation* is that the experience of using an application on a desktop computer should provide more to the user than the same type of application on a mobile device because, as users, we are accustomed to having much more power on the desktop than we do on a mobile device. In addition, many users assume that because an application is on the Web it might not have the same capacity level as a similar desktop application. For example, users might have lower expectations about a Web-based e-mail application because they don't believe it can offer the same e-mail capability that office productivity software such as Microsoft Office Outlook provides.

However, as platforms converge, user expectations are also increasing—and the term *rich* is now commonly used to describe an experience above the current baseline level of expectation. For example, the term *rich Internet application* was coined in response to the increased level of sophistication that Web users were seeing in applications powered by AJAX to provide a more dynamic experience in scenarios such as e-mail and mapping. This evolution in expectations has led to customers who now demand ever-richer experiences that not only meet the needs of the application in terms of functionality and effectiveness, but also address the perception of satisfaction that the user has with a company's products and services. This can lead to a lasting relationship between the user and the company.

As a result, Microsoft has committed to the User Experience (UX) and ships the tools and technologies that developers can use to implement rich UX applications. Additionally, these tools are designed to be coherent—that is, skills in developing UX-focused applications transfer across the domains of desktop and Web application development. So, if you're building a rich desktop application but need a Web version, you'll have cross-pollination between the two. Similarly, if you're building a mobile application and need an Internet version, you won't need two sets of skills, two sets of tools, and two sets of developers.

Regarding the Web, Figure 8-1 shows the presentation and programming models that are available today. As you can see, the typical browser-based development technologies are Cascading Style Sheets/Dynamic HTML (CSS/DHTML) in the presentation model and JavaScript/AJAX/ASP.NET in the development model. On the desktop, with .NET Framework 3.*x*, XAML provides the presentation model, and the framework itself provides the development model. These models overlap, and this is where the Silverlight-enhanced browser provides a "best of both worlds" approach.

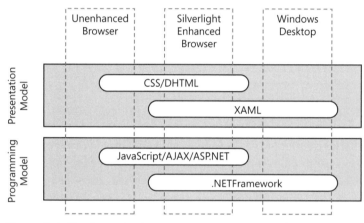

Figure 8-1 The interplay between presentation models

The typical rich interactive application is based on technologies that exist in the unenhanced browser category. The typical desktop application is at the other end of the spectrum, using unrelated technologies. The opportunity to bring these together into a rich application that is lightweight and runs in the browser is realized through the Silverlight-enhanced browser that provides the CSS/DHTML and XAML design model and the JavaScript/AJAX/.NET Framework programming model.

Silverlight achieves this coordination among models by providing a browser plug-in that enhances the functionality of the browser with the typical technologies that provide rich UIs, such as timeline-based animation, vector graphics, and audiovisual media. These technologies are enabled by the Silverlight browser-based XAML rendering engine. The browser receives the XAML and the plug-in renders it.

The architecture of a simple application running in the browser using Silverlight is shown in Figure 8-2.

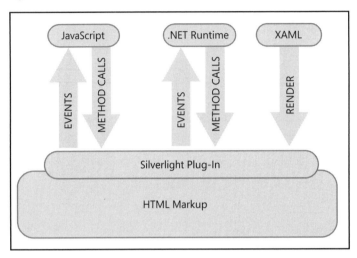

Figure 8-2 Diagram of a simple application using Silverlight

Applications that run in the browser typically are made up of HTML. This markup contains the calls to instantiate the Silverlight plug-in. As users interact with the Silverlight application, they raise events that can be captured by either JavaScript or .NET Framework functions. In turn, program code can make method calls against the elements in the Silverlight content to manipulate it, add new content, or remove existing content. Finally, XAML is read by the plug-in and rendered. The XAML itself can exist inline in the page, externally as a static file, or as dynamic XAML returned from a server.

Creating Your First Silverlight Application

You can develop Silverlight applications using either Microsoft Visual Studio 2008, with the Silverlight tools add-on or the Microsoft Expression suite of tools. In this chapter, we'll use the former.

If you don't have them already, you should install the Silverlight tools for Visual Studio 2008. These can be downloaded from *http://www.silverlight.net/getstarted*.

After they're installed, you'll see various Silverlight project types in the New Project dialog box.

After you select the Silverlight Application template and give it a name and location, click OK. This brings you to the next step, which is to select whether or not you want a Web project associated with this Silverlight application.

One of the choices available in the New Web Project Type drop-down list is ASP.NET Web Application Project. This project type builds a template project containing everything you need to create an ASP.NET application that delivers your Silverlight content. Or you can choose the ASP.NET Web site item, which is a lighter application that simply contains the HTML required to deliver a Silverlight application. An ASP.NET Web Application differs from a Web site in that it contains everything that Visual Studio needs to compile ASP.NET code into the binaries that can run on an ASP.NET server, as opposed to just flat HTML and JS files that are served up by a Web site.

For the rest of this chapter, you'll be using the ASP.NET Web Application Project type.

After you've selected this option, you'll see that Visual Studio creates two projects for you: the Silverlight project (FirstTouch) and the ASP.NET Web Application project (FirstTouch.Web). You can see the project layout in Solution Explorer, as shown here.

In the screen shot, you can see that the project contains the XAML files that were discussed earlier in this chapter in the Silverlight project. There are two XAML files: App.xaml, which declares the *Application* object and will handle events for application housekeeping such as starting up and ending; and MainPage.xaml, which defines the user interface for your Silverlight application.

If you open MainPage.xaml, you see code like this:

```
<UserControl x:Class="FirstTouch.MainPage"
    xmlns="http://schemas.microsoft.com/winfx/2006/xaml/presentation"
    xmlns:x="http://schemas.microsoft.com/winfx/2006/xaml"
    xmlns:d="http://schemas.microsoft.com/expression/blend/2008"
xmlns:mc="http://schemas.openxmlformats.org/markup-compatibility/2006"
    mc:Ignorable="d" d:DesignWidth="640" d:DesignHeight="480">
```

```
  <Grid x:Name="LayoutRoot">

  </Grid>
</UserControl>
```

The UI is implemented using a *UserControl* and defines a *Grid* that provides the layout for your application UI. As you can see, it's empty at the moment, so let's use a *TextBlock* control to render the ubiquitous "Hello, World!" message.

Your XAML looks like this:

```
<UserControl x:Class="FirstTouch.MainPage"
    xmlns="http://schemas.microsoft.com/winfx/2006/xaml/presentation"
    xmlns:x="http://schemas.microsoft.com/winfx/2006/xaml"
    xmlns:d="http://schemas.microsoft.com/expression/blend/2008"

    xmlns:mc="http://schemas.openxmlformats.org/markup-compatibility/2006"
    mc:Ignorable="d" d:DesignWidth="640" d:DesignHeight="480">
  <Grid x:Name="LayoutRoot">
        <TextBlock Text="Hello, World!"></TextBlock>
  </Grid>
</UserControl>
```

Running the application renders the "Hello, World" message in Silverlight, shown here.

Now this application runs within the browser, but with Windows 7 you're likely to want to have an application running on your shiny new desktop. So in the next section, we'll explain how you can do exactly this—make your application run out of the browser.

Building Out-of-Browser Applications in Silverlight

In version 3, Silverlight introduced the ability to take your applications out of the browser. This capability makes it easy for you to deploy applications to a desktop. Thus, if you have the Silverlight runtime installed, you don't need any dependencies to install your application; you can simply right-click on it to install it to your Start menu or desktop. In this section, you'll see how to do this as well as how easy it is to do this.

So, continuing with our "Hello, World!" application, go to Solution Explorer and right-click the FirstTouch project (not the FirstTouch.Web project or Solution). Then select Properties. You should see the user interface for setting properties, as shown here.

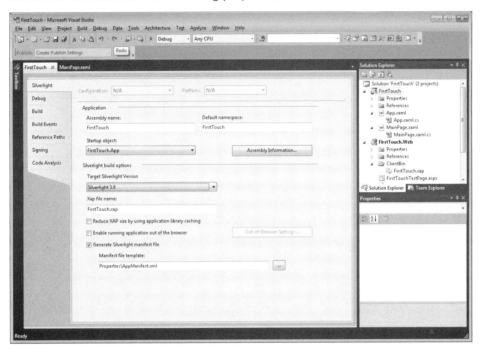

Make sure the Silverlight tab in the left pane is selected, as shown in the preceding screen shot. Then select the Enable Running Applications Out Of The Browser, which enables the Out-of-Browser Settings button. If you click this button, you see the following dialog.

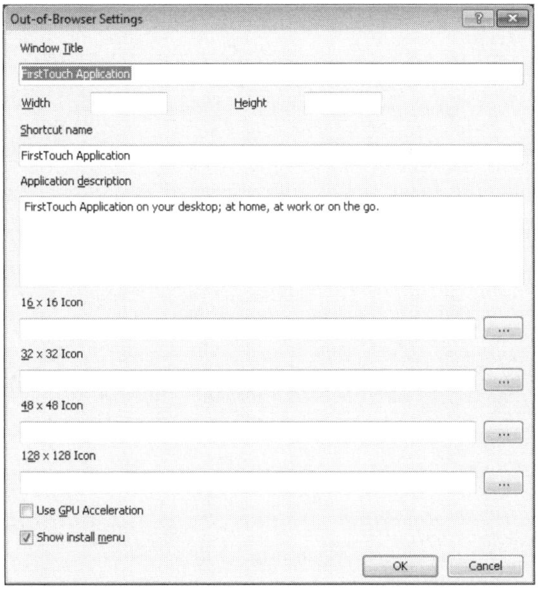

This dialog allows you to specify the title of the window your application will use, to which will be added the address of the server that the application was deployed from. It also allows you to set the following details:

- The window size

- The shortcut name

- The description of the application that will be given by Silverlight to your users when they try to install your application, as well as the application icons. (A default is used if you don't specify the icons to be used.)

- Whether or not you want to use GPU acceleration.

Click OK to exit this dialog and return to Visual Studio. Compile and re-run your application.

You'll see the "Hello, World!" message as you did earlier, but now if you right-click the application you see a new entry in the context menu, Install FirstTouch Application Onto This Computer, as shown here.

Selecting this link from the context menu gives you the Install Application dialog, which is built into Silverlight for installing the application to your desktop.

The icon that you see is presented when you don't define your own in the properties dialog box. If you define one, it is presented here instead of the default icon. Specify where you want the application to be deployed by selecting the Start Menu check box, the Desktop check box, or both. Click OK to deploy and launch the application.

You can see here what it looks like on the Windows 7 desktop.

When you launch your application, it runs in the Silverlight launcher.

Note the title bar, which appears as FirstTouch Application—localhost. This text specifies the name of the application *and* the server from which it was deployed so that users always know where it came from.

Now that you've created your first Silverlight application and you've seen how to run it outside of the browser, let's take a look at something a little more sophisticated. In the next section, you'll look at the Ink APIs in Silverlight and see how they can be used to build a single-touch application. Later, you'll see the Touch APIs, which are new in Silverlight 3, and learn how these can be used to extend your application for multitouch capabilities.

Using the Silverlight *InkPresenter* Control

As you've seen so far in this chapter, Silverlight empowers the designers of the next generation of Web applications by providing tools that allow you to add rich video, audio, vector graphics, animation, and other enhancements that improve the UX. Ink annotation—the creation of handwriting or drawing content using a device designed for this purpose—is another great way to make applications even more interactive and personal, and Silverlight's support for Ink-based programming brings this functionality to the Web. In this section, we'll investigate how Ink annotation is supported in Silverlight.

There are several types of devices that can be used for Ink-based applications:

- **Pen Input** Computers that support pen digitizers are typically Tablet PCs, but they can also be desktop computers that support external digitizers. These computers can take advantage of the pen input in Silverlight. They create *Ink* that can be integrated into Silverlight Web pages so that handwriting, drawing, annotation, and other input formats can be supported on the Web.

- **Touch Input** Touch screens are common in kiosk environments or other places where a stylus or keyboard is unwieldy or unnecessary. Silverlight with Ink annotation supports touch screens, allowing rich Internet applications with touch-based interactivity.

- **Mouse Input** The mouse can be used to provide digitized, penlike input similar to a Tablet PC pen. However, this Ink input has a lower resolution than if you used a true Tablet PC pen.

An Example of Ink Annotation in Silverlight

The Silverlight.net Web site provides a great example of an application that supports Ink annotation. It is the page-turner application hosted at *http://silverlight.net/samples/1.0/Page-Turn/default.html*, shown here

This application demonstrates how you can browse through images and other assets using an application that mimics turning the pages of a book. It's enhanced with Ink, which allows you to annotate the images—and the annotations you add remain associated with the image. Here it is in action.

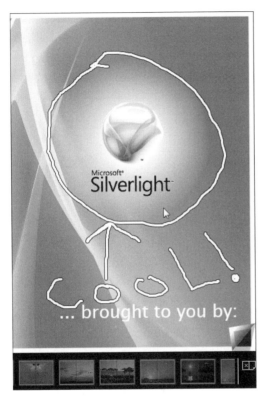

Silverlight Ink Classes for JavaScript Programmers

Support for Ink in Silverlight is straightforward. Every time you drag the input device across the screen, you generate one or more *StylusPoint* objects. These are collected into a *Stylus-PointCollection*, which forms the basis of a *Stroke*. The strokes are collected into a *StrokeCol-lection*, which makes up the list of graphics that are used to create the Ink that the *InkPre-senter* renders. If you consider the preceding screen shot, the letter "C" in *COOL* is a stroke that is made up of a number of points collected into its *StrokeCollection*. Each letter, the line and dot in the exclamation point, and the lines that make up the arrow and the circle are all strokes. Each of these strokes is a member of the *InkPresenter*'s *StrokeCollection*, and each of them is made up of *StylusPoints* held in the relevant stroke's *StylusPointCollection*. Each of these types provides an object-oriented interface with properties and methods that allow them to be programmable.

The *StrokeCollection* Type

The *InkPresenter* object contains the *Strokes* property, which is an instance of *StrokeCollection*. This collection, in turn, contains all the metadata that is required to represent the user's Ink input.

StrokeCollection Properties

When using JavaScript to program Silverlight, *StrokeCollection* exposes a *Count* property that can be used to return the number of strokes that are currently held within the collection.

StrokeCollection Methods

StrokeCollection exposes the following methods:

- **Add**   Allows you to add a new stroke to the collection.

- **Clear**   Clears the collection of strokes, which causes an immediate re-rendering (thus clearing the Ink that was previously created).

- **GetBounds**   Returns a rectangle (in a *Rect* structure) that represents the bounding box of the strokes.

- **GetItem(index)**   Retrieves the stroke that is stored at the specified index.

- **HitTest**   Passing this method a *StylusPointCollection*, returns the subset of strokes in *StrokeCollection* that intersect with these points.

- **Insert**   Similar to Add, except it allows you to insert a new stroke into the collection at a specific collection index.

- **Remove**   Removes a specific element from *StrokeCollection*.

- **RemoveAt**   Removes the indexed element from *StrokeCollection*.

The *Stroke* Type

The *StrokeCollection* you saw in the previous section is a collection of *Stroke* objects. A *Stroke* object represents a collection of points that corresponds to a stroke; the points are recorded with a single stylus action: stylus-down, stylus-move, or stylus-up. These objects, in turn, have their own set of properties and methods.

Stroke Properties

The *Stroke* object exposes these properties:

- ***DrawingAttributes***   Each stroke can have independent height, width, color, and outline color. These attributes are set using the *DrawingAttributes* type. To use this type, you create an instance of a *DrawingAttributes* object, set these properties, and then add the new *DrawingAttributes* object to the stroke.

- ***StylusPoints***   This property is a *StylusPointCollection* that contains the collection of *StylusPoint* objects that make up the stroke. *StylusPoint* is discussed in the following section.

Stroke Methods

The *Stroke* object exposes the following Ink-specific methods:

- ***GetBounds***   This method returns the bounding box of the *Stroke* as a *Rect* structure.

- ***HitTest***   If you pass this method a *StylusPointCollection* and if any of those points intersect the *Stroke*, this method returns *true*; otherwise, it is *false*.

The *StylusPointCollection* Type

This collection hosts a set of *StylusPoint* objects. It's used to store the stylus points for a *Stroke*, or in some cases, it can be passed to methods such as the *HitTest* method to determine whether or not strokes intersect.

StylusPointCollection Properties

The *StylusPointCollection* object exposes only one property—the *Count* property, which returns a count of the stylus points that are held in this collection.

StylusPointCollection Methods

The *StylusPointCollection* object exposes these methods:

- ***add***   Allows you to add a new *StylusPoint* to the end of the collection.

- ***addStylusPoints***   Allows you to add an existing *StylusPointCollection* to the bottom of the collection.

- ***clear***   Removes all *StylusPoint* objects from the collection.

- ***getItem***   Gets a specific *StylusPoint* from the collection. Use it with an integer value representing the index of the item you want to reference, such as *getItem(5)*.

- ***insert***   Inserts a new *StylusPoint* into the collection at the specified index.

- *remove*   Removes a specific *StylusPoint* from the collection.

- *removeAt*   Removes the *StylusPoint* at the specified index from the collection.

The *StylusPoint* Type

The *StylusPoint* type represents a single point that is collected while the user is executing Ink motions with a specific device—a pen, mouse, or touch screen. The point exposes a number of properties and methods for programmability.

StylusPoint Properties

The *StylusPoint* exposes the following properties:

- The *Name* property allows you to name the point. This is a unique identifier. When points are generated by user input, they are unnamed.

- The *PressureFactor* property indicates the pressure that the user puts on the pen or touch screen to generate a stroke. When a mouse is used, the pressure does not change from the default. The value is a *double* between 0.0 and 1.0, with a default value of 0.5. Based on the pressure factor, you can change the height and width of the *Stroke* programmatically through its *DrawingAttributes* property to give feedback to the user.

The coordinates of the stroke are returned using the *X* and *Y* properties. These are measured in pixels.

Mouse Event Arguments and Ink

When using Ink, events raised by the input device are treated as mouse events, and arguments received by your event handlers are *MouseEventArgs*.

The *MouseEventArgs* object contains methods that allow you to query the stylus information—to see if it is a mouse, stylus, or some other input device—and it contains methods that allow you to query for the collection of *StylusPoint* objects associated with this event. Note that this is the same *MouseEventArgs* object that is associated with the *MouseEnter*, *MouseLeave*, *MouseLeftButtonDown*, *MouseLeftButtonUp*, and *MouseMove* events.

MouseEventArgs Properties

The *MouseEventArgs* object exposes two Boolean properties, called *ctrl* and *shift*. These are *true* when the user holds down the equivalent key while raising the event.

MouseEventArgs Methods

The *MouseEventArgs* object exposes three methods:

- The *GetPosition* method takes an element as its parameter and returns a *Point* that represents the x and y coordinates of the mouse pointer relative to that element. If nothing is passed in, the *Point* contains the coordinates relative to the position of the control that raised the event.

- The *GetStylusInfo* method returns a *StylusInfo* object that contains information about the state of the stylus. *StylusInfo* has the following properties:

  o *IsInverted*: When a pen is inverted, it indicates that the user wants to use it to *erase* points instead of draw them. This property returns *true* in that circumstance.

  o *DeviceType*: This property returns a string containing the device type—Mouse, Stylus, or Touch.

- The *GetStylusPoints* method returns a clone of the stylus points that were collected since the last mouse event. This is a *StylusPointCollection* type.

Programming for Ink in Silverlight

When programming applications with Microsoft tools, the term *Ink* generally refers to handwriting or drawing content that is created by the user with the Ink-based devices described previously, such as a digital pen, touch screen, or mouse. When they are used in a Silverlight application, these devices fill a *StrokeCollection* object with individual *Stroke* objects. In turn, a *Stroke* maintains a record of the actions of a device—such as a pen—that include, for example, the pen-down, pen-move, and pen-up actions. A *Stroke* can represent a dot, straight line, or curve. It does this by maintaining a *StylusPointCollection* object, which contains *StylusPoint* objects that are collected from the digitizer associated with the pen, touch screen, or mouse. Attributes of the Ink are contained in the *DrawingAttributes* class.

As mentioned, Ink is collected by Silverlight using an instance of the *InkPresenter* class. This is effectively a subclass of the *Canvas* element, which also contains a collection of strokes in a *StrokeCollection*. When strokes are added to the *StrokeCollection*, the *InkPresenter* automatically renders them using the pertinent *DrawingAttributes*.

You typically add the *InkPresenter* to your XAML for your application at design time, but the *Stroke* objects within the *StrokeCollection* are added at run time using JavaScript.

Following is an example of using *InkPresenter* on a page, overlaying an image:

```
<Canvas xmlns="http://schemas.microsoft.com/client/2007"
        xmlns:x="http://schemas.microsoft.com/winfx/2006/xaml">
    <Image Source="sushi.jpg"></Image>
    <InkPresenter
```

```
        x:Name="inkEl"
        Background="transparent"
        Width="600" Height="400"
        MouseLeftButtonDown="inkMouseDown"
        MouseMove="inkMouseMove"
        MouseLeftButtonUp="inkMouseUp"/>
</Canvas>
```

The *InkPresenter* defines event handlers for *MouseLeftButtonDown*, *MouseMove*, and *MouseUp*. We'll look at how to manage these in JavaScript to build a simple inking application. Later in this section, you'll see how to create the same code in C#. The similarity is striking! These events will need event handler functions that handle the "start inking," "draw ink," and "stop inking" actions.

> **Note** Although Ink can be added with a pen, touch screen, or mouse, the API documentation uses the term *Mouse* throughout.

Before we look at these JavaScript event handler functions, we need to provide a few housekeeping details that will declare the global variables necessary to support these actions:

```
var theInk;      // Reference to the ink presenter
var newStroke;   // Reference to a stroke
var theControl;  // Reference to the Silverlight control
function handleLoad(control, userContext, rootElement)
{
    // The Load event returns a reference to the control
    // But other event handlers do not. So we're going
    // to make a reference to the control here
    theControl = control;

    // Here we will create a reference to the ink element
    theInk = control.content.findName("inkEl");
}
```

The Ink actions I mentioned are supported by functions that use these helper variables for the *InkPresenter*, the current stroke, and the Silverlight control itself. When the Silverlight control loads, it triggers the *handleLoad* function. This takes a reference to the Silverlight control as one of its parameters, but because the event handlers we're implementing for managing the mouse do not, we need to save a reference to the Silverlight control from within the *handleLoad* function. While processing in *handleLoad*, you might as well also get a reference to the *InkPresenter* by finding it based on its name (*inkEl*). This saves you from having to issue a *getHost* to get a reference to the parent UI element control to find the *InkPresenter* in each event handler invocation.

Now we're ready to learn more about the event handlers. First, let's look at what happens when the *MouseLeftButtonDown* event fires, in effect causing *inkMouseDown* to run. You want to capture the mouse movement in a fashion similar to the drag-and-drop processing you learned about in Chapter 7, "Building Multitouch Applications in Managed Code." After you have captured the mouse input, you create a new *Stroke* that contains a *DrawingAttributes* object that defines the visual characteristics of this stroke. In the example presented here, *DrawingAttributes* for the stroke provide it with a *Width* of 2, a *Height* of 2, a fill color of *White*, and an outline color of *White*. The *MouseEventArgs* type in Silverlight supports a *getStylusPoints* method, as you saw earlier in this chapter, that takes the *InkPresenter* as its sole parameter. This method returns an instance of the *StylusPointCollection* type that can be used with the stroke's *AddStylusPoints* method. You then add the stroke to the *InkPresenter*'s *StrokesCollection*. You can see the code here:

```
function inkMouseDown(sender,args)
{
    // Capture the mouse.
    theInk.CaptureMouse();

    // Create a new stroke.
    newStroke = theControl.content.createFromXaml('<Stroke/>');

    // Assign a new drawing attributes element to the stroke.
    // This, as its name suggests, defines how the stroke will appear
    var da = theControl.content.CreateFromXaml('<DrawingAttributes/>');
    newStroke.DrawingAttributes = da;

    // Now that the stroke has drawing attributes,
    // let's define them...
    newStroke.DrawingAttributes.Width = 2;
    newStroke.DrawingAttributes.Height = 2;
    newStroke.DrawingAttributes.Color = "White";
    newStroke.DrawingAttributes.OutlineColor = "White";


    newStroke.StylusPoints.AddStylusPoints(args.GetStylusPoints(theInk));
    theInk.Strokes.Add(newStroke);
}
```

Now, as you move the mouse over the canvas, if you are currently drawing a stroke (that is, *newStroke* is not *null*), you want to generate new points to add to this stroke, representing the track over which the mouse moved. Following is the code for this:

```
// Add the new points to the Stroke we're working with.
function inkMouseMove(sender,args)
{
    if (newStroke != null)
    {
        newStroke.StylusPoints.AddStylusPoints(args.GetStylusPoints(theInk));
    }
}
```

Finally, the *MouseLeftButtonUp* event fires after you finish the stroke by releasing the mouse button (or by lifting the pen from the screen). At this point, you want to clear the stroke and release the mouse capture. When the *newStroke* variable has been set to *null*, the mouse (or pen) movement across the screen no longer collects points to add to the stroke, and the stroke output will therefore not be drawn. Here's the code:

```
function inkMouseUp(sender,args)
{
    // Set the stroke to null
    newStroke = null;

    // Release the mouse
    theInk.releaseMouseCapture();
}
```

The following screen shot shows an example of an application before Ink annotation was added to it.

The next screen shot shows the same application after Ink annotation has been added to it—the annotation was drawn on it using a mouse or pen.

The previous example showed you how to program for Ink using Silverlight and JavaScript. The good news is that you can, of course, do the same with managed code. Here's the complete code-behind for C# to be able to build the same application:

```csharp
using System;
using System.Collections.Generic;
using System.Linq;
using System.Windows;
using System.Windows.Controls;
using System.Windows.Documents;
using System.Windows.Input;
using System.Windows.Media;
using System.Windows.Media.Animation;
using System.Windows.Shapes;
using System.Windows.Ink;

namespace NetInkSample
{
    public partial class Page : UserControl
    {
        Stroke newStroke;
        public Page()
        {
            InitializeComponent();
```

```
        }

        private void inkEl_MouseLeftButtonDown(
          object sender, MouseButtonEventArgs e)
        {
            inkEl.CaptureMouse();
            // Create a new stroke.
            newStroke = new Stroke();
            DrawingAttributes da = new DrawingAttributes();
            newStroke.DrawingAttributes = da;
            newStroke.DrawingAttributes.Width=2;
            newStroke.DrawingAttributes.Height=2;
            newStroke.DrawingAttributes.Color=Colors.White;
            newStroke.DrawingAttributes.OutlineColor=Colors.White;
            // Beta 2
            newStroke.StylusPoints.Add(
                e.StylusDevice.GetStylusPoints(inkEl));
            // Beta 1
            //newStroke.StylusPoints.AddStylusPoints(
                e.GetStylusPoints(inkEl));
            inkEl.Strokes.Add(newStroke);
        }

        private void inkEl_MouseMove(object sender, MouseEventArgs e)
        {
            if (newStroke != null)
            {
                //Beta 1
                //newStroke.StylusPoints.AddStylusPoints(
                  e.GetStylusPoints(inkEl));
                //Beta 2
                newStroke.StylusPoints.Add(
                  e.StylusDevice.GetStylusPoints(inkEl));

            }

        }

        private void inkEl_MouseLeftButtonUp(
          object sender, MouseButtonEventArgs e)
        {
            newStroke = null;
            inkEl.ReleaseMouseCapture();
        }
    }
}
```

In addition to showing the flexibility of Silverlight, which allows you to develop applications in either parsed JavaScript or compiled .NET languages, this example also demonstrates how straightforward it is to *migrate* from JavaScript to .NET. So you can see that if you have existing Silverlight applications in JavaScript, it is easy to upgrade them to Silverlight using managed code.

In the next section, you'll look at the raw touch APIs provided in Silverlight 3, and you'll see how these can be used to build Touch applications—in particular, *multitouch* applications running on Windows 7.

Using the Touch APIs in Silverlight

Silverlight 3 introduces a new *Touch* object that can be used to build single-touch or multitouch applications, depending on your touch hardware.

Using it is straightforward. To get started, you simply write an event handler for its *FrameReported* event, and then handle the touch arguments within this event handler. These arguments vary depending on your touch hardware and where you touch.

Let's first look at an example using a Tablet PC with a touch screen, a common piece of hardware that provides a single touch interface.

Create a new Silverlight application, and change its *MainPage.xaml* to look like the following code sample. Note that you are adding an *Ellipse* called *finger* as well as changing the *Grid* to a *Canvas*. Here's the XAML:

```
<UserControl x:Class="SecondTouch.MainPage"
    xmlns="http://schemas.microsoft.com/winfx/2006/xaml/presentation"
    xmlns:x="http://schemas.microsoft.com/winfx/2006/xaml"
    xmlns:d="http://schemas.microsoft.com/expression/blend/2008"

    xmlns:mc="http://schemas.openxmlformats.org/markup-compatibility/2006"
mc:Ignorable="d" d:DesignWidth="640" d:DesignHeight="480">
    <Canvas x:Name="LayoutRoot">
        <Ellipse Width="60" Height="60" Fill="Red" x:Name="finger"></Ellipse>
    </Canvas>
</UserControl>
```

Next, go to the MainPage.xaml.cs file and look for the class constructor. Add the definition of the event handler for the *FrameReported* event on the *Touch* object. Your code will look like this:

```
public MainPage()
{
    InitializeComponent();
    Touch.FrameReported += new TouchFrameEventHandler(Touch_FrameReported);
}
```

After you create the event handler declaration, Visual Studio creates the event handler code for you. It looks like this:

```
void Touch_FrameReported(object sender, TouchFrameEventArgs e)
{
    throw new NotImplementedException();
}
```

Note the second parameter, *TouchFrameEventArgs*—this object provides much of the functionality you need to handle both single touch and multitouch. We'll be using it extensively in
this chapter.

TouchFrameEventArgs provides a method called *GetTouchPoints*, which returns a collection of
touch points. Each element in the collection provides data about the touch point, such as the
x and y coordinates of where the user has touched to generate that touch point.

In a single-touch system, such as a Tablet PC, this collection has only one element. In systems
with multiple touch points, the maximum number of elements is equal to the maximum number of touch points the system supports, but only the touch points that are in use are populated. For example, if your system supports 10 touch points, but only three fingers are touching the screen, this collection is populated by three elements.

In our Tablet PC, single-touch example, we know that there will only be one touch point in
this collection, so we can create an instance of the *TouchPoint* class from the first element in
the collection, like this:

```
TouchPoint tp = e.GetTouchPoints(this)[0];
```

This *TouchPoint* class has a *Position* property, which is a *System.Windows.Point* that provides x
and y coordinates for where the screen has been touched. Recall that in our XAML we made
an ellipse called *finger*, so we can now move that ellipse to the point of the screen that the
user is touching.

Here's the code:

```
void Touch_FrameReported(object sender, TouchFrameEventArgs e)
{
    TouchPoint tp = e.GetTouchPoints(this)[0];
    finger.SetValue(Canvas.TopProperty, tp.Position.Y);
    finger.SetValue(Canvas.LeftProperty, tp.Position.X);
}
```

Now when you run your application and drag your finger or stylus around the screen, you'll
see that the ellipse follows it!

Expanding the Application for Multitouch

In the previous section, you saw that the *TouchFrameEventArgs* object exposed a *GetTouch-
Points* property that returned a collection of touch points. You built a sample application for a
single touch point by taking the first element in this collection. In this section, you'll see how

you can extend this to multitouch by using this collection and some classes to track multiple touch points.

Create a new Silverlight application, and add a new Class file to it called *finger.cs*. This class will be used to track a particular finger on a multitouch screen.

This class will have a number of properties: an ID that will be used to track which touch point it is for; x and y values for where the touch that corresponds to this finger took place, and a *TextBlock* that will be used to render the word *Finger* followed by the ID of the touch point. For example, if the touch point has the ID *1*, the *TextBlock* renders *Finger 1*.

Here's the full code for this class:

```
using System;
using System.Net;
using System.Windows;
using System.Windows.Controls;
using System.Windows.Documents;
using System.Windows.Ink;
using System.Windows.Input;
using System.Windows.Media;
using System.Windows.Media.Animation;
using System.Windows.Shapes;


namespace SilverlightTouch2
{

    public class Finger
    {
        public int FingerID { get; set; }
        public double X { get; set; }
        public double Y { get; set; }
        public TextBlock theText;
        public Finger()
        {
            theText = new TextBlock();
            theText.SetValue(Canvas.TopProperty, 0.0);
            theText.SetValue(Canvas.LeftProperty, 0.0);
        }
    }
}
```

Now let's edit the MainPage.xaml.cs to create the application. First, add the event declaration for the *Touch.FrameReported* event handler shown earlier:

```
Touch.FrameReported += new TouchFrameEventHandler(Touch_FrameReported);
```

You also need to add a *List<T>* that gives you a dynamic list of *Finger* instances so that you can keep track of how many fingers are touching the screen, and to ensure your application is flexible enough for devices that support a different number of touch points.

Here's the code:

```
List<Finger> myFingers = new List<Finger>();
```

Make this a class-level variable so that it's available to the event handler too.

Now let's see how to use *TouchFrameEventArgs* to manage multiple touch points.

First, you create a *TouchPointCollection* and initialize it to the return value of the *GetTouch-Points* of *TouchFrameEventArgs*:

```
TouchPointCollection t = e.GetTouchPoints(this);
```

Next, go through each element in this collection. Earlier we mentioned that it is a collection of *TouchPoint* objects, and each particular touch point has a unique ID associated with it—and here you will use that. If your device supports 10 touch points and you place a finger on it, that finger always has the same ID as long as it is touching the screen. Place a second finger on the screen, and similarly it has the same ID (which is different from the ID associated with the first finger), and so on.

What we'll do is go through the touch points and look at the ID of each one. If it's the ID of a touch that we have not yet seen, we'll add a new entry to the *List<Finger>* called *myFingers*; otherwise, we'll update the current entry on that list with the x and y values associated with this point.

Additionally, if you're adding a new finger to the *List<Finger>*, you also have to initialize its internal *TextBlock* by giving it the text *Finger* with the ID as discussed earlier (placing it in the appropriate x and y coordinates and adding it to the *Canvas* called *LayoutRoot*, which contains all your controls).

Here's the code to do this:

```
for (int lp = 0; lp < t.Count; lp++)
{
  int nID = t[lp].TouchDevice.Id;
  bool bFound = false;
  for (int nlp2 = 0; nlp2 < myFingers.Count; nlp2++)
  {
    if (myFingers[nlp2].FingerID == nID)
    {
      myFingers[nlp2].X = t[lp].Position.X;
      myFingers[nlp2].Y = t[lp].Position.Y;
      bFound = true;
      myFingers[nlp2].theText.SetValue(Canvas.TopProperty, myFingers[nlp2].Y);
      myFingers[nlp2].theText.SetValue(Canvas.LeftProperty, myFingers[nlp2].X);
```

```
      }
   }
   if (!bFound)
   {
      Finger newFinger = new Finger();
      newFinger.FingerID = nID;
      newFinger.X = t[lp].Position.X;
      newFinger.Y = t[lp].Position.Y;
      newFinger.theText.SetValue(Canvas.TopProperty, newFinger.Y);
      newFinger.theText.SetValue(Canvas.LeftProperty, newFinger.X);
      newFinger.theText.Visibility = Visibility.Visible;
      newFinger.theText.Text = "Finger " + nID;
      LayoutRoot.Children.Add(newFinger.theText);
      myFingers.Add(newFinger);
   }
}
```

And that's it! If you have a multitouch device, now you'll be able to track each finger touching the device and render the location of that finger. Here's a screen shot of this in action on a PC that supports 10 touch points.

The ID parameter is device-dependent, so it's not a good idea to do a one-to-one (1:1) mapping whereby finger 1 is ID 1, finger 2 is ID 2, and so on. As you can see here, the device we used for the preceding screen shot gave us the ID *5* for the first touch point, *6* for the second, and so on.

Silverlight 3 doesn't support gestures in the way that WPF does, as discussed in Chapter 5, "Touch Me Now: An Introduction to Multitouch Programming." So if you want to do some gesture support, you need to write your own gesture engine.

Summary

In this chapter, you learned about Silverlight—what it is and how it works. You learned how to use Silverlight to build a Windows 7 application using its out-of-browser mode. Then you looked at the various APIs for managing touch in Silverlight applications, including the JavaScript and .NET-based Ink APIs. (Recall that the JavaScript API works only in the browser.) You then worked with the Touch API, which works specifically with the Windows 7 multitouch system. Using this functionality, you saw how to build single-touch and multitouch applications by processing the raw inputs.

In the next chapter you will get your first look on the Windows 7 Sensor and Location platform and learn how to use sensors in your application to create dynamic and adaptive user interface that reacts to environmental changes.

Chapter 9
Introduction to the Sensor and Location Platform

In this chapter, you'll be introduced to the new Sensor and Location platform in the Microsoft Windows 7 operating system, which enables you to use some very cool implementations such as Location Base Services and to integrate ambient light sensors into your applications. We'll start by Understanding some of the reasons behind creating his new platform and learning about what problems the new platform is designed to solve. Next we'll dive into the architecture that supports the Sensor And Location interfaces and explain the role of each component in the system. Then we'll show you what the new platform API offers developers.

We'll start by looking at what information a sensor can provide and how to work with different sensor types and categories. Throughout the chapter, you'll see code snippets, both native and managed code, of a simple ambient light sensor application that we use for reference. At the end of the chapter, you can find additional reasons for building light-aware applications as well as information about the tools that you need to use during the development.

> **Note** The term *light-aware* refers to a program that uses light sensor data to optimize its content, controls, and other graphics elements. This data is used to create an optimum user experience in many different lighting conditions, ranging from darkness to direct sunlight.

Why Sensors?

In recent years, we have been witnessing sensors play an increasingly larger role in some exciting scenarios—from mobile devices that automatically change their screen orientation from portrait to landscape, to computers that automatically control their screen brightness when the lighting conditions change. Currently, most applications don't care if you are using your laptop outdoors in direct sunlight or on a train, where your lighting is constantly changing, because they can't react to changes in the environment that affect your use of the computer and your applications. Most applications that we use on a daily basis were designed for "normal" office-like environments. Let's face it, when was the last time you tested your application outdoors in direct sunlight?

Nowadays, laptops offer higher mobility than ever before, allowing us to use applications in different locations with different environmental conditions, such as changes in lighting conditions. Wouldn't it be nice to have an application that can adjust its look, feel, and behavior in response to changes in environment conditions? Ambient light sensors, for example, enable your computer to automatically adjust your screen's brightness based on the current lighting conditions. Furthermore, developers can also enable applications to optimize their content for readability, making applications easier to use in a range of operating environments. With the new Sensor and Location platform in Windows 7, it's easy for developers to get environmental information from sensors to optimize the experience their applications deliver in response to such environmental changes.

In the past, using sensors tended to be a very vertical solution. There was no specific definition of what a sensor was, what its date fields were, or how to access these fields. Lack of standardization made programming for sensors an arduous task. When using a sensor, like a GPS location sensor, you had to choose hardware from a wide range of vendors, and each vendor had a specific set of drivers and APIs you had to learn about to work with that piece of hardware. If you wanted to change your hardware or vendor, often you found yourself learning new APIs to access similar information.

In Windows 7, we address these problems by providing out-of-the-box support for sensors. The Windows 7 Sensor and Location platform provides a set of standard interfaces. The platform provides a standard device driver interface for integrating sensor hardware devices, and a set of standard application programming interfaces that enable developers to discover and receive data from sensors. By providing these standard interfaces, the Windows 7 Sensor and Location platform offers a win-win-win situation, wherein it's easier for developers to discover, access, and receive information from sensors, thus creating room for more developers to optimize their applications to environmental changes. In return, this creates greater demand for sensor hardware, and if you are a hardware provider you have a standardized way to target one set of APIs to integrate with Windows. And most importantly, the end user gets to experience an application that takes into account the environment the user is working in.

Ambient light sensors, which enable you to create a light-aware user interface (UI), are only one type of sensor. Other sensors, such as human presence and proximity sensors, can facilitate adherence to specific privacy and security requirements. Imagine the computer automatically detecting that you are leaving the immediate surroundings and locking itself or powering down to optimize its power consumption. Another popular scenario is enabled by the use of accelerometers (gravity sensors), which can enable UI reorientation, flipping between portrait and landscape when changing the device position, or it can even function as an input device for a general-purpose game.

Location-based sensors enable a wide range of location-based services, such as searching for specific computer game shops near your current location or helping to enforce a security policy by blocking specific content based on the computer location. The "Location" part of the Sensor and Location platform provides an easy way to retrieve data about a geographic location while protecting user privacy.

Note In this book, we cover only the Sensor and Location APIs that software developers use to discover, access, and read sensor input. This book will not address any drivers or hardware-related topics.

A Word on Security

As you'll soon discover, the Windows 7 Sensor and Location platform is a powerful piece of technology that unlocks new opportunities and scenarios for your application. But as always, with great power comes even greater responsibility. This is one of the reasons the platform takes special care of security and privacy issues. By default, each installed sensor is disabled. The end user has to enable each sensor before he can start using it. Providing permission for a sensor requires administrator rights, and users can do this from the Location And Other Sensors option located in the Control Panel. The following screen shot shows the sensors I have installed on my development machine, and you can see that only some are enabled.

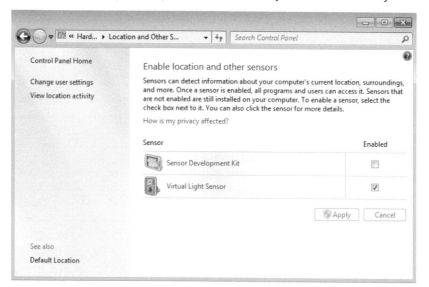

For privacy reasons, each sensor has an access control list that defines a list of user accounts on the local computer that can access the given sensors and read information. When enabled, a sensor device works for all programs running under a particular user account (or for all user accounts), including none-active users and services, such as ASPNET or SYSTEM. For example, if you enable a GPS sensor for your user account, only programs running under your user account have access to the GPS. If you enable the GPS for all users, any program running under any user account has access to the GPS. This approach to privacy is important to protect the user's location information (including history, as you can read in the next chapter).

But before we jump into the code, let's review the different components supporting the Windows 7 Sensor and Location platform.

Architecture of the Sensor and Location Platform

The first component of the Sensor and Location platform is the sensor hardware. This is a real physical device that measures physical phenomena such as the amount of light, temperature, humidity, relative gravity force, and other measureable physical phenomena. Shown in Figure 9-1 as number 1, sensors are typically hardware devices; however, a sensor can also be a logical device (also known as a *virtual sensor*). A virtual sensor is a software-based sensor that can perform sensor-type functionality with any type of back end providing the data, such as a Web service (which is widely used for IP location-based providers). Virtual sensors can be used to simulate real sensors to help the development process. The Windows 7 RC Software Development Kit (SDK) includes a virtual light sensor that we use in this chapter to simulate a light sensor.

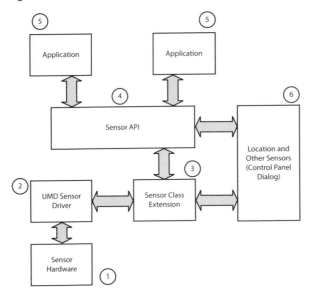

Figure 9-1 Windows 7 Sensor platform architecture

The sensor (hardware based or virtual) is integrated into the operating system via a user-mode device (UMD) sensor driver, depicted as number 2. A user-mode device driver is developed using the User Mode Driver Framework (UMDF), which allows you to write what is akin to a Win32 COM application instead of writing low-level kernel code that is complicated to develop and far more difficult to debug. To make it easier to write a device driver that exposes a sensor to Windows 7, the platform provides a sensor class extension, shown as number 3. This is essentially a driver utility library that implements common code that is required for sensor drivers. That way, you don't have to re-create the entire code that supports the Sensor and Location platform. Writing a sensor user-mode driver (or any other type of driver) is beyond the scope of this book. You can find additional information online at *http://www.microsoft.com/whdc/device/sensors.*

After a sensor is installed and integrated, it becomes discoverable to the application via the sensor API, shown as number 4 in Figure 9-1. The Windows 7 Sensor and Location platform enables different applications to receive information from the same sensor at the same time, depicted as number 5, which is one of the goals of the Sensor and Location platform. In previous Windows versions, devices usually used virtual COM ports to communicate with the system. One of the problems with virtual COM ports is that they don't scale and can't support multiple consumer applications at the same time; therefore, having a platform that supports multi-concurrency is a great advantage.

The last component of the Sensor and Location platform is the Location And Other Sensors dialog, which is part of the Control Panel. Shown as number 6 in the earlier illustration, this dialog communicates with both the hardware elements of the system and the software elements to enable users to control permissions settings. As you already saw in the previous section, this dialog allows users to configure specific permissions for each sensor for each user account, and it also shows the status of the sensor.

What Is a Sensor?

To better understand the Sensor And Location platform APIs, let's take a look at how sensors are represented in the operating system and review some of the concepts related to sensors in Windows 7. All the information about sensors in Windows 7 can be found in the two SDK "h files." The *sensors.h* and *sensorsapi.h* files are located in the Windows 7 SDK Include folder (by default—Program Files\Microsoft SDKs\Windows\v7.0\Include). These files define supporting structures and values used in the Sensor and Location platform, as well as the platform API's prototypes.

A sensor can be either a physical device or a logical (virtual) sensor. Regardless of the sensor's type, all sensors share similar properties like the state of the sensor, and events that all sensors expose, as explained in the following list:

- **Category**   *A collection of sensors types that are related. For example, a weather station might contain a wide variety of sensors, such as wind direction and speed, humidity, temperature, barometric pressure, and other related sensors. All these sensors do not necessarily provide similar data, but they all can be considered environmental sensors. Other categories defined by the platform include location, motion, electrical, biometric, orientation, mechanical, light, and scanner.*

- **Type** The physical phenomenon that is being "sensed" or measured, such as the voltage or current in an electrical sensor category or ambient light in the light category.

- **Properties** Metadata information that describes a sensor. Among the sensor's properties, you can find its type and friendly name, but you can also find information about the sensor's manufacturer and its model, serial number, description, and other properties. Some of the properties are read-only, such as the sensor model, and some are read-write. For example, you can update the report interval property, which defines the timeout between asynchronous data reports. Note that some properties might not be supported by a specific sensor device because vendors are not required to implement the entire properties list.

- **Data types** Measurements that sensors report. Sensor data types are a union of the phenomenon being measured and the units in which the measurements are reported. For example, location data types include, among other things, Latitude and Longitude data types, and you can expect to see these in any location-based sensor. But the location data types also include data types such as speed (in knots), heading (in degrees relative to magnetic north), or number of satellites in view (for GPS-based sensors). The location data types also include civic address information such as city and postal code. Being aware of the various data types available is important, and we'll return to this topic later in the "Reading Sensor Data Asynchronously and Handling Sensor Events" section.

- **Events** The main way the Sensor and Location platform communicates with your applications. By using events, sensors can notify you about new data, about changes in sensor state, when a sensor connects and becomes available, or when a sensor disconnects.

- **State** Defines the possible operational states for sensors and answers questions such as the following: "Is the sensor ready for use?" or "Has the user enabled the sensor?" The following is the list of supported sensor states:

  - **Ready** The sensor is ready to send data.

  - **Not Available** The sensor is not available for use by the application. Usually, this indicates an internal sensor problem.

  - **No Data** The sensor is ready for use, but it has no data to send to your application.

  - **Initializing** The sensor is available but performing initialization, so it is not ready to send data to your application.

- o **Access Denied**   *The sensor is available, but the user account does not have permission to access the sensor data. In this case, you need to ask for permission to enable the sensor.*

- o **Error**   *The sensor has raised an error.*

- o **Removed** *The sensor was removed from the system.*

Working with Sensors

As explained in the preceding section, a sensor provides a lot of information that you can handle. A given computer can include several sensors and sometimes more than one sensor per category. For example, an end-user computer can have a GPS location sensor and a WiFi triangulation sensor, which also is a location sensor even though it is a virtual sensor. You need to choose the best sensor for a given scenario. For example, use the GPS sensor when you're outdoors without any obstacles blocking the satellites, and use the WiFi triangulation sensor when you're indoors and the GPS sensor is not available. In the next chapter, we describe in detail the "location" piece of the Sensor and Location platform and explain how the Location API simplifies your work with location sensors.

Integrating Sensors into Your Application

When integrating sensors into your application, you need to follow a few basic steps:

1. Discovering the sensors. Before you can obtain a sensor, you need to discover which sensors are connected to the computer. In this step, you enumerate through the list of sensor devices that are connected to the computer and register to events that notify you when new sensor devices arrive.

2. Request sensor permissions. After you choose the sensor you want to use, you need to make sure you have permissions to access it. You need to prompt the user to enable your sensor; otherwise, your application won't be able to access the sensor's data.

3. Interact with the sensor. After obtaining a sensor whose data you have permission to access, you can read its various properties, read its data, and register for events and periodic data updates.

Each of these steps is covered in more detail in the following sections.

Discovering Sensors

The first step that every application that uses sensors needs to perform is obtaining a sensor (or sensors). To enable your application to do this, you need to use the *ISensorManager* COM interface. This sensor manager object maintains the list of available sensors. To use it, you must first call the COM *CoCreateInstance* method to create an instance of the sensor manager object and retrieve a pointer to its interface. You can think of this interface as the root interface for the sensor API. The following code snippet creates an instance of the sensor manager:

```
// Declare a smart pointer to receive the sensor manager interface pointer.
// Originally, this smart pointer is defined in the class prototype definition
// CAmbientLightAwareSensorManagerEvents
CComPtr<ISensorManager> m_spISensorManager;
HRESULT hr;
// Create the sensor manager
hr = m_spISensorManager.CoCreateInstance(CLSID_SensorManager);
```

The *ISensorManager* interface provides a set of methods for discovering and retrieving available sensors. It also exposes an event that is used for receiving notifications when a new sensor becomes available. We'll address that later in the chapter.

With an *ISensorManager* pointer in your hands, you can start searching for sensors. *ISensorManager* has three methods that help you search connected sensors:

- *GetSensorByID*

- *GetSensorsByCategory*

- *GetSensorsByType*

The first method returns a specific sensor by its ID, which is just a GUID. To retrieve a sensor by its ID, you must know the unique ID for the sensor. This ID is usually generated automatically when the sensor is first connected to the system, to support multiple sensors of the same make and model. Therefore, it's most likely that you'll use the last two methods, which return *ISensorCollection*, which is a collection of sensor objects.

It is possible that several sensors of the same category are connected to the same PC. For example, on my machine, I have one light sensor built in to the PC enclosure and another one as part of my Sensor Development Kit. It makes sense to use the light sensor built in to the enclosure because it provides the most accurate lighting condition reading from the PC. For an application, getting a collection of available sensors, using the Sensor Manager interface, by type or category is the best way to discover sensors and work with the right one from the list. The following code snippet is taken from the *Initialize* method of the *CAmbientLightAwareSensorManagerEvents* class. This is one of the classes in the Microsoft Foundation Classes (MFC) light-aware application that we are using throughout this chapter as a reference application. This class is a standard C++ class that supports *IUnknown* methods, and it's the main class for managing sensors. It also implements *ISensorManagerEvents* to receive updated information from the Sensor and Location platform API when a new sensor device is connected to the PC. The *Initialize* method is called during the initialization process

of the application's main dialog. The *CAmbientLightAwareSensorManagerEvents::Initialize*
method retrieves a collection of ambient light sensors that belong to the type named
SENSOR_TYPE_AMBIENT_LIGHT and register each sensor with the application event listeners.

```
HRESULT CAmbientLightAwareSensorManagerEvents::Initialize()
{
    HRESULT hr;
    // Create the sensor manager
    hr = m_spISensorManager.CoCreateInstance(CLSID_SensorManager);
    if (SUCCEEDED(hr))
    {
        hr = m_spISensorManager->SetEventSink(this);
        if (SUCCEEDED(hr))
        {
            CComPtr<ISensorCollection> spSensors;
            // Find all ambient light sensors
            hr = m_spISensorManager->GetSensorsByType(SENSOR_TYPE_AMBIENT_LIGHT,
                &spSensors);
            if (SUCCEEDED(hr) && NULL != spSensors)
            {
                ULONG ulCount = 0;
                hr = spSensors->GetCount(&ulCount);
                if (SUCCEEDED(hr))
                {
                    for(ULONG i=0; i < ulCount; i++)
                    {
                        CComPtr<ISensor> spSensor;
                        hr = spSensors->GetAt(i, &spSensor);
                        if (SUCCEEDED(hr))
                        {
                            // Helper function that sets up event sinking for a specific
                               sensor
                            hr = AddSensor(spSensor);
                            if (SUCCEEDED(hr))
                            {
                                // Read the sensor data and update the application's UI
                                hr = m_pSensorEvents->GetSensorData(spSensor);
                            }
                        }
                    }
                }
            }
        }
    }
    return hr;
}
```

Here you can see how after successfully obtaining an *ISensorManager* interface, you call
ISensorManager::GetSensorsByType, passing SENSOR_TYPE_AMBIENT_LIGHT and a pointer to
an *ISensorCollection* collection, *spSensors*. If successful, this function fills *ISensorCollection* with

all the available ambient light sensors. Next, you iterate through the sensors collection, and for each sensor you call the *AddSensor* helper function, which sets up event sinking for a sensor by registering the sensor to *m_pSensorEvents*, which is a *SensorEvents* implementation class used for event sinking that we explain later in the chapter. Last, you call another helper method, *GetSensorData*, to read data from the sensor and to update the LUX value in the application's UI. Please note, we omitted a few lines of code from this snippet that we'll add and describe later, as they are more relevant to the "Requesting Sensor Permissions" section later in this chapter and we didn't want to clutter this sample.

During the runtime of the application, new light sensors might get connected to the PC. On the same topic, during the runtime of any given application or service, new sensor devices might get connected to the PC. Therefore, you need a mechanism of notifying applications when new sensor devices are connected to the PC. The *ISensorManager* interface contains a *SetEventSink* method that is used to set an event sinking implementation class. This function receives an *ISensorManagerEvents* callback interface that receives the event notifications when a new sensor device gets connected. This event sink acts as a listener that handles the single event the *ISensorManagerEvents* interface has, *OnSensorEnter*. Note that in the code sample, you call *SetEventSink* right after the successful creation of the *ISensorManager* interface and pass *"this"* as the input parameter. This means that the *CAmbientLightAwareSensorManagerEvents* class implements the *ISensorManagerEvents* interface. Therefore, in this class you can find the implementation for the *ISensorManager::OnSensorEnter* event, which looks like the following code snippet:

```
HRESULT CAmbientLightAwareSensorManagerEvents::
        OnSensorEnter(ISensor* pSensor, SensorState state)
{
    HRESULT hr = S_OK;
    if (NULL != pSensor)
    {
        SENSOR_TYPE_ID idType = GUID_NULL;
        hr = pSensor->GetType(&idType);
        if (SUCCEEDED(hr))
        {
            // we are interested only in light sensors
            if (IsEqualIID(idType, SENSOR_TYPE_AMBIENT_LIGHT))
            {
                //Helper function that sets up event sinking for a specific sensor
                hr = AddSensor(pSensor);
                if (SUCCEEDED(hr))
                {
                    if (SENSOR_STATE_READY == state)
                    {
                        //Read the sensor data and update the UI
                        hr = m_pSensorEvents->GetSensorData(pSensor);
                    }
                }
            }
        }
    }
```

```
    }
    else
    {
        hr = E_POINTER;
    }
    return hr;
}
```

Here you can see that the *OnSensorEnter* method receives a pointer to the newly connected sensor device and the state status of the sensor. Assuming the sensor pointer is valid (not null), first you read the sensor's type by calling the *GetType* method on the *ISensor* interface. Because in your light-aware application you are interested only in light sensors, you check if the newly connected sensor device is a light sensor by checking its type. Remember that *ISensorManager* receives notification of any type of sensor devices that are connected to the PC. Assuming your sensor is a light sensor, you then call the same *AddSensor* helper function that you use in the *Initialize* method to set up event sinking for specific sensors. (Don't get confused with the *ISensorManager* event sinking.) The last thing you do is check whether the sensor is in a ready state. If it is, you read the sensor's data and update the application's UI.

You might ask yourself where the *OnSensorLeave* event is handled if not in the *ISensorManagerEvents* interface. All sensor-related events, other than detecting a new connected one, are handled by the *ISensorEvents* interface, which defines the callback interface you must implement if you want to receive sensor events. But we'll deal with the *ISensorEvent* later in this chapter in the "Reading Sensor Data Asynchronously and Handling Sensor Events" section.

Discovering Sensors Using Managed Code

So far, you have seen C++ and COM examples of the Sensor and Location platform. Now let's take a look at how managed code developers can use the platform. Using the Windows API Code Pack for the .NET Framework, which you already saw in action in Chapter 2, "Integrate with the Windows 7 Taskbar, Part 1," and Chapter 3, "Integrate with the Windows 7 Taskbar, Part 2," you can follow the same programming model, discovering sensors before starting to use them.

The main namespace for sensors in the Windows API Code Pack is *Microsoft.WindowsAPICodePack.Sensors* implemented in the Microsoft.WindowsAPICodePack.Sensors.dll assembly. In that namespace, you can find the *SensorManager* class, which manages sensor devices that are connected to the PC. This class exposes a very similar set of methods as the native *ISensorManager* interface does. These methods include *GetSensorsByCategoryId*, *GetSensorsByTypeId*, and *GetSensorsBySensorId*, the last of which receives as an input parameter a GUID that either represents a sensor category, type, or single sensor ID. In addition, you can also find the *GetAllSensors* method, which returns all the sensors that are connected to the system regardless of type or category.

The Windows API Code Pack provides a list of all the GUIDs that are available in Sensors.h. The *SensorPropertyKeys* and *SensorCategories* classes contain the public read-only property of GUID objects that correspond to the same values in the Sensors.h file. However, this is not the usual programming model that .NET developers are accustomed to, mainly because the sensor objects are not strongly typed and you have to use the more generic GUID system to access a sensor's data. This doesn't allow you to use all the great features .NET offers, such as data binding, type safety, and properties. Therefore, the *Microsoft.WindowsAPICodePack.Sensors* namespace includes several strongly typed sensor classes that allow you to bind to their properties. For example, you can find *AmbientLightSensor*, which has one public property, *CurrentLuminousIntensity*, which represents the current amount of light (luminous) detected by the sensors.

The *Microsoft.WindowsAPICodePack.Sensors* namespace offers an extensibility model that allows you to create any strongly typed sensor. When this is combined with the extensibility offered by the native API, you can create any type of sensor you want with any data values. However, this topic is outside the scope of this introductory book. You can read more about the Sensor and Location platform extensibility module at the Sensor and Location Platform Web site: *http://www.microsoft.com/whdc/device/sensors/*.

With a strongly typed sensor class, the Windows API Code pack can define a .NET Generics version of the *Get* methods. For example, *GetSensorsByTypeId<S>*, where *S* is a type derived from the *Sensor* base class. The prototype looks like this:

```
public static SensorList<S> GetSensorsByTypeId<S>( ) where S: Sensor
```

When using this function, you need to predefine a specific *SensorList< >* of the desired sensor type (*AmbientLightSensor*, in our example), and then call the method requesting the sensor's manager to return only *AmbientLightSensor* sensors. The following code snippet illustrates this process:

```
// Strongly typed SensorList of type AmbientLightSensor
SensorList<AmbientLightSensor> alsList = null;
try
{
    alsList = SensorManager.GetSensorsByTypeId<AmbientLightSensor>();
}
catch (SensorPlatformException)
{
    //handle error when no sensor device is accessible
}
```

The *SensorManager* class contains one event called *SensorChanged*, which is equivalent to the native *ISensorManager::OnSensorEnter* event. The one main difference between the native and managed code implementations is that the managed code implementation, in addition to receiving an event when a new sensor device is connected to the PC, also generates an event when a sensor gets disconnected. Therefore, *SensorsChangedEventArgs*, the arguments passed to the *SensorManager.SensorChanged* event handler, includes a *SensorAvailabilityChange* member that defines the type of change for each sensor, which can be *Addition* for new sensor devices and *Removal* when sensors are disconnected from the PC. In this simple application, the best place to register for this event is in the main form's constructor, as shown in the following code snippet:

```
SensorManager.SensorsChanged += new SensorsChangedEventdHandler(
SensorManager_SensorsChanged );
```

SensorManager_SensorsChanged is the function that handles the *SensorsChanged* event in our application, and it looks like this:

```
void SensorManager_SensorsChanged( SensorsChangedEventArgs change )
{
    // The SensorsChanged event comes in on a non-UI thread.
    // Whip up an anonymous delegate to handle the UI update.
    BeginInvoke( new MethodInvoker( delegate
    {
        PopulatePanel( );
    } ) );
}
```

The *SensorsChanged* event is dispatched on a different thread than the application's main form (UI) thread. Because Windows Forms does not allow you to update the UI of the application from a non-UI thread, for any Windows application with window-based UI, it is highly recommended that you use a different a thread than the main UI thread to execute long computations or any I/O-bound communication (as we do in our example when you synchronously read sensor data). Therefore, to properly handle non-UI-thread UI updates, you should use *BeginInvoke* to execute the specified delegate asynchronously on the thread that the form's underlying handle was created on. The *PopulatePanel* method iterates through all the ambient light sensors and updates the application UI. We'll see the complete implementation of *PopulatePanel* later in the chapter.

Requesting Sensor Permissions

You've seen how to get a list of sensors and obtain a specific sensor from that list. After you obtain a sensor, either using C++ or .NET, you need to verify that you have permission to access that sensor data (by checking if the sensor is enabled). Even without permission to access the sensor's data, there's still a lot you can do with a sensor. For example, you can retrieve some property values from a sensor before the user has enabled it. Information such as the manufacturer's name, the model of the sensor, or the field's supported value data types can help you to decide whether your program can use a particular sensor. You should ask for permission to access a particular sensor's data only after you've ascertained that you need that sensor.

Assuming you do need to request permission to access the sensor's data, which you'll see how to do so, right after this short explanation, you can request the user to enable that sensor so that it allows your application to access its data. For consistency and to help you implement strict privacy and security policies across all applications that use sensors, the Sensor and Location platform provides a standard way for asking the user to enable sensors. The platform provides a Windows dialog box that prompts users to enable sensor devices. To show this dialog, you need to call the *ISensorManager::RequestPermissions* method. All you need to pass is an HWND for the parent window, a pointer to a list of sensors to request access for, and a Boolean indicating whether the dialog is a modal or not. It's easy to do, as illustrated by this single line of code, where *spSensors* is a collection of sensors that you want the user to enable:

```
m_spISensorManager->RequestPermissions(NULL, spSensors, true);
```

Using the preceding code to call the method results in a system dialog box that requests the user to give permission to access the sensor data.

How do you know when to ask for permission and for which sensors? The answer is simple: whenever you want to read the sensor's data (not general properties such as friendly name or manufacturer), you should check whether the sensor is in its ready state, SENSOR_STATE_READY for C++ and *SensorState.Ready* for .NET. If the sensor is in any other state (Initializing, Not Available, or Error), your application logic should handle that and display some friendly message to the user. However, if the sensor is in an access-denied state (SENSOR_STATE_ACCESS_DENIED or *Sensor.NotAvailable*), you should request the user to give permission to access that sensor's data using the *RequestPermission* method.

Let's update the *CAmbientLightAwareSensorManagerEvents Initialize* method described earlier to include the relevant code for requesting permission for any light sensor devices that are not already enabled. The updated method code looks like this:

```
HRESULT CAmbientLightAwareSensorManagerEvents::Initialize()
{
    HRESULT hr;
    // Create the sensor manager
    hr = m_spISensorManager.CoCreateInstance(CLSID_SensorManager);
    if (SUCCEEDED(hr))
    {
        hr = m_spISensorManager->SetEventSink(this);
        if (SUCCEEDED(hr))
        {
            // Find all ambient light sensors
            CComPtr<ISensorCollection> spSensors;
            hr = m_spISensorManager->GetSensorsByType(SENSOR_TYPE_AMBIENT_LIGHT,
                                                      &spSensors);
            if (SUCCEEDED(hr) && NULL != spSensors)
            {
                ULONG ulCount = 0;
                hr = spSensors->GetCount(&ulCount);
                if (SUCCEEDED(hr))
                {
                    for(ULONG i=0; i < ulCount; i++)
                    {
                        CComPtr<ISensor> spSensor;
                        hr = spSensors->GetAt(i, &spSensor);
                        if (SUCCEEDED(hr))
                        {
                        // Helper function that sets up event sinking for a specific sensor
                            hr = AddSensor(spSensor);
                            if (SUCCEEDED(hr))
                            {
                                // Check the current sensor state.
                                SensorState state = SENSOR_STATE_READY;
                                hr = spSensor->GetState(&state);
                                if(SUCCEEDED(hr))
                                {
                                    if(state == SENSOR_STATE_ACCESS_DENIED)
                                    {
                                        hr = m_spISensorManager->RequestPermissions
                                                        (NULL, spSensors, true);
                                        if(hr == HRESULT_FROM_WIN32(ERROR_ACCESS_DENIED) ||
                                           hr == HRESULT_FROM_WIN32(ERROR_CANCELLED))
                                        {
                                            /*handle user access denied*/
                                        }
                                    }
                                }
                                if(state == SENSOR_STATE_READY)
```

```
                                        {
                                            // Read the sensor data and update the application's UI
                                            hr = m_pSensorEvents->GetSensorData(spSensor);
                                        }
                                    }
                                }
                            }
                        }
                    }
                }
            }
        return hr;
    }
```

There are few important topics to review in this code snippet. First, you probably noticed that you check the sensor state after calling the *AddSensor* method. The *AddSensor* method saves the sensor in a private sensor array member of the application and also sets the event sinking object on the sensor. After the event sinking object is set, the application starts receiving events (like state change) from that sensor. This is important because next you test the state of the sensor, and if the sensor's state is "access denied," you call the *RequestPermission* method. Assuming the user enables the sensor device, the Sensor and Location platform generates a *SensorState* event (*ISensor::OnStateChanged*) indicating that the sensor state has changed. You can read more details in the "Interacting with Sensors" section. But for now, all you need to know is that in the event implementation you can read the sensor's data. In the preceding code, you explicitly check the sensor to see if it's in a ready state and then perform a synchronous data read. This code is required in case the sensor is already in a ready state and you don't need to ask for permission.

The second possibility to consider is that the user might deny the request and not enable the sensor device. In Windows 7, Microsoft emphasizes security and privacy issues. The Sensor and Location platform is no exception. If the user denies a request to enable a sensor, calling *RequestPermission* a second time will not prompt the dialog window again. This behavior is designed to prevent patsy applications from calling this method repeatedly and annoying the user. Therefore, you might want to consider prompting the user with a specific message before showing the system's sensor permission dialog to make sure the user understands the importance of enabling the sensor. Similarly, if a sensor is already enabled and you call the *RequestPermission* method, the system ignores your call and does not display the request permission dialog box for any sensors that are already enabled.

Requesting Sensor Permissions Using Managed Code

Similar to the native code implementation, in managed code you should follow the same guidelines and check the state of the sensor before reading its data. It shouldn't be a surprise that the following code snippet is similar to the native *Initialize* method described previously. The following code snippet is the complete *PopulatePanel* method that gets called in the application's main form handler of the *Shown* event, triggered the first time the form is displayed:

```
private void PopulatePanel()
{
    SensorList<AmbientLightSensor> alsList = null; //better be explicit
    try {
        alsList =SensorManager.GetSensorsByTypeId<AmbientLightSensor>();
    }
    catch (SensorPlatformException)
    { //handle error when no sensor device is accessible  }

    panel.Controls.Clear( );
    int ambientLightSensorsCount = 0;
    if (alsList != null)
    {
        foreach (AmbientLightSensor sensor in alsList)
        {
            // set sensor data report change and sensor state change events
            sensor.ReportInterval = 0;
            sensor.DataReportChanged += new DataReportChangedHandler(DataReportChanged);
            sensor.StateChanged += new StateChangedHandler(sensor_StateChanged);
            // if the state is access denied, request permission
            if (sensor.State == SensorState.AccessDenied)
            {
                SensorList<Sensor> toApprove = new SensorList<Sensor>();
                toApprove.Add(sensor);
                SensorManager.RequestPermission(this.Handle, true, toApprove);
            }
            else if (sensor.State == SensorState.Ready)
            {
                // read data synchronously
                CreateSensorUIElements(sensor, ambientLightSensorsCount);
                ambientLightSensorsCount++;
            }
        }
    }
    if( ambientLightSensorsCount == 0 )
    {
        UIForNoSensorsDetected();
    }
}
```

Here you can see that the *SensorManager* object is used to get a list of ambient light sensors. For each sensor, first you set event handlers for *Sensor.StateChanged* and *Sensor.DataReportChanged*. Next, you check the state of the sensor. If the sensor state is *SensorState.AccessDenied*, you call the *SensorManager.RequestPermission* method, passing the handle to the current window, along with a list of sensors to approve. In the preceding code, this list always contains a single sensor. And as before, assuming the user allows access to the sensor, a *Sensor.StateChanged* event will be raised by the system and handled by the *sensor_StateChanged* method, which you set at the beginning of the *foreach* loop.

If the sensor is in a ready state, you call *CreateSensorUIElements*, which is a helper function that creates a progress bar and two labels for each sensor that display the LUX value from the sensor, as shown in the following illustration. The upper part of the image is the Virtual Light Sensor which ships with the Windows 7 SDK. We use the Virtual Light Sensor to simulate different lighting conditions, the slider changes the value of the "Current light intensity". The lower part is the managed application that reads the light sensor values.

The Virtual Light Sensor application included as part of the Windows SDK simulates the functionality of a light sensor. Behind the scenes, this application implements the Windows 7 Sensor and Location Driver module. The application can be found in the Windows 7 SDK Bin folder (C:\Program Files\Microsoft SDKs\Windows\v7.0\Bin\x64\VirtualLightSensor.exe). After it is installed, you can use this application to simulate different LUX values by changing the slider position. This application sends data, as described in the "Architecture of the Sensor and Location Platform" section, that any Windows 7 application can access and read, assuming the sensor is enabled. We'll use this application while developing and testing the Ambient Light application.

Interacting with Sensors

So far, you have seen how to obtain a sensor and request permissions to access its data. During that process, you also saw specific sensor events such as *Sensor.StateChanged* and *Sensor.DataReportChanged*. But we didn't provide any detailed explanation about the sensor's APIs. It's time we take a closer look at how to interact with a sensor.

Looking at the Sensor API (found in Sensorsapi.h) reveals the *ISensor* interface. This COM interface represents a sensor object that enables you to do the following:

- *Retrieve metadata about the sensor, such as its ID, type, or friendly name.*

- *Retrieve information about a specific data field the sensor can provide.*

- *Retrieve state information, such as whether the sensor is ready to use or is initializing.*

- *Specify the callback interface the Sensor API can use to provide your program with event notifications.*

- *Retrieve sensor data synchronously.*

As you already read earlier in the chapter, the Sensor and Location platform allows you to operate a sensor even if you don't have permission to access its data. With a sensor object at hand, you can do all of the above-mentioned operations in addition to retrieving sensor data, either synchronously or asynchronously. This is a rather important piece of the platform because it enables you to retrieve a sensor's property values even before the user has enabled the sensor. Information such as the manufacturer's name or the model of the sensor can help you to decide whether your program can use the sensor and even whether it's worth asking the user to grant permission to the specific sensor device. You can choose to retrieve a single sensor property value by using *ISensor::GetProperty* or to retrieve a collection of sensor properties values by using *ISensor::GetProperties*.

The managed code *Sensor* class provides similar functions. Let's review the following code snippet, which retrieves a few sensor properties and prints them to the debug output console:

```
private void PrintSensorProperties(Sensor sensor)
{
    PropertyKey[] SensorsPropertiesKeys =
                {
                        SensorPropertyKeys.SENSOR_PROPERTY_MANUFACTURER,
                        SensorPropertyKeys.SENSOR_PROPERTY_SERIAL_NUMBER,
                        SensorPropertyKeys.SENSOR_PROPERTY_DESCRIPTION,
                        SensorPropertyKeys.SENSOR_PROPERTY_FRIENDLY_NAME,
                        SensorPropertyKeys.SENSOR_PROPERTY_MODEL,
                        SensorPropertyKeys.SENSOR_PROPERTY_MIN_REPORT_INTERVAL,
                        SensorPropertyKeys.SENSOR_PROPERTY_CURRENT_REPORT_INTERVAL
                };

    IDictionary<PropertyKey, object> SensorsProperties =
        sensor.GetProperties(SensorsPropertiesKeys);

    for (int currentProperty = 0;
         currentProperty < SensorsProperties.Count;
         currentProperty++
         )
    {
        Debug.WriteLine(
            SensorsProperties.Keys.ElementAt(currentProperty).PropertyId.ToString() +
            " = " +
            SensorsProperties.Values.ElementAt(currentProperty).ToString()
```

```
            );
      }
   }
```

In this code snippet, you call the *Sensor.GetProperties* method that expects an array of *PropertiesKeys* that are defined in the *SensorPropertyKeys* class, which is just a representation of all the equivalent sensors' properties GUID values found in Sensors.h. You populate the property key array with all the specific properties you want to read from the sensor. There is a wide variety of properties you can use, and you can choose which properties you want to read from the sensor. Just remember that not all properties are supported by all sensors. Next, you call *Sensor.GetProperties* and then iterate through the array, printing all the returned values to the Debug console. The result looks like this:

```
6 = Microsoft
8 = 47162083952637-01827915268783
10 = Ambient Light Sensor
9 = Ambient Light Sensor
7 = Virtual Light Sensor
12 = 0
13 = 750
```

The native API provides the same functionality using the same method names; it just uses a different programming model and a lot more lines of code. If you want to review the specific native API in action, refer to the sensor section of the Windows 7 SDK. You can also refer to this chapter's sample code.

Getting and Setting Sensor Properties

The last two properties that we read from the sensor in the preceding code sample were the minimum and current report time intervals. Both of these values relate to the asynchronous data report the sensor generates that you'll read about in the next section, "Reading Sensor Data Asynchronously." For now, let's treat these as sensor property values that you want to read and that you also want to write to. Not all sensor properties can be set. For example, you can't set the manufacturer name or serial number properties.

The data report time interval is one of the sensor's properties that you can write to. You can control the report time interval and set it according to your application's needs. You need to set the report time interval to a short period of time in case your application requires frequent data reports. For example, a navigation application might need frequent updates to display the accurate location, whereas a room's climate-control application might need to read the room's temperature every minute or at longer intervals.

Before you can set property values for a sensor, the user must enable the sensor and have similar permissions that are required for reading the sensor's data. The following code snippet illustrates how you can set the current report interval:

```
HRESULT CAmbientLightAwareSensorEvents::
        SetCurrentReportInterval(ISensor* pSensor, ULONG ulNewInterval)
{
    HRESULT hr = S_OK;
    if(NULL == pSensor) {
        return E_POINTER;
    }
    CComPtr<IPortableDeviceValues> spPropsToSet; // Input
    CComPtr<IPortableDeviceValues> spPropsReturn; // Output
    // Create the input object.
    hr = spPropsToSet.CoCreateInstance(__uuidof(PortableDeviceValues));
    if(SUCCEEDED(hr))
    {
        // Add the current report interval property.
        hr = spPropsToSet->SetUnsignedIntegerValue
                            (SENSOR_PROPERTY_CURRENT_REPORT_INTERVAL, ulNewInterval);
    }
    if(SUCCEEDED(hr))
    {
        // Only setting a single property, here.
        hr = pSensor->SetProperties(spPropsToSet, &spPropsReturn);
    }
    // Test for failure.
    if(hr == S_FALSE)
    {

        // Print an error message.
        wprintf_s(L"\nSetting current report interval failed with error 0x%X\n", hrError);
        //Return the error code.
        hr = hrError;
    }
    else if(hr == E_ACCESSDENIED)
    {
        // No permission. Take appropriate action.
    }
    return hr;
}
```

In the preceding code, you use an *IPortableDeviceValues* interface that holds a collection of PROPERTYKEY/PROPVARIANT pairs. Because the Sensor and Location platform is a COM-based API, you need to use *CoCreate* with *IPortableDeviceValues* before you can use it. The *spPropsToSet* collection is your properties collection and is the equivalent of the .NET *PropertyKey* array from the previous example. After initializing the collection, you add a single integer value by calling the *SetUnsignedIntegerValue* method and passing a GUID indicating the property you want to set—in this case, the report time interval (SENSOR_PROPERTY_CURRENT_REPORT_INTERVAL) and an integer value (*ulNewInterval*), which will soon become the new report time interval.

Next, you call the *ISensor.SetProperties* method, passing the *spPropsToSet* and *spPropsToReturn* collections. The first collection is an input parameter that you just created with *CoCreateInstance* and set. The second collection is an output parameter that lists, after the method returns, an HRESULT value (indicating whether setting the property succeeded) for each property in *spPropsToSet*. The result of calling the *ISensor.SetProperties* method can be S_OK, indicating the method succeeded. It also can be S_FALSE, indicating that the request to set one or more of the specified properties failed. Or it can be E_ACCESSDENIED, indicating that your application doesn't have permission to access the sensor device. If you receive a return value of "access denied," you should ask the user to enable the sensor device as explained in the previous section.

As expected, the .NET *Sensor* class has similar methods for setting properties. The *Sensor.SetProperties* method can be used to set the values of multiple properties by passing an array that contains the *Dictionary* collection containing property keys and their corresponding values. However, the managed code API provides additional .NET-style properties for a number of specific sensor properties as a quick and convenient way to access such properties. You can find a sensor's read-only properties (such as Description, Model, or Manufacturer) and also a sensor's read-write properties (such as *ReportInterval*).

Reading Sensor Data Synchronously

By now, you know almost everything you need to know about working with sensors. You know how to obtain a sensor, ask for permission to access its data, and change properties that affect how often the sensor generates a data report. But you still need to learn one very important task—how to read sensor data that is the actual physical values the sensor is measuring. There are two ways to read sensor data:

- *Synchronously, by calling the* ISensor::GetData *method, which is a blocking method*

- *Asynchronously, by registering and implementing the* ISensorEvents::OnDataUpdate *event*

After you have obtained a sensor object and you have permission to read its data, you can synchronously call *ISensor::GetData* to read the sensor's data. Note that this is a blocking method. You need to pass a pointer to an *ISensorDataReport* interface, and if the method succeeds, this interface contains the most recent data report generated by the sensor.

The amount and frequency of data generated by sensors varies from one sensor to the other. For example, a sensor that detects whether or not a door is open generates a small amount of Boolean data, whereas a motion sensor might continuously generate multiple, more complex data streams of data. To provide a consistent programming model for your program to receive data, the Sensor API uses the sensor data report object that is represented by the *ISensorDataReport* interface. Using the *ISensorDataReport* interface, you can access the information in a sensor data report by reading the different data fields (values) of the sensor.

Sensor data reports contain the data field values generated and a time stamp that indicates when the data report was created.

The following code snippet is the *GetSensorData* method from the *CAmbientLightAwareSensorEvents* class that we described earlier in the chapter. This method gets called when a new light sensor device is contacted by the system:

```
HRESULT CAmbientLightAwareSensorEvents::GetSensorData(ISensor* pSensor)
{
    HRESULT hr = S_OK;
    if (NULL != pSensor)
    {
        CComPtr<ISensorDataReport> spDataReport;
        hr = pSensor->GetData(&spDataReport);
        if (SUCCEEDED(hr))
        {
            // helper function that reads a sensor's data report and updates the UI
            hr = GetSensorData(pSensor, spDataReport);
        }
        else
        {
            // handle error getting sensor data report
        }
    }
    else
    {
        hr = E_POINTER;
    }

    return hr;
}
```

Here you call the sensor's *GetData* method, passing a pointer to an *ISensorDataReport* interface. Next, you call the *GetSensorData* helper function, passing to it the sensor object and the newly obtained sensor data report. This helper function reads the LUX value from the sensor report and updates the application's UI with the new values, as shown in the following code snippet:

```
HRESULT CAmbientLightAwareSensorEvents::GetSensorData(ISensor *pSensor,
                                                ISensorDataReport *pDataReport)
{
    HRESULT hr = S_OK;
    if (NULL != pSensor && NULL != pDataReport)
    {
        SENSOR_ID idSensor = GUID_NULL;
        hr = pSensor->GetID(&idSensor);
        if (SUCCEEDED(hr))
        {
            PROPVARIANT pvLux;
            PropVariantInit(&pvLux);
```

```
        hr = pDataReport->GetSensorValue(SENSOR_DATA_TYPE_LIGHT_LEVEL_LUX, &pvLux);
        if (SUCCEEDED(hr))
        {
            // Save the lux value into our member variable
            m_mapLux[idSensor] = V_R4(&pvLux);
            hr = UpdateLux();
        }
        PropVariantClear(&pvLux);
    }
}
else
{
    hr = E_INVALIDARG;
}
return hr;
}
```

Here you read the light LUX value from the sensor data report using the *ISensorDataReport::GetSensorValue* method that retrieves a single data field value from the data report. This method expects a REFPROPERTYKEY as an input parameter that indicates the specific data field you want to read from the report and a pointer to PROPVARIANT as an output parameter that is filled with the actual data field value. Note that at this time in the application development you must know the exact data field you want to read. In our application, it is the LUX level; therefore, you pass SENSOR_DATA_TYPE_LIGHT_LEVEL_LUX as a REFPROPERTYKEY.

The reason the *GetSensorValue* method expects PROPVARIANT as an output parameter is rather simple. *ISensorDataReport* is a generic interface used by all sensors, and therefore it needs to represent any number of data fields that can have any data type. Because the Sensor API is COM based, using PROPVARIANT is an easy way to represent any give data type. However, you still need to know what the exact type is that PROPVARIANT contains (an integer, float, or bool). This is the reason we use the V_R4 macro in our application; it extracts a float value from PROPVARIANT. This means that when you read a sensor data report, you need to know exactly which data field you want to read and eventually what its type is. In our Ambient Light application, we are reading a LUX value that is of type float.

Reading Sensor Data Asynchronously and Handling Sensor Events

As we mentioned in the previous section, you can also read sensor data asynchronously. To do so, you need to use the Sensor API events, which provide event notifications for sensor data updates and state changes. To receive sensor event notifications, you must implement a set of callback methods defined by the *ISensorEvents* COM Interface:

- **OnEvent**   *Provides a generic event notification that includes an ID indicating which event was received: data update, sensors leave, or sensor state change*

- **OnDataUpdated**   *The event you want to use to receive sensor data updates and read new sensor data values*

- **OnLeave**   *The event you'll need to handle when a sensor is no longer available*

- **OnStateChanged**   *Provides a notification that a sensor state has changed*

ISensorEvents is a COM interface that inherits from *IUnknown*. If you want to read sensor data asynchronously, you need to implement the *ISensorEvents.OnDataUpdate* callback method. This method receives pointers to a *ISensor* object and to a *ISensorDataReport* as shown in the following code snippet:

```
HRESULT CAmbientLightAwareSensorEvents::OnDataUpdated(ISensor *pSensor, ISensorDataReport
*pNewData)
{
    HRESULT hr = S_OK;
    if ((NULL != pSensor) && (NULL != pNewData))
    {
        // Helper function, gets LUX data from a sensor and updates the application's UI
        hr = GetSensorData(pSensor, pNewData);
    }
    else
    {
        hr = E_UNEXPECTED;
    }
    return hr;
}
```

Here you can see that after verifying that the sensor and its data report are valid (not null pointers), you call a helper function, *GetSensorData*, that reads the LUX value from the sensor report and updates the application's UI. This is the same helper function we described in the "Reading Sensor Data Synchronously" section.

The *OnStateChange* event is also an important event to handle. This is mainly because when you ask a user to enable a sensor, if the user does enable the sensor, you can expect the sensor to generate a state change event. In this case, the state change event indicates that the sensor state has changed from SENSOR_STATE_ACCESS_DENIED to SENSOR_STATE_READY. When implementing the *OnStateChanged* event handler, you should handle all the possible states a sensor can have, which were described in the "What Is a Sensor?" section earlier in the chapter. The following code snippet is the simple (and not complete) implementation of the *OnStateChanged* method in our Ambient Light application.

```
HRESULT CAmbientLightAwareSensorEvents::OnStateChanged(ISensor *pSensor, SensorState state)
{
    HRESULT hr = S_OK;
    if (NULL != pSensor)
    {
```

```
        SENSOR_ID idSensor = GUID_NULL;
        hr = pSensor->GetID(&idSensor);
        if (SUCCEEDED(hr))
        {
            if (SENSOR_STATE_READY == state)
            {
                hr = GetSensorData(pSensor);
            }
            else
            {
                // If the sensor is not ready, its lux value is ignored
                m_mapLux[idSensor] = -1.0;
                hr = UpdateLux();
            }
        }
    }
    else
    {
        hr = E_POINTER;
    }
    return hr;
}
```

Here you can see that first you verify the sensor state, and if it's ready, you synchronously read its data using the *GetSensorData* method that we described in the "Reading Sensor Data Synchronously" section.

Setting Sensor Event Sinking

There is just one more thing you need to do to receive sensor events. You need to register your *ISensorEvents* implementation to specify the interface that receives sensor event notifications. We touched upon this topic in the "Discovering Sensors" section earlier in the chapter. During the Ambient Light application initialization phase, for each sensor you discover, you call the *AddSensor* function. This is a helper function that sets up event sinking for a specific sensor, and its code looks like this:

```
HRESULT CAmbientLightAwareSensorManagerEvents::AddSensor(ISensor *pSensor)
{
    HRESULT hr = S_OK;
    if (NULL != pSensor)
    {
        hr = pSensor->SetEventSink(m_pSensorEvents);
        if (SUCCEEDED(hr))
        {
            // Get the sensor's ID to be used as a key to store the sensor
            SENSOR_ID idSensor = GUID_NULL;
            hr = pSensor->GetID(&idSensor);
            if (SUCCEEDED(hr))
            {
                // Enter the sensor into the map and take the ownership of its lifetime
                pSensor->AddRef(); // the sensor is released in the destructor
                m_Sensors[idSensor] = pSensor;
```

```
            }
        }
    }
    else
    {
        hr = E_POINTER;
    }
    return hr;
}
```

Here you can see that you call the *ISensor::SetEventSink* method for a sensor to set up event sinking for the sensor. You pass *m_pSensorEvents*, which is a pointer to the *CAmbientLightAwareSensorEvents* class that implements the *ISensorEvents* interface. This is the class that implements, among other things, *OnStateChanged*, which you saw in the previous section.

Reading Sensor Data Using Managed Code

As expected, the *Microsoft.WindowsAPICodePack.Sensors* namespace provides similar functionality to the native API. You can read sensor data synchronously as well as register for events such as state changes or data report changes. The sensor leave event is handled by the *SensorManager* class, as explained in the "Discovering Sensors Using Managed Code" section earlier in the chapter. There is no managed code event equivalent to the *ISensorEvents::OnEvent*.

Although using the native API, you need to know which data fields you want to read from, the data report, and the data types. However, when using the *Microsoft.WindowsAPICodePack.Sensors* namespace you have another option. The *Microsoft.WindowsAPICodePack.Sensors* namespace includes several strongly typed sensor classes that expose .NET properties, and these classes represent specific values of a given sensor data report. For example, you can find *AmbientLightSensor* (a strongly typed light sensor), which has a public property, *CurrentLuminousIntensity*, that represents the latest amount of light (LUX) detected by the ambient light sensor. This is the same float value you saw in the previous section that can be found in *ISensorDataReport* for an ambient light sensor. Therefore, when using the Windows Code pack API, you can use the typed sensor classes and easily access their data values. The following code snippet illustrates how easy it is to read a data report from a strongly typed sensor class:

```
// Try read a new data report and update the managed data values
if (als.TryUpdateData())
{
    float current = als.CurrentLuminousIntensity.Intensity;
    // set intial progress bar value
    pb.Value = Math.Min((int)current, maxIntensity);
```

```
    _lblLux.Text = current.ToString();
}
```

First you synchronously call the *als.TryUpdateData* method, which is a wrapper method that calls the native *ISensor::GetData*. If this method requests a data update from the sensors and returns true if the platform successfully obtained new read from the light sensor, and it is safe to read the LUX value using a special property of *AmbientLightSensor*. Then we simply update the different UI elements in the form to reflect the new values. As with the native API, *Sensor.TryUpdateData* is a blocking method. This was done to try and follow similar programming API and promotes consistency with the native API. The internal wrapper also updates the sensor internal data report structure with the latest data report values. The managed Sensor API also exposes the *Sensor.UpdateData* method, which, like the *TryUpdateData* method, synchronously request data update from the sensor. But this method throws an exception if the request failed. Internally both the *UpdateData* and *TryUpdateData* are using the same interop layers to request sensor data update. You can look for yourself in the Windows API Code pack code for Sensor.cs.

If you want to read the sensor's data values using its data report, you can use the *Sensor.DataReport* object, as shown in the following code snippet:

```
// Using generic sensor data report to extract Light Sensor data report values
IList<Object> value;
float luxVal;
SensorReport sensorDataReport = sender.DataReport;
SensorData sensorDataReportValues = sensorDataReport.Values;
if (sensorDataReportValues.TryGetValue
    (
        SensorPropertyKeys.SENSOR_DATA_TYPE_LIGHT_LUX.FormatId,
        out value
    )
  )
{
    luxVal = (float)value.ElementAt<object>(0);
}
else
{
    //handle error
}
```

In this example, you can see how you read a sensor data report, *Sensor.DataReport*, and then extract all the values of that report into a *SensorData* object, which is a dictionary of GUID keys and a list of objects that are used as values. These are the actual native API GUID keys and values of the Sensor API. You call the *TryGetValue* method on the *sensorDataReport.Values* object to extract a single value, the Light LUX value. Note that you pass a GUID-based key in the form of *SensorPropertyKeys.SENSOR_DATA_TYPE_LIGHT_LUX.FormatId*, which is the same GUID you used in the native example shown in the previous section.

Handling Sensor Events Using Managed Code

To asynchronously receive data reports from a sensor, you need to register your implementation for the *Sensor.DataReportChangedEventHandler*. After adding your handler to the sensor's *DataReportChanged* event, you are set to receive and handle the sensor's data change event. As with any .NET event handler, the *DataReportChangedEventHandler* includes two parameters: a sender object that is a *Sensor* object, and an *EventArgs* object that in this case is just an empty argument object (because the updated data is found in the sensor data report). The following code snippet shows the implementation of the event handler of the changed data report:

```
void DataReportChanged(Sensor sender, EventArgs e)
{
    /* Using strongly typed AmbientLightSensor special properties */
    AmbientLightSensor als = sender as AmbientLightSensor;
    float luxVal = als.CurrentLuminousIntensity.Intensity;
    // Update UI on a different thread because the sensor event is received on the non UI
        thread

    BeginInvoke(

        new UpdateSensorUIValuesDelegate(UpdateSensorUIValues),

        new object[] { sender.SensorId, luxVal }

            );

}
```

In this code, you cast the *Sender* object to a strongly typed *AmbientLightSensor* object. After that, you call *AmbientLightSensor*-specific properties to read the sensor's data report values, such as the *CurrentLuminousIntensity* value. Last, you call *BeginInvoke*, passing a delegate that is basically a function that updates the UI. You need to call *BeginInvoke* because the *Sensor* and *Location* events arrive on a non-UI thread and therefore are not allowed to directly change any UI elements.

The *Microsoft.WindowsAPICodePack.Sensors* namespace also allows you to handle the sensor state change event. Similar to the data report change event, your implementation of *Sensor.StateChangedEventHandler* is a standard .NET event handler that receives a sender object, which is a *Sensor* object and an empty *EventArg*. As before, you cast the sender object to an *AmbientLightSensor* and simply use its .NET properties, which is a lot easier than using directly the sensor data report as shown in the following code snippet:

```
void sensor_StateChanged(Sensor sender, EventArgs e)
{
    AmbientLightSensor als = sender as AmbientLightSensor;
    if (als != null &&
        als.State != SensorState.Ready)
    {
        // The sensor's changed event comes in on a non-UI thread.
        // Whip up an anonymous delegate to handle the UI update.
        BeginInvoke(new MethodInvoker(delegate
        {
            PopulatePanel();
        }));
    }
    else
    {
        DataReportChanged(sender, e);
    }
}
```

Ambient Light Sensor Application

Throughout the chapter, you have seen code snippets and the partial implementation of methods of light-aware applications: one using the native API and another using the .NET-managed code API. But in addition to just showing you how to use the API, we want to further explain the reasons for using the Sensor and Location platform to build light-aware applications.

Because we wanted to focus on the API, our application is a simple ambient light–aware application. This application illustrates how to use the Sensor and Location platform APIs and skips the fancy graphics. Thus, this application has a very simple user interface that displays the amount of light detected by a light sensor, the number of light sensors, and optimized text. The following picture shows the application before connecting any light sensors to the computer. Note there are zero sensors and no LUX value.

This application is a light-aware application. Perhaps the most important optimizations of such applications are improvements to legibility and improving user interactions in direct sunlight because screens do not typically perform well in these conditions. Windows 7 ships with the Adaptive Brightness service, which monitors ambient light sensors to detect changes in ambient light and adjust the primary display brightness. But if you want to further optimize the end user's experience with your application, to provide better readability under strong lighting conditions (such as direct sunlight) you can consider performing the following steps:

- ***Increasing the displayed content contrast.***   *When your screen is exposed to a strong light source, it's saturated with light, which makes it harder to distinguish between the various dark areas on the screen. Increasing the contrast increases the separation between the different areas, thus making it easier to distinguish between them.*

- ***Reducing the use of color to increase the contrast.***   *Using a wide range of color creates a very compelling user interface. However, most of the colors get lost if the computer screen is exposed to a strong light source. The subtle differences separating the colors get lost under these conditions. Gradually reducing the use of colors in the application as the amount of detected light (by the sensors) increases results in a bigger contrast, which yields a better reading experience.*

- ***Scale.***   *In general, larger objects are easier to see. When the computer is in adverse lighting conditions, making content larger can help to improve the legibility of that content. This is especially true for font size. Increasing the font size in the application as the amount of detected light (by the sensors) increases will yield a far better reading experience under direct sunlight than a nonoptimized version of the application.*

The following image shows the Virtual Light Sensor that ships in the Windows 7 SDK.

Summary

In this chapter, you were introduced to the Sensor and Location platform in Windows 7. By now, you should understand what a sensor is and how sensors interact with the operating system and with your application. First, you need to obtain a sensor by reviewing all the available sensors, and then you can try reading the sensor data, changing sensor properties, or registering to receive notifications from the sensor. We focused on the Sensor API, and you saw both native and managed code implementations. Last, we explained some reasons and techniques for creating a light-aware application that optimizes the way content is displayed.

In the next chapter, we'll focus on the *location* part of the Sensor and Location platform.

Chapter 10
Tell Me Where I Am: Location-Aware Applications

In the previous chapter, you were introduced to the Sensor API of the Sensor and Location Platform. This chapter talks about the second part of that platform, known as the Location API. The Location API is built on top of the Sensor API and focuses on providing an answer to a single question: Where am I? Or, more specifically, what is my current, most up-to-date, location?

In this chapter, you will learn the reasons for having a dedicated set of APIs only for Location, as a subset of the Sensor and Location Platform. You will learn how the Location API uses the Sensor APIs to provide a higher level of abstraction for developers. Then we dive into the API and go through the specifics of working with the Location API to create a console application that prints your current location geo-coordinates and address.

Although the Location API can be viewed, and certainly learned, as an independent set of APIs, some concepts in this chapter are based on the Sensor API and are explained in great detail in Chapter 9, "Introduction to the Sensor and Location Platform." Therefore, we recommend that you review that chapter first to get a complete picture of the entire platform.

Why Location Awareness Is So Important

Let's begin with a short explanation of why a different set of APIs is used just for getting location information. Location-based services are becoming very popular on mobile devices because they offer great productivity gains and ease of use. Because more and more mobile PCs are being sold, it makes sense to add a location API to Microsoft Windows. Location awareness can enable some interesting scenarios. For example, when you're traveling to a different time zone, it would be nice if your computer automatically detected the change in location and adjusted the time, just as many mobile phones do today. Similarly, it would be nice if all other location-related information changed also, such as weather information. Another nice feature would be automatic geo-tagging of photos or any other information related to your location. When I am on the road, I like to taste local cuisine; it would be helpful to be able to just type "Great Italian restaurants within a 5-mile radius" in the browser search box and press Enter. The returned results would then display Italian restaurants within a five-mile radius of my current location.

There are other implementations for location-aware functionality, such as security. For example, imagine a computer that works or provides some unique functionality only when located in a specific and predefined area. With the Location API, the computer knows its location and can detect changes. If the computer leaves the allowed area, it notifies the user and eventually locks the specific features. Other scenarios include tracking inventory or managing large computer deployments in an IT organization. Imagine computers knowing their exact location based on Internet Protocol and the triangulation of Wi-Fi hot spots.

There are more obvious applications of this functionality, such as navigation. For example, Microsoft Street and Trips displays an interactive map showing your current location based on Global Positioning System (GPS) provider (device). But when running on Windows 7, such applications can use the Location Platform and other location providers, rather than just being bound to a physical GPS device.

These are just a few examples of location-aware applications. They illustrate common scenarios that can be incorporated into many existing applications and are therefore good reasons for Microsoft creating a specific Location API.

Because the Location API is based on the Sensor API, it inherits all of the Sensor API capabilities that we described in the previous chapter. This includes *concurrency*, or enabling multiple applications to access location information at the same time. Also, because the Location API is based on the Sensor API, there is no need for you to learn vendor-specific APIs for a GPS device or even an IP resolver. You just use the simple API that the platform provides.

Location Platform Architecture

The *location* part of the Sensor and Location Platform focuses on providing accurate and up-to-date location information as well as an easy way to access that information. When thinking about location devices, your first thought might be a GPS device. However, there are other location devices, such as Wi-Fi and broadband triangulation, IP Resolver, or user-entered data (for example, the user's address). As we mentioned before, in Windows 7 Sensor and Location Platform all these devices are actually sensors. To be accurate, all these share the same *SensorCategoryID* value: SENSOR_CATEGORY_LOCATION. Therefore, they are considered location sensors. Except for the GPS sensors, all the above-mentioned location sensors are virtual sensors.

As with any regular sensor, you can access these directly using the Sensor API. However, if you choose to go down that path, you are forced to access each location sensor and extract the location information from its data report. In this case, it is your responsibility to decide which sensor provides more accurate location information and to manage any change to the sensor's state. Also, you are expected to understand the scenario and decide which location device is the best to use. Do you use the more accurate GPS, which works well only in outdoor conditions, or do you use the IP Resolver, which works great indoors?

This is where the location part of the Location and Sensor Platform kicks into action. The Location API uses the Sensor API to abstract all the information about the different location sensors that are connected to the computer: their availability and what location information they provide. The Location API focuses on providing the most accurate and up-to-date location information regardless of which sensor device actually contributed the location data report. As shown in Figure 10-1, the Location API is an additional layer above the Sensor API that uses the Sensor API as any other application would to manage the most accurate location information.

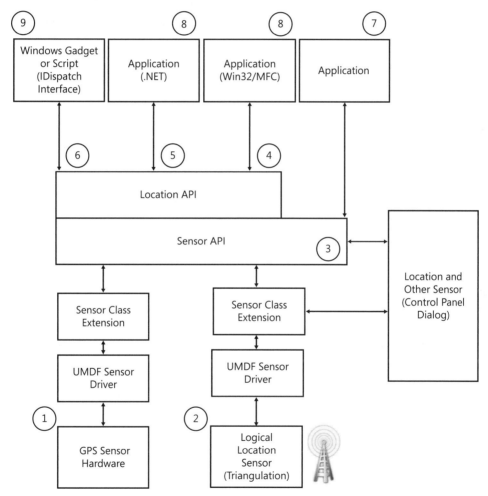

Figure 10-1 Sensor and Location Platform architectural diagram

This is the complete Sensor and Location Platform architecture diagram. In this diagram, we added the location pieces of the platform to the version shown in the previous chapter.

As mentioned before, location devices are sensors; therefore, it all starts with a sensor device—in our case, a GPS sensor. A GPS sensor is a physical hardware device that is connected to the computer, as shown by number 1 in Figure 10-1. To properly work with the Windows 7 Sensor and Location Platform, any sensor device (physical or logical) requires a Windows 7 Sensor and Location driver.

We explained the role of the User Mode Driver and Sensor Class Extensions in the previous chapter. In the previous chapter, we also mentioned that sensors can be logical (virtual) sensors, and that is the case with most other location sensors that are not GPS based. IP Resolver, Wi-Fi, and broadband triangulation are all logical location sensors that are connected to the computer, as shown by number 2. After a sensor (physical or logical) is installed and integrated, this sensor becomes discoverable to an application via the Sensor API, shown as number 3. Any application can directly access sensors using the Sensor API, as depicted by number 7 and as explained in the previous chapter.

The Sensor and Location Platform, through the Location API, exposes three sets of programming models to retrieve location information. A C++ COM-based API that exposes a set of interfaces and objects that you can work with to get location data reports and notification about changes in the location, as shown as number 4. There is an equivalent managed code API for .NET developers, shown as number 5, which we describe later in the book in the "Application Using .NET" section. Any application can access the Location API, shown as number 8. Note that, as with the Sensor API, the Location API supports concurrent access, thereby enabling multiple applications to retrieve location information using the Location API at the same time.

The third programming model that exposes location information is the scripting model; it does this by using the Location IDispatch Interface, shown as number 6. This is an ActiveX object that enables scripting languages, such as Java Script, access to the location information. These objects provide similar functionality as the C++ API, and they enable you to create Windows gadgets and Web pages that are location aware. For example, Figure 10-2 shows two gadgets: on the left, a location-aware weather gadget that ships with Windows 7; on the right, a locations gadget that displays different types of venues within a certain radius from the user's current location like coffee shops, restaurant, movie theaters, or in our example, public parks.

Figure 10-2 Location-aware gadgets in Windows 7

Note that the Location API is not marked as safe for scripting. It is designed to be used in scripts that run in the Local Computer zone, and therefore is perfect for Windows Gadgets.

Location Devices Are Regular Windows 7 Sensors

A location device is just a regular Windows 7 sensor. You can access any Windows 7 Location sensor directly via the Sensor and Location APIs, as we explained in Chapter 9. However, if you choose to access location devices directly and not use the Location API, you have to perform a few tasks to make sure you have the most updated and accurate location information. Because there might be multiple location sensors connected to your PC, you need to obtain all the location sensors and be aware of their status and availability. You also need to register for DataReport notifications and handle any data updates for all the location sensors. Then you need to read each data report from each location sensor, understand the sensor type and its data report data values, extract the location information, and then compare all sensors to conclude which location sensor provides the most accurate and up-to-date location information. (Any location sensor's data report includes an error radius data field that can be used to compare accuracy.) Assuming you are familiar with the Sensor API, performing all these procedures is not that difficult. However, because location-based services are a common user need, and because nearly every computer connected to the Internet has a valid IP address, most computers can have an IP Resolver location sensor (a virtual sensor) installed. Therefore, it makes sense for Windows to provide a platform that will do all the previously mentioned heavy lifting for you and shield you from interacting directly with the lower-level Sensor API, which is exactly what the Location API is doing for you.

Because location devices are sensors, you can access all the sensor properties (via the Sensor API), such as the sensor's friendly name or the manufacturer's name. You can also access specific sensor data report values. For a sensor to be considered a location sensor, the following three data values must be included in its data report:

- **Latitude**   The angular distance north or south of Earth's equator, measured in degrees along a meridian, as on a map or globe.

- **Longitude**   The angular distance on Earth's surface, measured east or west from the prime meridian at Greenwich, England, to the meridian passing through a position, expressed in degrees (or hours, minutes, and seconds).

- **Error Radius**   Measured in meters and combined with the reported location as the origin, this radius describes the circle within which the actual location might exist.

These are the minimum fields required from each location sensor. Most likely, you'll find additional information in the location sensor data report. However, to access that information you will need to use the Sensor API and know exactly which data values you want to obtain. From the location data report, you can get the sensor ID of the sensor that contributes the current location data report. Using that sensor ID, you can obtain a pointer to the *ISensor* interface. With an *ISensor* interface at hand, you can get extra information—for example, a GPS location sensor might include in its data report the number of satellites in its view or your current speed if you are in motion (as with a navigation application).

Location Information Is Sensitive Information

Because location devices are sensors and the Location API is based on the Sensor API, it inherits the Sensor Platform's security model. Also, because location devices can reveal sensitive information about your whereabouts, location providers are not enabled by default. As with the any other sensor, a location sensor needs to be enabled by the user in advance to enable your application to access and receive location data reports from it. Therefore, just like any other sensor, you have to ask the user to enable any location sensor that is not enabled. We'll describe how to request a user to enable a location sensor later in this chapter in the "Requesting Location Permissions" section.

If at least one location sensor is connected to the computer and enabled, the Location API caches its location data. This means that location information is stored on the computer; it can be detailed information about the current location or a history of location information. Because location information is sensitive, you might not want to share it with anyone else. Because the Location Platform caches location data, it is important to remove that information at some point. Therefore, in addition to requesting the user to enable location devices, the Location Platform makes sure that any data that has been collected from a given location sensor is deleted after a location device is disabled (from the Location And Other Sensors dialog found in Windows 7 Control Panel) or disconnected from the computer (in the case of physical devices).

Working with the Location API

It is time to dive into the Location API. We'll do so while creating a Win32 console application that reads a location report, handles location events, and then prints this information to the console. Because the Location API is built on top of the Sensor API, the flow of applications that use the Location API is similar to the flow used in applications that use the Sensor API. The flow looks like this:

- Obtaining a location interface, *ILocation*, which is a COM interface. This is the main interface, and it provides methods used to manage location reports, event registration, and sensor permissions.

- Requesting permission for any location providers that are not enabled.

- Interacting with the location interface by reading location reports and handling location events.

Understanding How the Location API Works

ILocation is main interface through which you gain access to location reports, register for location events, and ask for location sensor permission. You can think about this interface as being equivalent to the *ISensorManager* interface found in the Sensor API (and described in detail in Chapter 9). However, there is one fundamental difference between the function that *ISensorManager* performs and the function *ILocation* does. The *ISensorManager* interface's main function is to provide you with a channel through which you can discover sensors that are connected to the computer and through which you can gain access to an individual sensor (to request permission for a sensor and obtain the *ISensor* interface). Then you can read the sensor's data report or register for events. On the other hand, the *ILocation* interface's main function is to provide methods to access location reports and to register for location change notification events. The difference between *ISensorManager* and *ILocation* is that the *ILocation* interface is used to access actual location data, in the form of location reports, and not just location sensors.

You can think of the *ILocation* interface as a façade for all the location sensors. The main goal of the *ILocation* interface is to provide you with the most accurate and up-to-date location reports. You should not really care whether the data found in the location report originated from the GPS sensor or from an IP Resolver sensor, as long as the location report is accurate and up to date.

The Location Platform performs all the heavy lifting for you, working with all the location sensors at the same time. It aggregates all the location information from all the enabled location sensors, and it presents you with a single location report that contains the most accurate location data, as shown in Figure 10-3.

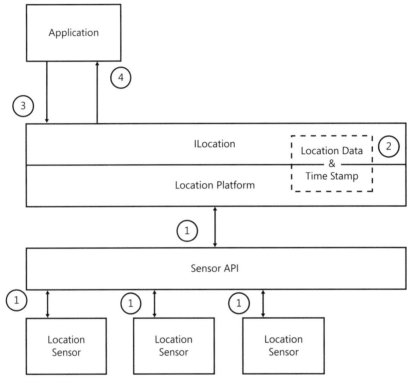

Figure 10-3 Location API process for retrieving accurate location information

The Location Platform reads sensor data reports from all enabled location sensors, as depicted by step number 1 in Figure 10-3. Then it calculates which sensor data report represents the most accurate location data. This can be done because the error radius value is found in each location sensor data report. The Location Platform also registers for data and status updates from all the enabled location sensors. Therefore, each time one of the enabled location sensors generates a data update event (*ISensorEvents::OnDataUpdated*), the Location Platform checks whether this new location sensor report contains more accurate location information than the already existing location report, again based on the error radius. If the new sensor location data report is more accurate than the existing one, the Location Platform caches the new sensor data report and its received time stamp, as shown by number 2. At this point, the Location Platform has new location information that is available to read (or to notify the user of) through the *ILocation* interface. When you read a location report using the *ILocation* interface, you receive the latest and most accurate location report, as shown by number 3.

You can also register to receive location notifications, generated when new location data is available, as shown by number 4.

A location report contains a *GetSensorID* method through which you can gain access to the actual sensor that contributed the location information to the current location report. By doing so, you can bypass the Location API and interact directly with the location sensor the same way you do while using the Sensor API. However, if you are just interested in the location information, there is no need to access individual location sensors.

Working with the *ILocation* Inferface

The *ILocation* interface is your main interface with the Location Platform. After you obtain this interface, you can do the following:

- **Request permissions to enable location providers**   This is useful if not all location sensors are enabled.

- **Request location reports**   This allows you to read the location report synchronously.

- **Subscribe to location report events**   This enables you to receive notifications when new location data is available.

- **Unsubscribe from location report events**   This enables you to stop listening for notifications about location data.

- **Check the status of a type of report**   This allows you to check whether the status of a particular location report is valid.

- **Get or set the time interval between report events**   This allows you to set the data report interval just as you can do with the Sensor API; you can retrieve or set the minimum amount of time, in milliseconds, between report events.

Obtaining a Location Interface

By now, you understand that you need to get your hands on an *ILocation* interface. So let's get one. Before using the Location API interface, you must first call the COM *CoCreateInstance* method to create an instance of the *ILocation* interface. The code is really simple, as shown in the following code snippet:

```
// This is the main Location interface
CComPtr<ILocation> spLocation;
// Create the Location object
if (FAILED(spLocation.CoCreateInstance(CLSID_Location)))
{
    //handle error
    wprintf(L"Failed to create Location COM object.\n");
    return 1;
}
```

Assuming you succeed in creating the *ILocation* interface, you are all set to start working with the Location Platform. Your first step is to make sure that there are some enabled location sensors; if there are not any enabled location sensors, you need to request the user to enable some of these location sensors.

Requesting Location Permissions

Just like the Sensor API, the Location API provides a method you can use to prompt the user for permission to enable a location provider. It is required that users enable location providers before your program can access any location data.

If there are disabled location sensors that must be enabled for a report type to work, you can have your application request permission to enable these sensors by calling the *ILocation::RequestPermissions* method, as shown in the following code snippet:

```
// Array of report types of interest.
IID REPORT_TYPES[] = { IID_ILatLongReport, IID_ICivicAddressReport };
// Request permissions for this user account to receive location data for all the
// types defined in REPORT_TYPES

if (FAILED(spLocation->RequestPermissions
                        (NULL,
                        REPORT_TYPES,
                        ARRAYSIZE(REPORT_TYPES),
                        TRUE))) // TRUE means a synchronous request
{
    //handle error
    wprintf(L"Warning: Unable to request permissions.\n");
}
```

Here you can see that the *RequestPermissions* method expects an array of report types, REPORT_TYPES, that you want to enable, and we also need to pass the size of the array. Depending on whether any location sensors have been installed, the dialog box displayed to the user might be the Enable Location Sensors dialog box, as shown in the following image:

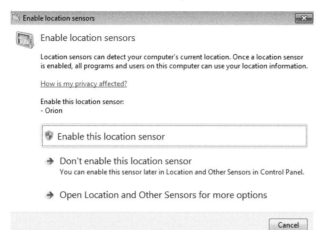

Default Location

There are some scenarios where all the location sensors on a computer are unavailable—for example, if the computer is situated indoors, the GPS receiver has no reception, and there is no available IP to trace. To provide some sort of back-up location information, the Sensor and Location Platform is equipped with a way for you to set the default location. To access the Default Location dialog, you need to open Control Panel and click on Location And Other Sensors. Then click the Default Location link in the bottom right corner. Another option for displaying this dialog is by calling the *ILocation::RequestPermissions* method. If no location sensors are installed and no default location has been provided in Control Panel, Windows opens the Enter A Default Location dialog for this computer.

The Location API provides a default location interface: the *IDefaultLocation* interface. Using this interface, you can set and get the default location information.

Interacting with the Location Interface

So far, you've seen how to obtain a location interface and ask for permission to access the different location sensors. It is almost time to read your first location report. However, before reading a location report, you need to understand the different location report types and then verify the report's status to make sure you can read it.

Location Reports Type

The Location Platform provides convenient reports through which you can access actual location information. For example the Lat-Long report, exposed through the *ILatLongReport* interface, includes information such as the latitude and longitude coordinates. Another useful report is the Civic Address report, exposed through the *ICivicAddressReport* interface, which we describe later in this section. The Lat-Long and Civic Address reports are the two most used location reports the Location API provides.

The *ILocationReport* is the base interface for all the different types of location reports. You can obtain a location report by calling the *ILocation::GetReport* method. After you obtain an *ILocationReport* interface, you can call the following methods:

- **GetSensorID**   The return value represents the identification number of the location sensor that contributed the current (in this data report) location information. If you want to interact directly with the sensors, you can pass the sensor ID to the *ISensorManager::GetSensorByID* method to obtain an *ISensor* interface. Doing so gives you full access to the sensor through the *ISensor* interface that is part of the Sensor Platform.

- **GetTimeStamp**   This value represents the time stamp indicating when the report was received by the Location API. This time value reflects the computer's local time.

- **GetValue**   Retrieves a property value from the location report. This method is equivalent to the *ISensor::GetProperty* method that is used to retrieve property values in a sensor. With this, you can get values such as the sensor's friendly name, its model, or its serial number. For example, by passing the SENSOR_PROPERTY_LOCATION_DESIRED_ACCURACY value as input parameter you can read the value that indicates the type of accuracy-handling requested by the client application, that is, your application.

The *ILocationReport* methods are very basic and don't really provide any extra value over using the Sensor API. You need to remember that the *ILocationReport* interface is the base interface for two other much more useful location reports: *ILatLongReport* (Lat-Long report) and *ICivicAddressReport* (Civic Address report), which are introduced next. However, the *ILocationReport::GetValue* method provides you an extendibility point through which you can query extra information directly from the location sensor. For example, if you know the sensor ID, you can check whether the sensor is a GPS location sensor. If the sensor's type is a GPS type, you can use the *GetValue* method to try and retrieve extra information that is specific to a GPS location sensor. It is most likely that in addition to the latitude and longitude value, a GPS sensor data report includes a data field that represents the number of satellites in view. A careful look in the Sensors.h file (part of the Windows 7 SDK) reveals a wide range of GPS data type values in the form of GUIDs, such as SENSOR_DATA_TYPE_SATELLITES_IN_VIEW. Passing this GUID to the *GetValue* method results in a *propvariant* return value, which holds an integer representing the number of satellites in view.

The following list provides detailed information about the two most used location reports: the Lat-Long and Civic Address reports.

The *ILatLongReport* interface represents a location report that contains location data values such as longitude and latitude. This interface inherits from the *ILocationReport* interface and provides additional functionality, such as the following:

- **GetLongitude** and **GetLatitude** **methods**   Each method returns a double type value representing the current latitude and longitude values.

- *GetErrorRadius* **method**   The returned value of this method indicates the error radius of the location sensor. Combined with the reported location (longitude and latitude values) as the origin, this radius describes the circle within which the actual location might exist. The value of the error radius depends on the GPS hardware and number of satellites in view. But GPS devices tend to be accurate location devices, and the error radius value is usually less than 25 meters (about 75 feet).

- *GetAltitude* **and** *GetAltitudeError*   These values indicate the current altitude and the error radius, respectively. Combining the location information, location error radius, altitude, and altitude error, you can create a sphere within which the actual location might exist. Note that not all location drivers support altitude and altitude error values, and therefore they are optional.

The *ICivicAddressReport* interface represents a location report that contains location information in the form of a street address and includes data values such as address 1, city, and postal code. This interface inherits from the *ILocationReport* interface and provides additional functionality, such as the following:

- *GetAddressLine1, GetAddressLine2, GetCity, GetCountryRegion, GetPostalCode, GetStateProvince*   All these functions return the corresponding values of the default location, as shown in the "Default Location" section earlier in this chapter.

- *GetDetailedLevel*   Retrieves a value that indicates the level of detail provided by the Civic Address report. This value indicates the accuracy of the Civic Address report. The detail level of the Civic Address report is based on a scale of 1 through 5, depending on how much data has been entered in the Location And Sensor Default Location dialog. The following table defines the detailed values according to the location data values:

Detail level	Meaning
1	Address 1 or Address 2
2	Postal code
3	City
4	State or province
5	Country or region

The accuracy of the Civic Address report is equal to the lowest number that has values for every preceding field (as shown in the preceding table). For example, if the country and city names are filled in, the accuracy of the Civic Address report is 3. But if the country and the postal code values are filled in, the accuracy of the Civic Address report is 2, because the postal code provides better location resolution than just the name of the city.

Understanding the Location Report Status

The previous section introduced the concept of location reports. To get one of the two report types provided by the Location API (either Lat-Long or Civic Address), you need to use the *ILocation::GetReport* method. Each location report type has a Report Status value. This value summarizes the ability of the location API to provide valid location information for each report type. Because the *ILocation* interface acts as a façade for all the location sensors, to get a specific location report status, you need to call the *ILocation::GetReportStatus* method.

To provide clarity with regard to the Location API's ability to provide accurate location information, the *ILocation* interface exposes the *GetReportStatus* method. The report status return value, returned through the second parameter (which is an out parameter) of this method defines the possible operational states for the Location API with regard to new reports of a particular report type. The *ILocation::GetReportStatus* method expects a report type as an input parameter, which defines the specific report type. The second parameter is a pointer to a LOCATION_REPORT_STATUS enumeration (enum) that will hold the report type status value, which indicates the ability of the *ILocation* interface to provide you with accurate information regarding that report type location report.

Here are the values of the LOCATION_REPORT_STATUS enumeration:

- **REPORT_NOT_SUPPORTED**   Indicates that the requested report type is not supported by the API. Generally, this value indicates there is no such location device installed. In the case of a Civic Address report, this value indicates that the default location is not set.

- **REPORT_ERROR**   Indicates that there was some internal error while creating the report.

- **REPORT_ACCESS_DENIED**   Indicates that you don't have permission to access any of the location sensors that support the requested location report type.

- **REPORT_INITIALIZING**   Indicates that the sensor is not ready to provide location information. For example, a GPS location sensor that is waiting to lock additional satellite signals might be in its initializing state.

- **REPORT_RUNNING**   Indicates that the report is valid and you can read accurate up-to-date location information.

By default, the default location is not set. The user has to manually type his default location if he wants to provide this location for programs to use when a location sensor, such as a GPS, is unavailable. Note that once this is set, all programs on the computer can use the default location. This means that once it is set, the report status for the Civic Address report type is REPORT_RUNNING. If the default location is empty, the report status for the Civic Address report type is REPORT_NOT_SUPPORTED.

The following code snippet illustrates how to get the status of a Lat-Long location report:

```
// The LOCATION_REPORT_STATUS enumeration is defined in locationapi.h in the SDK
LOCATION_REPORT_STATUS status = REPORT_NOT_SUPPORTED;
// Get the status of this report type
if (FAILED(spLocation->GetReportStatus(IID_ILatLongReport, &status)))
{
    //handle error
    wprintf(L"Error: Unable to obtain lat/long report status.\n");
    return 1;
}
switch (status)
{
    case REPORT_RUNNING:
        // If the status for the current report is running,
        // try reading the location report
        break;
    case REPORT_NOT_SUPPORTED:
        wprintf(L"\nNo devices detected.\n");
        break;
    case REPORT_ERROR:
        wprintf(L"\nReport error.\n");
        break;
    case REPORT_ACCESS_DENIED:
        wprintf(L"\nAccess denied to reports. Report not enabled.\n");
        break;
    case REPORT_INITIALIZING:
        wprintf(L"\nReport is initializing.\n");
        break;
}
```

As you can see, the code is self-explanatory. If you want to get the status report of the Civic Address location report, all you need to do is pass *IID_ICivicAddressReport* instead of *IID_LatLongReport*.

Reading Location Reports

Finally, after all the introductions, we can go ahead and read a location report. We already mentioned that the name of the method, *ILocation::GetReport*, is used to read a location report. Now it is time to explain how this method works and see a few code examples.

The following code illustrates how to read a Lat-Long location report. Assuming the status of the Lat-Long report is valid (REPORT_RUNNING), it is safe to read the location report. You need to call the *ILocation::GetReport* method, passing the type of location report you want to read (*IID_ILatLongReport*, in our case) and a pointer to *ILocationReport*. Remember that *ILocationReport* is the base interface for all location reports; therefore, it is safe to return as the out parameter of the *GetReport* method for all report location types. Next, you need to cast (actually, convert) the generic *ILocationReport* to the desired report type (*ILatLongReport*, in our case). You do this using the *QueryInterface* method, passing a pointer to the desired location report type pointer interface (using ATL and smart pointers). You then double-check that the conversation was successful by making sure the pointer of the desired location report is not null. This code snippet adds code to the REPORT_RUNNING case of the report status switch case shown in the previous code snippet:

```
case REPORT_RUNNING:
    // Get the current location report; then get the ILatLongReport interface from
ILocationReport
    // using QueryInterface; then ensure that it isn't NULL
    if ((SUCCEEDED(spLocation->GetReport
                    (IID_ILatLongReport, &spLocationReport))) &&
        (SUCCEEDED(spLocationReport->QueryInterface
                    (IID_PPV_ARGS(&spLatLongReport)))) )
    {
        // Print the Timestamp
        SYSTEMTIME systemTime;
        if (SUCCEEDED(spLatLongReport->GetTimestamp(&systemTime)))
        {
            PrintTimestamp(systemTime);
        }
        // Print the Sensor ID GUID information
        GUID sensorID = {0};
        if (SUCCEEDED(spLatLongReport->GetSensorID(&sensorID)))
        {
            PrintSensorGUID(sensorID);
        }
        // Print the report
        PrintLatLongReport(spLatLongReport);
    }
    else
    {
        //handle error
    }
    break;
```

After you get an *ILatLongReport* interface, you can read its various data values, such as the report's time stamp. Here you can see that you use few helper functions to print the actual values you read. The interesting helper function is *PrintLatLongReport*. This function, shown in the following code snippet, illustrates how to read different values from *ILatLongReport*:

```
void PrintLatLongReport(ILatLongReport *pLatLongReport)
{
    DOUBLE latitude = 0, longitude = 0, altitude = 0, errorRadius = 0, altitudeError = 0;
    wprintf(L"\nReport:\n");
    // Print the Latitude
    if (SUCCEEDED(pLatLongReport->GetLatitude(&latitude)))
    {
        wprintf(L"Latitude: %f\n", latitude);
    }
    else
    { /* handle error */ }
    // Print the Longitude
    if (SUCCEEDED(pLatLongReport->GetLongitude(&longitude)))
```

```
{
    wprintf(L"Longitude: %f\n", longitude);
}
else
{ /* handle error */ }
// Print the Error Radius
if (SUCCEEDED(pLatLongReport->GetErrorRadius(&errorRadius)))
{
    wprintf(L"Error Radius: %f\n", errorRadius);
}
else
{ /* handle error */ }
// Print the Altitude
if (SUCCEEDED(pLatLongReport->GetAltitude(&altitude)))
{
    wprintf(L"Altitude: %f\n", altitude);
}
else
{
    // Altitude is optional and may not be available
    wprintf(L"Altitude: Not available.\n");
}
// Print the Altitude Error
if (SUCCEEDED(pLatLongReport->GetAltitudeError(&altitudeError)))
{
    wprintf(L"Altitude Error: %f\n", altitudeError);
}
else
{
    // Altitude Error is optional and may not be available
    wprintf(L"Altitude Error: Not available.\n");
}
}
```

After you have a valid report object in hand, working with it is easy. Simply call the method that represents the data values you want to read. You might want to note that each Lat-Long location report must include valid latitude, longitude, and error radius values. All other values are optional. The result of calling the preceding code appears like this:

```
Lat./long. Report status: Report ready.
Timestamp: YY:2009, MM:8, DD:24, HH:6, MM:19, SS:12, MS:858
SensorID: {682F38CA-5056-4A58-B52E-B516623CF02F}
Lat-Long Report:
Latitude: 47.640352
Longitude: -122.130718
Error Radius: 0.000000
Altitude: 0.000000
Altitude Error: 0.000000
```

Registering for Location Events

In the last section, you saw how to synchronously read a Lat-Long location report. The Location API also provides event notifications through callback interfaces, supporting asynchronous reading of location reports and location report type status. To start getting location event notifications, you need to register your callback implementation. Before we jump into the actual callback implementation, let's take a look at how to register to start receiving location event notifications.

Our callback implementation class is *CLocationEvents*. This class has to inherit the *ILocationEvents* interface to enable the Location API to send event notifications to our class. First, you need to create an instance of this class. Our implementation uses ATL, so creating a new instance of *CLocationEvents* looks like this:

```
CComObject<CLocationEvents>* pLocationEvents = NULL;
// Create the object
if (FAILED(CComObject<CLocationEvents>::CreateInstance(&pLocationEvents)))

{
    // handle error
        wprintf(L"Error creation Location events sink.\n");
        return 1;
}
```

Now, you can register this class with the Location API as the callback implementation of *ILocationEvents*. To do so, you need to call the *ILocation::RegisterForReport* method. This method expects three input parameters: a pointer to the *ILocationEvents* implementation you just created; a report type ID, which is a GUID that represents the desired location report (either a Civic Address or Lat-Long report); and the last parameter, which is a requested report interval that specifies the desired elapsed time, in milliseconds, between event notifications for the specified report type. Here is a code snippet illustrating this registration process:

```
// Register for reports for ICivicAddressReport
pLocationEvents->AddRef();
if (FAILED(spLocation->RegisterForReport(pLocationEvents, IID_ICivicAddressReport, 0)))
{
    pLocationEvents->Release();
    wprintf(L"Error registering for report.\n");
    return 1;
}
// Register for reports for ILatLongReport
if (FAILED(spLocation->RegisterForReport(pLocationEvents, IID_ILatLongReport, 0)))
{
    pLocationEvents->Release();
    wprintf(L"Error registering for report.\n");
    return 1;
}
```

Note that you need to call *ILocation::RegisterForReport* twice, once for each report type. After you call these methods, the Location API starts sending location and status changed events to your callback implementation.

There is one more thing to remember. To stop receiving location events, or during application termination, you need to clean up and unregister the callback implementation. You need to unregister each report type callback implementation, as shown in the following code snippet:

```
//clean up
if (NULL != pLocationEvents)
{
    // Unregister for reports
    spLocation->UnregisterForReport(IID_ICivicAddressReport);
    spLocation->UnregisterForReport(IID_ILatLongReport);
    pLocationEvents->Release();
}
```

Handling Location Events

In the previous section, you saw how to register your callback implementation to location events to receive location event notifications. Let's review the *ILocationEvents* interface and see its implementation:

- **OnLocationChanged**   Called when a new location report is available

- **OnStatusChanged**   Called when a specific report status has changed

Note that both methods include a report type input parameter that specifies the report type associated with the events. For example, if you have a GPS location sensor attached to your computer, you can expect to receive *OnLocationChanged* and *OnStatusChanged* events with a Lat-Long report as the report type parameter.

The following code snippet illustrates an implementation of the *ILocationEvents::OnLocationChanged* callback method:

```
STDMETHODIMP CLocationEvents::OnLocationChanged
                          (REFIID reportType,
                           ILocationReport* pLocationReport)
{
    if (IID_ICivicAddressReport == reportType)
    {
        CComPtr<ICivicAddressReport> spCivicAddressReport;
        // Get the ICivicAddressReport interface from ILocationReport
        if ((SUCCEEDED(pLocationReport->QueryInterface
                    (IID_PPV_ARGS(&spCivicAddressReport)))) &&
            (NULL != spCivicAddressReport.p))
        {
            wprintf(L"Civic address location changed:\n\n");
            PrintCivicAddress(spCivicAddressReport);
        }
    }

    if(IID_ILatLongReport == reportType)
    {
        CComPtr<ILatLongReport> spLatLongReport;
```

```
        if ((SUCCEEDED(pLocationReport->QueryInterface
                        (IID_PPV_ARGS(&spLatLongReport)))) &&
            (NULL != spLatLongReport.p))
        {
            wprintf(L"Lat Long location changed:\n\n");
            PrintLatLongReport(spLatLongReport);
        }
    }
    return S_OK;
}
```

Here you can see that you check the type of the report and handle each report type differently. The second input parameter is the base class *ILocationReport* interface. After the report type is identified, you need to call the COM casting method, *QueryInterface*, passing the desired location report type. Last, you need to do something useful with the new location information. In our application, we simply print the location information to the console by calling the *PrintCivicAddress* helper function that is shown in the following code snippet:

```
void CLocationEvents::PrintCivicAddress(ICivicAddressReport *pCivicAddressReport)
{
    HRESULT hr = S_OK;
    DWORD dwDetailLevel;
    CComBSTR bstrAddress1;
    CComBSTR bstrAddress2;
    CComBSTR bstrPostalCode;
    CComBSTR bstrCity;
    CComBSTR bstrStateProvince;
    CComBSTR bstrCountryRegion;

    hr = pCivicAddressReport->GetAddressLine1(&bstrAddress1);
    if ((SUCCEEDED(hr)) && (bstrAddress1.Length() != 0))
    {
        wprintf(L"\tAddress Line 1:\t%s\n", bstrAddress1);
    }

    hr = pCivicAddressReport->GetAddressLine2(&bstrAddress2);
    if ((SUCCEEDED(hr)) && (bstrAddress2.Length() != 0))
    {
        wprintf(L"\tAddress Line 2:\t%s\n", bstrAddress2);
    }

    hr = pCivicAddressReport->GetPostalCode(&bstrPostalCode);
    if ((SUCCEEDED(hr)) && (bstrPostalCode.Length() != 0))
    {
        wprintf(L"\tPostal Code:\t%s\n", bstrPostalCode);
    }

    hr = pCivicAddressReport->GetCity(&bstrCity);
    if ((SUCCEEDED(hr)) && (bstrCity.Length() != 0))
    {
        wprintf(L"\tCity:\t\t%s\n", bstrCity);
    }
```

```
    hr = pCivicAddressReport->GetStateProvince(&bstrStateProvince);
    if ((SUCCEEDED(hr)) && (bstrStateProvince.Length() != 0))
    {
        wprintf(L"\tState/Province:\t%s\n", bstrStateProvince);
    }

    hr = pCivicAddressReport->GetCountryRegion(&bstrCountryRegion);
    if (SUCCEEDED(hr))
    {
        // Country/Region is an ISO-3166 two-letter code.
        wprintf(L"\tCountry/Region:\t%s\n\n", bstrCountryRegion);
    }
}
```

Putting It All Together

By now, you know all there is to know about the Location API. You saw how to obtain an *ILocation* interface through which you can request permission to enable location sensors, read location reports, and register to receive location event notifications. If you followed the code throughout this chapter, you have seen about 90 percent of our console application implementation. This application reads both the Lat-Long and Civic Address location reports, prints the reports to the console, and then registers to receive location event notifications for both Lat-Long and Civic Address reports. So, you should ask, "How can I test my great application?"

There are a few options for testing Sensor and Location Platform applications. By far the easiest way to test your new location-aware console application is to change the default location. By default, the Default Location field is empty. Once you click Apply to save to your new default location, the Location API triggers an *OnLocationChanged* notification for the Civic Address report. If your console-aware application is running at the same time you set the default location, you will see the results of the new location printed in the console, as shown in the following image.

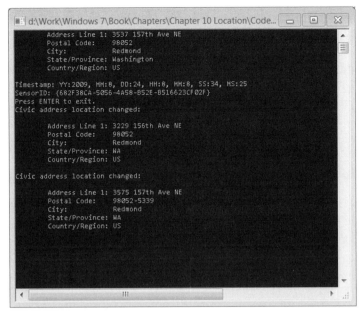

You can see that first the application reads and prints the existing civic address (because this is not the first time I have run the application). Next, the Default Location value is changed; the application receives a location event notification, reads the new Civic Address location reports, and prints the new civic address data field values. Similarly, if you delete the default location information, your application gets an *OnStatusChanged* event notification stating that the Civic Address report type is not supported.

Writing a Location-Aware Application Using .NET

Throughout the book, we used the Windows API Code Pack for the .NET Framework as our main .NET library for supporting new Windows 7 features. We used the Windows API Code Pack in Chapter 9 to work with the Sensor API. Unlike the Sensor API, the .NET version of the Location API was left out of the Windows API Code Pack. However, there is a set of .NET Location API wrappers that can be found on the Sensor and Location Web page on MSDN Developer for Windows 7 Web site (*http://code.msdn.microsoft.com/SensorsAndLocation*). From this Web site, you can download the Windows 7 Sensor and Location .NET Interop Sample Library, which is a fully working set of .NET assemblies for working with the Windows 7 Sensor and Location Platform. If you need to use sensors in your application, it is highly recommended that you use the Windows API Code Pack. However, because the Location API didn't make it into the Windows API Code Pack, it is recommended that you use this library for .NET location-aware applications. This is exactly what we are going to do right now. We are going to write a .NET console application that is similar in functionality to the native application we've seen so far.

In the .NET library, you will find Windows7.SensorAndLocation.dll, which holds the .NET location API namespace. The main namespace for the .NET Location API is *Windows7.Location*. Within that namespace, you can find the *LocationProvider* abstract class, which is the base class for the other location providers. This is the main difference between the .NET Location API and the native one. There is no equivalent .NET "Location Manager" class in the form of the native *ILocation*. *LocationProvider* is an abstract class that exposes the .NET methods, functions, and events equivalent to the native Location API that you saw earlier in this chapter. But you can't create a new instance of the *LocationProvider*. Instead, you have to use one of the location provider implementations: *LatLongLocationProvider* or *CivicAddressLocationProvider*.

By working with a specific location provider, the .NET API enables the creation of strongly typed objects in the form of specific location providers. Basically, these strongly typed location providers are a location report type that is a customized version of the native *ILocation* interface, which performs all the functions of a "location manager" for the specific location report type, such as Civic Address or Lat-Long.

Note that these .NET wrappers are just a thin layer of .NET glue and a little bit of logic to make it easy for .NET developers to work in a .NET-natural way with the Location API. Underneath the surface, everything that we described so far in this chapter still applies; that is, you still need to obtain a specific location provider, make sure the location sensors are enabled and, if they are not, ask permission to enable them. Next, you need to verify the status of the location provider, verifying its ability to provide a valid location report. Then you can read location information synchronously or register for location events for an asynchronous programming model.

LocationProvider includes the following public functions, events, and .NET properties you need to see before starting to program with the specific location provider:

- **ReportStatus**   Returns the current provider status. Similar to the way you used *ILocation::GetReportStatus* to check the availability of the Location API to provide the desired location report. This property provides the enumeration values for the specific report you are working with.

- **GetReport**   Synchronously returns a location report class, *LocationReport*, which is an abstract base class you need to cast to the desired location report type.

- **ReportInterval**   Gets or sets the desired update frequency of the location report interval, in milliseconds.

- **RequestPermission**   Requests the user's permission to access the given report types and location providers if the location sensors are disabled.

- **LocationChanged**   The event that generates notifications about location changes.

- **StatusChanged**   The event that generates notifications about provider status changes. For example, this event is called when a GPS location sensor loses all its satellites and can't provide a location report. *LatLongLocationProvider* sends this event, and *LatLongLocationProvider.Status* changes to reflect this change.

Looking into the *LocationProvider* class, you might notice a few functions that we did not mention yet—for example, *LocationProvider.GetDesiredAccuracy* and *LocationProvider.SetDesiredAccuracy*. These are used when you want to set the accuracy of the location report notification—that is, set the maximum error radius that you are willing to tolerate. Any report with a larger error radius will not be reported to your application; for example, if a given location sensor has a new location report, the new location report error radius value is 100, and you have set (using *LocationProvider.DesiredAccuracy*) the maximum error radius to 50, you will not receive the *LocationChanged* event. By default, the accuracy value is not set and any new location report, with any error radius, triggers the *LocationChanged* event. This is true for both the native and managed APIs.

Reading Location Reports and Handling Location Events

As we already mentioned, when using .NET you are using a strongly typed location provider. These are just regular classes that you can initiate. After you obtain such a location provider class, you can simply start using it. In our example, we use the *CivicAddressLocationProvider*, as shown in the following code snippet:

```
CivicAddressLocationProvider civicAddressLocationProivder
    = new CivicAddressLocationProvider(1000);
ReportStatus locationReportStatus =
    civicAddressLocationProivder.ReportStatus;
if (locationReportStatus == ReportStatus.Running)
{
    locationListener.PrintLocationReport(
        (CivicAddressLocationReport)
         civicAddressLocationProvider.GetReport());
}
//register for location events
civicAddressLocationProvider.LocationChanged +=
    locationListener.LocationChangedEventHandler;
civicAddressLocationProvider.StatusChanged +=
    locationListener.StatusChangedEventHandler;
```

The *locationListener* class will soon be used as our event handler for handling the location events. This class also includes several helper functions for printing location reports.

First, you need to create a new instance of *CivicAddressLocationProvider*. The constructor of all location providers expects an integer (*uint*) value that defines the initial value of the minimum report interval. You can later change this value using the *ReportInterval* property.

Next, you can check the status of the report. Any location provider has a *ReportStatus* value that indicates the operational state of the location provider. We already covered the exact states in the "Understanding the Location Report Status" section earlier in this chapter. Similar to the native API, the Civic Address location report status might be in a *ReportStatus.NotSupported* state—that is, if the default location is not set.

However, assuming the default location is defined, you can call the location provider *GetReport* function. This function returns a *LocationReport* that is the base class for all the reports—again, it's equivalent to the native *ILocationReport* interface. Therefore, you need to cast the return value to the desired report type, which in our case is *CivicAddressLocationReport*. Then you pass this location report to a helper function that prints the report to the console application.

The last two lines in the code snippet register an event listener to the two events that *CivicAddressLocationProvider* exposes. Again, these events are identical to the native events defined in the *ILocationEvents* interface. The following code snippet shows the implementation of *LocationChangedEventHandler* in our .NET console application:

```
public void LocationChangedEventHandler
    (LocationProvider locationProvider, LocationReport newLocation)
{
    if (locationProvider.ReportStatus == ReportStatus.Running)
    {
        LatLongLocationReport latLongLocationReport
            = newLocation as LatLongLocationReport;

        if (latLongLocationReport != null)
        {
            Console.WriteLine("new Lat Long Location");
            PrintLatLongLocationReport(latLongLocationReport);
            return;
        }

        CivicAddressLocationReport civicAddressReport
            = newLocation as CivicAddressLocationReport;

        if (civicAddressReport != null)
        {
            Console.WriteLine("New Civic Address Location");
            PrintCivicAddressLocationReport(civicAddressReport);
        }
    }
    else
    {
        //handle error
    }
}
```

Here you can see that *LocationChangedEventHandler*, called when the *LocationChanged* event fires, receives two input parameters: a location provider and a location report. Both are abstract base classes for more specific classes. Therefore, you use this function as a more generic event handler that handles events for both the Lat-Long and Civic Address location providers.

First, you need to check the status of the report. Assuming the status of the location provider is in its running state, you can next cast to the desired report type. In this case, you simply try to cast the input location report object, *newLocation*, into both location report types, using the .NET *as* statement. First in order is the Lat-Long location report type. If the *newLocation* object is of type *CivicAddressLocationReport*, the *newLocation as LatLongLocationReport* returns null and you try your luck with the second cast, which is the Civic Address report. Then you call the relevant print function to print the report values.

You can test this application in the exact same way we tested the native application shown earlier. However, there is a much cooler way to do so: use the enhanced default location provider.

Using the Enhanced Default Location Provider Tool for Testing

The enhanced default location provider (eDLP) tool is a Windows Presentation Foundation (WPF) open-source example that the Windows Sensor and Location team put together to illustrate the use of the .NET Location API. The binaries of this tool can be found with the rest of the code samples for this chapter. The entire source code of the eDLP and the .NET Location API, can be found at the MSDN Developer for Windows 7 site (*http://code.msdn.microsoft.com/SensorsAndLocation*).

The eDLP displays Virtual Earth maps within a Web browser control, as shown in the following image. You can right-click any location on the map to set the location values. You will see the geographic coordinates (latitude and longitude) change each time you right-click on a different location on the map. The Address values will be set only if you right-click within the boundaries of any known city or town.

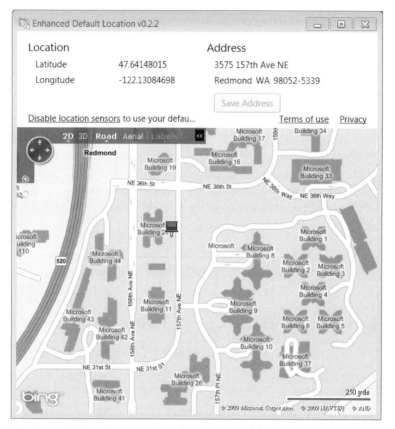

The Save Address button saves the current address as your Default Location value in the Location And Other Sensors Default Location dialog, shown in the "Default Location" section earlier in this chapter. Therefore, if you run the eDLP tool alongside your application, each time you save a new address you will see the new address in your console application as a result of handling the location change event. This application requires administrator rights because you are changing the value of the default location.

Summary

In this chapter, you saw the second part of the Sensor and Location Platform, the *location* piece. You learned why location received special treatment in the form of its own set of Location APIs. Next, you saw the complete architecture diagram of the Sensor and Location Platform, including the missing elements of the location part that we didn't review in Chapter 9. Then we dove into the native Location API and showed you how to use the different objects to receive accurate and up-to-date location information. The last topic we introduced in this chapter was managed code for the Location API, and you saw how easy it is to use this API to extract valuable location information.

This was the second chapter explaining the Sensor and Location Platform. After reading both chapters, you should now have a solid understanding of the platform's capabilities and the new and exciting scenarios you can introduce into your application to create a better user experience for your end users.

Chapter 11
Develop with the Windows Ribbon, Part 1

This is the first chapter of two that show how to build a modern, more productive user interface using the Microsoft Windows Ribbon framework. The Windows 7 Microsoft Ribbon framework is based on the new Fluent User Interface invented by the Microsoft Office team. The Fluent User Interface is a User Interface that makes it easier to work with an application and to get better and fast results. The Fluent User Interface provides cleaner User Interface elements layout with logical grouping. The Windows Ribbon Framework is one of many implementations of the Office Fluent User Interface. All of these implementations share the same ideas because they follow the same guideline. So if you choose to use the WPF Ribbon toolkit, or the Visual Studio 2008 SP1 MFC Ribbon controls and not the Windows 7 Ribbon framework APIs, you can still benefit from reading the following two chapters. The Windows Ribbon framework will be also available on Windows Vista.

In this chapter, you will get answers for questions such as, "What is a Ribbon, and how should I design my application to use the fluent user interface?

In this chapter, you will learn how to build the user interface of the Ribbon, while the following chapter will teach you how to interact with it from your code.

History

The designing of Office 2007 was started in August 2003. The general perception of the development team regarding Office 2003 was that it was good enough, it was complete, and there was no real innovation needed. But when asking real people about it, the Office team heard a totally different story, such as responses like this:

> *"I'm sure there's a way to do this, but I can't figure out how."*

> *"Office is so powerful; I would be better at my job if I knew how to use it more."*

The conclusion of the team was this:

> *"The user interface was failing the users."*

With every new release of Office, new features had been added, but too few users found or used them. The product became more and more complicated. People wanted a better way to get things done, but the assumption was that the product would never change to satisfy that need.

The traditional user interface (UI) of Office Word 2003 with drop-down menus and toolbars resembles the user interface of Office Word 2.0, which was released in 1992. Over the years, more toolbars were added, from two in Word 2.0 to eight in Word 6.0 (1994) to nine in Word 95 to 18 in Word 97. The Office UI became bloated. Of course, there were many other UI innovations, such as the red squiggle for calling attention to spell-checking errors, the green squiggle for noting grammar errors, the addition of Microsoft IntelliSense, on-the-fly spelling corrections, and so forth.

In Word 2000, a few more toolbars were added, bringing the total number to 23. But there was a big effort to clear the UI and to change the impression that the Office UI was bloated. As part of this effort, the team invented new UI concepts, such as Intelli-Menu (an expandable menu with a chevron button), Show/Hide toolbar buttons that change based on frequency of use, a toolbar that can be expanded by clicking on a chevron button, a window on the taskbar for each document (Tabbed Multi-Document Interface), and a side pane for help.

Instead of reducing the complexity of the product, Office 2000 tried to hide it. This approach caused great confusion. The UI was not consistent, and users could not find the commands they needed. The perception that Office was too complex had not changed.

In Office Word 2002, the number of toolbars reached 30. The Office team ran out of ideas about how to solve the complexity problem. To make a change in this direction, they created the task pane, a new side pane capable of holding more commands. In Office Word 2002, there were eight task panes.

Office Word 2003 had 31 toolbars and 19 task panes. With so many toolbars and task panes, the screen was even more cluttered. The working area that remained for writing an actual document was too small, even on large 24-inch monitors.

Figure 11-1 shows the increase in toolbars and task panes over the years with each new version of Microsoft Office Word.

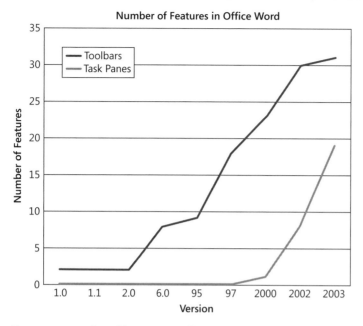

Figure 11-1 Number of features per Office Word version

The first time that Office 12 and the new Fluent UI were presented was during the 2005 Microsoft Professional Developer Conference (PDC). The keynote address at the 2005 PDC was a real show. Microsoft revealed, one by one, its new technologies, including Windows Vista, Ajax, the .NET Framework 3.0, LINQ, Windows Mobile (discussed in the upcoming sidebar), and of course Office 12 (which is known as Office 2007).

How I Did Not Miss the First Presentation of Office 2007

I was lucky to be at PDC 2005. During the first period of the PDC 2005 keynote address, Microsoft Platforms Group Vice President, Jim Allchin, offered to sell I-Mate JASJAR devices for $149 instead of the list-price of more than $1000. He said that there were about 1000 devices to be sold starting immediately!

I was with a bunch of my colleagues. Very quickly, we understood there were not enough devices for everyone. A few seconds later, I was alone in the audience with only one colleague because all my other colleagues went to get in line to buy the device. Because I stayed, I was able to see the first Office 12 Demo! My colleagues did not. Later, I was one of the first people to leave at the end of the keynote address and succeeded in buying one of the last devices. I went to one of the available computers, logged-in, and started the purchasing process. When I clicked the final OK button, I heard someone nearby say the words "Sold out.". I bought the 997th device out of the 1000 available.

In Office 2007, the Office team took another, refreshing UI design approach—instead of thinking in terms of *commands*, they thought in terms of *features*. They referred to this approach as *results-oriented design*. One of the main features of the result oriented approach is the usage that Office Applications do with the power of the modern CPU combined with visual galleries. Office 2007 can preview the outcome of an action whenever the mouse pointer is hovering over the command icons. For example, when a user needs to select a paragraph style, she simply hovers the mouse pointer about each style icon she wants in the style gallery to preview the effects on the document. When the right style is found, the user clicks on the button to validate the choice that makes the document look the best. Focusing on features influence the grouping of commands as well as the context that group of commands will be presented in the Office User Interface. When working with Office 2007 application, it changes its User Interface according to the action that the user takes, for example a new tab for picture editing features is appear when the user select a picture. This features-based design made Office 2007 much more productive than any older version of Office.

The Office team has put enormous effort into designing and inventing the Office Fluent UI and Ribbon concepts. As you might know, the Office team is the one of the main sources for creating many of the perceptions about what a UI should do; they influence the UI standard at Microsoft and, by extension, other 3rd party applications that running on the Windows platform. The Office team knew that other developers will mimic the Office UI. They wanted to make sure that developers will do it in the right way. They know there are many pitfalls you can encounter while implementing the user interface. To ensure a smooth release of the technology to partners and other independent software vendors (ISVs) and help vendors create compliant implementations of it, they created a guideline. The control suite vendor has to sign an agreement stating they will follow this guideline. For example, to download the Windows Presentation Foundation (WPF) Ribbon library which let you implement the Office Fluent User Interface in your WPF based application, you need to sign this agreement.

Here's the Office team's take on the license agreement:

> *"The license is available for applications on any platform, except for applications that compete directly with the five Office applications that currently have the new UI (Microsoft Office Word, Excel, PowerPoint, Outlook, and Access). We wanted to make the IP available broadly to partners because it has benefits to Microsoft and the Office ecosystem. At the same time, we wanted to preserve the uniqueness of the Office UI for the core Office productivity applications. "*

Do you, as a developer, need to sign this agreement to use the Windows 7 Ribbon? To use the Windows 7 Ribbon, you need to install the Windows 7 Software Development Kit (SDK). The SDK license doesn't instruct you to sign any agreement. Also, at PDC 2008 Nicolas Brun, Senior Development Lead at Microsoft Corporation, was asked about the license agreement during his speech[1]. He said that because the Windows Ribbon platform is consistent with the Office Fluent UI guidelines you can freely use it. In his words: *"The answer is no, you do not need to sign up the office fluent guideline anymore. Actually, the end user agreement that you get and accept when you install the Windows SDK is all you need."*

Bear in minds that this is only the case with the Windows Ribbon framework. When using the application wizard of Microsoft Visual Studio 2008 Service Pack (SP1) to create the Microsoft Foundation Classes (MFC)–based Ribbon, you get the following lines in each of the generated files:

```
// This MFC Samples source code demonstrates using
// MFC Microsoft Office Fluent User Interface
// (the "Fluent UI") and is provided only as referential material to supplement the
// Microsoft Foundation Classes Reference and related electronic documentation
// included with the MFC C++ library software.
// License terms to copy, use or distribute the Fluent UI are available separately.
// To learn more about our Fluent UI licensing program, please visit
// http://msdn.microsoft.com/officeui.
//
// Copyright (C) Microsoft Corporation
// All rights reserved.
```

Using the Ribbon

A good developer has to be a good user. This means that to build a state-of-the-art user interface in your application, you have to know all about the control suite that you use. Windows 7 comes with built-in support for the Ribbon, also known as the Windows Ribbon Framework. Good examples for the User Interface change that the Ribbon can make are the two Windows built-in applications: Microsoft WordPad and Microsoft Paint. You can compare between the user interface and user experience of these two applications on Windows XP/Vista to the new Windows 7. Figure 11-2 shows the new Paint UI comparing the Vista Paint UI.

---

[1] http://channel9.msdn.com/pdc2008/PC14/ (57:30)

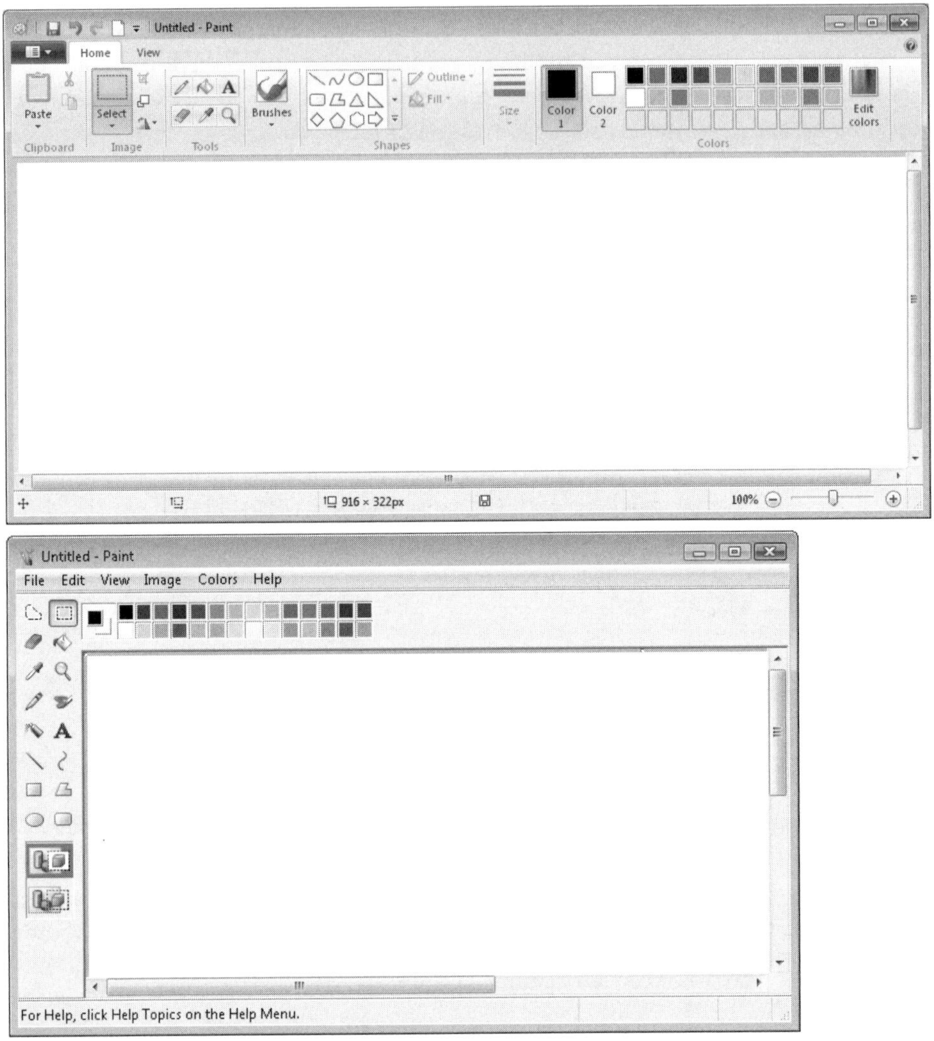

Figure 11-2 The new and old look of Paint.

Figure 11-3 shows new WordPad UI comparing to the UI in Vista.

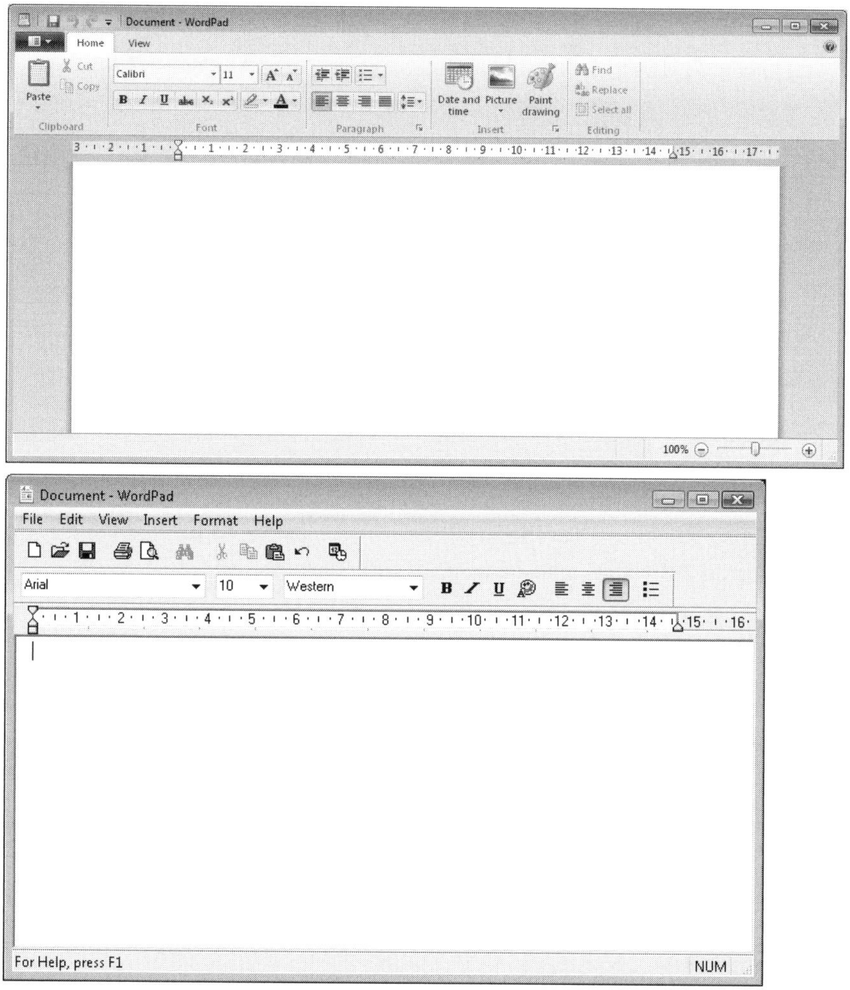

Figure 11-3 The new and old look of WordPad.

I encourage you to play with the Ribbon in these applications as well as the Ribbon of Office 2007 so that you can become familiar with the various options they contain. Let's take a short tour of Ribbon land, beginning with Figure 11-4.

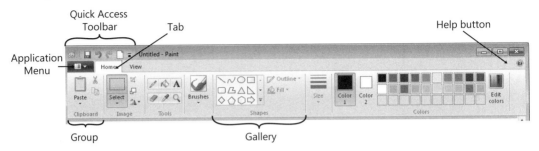

Figure 11-4 The Ribbon components.

We'll start from the top-left corner. First you see the Quick Access Toolbar (QAT), which is a small toolbar populated with a few tiny icons. The most frequently used commands can be found there.

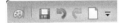

You can add any control of the ribbon to the QAT by right-clicking on that control and selecting Add To Quick Access Toolbar. You can remove an item from the QAT by right-clicking the control and selecting Remove from Quick Access Toolbar.

The QAT contains a customization menu that enables you to easily add or remove selected items from the QAT. If there is not enough room to show all the icons in the QAT, it can be expanded by clicking the expand button (the double-arrow icon).

Play with the menu options. You'll see what the Show Quick Access Toolbar Below The Ribbon option does. You should also try the Minimize The Ribbon option.

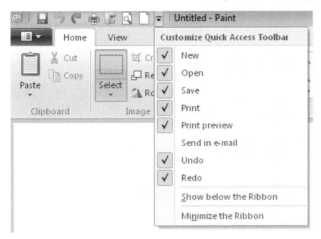

Below the QAT in the left corner, you can find the main application button. Clicking this button opens the application menu, a remnant of the old menu that contains the most usable menu items that used to be in the top-level menu, especially items from the File menu.

Near the application menu, you find a series of tabs. In the case of Paint, there are two tabs: Home and View. You'll find the same tab names and items in applications as you did with the old menu-based UI. Usually, the Home tab contains the most frequently used commands for manipulating the document, editing, and so on. The View tab handles view settings such as zoom in, zoom out, hide the status bar, and toggle full-screen mode.

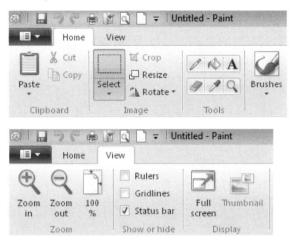

In addition to the resident tabs, you might also have a contextual tab. A contextual tab is one that appears in a specific context—for example, in Paint, the Text tab appears whenever the user chooses the text tool.

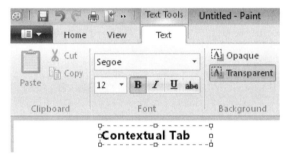

When you select a different tab, you switch the content of the body of the Ribbon. The body contains groups of icons, each representing an action or command. You have many group layouts you can choose from: on the View tab, the zoom group has three big icons in a row; in the Clipboard group on the Home tab, there is one big Icon for paste and two small icons for the cut and copy operations. Each icon might also have a ToolTip. ToolTips help the user understand the purpose of the icon, even though a picture is supposedly worth a thousand words.

Groups can contain many different UI elements, such as buttons, check boxes, drop-down buttons, as well as the most exciting element, the gallery. In Paint, you can see the Shapes gallery and the Brushes gallery for example.

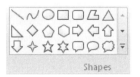

Galleries provide Live Preview. To see Live Preview in action, select a shape from the Shapes gallery and draw it. Leave the shape selected. Select a color by clicking on one of the colors in the Color gallery, and then click the Fill button. On the drop-down menu that appears, hover your mouse cursor over the various fill options. Can you see how the filling for the selected shape changes as you do this? Now choose one of the filling options to actually apply the change.

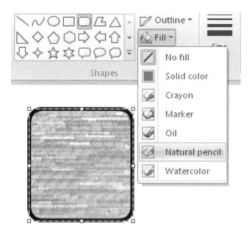

Programming with the Windows Ribbon Framework

The first impression you might have is that a Ribbon is a container for regular *user32*-based controls, but it is not. The Office team wanted to make sure that other Ribbon implementations adhere to the Office Fluent UI guideline, so they took a legal-based approach. The Windows team, on the other hand, decided to make sure that the user follows the guideline by making it hard (or impossible) to break the rules. The Windows Ribbon is rich, with many control types and many group layouts and sizing policies. But it is not flexible. You cannot put your own control or owner draw controls in the Ribbon. You can choose the pictures for the icons, or you can use galleries with your images. For Windows, the Ribbon is one control[2]. Using Spy++, you find that the main Ribbon has a Windows class named "NetUIHWND" and that it has no child windows.

Figure 11-5 shows the Spy++ output for the main Ribbon window (control).

---

[2] For drop-down elements such as menus and galleries the Ribbon framework uses more *user32* controls

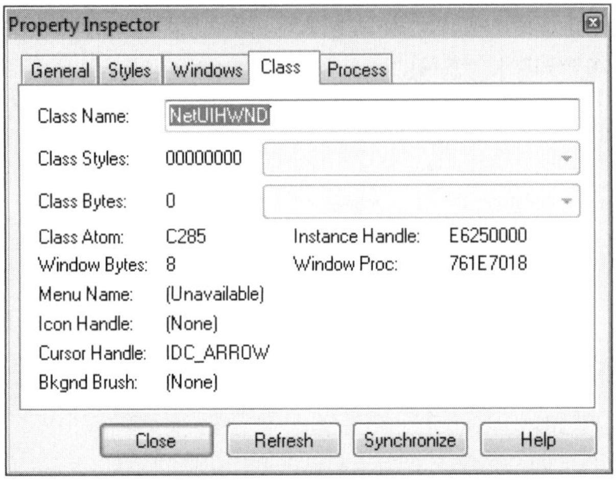

Figure 11-5 The one *user32* HWND handle for all the ribbon controls.

Figure 11-6 shows the Windows relationship of the main Ribbon window.

Figure 11-6 The Ribbon has no child window.

If you're familiar with programming user interfaces, you know that working with the bare *user32* APIs is hard, mainly because you have to deal with many tiny details. Think about the *CreateWindow()* API compared to creating *CWnd* in MFC, *Form* in WinForms, or *Windows* in WPF. To simplify UI programming, we want and need a UI framework.

The Windows Ribbon Framework team decided that this is a good opportunity to change not just the way the user interacts with the application, but also the way the native developer interacts with the UI APIs. They have created a new UI framework that is based on the concept of separating the UI from code.

Using declarative programming is not a new approach. WPF, Silverlight, and Media Center Markup Language are all following it. In this approach, the UI content, layout, and even UI behavior is scripted using an XML-based language, while the command execution logic is written in a code-behind file using an imperative programming language. In WPF and Silverlight, the UI is written using XAML and the code-behind file is written usually in C# or Visual Basic .NET. In the Windows Ribbon UI framework, the UI is scripted using XML with XAML-like syntax and the code-behind file is written using C/C++ and COM.

Dialog Template

You can argue that the separation of the UI and code is not new to native code. Dialog templates can be used with *user32* APIs without any framework such as MFC. The dialog template defines the controls and the layout of the dialog, while in runtime the *DialogBoxParams()* API loads it and uses the "dialog with code-behind file" approach. However, dialog templates are not based on XML and do not contain UI behavior, just a static layout of *user32* controls.

To use the Ribbon UI, the XML file has to be compiled to a binary file. The compiled binary file needs to be embedded as a Win32 resource in one of the application modules. You'll see how to do it soon, but first let's look at XML.

Ribbon Markup

The Ribbon markup language is somewhat similar to XAML: it looks the same, but it does not have all the XAML extensions. What it does have in common with XAML is the ability to use property element syntax. Property elements are a way to declare XML attributes outside the tag declaration. For example, these two XML snippets have the same meaning:

```
<Command Name='Paste' LabelTitle='MyPaste'/>
```

```
<Command>
      <Command.Name>Paste</Command.Name>
      <Command.LabelTitle>MyPaste</Command.LabelTitle>
</Command>
```

You might be wondering what the property element syntax is good for. This syntax enables the usage of inner elements of an attribute value—for example:

```
<Command Name='Paste' LabelTitle='MyPaste'>
      <Command.SmallImages>
        <Image Source='res/PasteHS.bmp'/>
      </Command.SmallImages>
      <Command.LargeImages>
        <Image Source='res/PasteHS.bmp'/>
```

```
        </Command.LargeImages>
    </Command>
```

The Ribbon markup is defined in a schema. The schema file can be found under the binary directory of the Windows SDK. This is the path to the schema on my computer:

```
C:\Program Files\Microsoft SDKs\Windows\v7.0\Bin\UICC.xsd
```

The Visual Studio XML editor can assist you with Microsoft IntelliSense and XML schema validation if it knows about the schema. Use the Schemas option in the XML menu, shown in Figure 11-7, to add it.

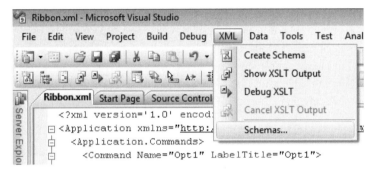

Figure 11-7 Adding the UICC.xsd schema.

Figure 11-8 shows the screen you see after selecting the Schemas option.

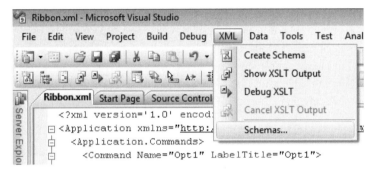

Figure 11-8 Visual Studio 2008 schema set window

Another way to introduce the schema to Visual Studio is to copy the schema file to the Visual Studio schema folder. On my computer the location is here:

```
C:\Program Files (x86)\Microsoft Visual Studio 9.0\Xml\Schemas
```

According to the schema, the minimal valid Ribbon markup is as follows:

```
<?xml version="1.0" encoding="utf-8"?>
<Application xmlns='http://schemas.microsoft.com/windows/2009/Ribbon'>
```

```
    <Application.Views>
      <Ribbon>
      </Ribbon>
    </Application.Views>
  </Application>
```

The *Application.Views* section defines the layout of the Ribbon. Here you define the tabs, groups, and contextual menu. Views are populated with commands. We'll start with the *Application.Commands* section and then dive into the different *Views* options. But before doing that we need to know how we can take the Ribbon markup file and convert it to a binary resource.

The Ribbon markup XML file has to be compiled and added as a Win32 resource to an application that knows how to handle the Windows Ribbon UI framework. In the Bin directory of the Windows 7 SDK, there is a tool called *UICC.EXE*, which stands for *UI Command Compiler*.

```
C:\Program Files\Microsoft SDKs\Windows\v7.0\Bin>uicc
Microsoft (R) Ribbon Markup Compiler Version 6.1.7600.16385 for x86, Retail Build
Copyright (C) Microsoft Corporation.  All rights reserved.

Usage: UICC <ribbonFile> <binaryFile> [options]

  - OPTIONS -

 /header:<headerFile>
   Emit header file named <headerFile>. If omitted, a header file will not be
   generated.

 /res:<resourceFile>
   Emit resource file named <resourceFile>.

 /name:<ribbonName>
   Resource name for the ribbon binary.  The default is APPLICATION_RIBBON.

 /W{0|1|2}
   Specify warning level 0-2. The default is 2.

  - EXAMPLE -

 UICC.exe MyApp.ribbon MyApp.bin /header:MyRibbon.h /res:MyRibbon.rc
```

Try to compile the minimal valid Ribbon.

```
C:\temp>uicc MinimalRibbon.xml MinimalRibbon.bin /res:MinimalRibbon.rc
MinimalRibbon.xml(4): warning SC2002 : Undefined property: 'ApplicationMenu'. Using default
value.
MinimalRibbon.xml(4): warning SC2002 : Undefined property: 'Tab'. Using default value.
MinimalRibbon.xml(4): warning SC2002 : Undefined property: 'QuickAccessToolbar'.  Using
default value.
MinimalRibbon.xml : warning SC2001 at
```

```
/Application/Application.Views/Ribbon/Ribbon.ApplicationMenu/ApplicationMenu: Undefined
Command on element.
MinimalRibbon.xml : warning SC2001 at /Application/Application.Views/Ribbon/Ribbon.Tabs/Tab:
Undefined Command on element.
Header file generation successful: '(null)'.
Ribbon markup file validation successful: 'MinimalRibbon.xml'.
Ribbon resource file generation successful: 'MinimalRibbon.rc'.
```

Compiling a Ribbon markup file generates a resource file. String values such as labels and
ToolTips go to the String Table. Images are defined using the *BITMAP* resource entry, and the
Ribbon layout setting and views go to a binary file that is also embedded in the resource. This
is the resulting resource file (`MinimalRibbon.rc`):

```
// ********************************************************************************
// * This is an automatically generated file containing the ribbon resource for *
// * your application.                                                           *
// ********************************************************************************

STRINGTABLE
BEGIN
    60001 L"Label:InternalCmd2" /* LabelTitle InternalCmd2_LabelTitle_RESID: (null) */
END

STRINGTABLE
BEGIN
    60002 L"Label:InternalCmd4" /* LabelTitle InternalCmd4_LabelTitle_RESID: (null) */
END


APPLICATION_RIBBON    UIFILE    "MinimalRibbon.bin"
```

The resource file is a text file. To use it as a Win32 resource, you need to compile it to binary
using the Resource Compiler. The *RC.EXE* tool also comes with the Windows SDK, and it
resides in the same Bin directory as the *UICC.EXE*. I am using the */v* option to show the actions
that the Resource Compiler tool takes:

```
C:\temp>rc /v MinimalRibbon.rc
Microsoft (R) Windows (R) Resource Compiler Version 6.1.7600.16385
Copyright (C) Microsoft Corporation.  All rights reserved.

Using codepage 1255 as default
Creating MinimalRibbon.res

MinimalRibbon.rc...
Writing UIFILE:APPLICATION_RIBBON,    lang:0x409,    size 1042
Writing STRING:3751,    lang:0x409,    size 104
```

The resulting `MinimalRibbon.res` is a binary resource file that can be linked to an executable
or dynamic-link library (DLL). Because the Ribbon uses string tables, it is easy to localize it.
You can also create a resource-only DLL for each language. You can use the LINK.EXE
command, which is part of VC++:

```
C:\temp>link /VERBOSE /MACHINE:x64 /NOENTRY /DLL /OUT:ribbon.dll MinimalRibbon.res
Microsoft (R) Incremental Linker Version 9.00.30729.01
Copyright (C) Microsoft Corporation.  All rights reserved.


Starting pass 1

Searching libraries

Finished searching libraries

Finished pass 1


Invoking CVTRES.EXE:
 /machine:amd64
 /verbose
 /out:"C:\Users\Book\AppData\Local\Temp\lnk9A19.tmp"
 /readonly
 "MinimalRibbon.res"
Microsoft (R) Windows Resource To Object Converter Version 9.00.21022.08
Copyright (C) Microsoft Corporation.  All rights reserved.

adding resource. type:UIFILE, name:APPLICATION_RIBBON, language:0x0409, flags:0x30,
size:1042
adding resource. type:STRING, name:3751, language:0x0409, flags:0x1030, size:104
Starting pass 2
     MinimalRibbon.res
Finished pass 2
```

You can see that LINK.EXE uses another tool called CVTRES.EXE that converts the text resource to an object file.

When using Visual Studio, you first need to integrate Windows SDK 7.0. Integrating the SDK is a matter of telling Visual Studio to use the header files, libraries and tools from the Windows 7 SDK. You can do so manually by going to Visual Studio menu "Tools\Options\Projects and Solutions\VC++ Directories" or much easier by using the Windows SDK Configuration Tool that comes with the SDK.

Figure 11-9   How to set the current SDK in Visual Studio (1)

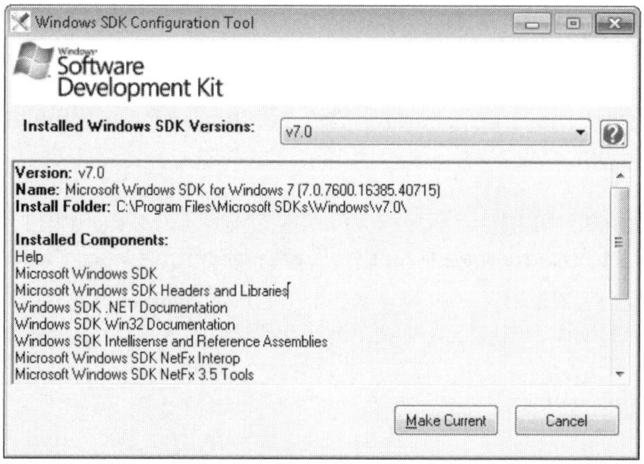

Figure 11-10   How to set the current SDK in Visual Studio (2)

Figure 11-9 and 11-10 above Show how to set the current SDK in Visual Studio

To automatically have the Ribbon.xml part of the project build, you can use the Custom Build Step option. Right-click on the XML file to access the dialog box shown in Figure 11-11, select the General item under "Custom Build Step" on the left and set the command line with what is shown in the Command Line dialog box of the screenshot. As long as you add the resulting resource (rc) file to the project resource section and include the resulting header file, you are done. Visual Studio knows how to compile text resource files and to link them to the executable.

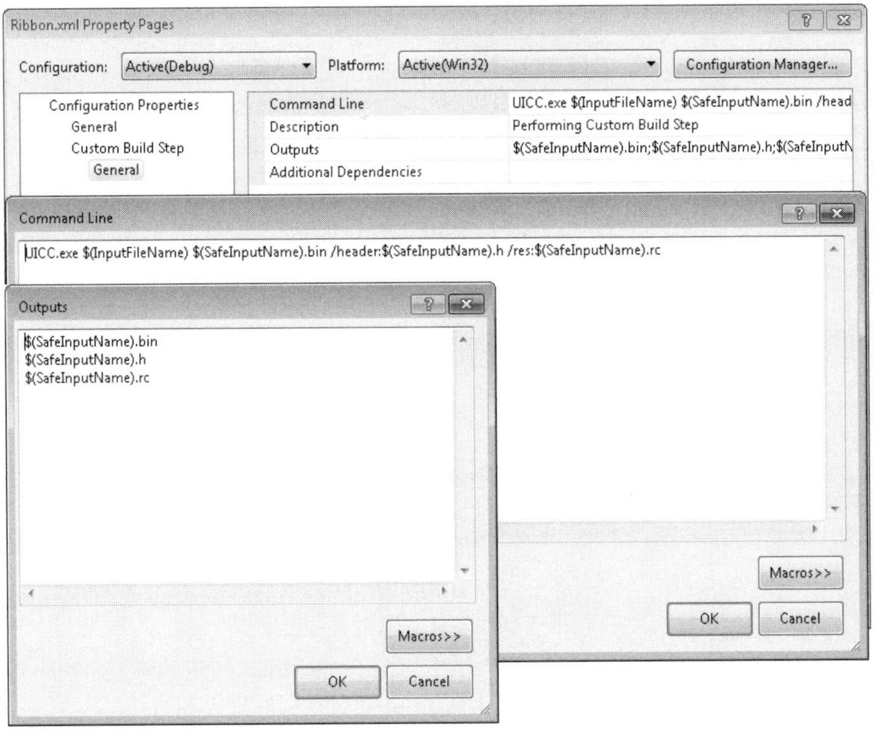

Figure 11-11 Using the Visual Studio property page to set a custom build action.

Figure 11-12 is a diagram that shows how the C++ compilation and linking process of an application embedding a Ribbon.

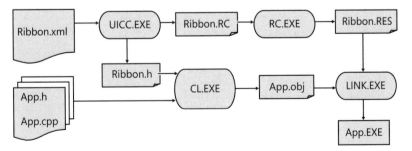

Figure 11-12 Ribbon compilation and linking process.

To see the resulting Ribbon, you need an application that knows how to start the Ribbon framework and load the embedded resource. In the book source code folder, you can find the MinimalRibbon project, which does exactly that. You'll understand the steps required to build such an application in the next chapter, which deals with the code-behind part. For this chapter, to be able to play with the markup language you'll use an application that we have built for this purpose, the RibbonExplorer (*Sources and executable can be found in the book source folder*). RibbonExplorer is a tool that takes the Ribbon markup and executes the three compilation steps. It creates a satellite DLL that contains the Ribbon binary resource, and then it loads and shows the resulting Ribbon. The tool also shows the output of each of the compilation steps as well as the generated resource and header file. The generated header file contains the constant definitions that are needed to interact with the Ribbon from the code-behind file.

The best way to learn how to use the Ribbon and the Ribbon markup is to play with it. RibbonExplorer makes it easy to experience every tiny detail. We encourage you to use it while you continue reading through the material in this chapter.

Enter the minimal Ribbon XML, and test it. (See Figure 11-13.)

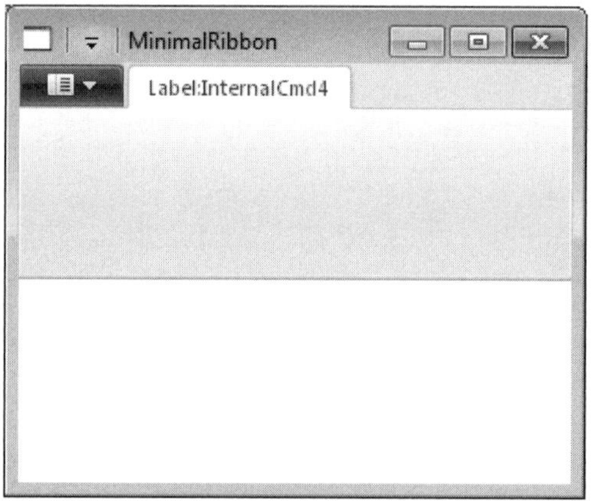

Figure 11-13 The minimal Ribbon.

The Application.Commands Section

The Windows team calls the new UI concept *Intent UI*, and the name reveals the perception. The focus is not on the "how," but on the "what." The markup file gives a description for the UI framework, telling it what it is that you want. The framework knows how to render the Ribbon and let the end user interact with it.

The first section that you have to create is the *Application.Commands* section. Commands hold all the information that is needed to render and interact with UI elements. Each command contains XML attributes and elements that set the command's properties. For example, you can give a name for the command, assign a small or large icon, assign a label, a tooltip and there are several more properties. Without commands, you cannot populate the various application views. Application view controls refer to commands by using the command's name property.

To test a command, you may use the RibbonExplorer. To be able to compile the markup, the icon's bitmaps should be put in a location relative to the directory of the markup file. There are two main conventions, the first is to put the icon's bitmap in the same folder of the ribbon markup file, the second is to put all graphics under the `res` folder and add the `res` folder prefix to the `Image Source` file path.

To see a command in action, try the following XML text in RibbonExplorer. Make sure that you copy the `PasteHS.bmp` file to a folder named `res` that is placed in the same location of the Ribbon XML file.

```
<?xml version="1.0" encoding="utf-8"?>
<Application xmlns='http://schemas.microsoft.com/windows/2009/Ribbon'>
  <Application.Commands>
    <Command  Name='Paste' LabelTitle='MyPaste'>
      <Command.SmallImages>
        <Image Source='res/PasteHS.bmp'/>
      </Command.SmallImages>
    </Command>
  </Application.Commands>
  <Application.Views>
    <Ribbon>
      <Ribbon.Tabs>
        <Tab>
          <Group>
            <Button CommandName='Paste'/>
          </Group>
        </Tab>
      </Ribbon.Tabs>
    </Ribbon>
  </Application.Views>
</Application>
```

The result is the following:

As you can see from the last code snippet, there is one Command, The *'Paste'* and it is correlated to one control, the Button. The correlation is done via the *CommandName* attribute of the Button control: `<Button CommandName='Paste'/>`.

UICC.EXE uses default values. This is why you see Label:InternalCmd2 and Label:InternalCmd4. To fix this problem, you also have to define commands for the tab and the group.

To enrich the result, and learn about other Command element's attributes let's add some other properties to the commands. The *Keytip* adds keyboard navigation capabilities. To activate and view the *Keytip* support the user has to press on the Alt key. The *TooltipTitle* and *TooltipDescription* are shown when the user hoover on top of the command associated control, the *TooltipTitle* is a short title of the command and is more important for commands that has no label or in cases that the label is not shown. The *TooltipDescription* should supply more information about the command. Like *TooltipDescription* the *LabelDescription is* used to supply more information about the command. When compiling the Ribbon, the UICC.EXE can generate a header file (using the /header option). The header file is used to interact with the Ribbon commands from code. The *Id, Symbol* and *Comment* are used to generate the command entry in the header file:

```
#define <Symbol> <Id> /* <Comment> */
```

Omitting the *Id* and *Symbol* attributes resulting a generation of automated values. The following markup demonstrates richer command content:

```
<?xml version="1.0" encoding="utf-8"?>
<Application xmlns='http://schemas.microsoft.com/windows/2009/Ribbon'>
  <Application.Commands>
    <Command Name='Home' LabelTitle='Home' Keytip='H' Id='100' Symbol='strHome'
            TooltipTitle='Main Tab'/>
    <Command Name='Clipboard' LabelTitle='ClipBoard'/>
    <Command Name='Paste' LabelTitle='MyPaste' Keytip='V' Id='101' Symbol='strPaste'
            TooltipTitle='Paste'>
      <Command.Comment>This is the paste command</Command.Comment>
      <Command.LabelDescription>Select to execute MyPaste</Command.LabelDescription>
      <Command.TooltipDescription>
              Press here to insert the Clipboard content
      </Command.TooltipDescription>
      <Command.SmallImages>
        <Image Source='res/PasteHS.bmp'/>
      </Command.SmallImages>
      <Command.LargeImages>
        <Image Source='res/PasteHS.bmp'/>
      </Command.LargeImages>
    </Command>
    <Command Name='PasteSpecial' LabelTitle='Paste Special'
            TooltipTitle='Paste Special'>
      <Command.SmallImages>
        <Image Source='res/PasteHS.bmp'/>
      </Command.SmallImages>
      <Command.LargeImages>
        <Image Source='res/PasteHS.bmp'/>
      </Command.LargeImages>
    </Command>
  </Application.Commands>
```

```
<Application.Views>
  <Ribbon>
    <Ribbon.Tabs>
      <Tab CommandName='Home'>
        <Group CommandName='Clipboard'>
          <Button CommandName='Paste'/>
        </Group>
      </Tab>
    </Ribbon.Tabs>
    <Ribbon.ApplicationMenu>
      <ApplicationMenu>
        <MenuGroup>
          <SplitButton>
            <SplitButton.ButtonItem>
              <Button CommandName="PasteSpecial"/>
            </SplitButton.ButtonItem>
            <SplitButton.MenuGroups>
              <MenuGroup Class="MajorItems">
                <Button CommandName="Paste"/>
              </MenuGroup>
            </SplitButton.MenuGroups>
          </SplitButton>
          <Button CommandName="Paste"/>
        </MenuGroup>
      </ApplicationMenu>
    </Ribbon.ApplicationMenu>
  </Ribbon>
</Application.Views>
</Application>
```

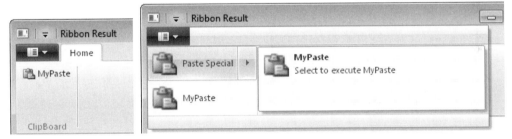

The default labels are gone, and now you have icons and ToolTips with ToolTip descriptions. You've also added the Application menu in the Ribbon element of the Application view. In the Application menu, you can see the use of the same *MyPaste* command, and here you can see the label description. Pressing the Alt key reveals the use of *KeyTip* to navigate and execute commands using the keyboard:

Other properties, such as *Symbol, Id and Comment*, are reflected in the generated header file;

```
...
<Command Name='Paste' … Id='101' Symbol='strPaste' …>
    <Command.Comment>This is the paste command</Command.Comment>
</Command>
...
```

The generated header file:

```
// ********************************************************************************
// * This is an automatically generated header file for UI Element definition  *
// * resource symbols and values. Please do not modify manually.                *
// ********************************************************************************

#pragma once

#define strHome 100
#define strHome_LabelTitle_RESID 60001
#define strHome_Keytip_RESID 60002
#define strHome_TooltipTitle_RESID 60003
#define Clipboard 2
#define Clipboard_LabelTitle_RESID 60004
#define strPaste 101   /* This is the paste command */
#define strPaste_LabelTitle_RESID 60005
#define strPaste_LabelDescription_RESID 60006
#define strPaste_Keytip_RESID 60007
#define strPaste_TooltipTitle_RESID 60008
#define strPaste_TooltipDescription_RESID 60009
#define strPaste_SmallImages_RESID 60010
#define strPaste_LargeImages_RESID 60011
#define PasteSpecial 3
#define PasteSpecial_LabelTitle_RESID 60012
#define PasteSpecial_TooltipTitle_RESID 60013
#define PasteSpecial_SmallImages_RESID 60014
#define PasteSpecial_LargeImages_RESID 60015
#define InternalCmd2_LabelTitle_RESID 60016
#define InternalCmd4_LabelTitle_RESID 60017
```

A quick look at the previous example, the *ApplicationViews* section, reveals that commands are also used for tabs, groups, and other container controls. These elements also need properties such as *LabelTitle* and *KeyTip*, and the command can also be used to interact with container controls from code. Table 11-1 summarizes the command attributes.

Table 11-1 Command Attributes

Command Attribute	Description
Name	Associates a name with the command. The *ApplicationViews* section has many elements (such as tabs, groups, menus, and buttons). All of them have the *CommandName* attribute, which takes the command name. Each command must have a unique name.
Id	A unique numeric identifier for the command. The range can be from 2 to 59999 or 0x2 to 0xEA5F. If this attribute is omitted, the UICC.EXE generates a default unique ID. The Id is associated with the Ribbon Command and it enables to distinguish between commands in code.
KeyTip	A string value that represents the shortcut key for the command. When the user presses the Alt key, she can navigate and execute commands using the keyboard.
LabelTitle	Represents the text that will be used when presenting the command in a control. If the command is associated with a menu item and an ampersand precedes one of the letters, the system treats this letter as the keyboard accelerator. For example, in `<Command ... LabelTitle="&amp;Open"/>`, the *O* becomes the keyboard accelerator as well as the Ribbon KeyTip. In controls other than *Menu*, the ampersand is ignored and the KeyTip value is used. Use `&amp;&amp;` to insert one ampersand (&) character.
LabelDescription	Contains additional information regarding the command. It's presented in only a few cases, as shown in the earlier example.
TooltipTitle	The ToolTip text.
TooltipDescription	Extended information that can be shown with the short ToolTip.
SmallImages, LargeImages, SmallHighContructImages, LargeHighContructImages	Provide a set of images to the view to choose from. The image element is used to provide the image file. More than one image element can be provided, each with a different dots-per-inch (DPI) setting. The Ribbon UI framework chooses the best image that fits the size and the screen DPI. In any case, the system knows to resize the image, but the result might be blurry. For more information, see the "Ribbon Image Resource Format" section.
Symbol	The definition name in the header file. It has to have a valid C/C++ macro identifier. If this attribute is omitted, a default symbol is generated.
Comment	Adds a comment to the command definition in the generated header file. The maximum length is 250 characters, and no new lines are allowed in the text.

Ribbon Image Resource Format

For an image to be used in the Ribbon, it has to meet specific criteria. It has to be a 32-bits-per-pixel .bmp file in the ARGB format. This format supports an alpha channel for 256 (8-bit) transparency levels. To create such an image, you should use a tool that preserves and supports an alpha channel. Unfortunately MS-Paint does not support this format. A good tool that does support this format is the PixelFormer, a new tool from Qualibyte Software (http://www.qualibyte.com/pixelformer/). When setting Windows to use a high-contrast theme, a 4-bit-per-pixel format should be used. The recommended approach is to create many different images with different resolution that fit both regular and high contrast Windows theme for the same icon. The Ribbon framework chooses the best image that fits the required size and the screen DPI setting. (See the upcoming "High DPI" side bar.) Table 11-2 provides the recommended image sizes.

Table 11-2 Recommended Image Sizes

DPI	Small Image size	Large Image Size
96	16 by 16	32 by 32
120	20 by 20	40 by 40
144	24 by 24	48 by 48
192	32 by 32	64 by 64

High DPI

The ability to set the dots-per-inch in the Display Control Panel applet is not new. However, in the Windows 7 time frame, many more systems will use a higher DPI setting than the default 96 DPI. In the past, to make the text and icons larger the user could change the screen resolution. CRT-based monitors handle different resolution settings easily and provide a good quality picture. LCD monitors do not handle very well a resolution that is different from their natural resolution of an exact one-to-one pixel mapping. To get a large-enough picture that is smooth, you need to have more pixels per letter or icon. The way to do that is to set the screen DPI to a higher value. When you install Windows 7 as a clean install, the system chooses the best DPI setting according to the monitor ability. Also, in Windows 7, it's easier to find how to change the DPI setting[3]. The setting is per user, and it does not require a reboot, just logging off the user.

---

[3] To set the Windows theme right-click on empty spot in the Desktop and choose Personalize. To change the System DPI press Display on the command-link in the side pane.

Localized the Ribbon

There are three possible approaches. The first is to have a Ribbon markup for each language. This approach is hard to maintain since you have to edit all of the files for each change in the Ribbon markup. The second approach is to use the resulting resource (rc) file. The UICC.EXE Ribbon markup compiler extracts all strings from the markup files and put them in a standard Win32 Resource String Table in the resulting resource (rc) file. You can create a resource file for each language by making a copy of the generated resource file and edit the String Table. For automated process you need to have a script or tool that replaces the original string with the locale text. The last approach is not to have any text in the markup file and supply the text at runtime. The Ribbon framework calls your code and requests the missing properties, those properties that you did not supply in the markup file. You should reply with the corresponding text according to the current user locale.

Presenting Commands

Commands represent the connection between the UI elements, also known as controls, and the code-behind file. The generated header file contains information that is derived only from the *Application.Commands* section. To present a command, you need a control. Unlike traditional UI code, in the Windows Ribbon framework, the system manages and renders the controls for you. Each control has the *CommandName* attribute. The *CommandName* binds the control with the underlying command.

The *Application.Views* section contains the needed information for presenting controls. Controls may appear in different places, layouts and groups. Windows Ribbon has three types of controls: basic, containers, and specialized controls.

Basic Controls are the simple familiar controls such as the button, checkbox and spinner control. The most basic and self-explanatory control is the *Button* control. In addition to the *CommandName* attribute, *Button* has only two additional attributes, *ApplicationDefaults.IsChecked* and *ApplicationMode*, and they are both relevant only when the button is used in a specific place.

ApplicationDefaults.IsChecked is relevant if *Button* is part of the Quick Access Toolbar (QAT). (We'll discuss that case in the Quick Access Toolbar section.) Application mode is a state that is represented by a number from 0 through 31. You can associate several modes with the same control for example: `ApplicationModes='0, 1, 4'`. Programmatically you can set the current application mode of the Ribbon. When the program sets a mode number that is not associated with the control, the control disappears. Usually, *ApplicationMode* is related to container controls such as *Group*. In case of the *Button* control the *ApplicationMode* is relevant only when the button is hosted in the left column of the Application menu. You can use RibbonExplorer to set the application mode and see how the related controls appear or disappear. You'll see how to set the current application mode from code in Chapter 12. Figure 11-14 shows the basic controls.

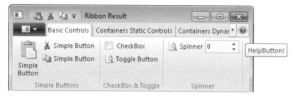

Figure 11-14 Basic controls include Button, CheckBox, ToggleButton, Spinner, and HelpButton.

The *CheckBox* and *ToggleButton* controls are similar to the *Button* control, but they have a toggle state. You can't set the starting state in markup; you need to do it from code.

HelpButton is a special control that is similar to the *Button* control, but it's restricted to appearing only once in a Ribbon, in the *Ribbon.HelpButton* element. The framework provides the image for the help button. The associated command can provide the ToolTip and the *Keytip*. The purpose of the help button is to have a common place that the user can refer (click) to get help about the application.

The *Spinner* control is a combination of two controls: an edit box that takes decimal values, and up/down arrows that increment or decrement the value. Setting the initial values and controlling the limits is done via code. The following markup segment shows the markup behind Figure 11-14:

```
<Application.Views>
    <Ribbon>
      <Ribbon.HelpButton>
        <HelpButton CommandName='cmdHelpButton'/>
      </Ribbon.HelpButton>
      <Ribbon.Tabs>
        <Tab CommandName='cmdBasicControls'>
          <Tab.ScalingPolicy>
            <ScalingPolicy>
              <ScalingPolicy.IdealSizes>
                <Scale Group='cmdGrpButtons' Size='Medium'/>
                <Scale Group='cmdGrpCheckBoxToggleButtons' Size='Large'/>
                <Scale Group='cmdGrpSpinner' Size='Large'/>
              </ScalingPolicy.IdealSizes>
            </ScalingPolicy>
          </Tab.ScalingPolicy>
          <Group CommandName='cmdGrpButtons'
                 SizeDefinition='ThreeButtons-OneBigAndTwoSmall'>
            <Button CommandName='cmdButton1'/>
            <Button CommandName='cmdButton2'/>
            <Button CommandName='cmdButton3'/>
          </Group>
          <Group CommandName='cmdGrpCheckBoxToggleButtons'>
            <CheckBox CommandName='cmdCheckBox'/>
            <ToggleButton CommandName='cmdToggleButton'/>
```

```
        </Group>
        <Group CommandName='cmdGrpSpinner'>
          <Spinner CommandName='cmdSpinner'/>
        </Group>
      </Tab>
    </Ribbon.Tabs>
    ...
```

Container Controls   Containers hold collections of controls. Tabs, groups, the Application menu are all examples of containers. Containers can be associated with commands, to give them text values and also to enable interacting with them from code. There are two types of containers: static and dynamic. Dynamic containers are a little bit more complicated because their content is changed during runtime, usually from the code. Static containers get their content from the markup file; hence, they're easy to maintain and prototype. We'll start by examining static containers.

Static Containers   The following markup snippet represents a Ribbon with one tab that has one group:

```
<Application.Views>
  <Ribbon>
    <Ribbon.Tabs>
      <Tab CommandName='cmdHome'>
        <Group CommandName='cmdClipboard'>
          <Button CommandName='cmdPaste'/>
        </Group>
      </Tab>
    </Ribbon.Tabs>
  </Ribbon>
</Application.Views>
```

Let examine the Microsoft Paint program. You see two core tabs: Home and View. Switching between the two tabs changes the content of the Ribbon. Each of the tabs has its own tab groups. If you select the Text tool and start to enter some text, a special contextual tab appears at the top of the screen with the highlighted name "Text Tools." Also, a Text contextual tab is added to the Ribbon's tabs for the text manipulation:

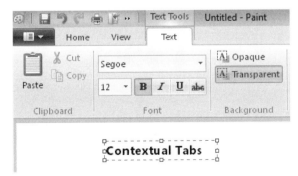

Contextual tabs are defined in the *Ribbon.ContextualTabs* section as child elements of *TabGroup*. You can have more than one *TabGroup;* each has more than one tab. As in the case of Paint, contextual tabs are displayed only when needed, usually when a specific object is selected. You'll see how to activate contextual tab from code in the next chapter, meanwhile you can use the RibbonExplorer to preview contextual tabs.

Figure 11-15 shows the Paint Print Preview. When the user chooses the Print Preview, the Home and View tabs disappear and the Print Preview tab replaces them. The Print Preview tab is a *modal* tab. It has an application mode number associated with it. When the user selects Print Preview, the Paint code sets a different application mode that is only associated with the Print Preview Tab. Because Home and View have not been associated with the same application mode as Print Preview, they disappear.

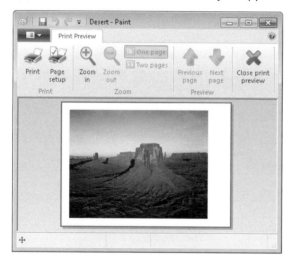

Figure 11-15 The Paint Print Preview Modal tab

Contextual tabs and application modes look the same. However, contextual tabs come to assist in cases where a special UI is needed in addition to all the other tabs, while application modes are handy in cases where you need to hide some of the UI controls—such as in the case of Paint Print Preview or when you need to hide a group of controls that let the user browse the Internet when there is no network connection.

The *Group* container holds a group of controls within a tab. *Group* can be associated with one or more application mode numbers, which enables hiding the group when needed. The most interesting attribute of the *Group* control is *SizeDefinition*. The size definition defines the layout of the controls in the group. *SizeDefinition* will be explained in the "Controlling Scaling Behavior" section.

Two special containers are the *DropDownButton* and *SplitButton* controls. In Paint, in the Home tab Image group, Paste is implemented as a *SplitButton* control and Rotate is implemented as a *DropDownButton* control. *SplitButton* is a button with drop-down list. You can click the button or choose an item from the list, as shown in the following screen shot on the left. *DropDownButton* is a button that is used to spawn a control list when clicked, as shown in the following screen shot on the right. *SplitButton* is best used in those places that a default action exists.

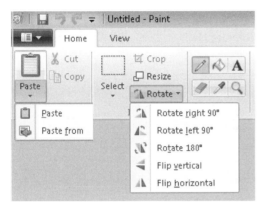

Two other container controls are *ApplicationMenu* and *ContextPopup*. *ApplicationMenu* is the main menu that holds commands for performing operations with the document, such as open, save, print, and so forth. *ContextPopup* is the top container of one of more composite context menus and a toolbar. This context menu is similar to the traditional right-click context menu, but it also can display a mini-toolbar. The commands in the floating menu and toolbar are usually in the context of the current selected item on the screen. The application should display the context popup near the selected item.

The following markup demonstrates how to create a *ContextPopup*:

```
<ContextPopup>
    <ContextPopup.MiniToolbars>
      <MiniToolbar Name='ClipBoard'>
        <MenuGroup>
          <Button CommandName='cmdPaste'/>
          <Button CommandName='cmdCut'/>
          <Button CommandName='cmdCopy'/>
          <Button CommandName='cmdDelete'/>
        </MenuGroup>
      </MiniToolbar>
    </ContextPopup.MiniToolbars>

    <ContextPopup.ContextMenus>
      <ContextMenu Name='PrintMenu'>
        <MenuGroup>
```

```
            <Button CommandName='cmdPrint'/>
            <Button CommandName='cmdPrintPreview'/>
            <Button CommandName='cmdPortrait'/>
            <Button CommandName='cmdLandScape'/>
            <Button CommandName='cmdPortraitLandScape'/>
        </MenuGroup>
      </ContextMenu>
    </ContextPopup.ContextMenus>
    <ContextPopup.ContextMaps>
      <ContextMap CommandName='cmdContextualUI' ContextMenu='PrintMenu'
                  MiniToolbar='ClipBoard'/>
    </ContextPopup.ContextMaps>
  </ContextPopup>
```

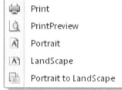

As you can see in the previous markup the *ContextPopup.ContextMaps* element combines the *ContextPopup.MiniToolbars* and *ContextPopup.ContextMenus* to one Context Popup view. *MiniToolbar* represents a popup toolbar and *ContextMenu* represent the traditional right-click menu. The application can show a *ContextPopup* element by using the *ContextMap* associated command. You will see how to do it in the next chapter. You can also use RibbonExplorer to play with it without the need to write code.

For each Ribbon, there can be only one *ApplicationMenu* element. *ApplicationMenu* may have one *ApplicationMenu.RecentItems* and many menu groups. *ApplicationMenu.RecentItems* represents the Most Recently Used (MRU) list, which in turn is a dynamic container control that needs to be populated from code. You'll see how to manage the recent item list in the next chapter. Menu groups appear one below the other with a separator between them like the two groups defined in the following markup and shown in Figure 11xx16.

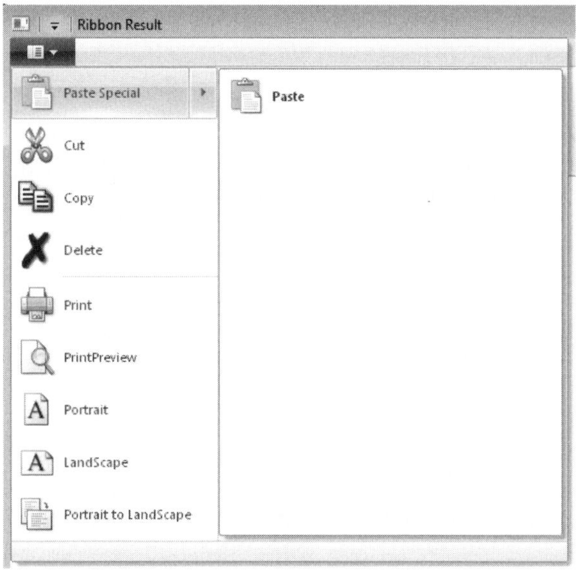

Figure 11-16 An Application Menu example

```xml
<Ribbon.ApplicationMenu>
  <ApplicationMenu>
    <MenuGroup>
      <SplitButton CommandName='cmdSplitButton'>
        <SplitButton.ButtonItem>
          <Button CommandName="cmdPasteSpecial"/>
        </SplitButton.ButtonItem>
        <SplitButton.MenuGroups>
          <MenuGroup Class="MajorItems">
            <Button CommandName="cmdPaste"/>
          </MenuGroup>
        </SplitButton.MenuGroups>
      </SplitButton>
      <Button CommandName="cmdCut"/>
      <Button CommandName="cmdCopy"/>
      <Button CommandName='cmdDelete'/>
    </MenuGroup>
    <MenuGroup>
      <Button CommandName='cmdPrint'/>
      <Button CommandName='cmdPrintPreview'/>
      <Button CommandName='cmdPortrait'/>
      <Button CommandName='cmdLandScape'/>
      <Button CommandName='cmdPortraitLandScape'/>
    </MenuGroup>
  </ApplicationMenu>
</Ribbon.ApplicationMenu>
```

You can get a sub-menu hierarchy by inserting a *SplitButton* as an element in the *MenuGroup*.

Dynamic Containers Dynamic containers are containers whose content might change during runtime. Most of the dynamic containers are based on the concept of galleries. Galleries get populated at runtime and can be changed in response to a change in the application state. Each control in the gallery has an index and can be manipulated using this index. *DropDownGallery* and *SplitButtonGallery* are similar to their static-container counterparts, but their content can be altered at runtime instead of being defined only in markup. In the Ribbon framework, a *ComboBox* is also implemented as a gallery-based control. *InRibbonGallery* is a rectangular control that holds a list of items. If there is not enough room to show all the containing controls, it can be expanded to show all of them. In Paint, the Shapes group contains *InRibbonGallery*.

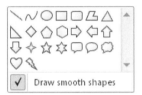

You'll learn how to use galleries from markup and code in the "Managing Galleries" section of the next chapter.

Another two dynamic containers are *Ribbon.QuickAccessToolbar* (which is the QAT you met earlier in the chapter) and *ApplicationMenu.RecentItems*. The QAT is a small toolbar that by default appears at the top of the Ribbon. Although the QAT is a dynamic control, the Ribbon framework handles its content. Whenever the user is choosing to add or remove an item, the framework does it with no need of intervention from code. However, if needed, it can be controlled. The *ApplicationDefault* section provides a quick way to customize the application-chosen defaults. The default control set can contains one or more controls from the *Button*, *CheckBox*, and *ToggleButton* control types. Each of these controls has the attribute *ApplicationDefaults.IsChecked*, which defines the default setting of this item in the QAT. The following code snippet shows how to populate the QAT and set its default commands:

```
<Ribbon.QuickAccessToolbar>
  <QuickAccessToolbar>
    <QuickAccessToolbar.ApplicationDefaults>
      <Button CommandName='cmdPaste' ApplicationDefaults.IsChecked='true'/>
      <Button CommandName='cmdCut' ApplicationDefaults.IsChecked='true'/>
      <Button CommandName='cmdCopy' ApplicationDefaults.IsChecked='true'/>
      <Button CommandName='cmdDelete' ApplicationDefaults.IsChecked='false'/>
      <CheckBox CommandName='cmdCheckBox'  ApplicationDefaults.IsChecked='false'/>
      <ToggleButton CommandName='cmdToggleButton'
                    ApplicationDefaults.IsChecked='false'/>
    </QuickAccessToolbar.ApplicationDefaults>
  </QuickAccessToolbar>
</Ribbon.QuickAccessToolbar>
```

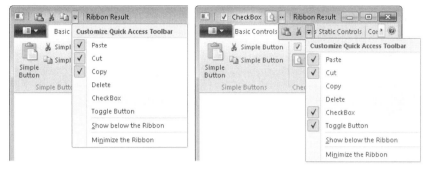

Another attribute that extends the QAT customization menu is *CustomizeCommandName*. This feature adds a new More Commands menu entry to the Customize Quick Access Toolbar menu. The command name that is given to this attribute is the command that will be sent to the application to take action when the user chooses it. Usually, the application pops up a dialog that shows all the commands. Using this dialog, the user can manage the commands that are shown in the QAT. The Ribbon framework dos not supply this dialog. You need to build it on your own.

ApplicationMenu.RecentItems is a special menu entry for populating MRU items, such as files and projects. The header text comes from the *LabelTitle* attribute of the associated command. The content comes from the code. You can set the maximum number of items and whether items can be pinned, as shown in the following code:

```
<Command Name='cmdRecent' LabelTitle='Recent Pictures'/>
...
<Ribbon>
  <Ribbon.ApplicationMenu>
    <ApplicationMenu>
      <ApplicationMenu.RecentItems>
        <RecentItems EnablePinning='false' MaxCount='10' CommandName='cmdRecent'/>
      </ApplicationMenu.RecentItems>
...
```

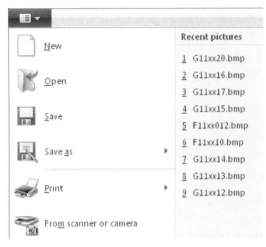

Specialized Controls   This group of controls contains two controls that are composed from many other controls. *DropDownColorPicker* is a composite control that presents a color pallet. *FontControl* presents a font-picker UI. These two controls are very rich. They mimic the color and font manipulation UI elements of the Microsoft Office suite of products.

You cannot get directly to the subcontrol group; instead, these controls take a template that defines the look and functionality of the inner controls. You can also access the subcontrol information using code.

DropDownColorPicker has three looks that are defined by the *ColorTemplate* attribute, as shown in the following screen shot. The value of the attribute can be *ThemeColors*, *StandardColors*, or *HighlightColors*. You can choose the template that is best for your needs.

```
<Ribbon.Tabs>
 <Tab CommandName="cmdHome">
  <Group CommandName="cmdColorGroup" SizeDefinition="ThreeButtons">
   <DropDownColorPicker CommandName="cmdThemeColors" ColorTemplate="ThemeColors"/>
   <DropDownColorPicker CommandName="cmdStandardColors"
                        ColorTemplate="StandardColors"/>
   <DropDownColorPicker CommandName="cmdHighlightColors"
                        ColorTemplate="HighlightColors"/>
  </Group>
 </Tab>
       …
```

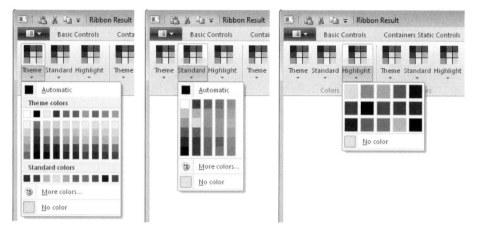

The other attributes control the number of column and rows of *chips* that the color pallet shows, the size of each chip (small, medium, or large) and whether to show or hide some of the control buttons. Note that there are some attributes that are valid only for specific templates. The following markup demonstrates these attributes:

```
<Ribbon.Tabs>
  <Tab CommandName="cmdHome">
    <Group CommandName="cmdColorGroup" SizeDefinition="ThreeButtons">
      <DropDownColorPicker ChipSize="Large" Columns="2" ThemeColorGridRows="3"
                           StandardColorGridRows ="4" CommandName="cmdThemeColors"
                           IsAutomaticColorButtonVisible ="false"
                           IsNoColorButtonVisible="false" RecentColorGridRows="6"
                           ColorTemplate="ThemeColors"/>
      <DropDownColorPicker CommandName="cmdStandardColors" ChipSize="Small"
                           Columns="30" ColorTemplate="StandardColors"/>
      <DropDownColorPicker ChipSize="Medium" Columns="3"
                           CommandName="cmdHighlightColors"
                           ColorTemplate="HighlightColors"/>
    </Group>
  </Tab>
</Ribbon.Tabs>
```

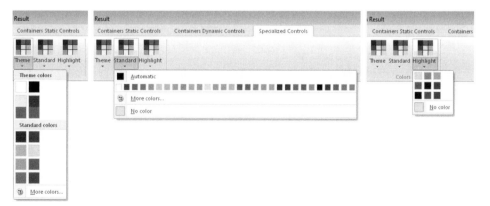

The *FontControl* control is somewhat similar to *DropDownColorPicker*. Like *DropDownColorPicker*, it provides a consistent experience in the configuration and selection of fonts for applications that need to manipulate text. Like the color-picker control, the font control has three different templates that define its look and functionality. To set a template, use the *FontType* attribute. The attribute takes one of the following values: *FontOnly*, *FontWithColor*, and *RichFont*. If the *FontType* attribute is omitted, *FontOnly* is the default template. The following code demonstrates the three types:

```
<Ribbon>
  <Ribbon.Tabs>
    <Tab CommandName="cmdHome">
      <Group CommandName="cmdFontOnlyGroup">
        <FontControl CommandName="cmdFontOnly" FontType="FontOnly" />
      </Group>
      <Group CommandName="cmdFontWithColorGroup">
        <FontControl CommandName="cmdFontWithColor" FontType="FontWithColor" />
      </Group>
      <Group CommandName="cmdRichFontGroup">
        <FontControl CommandName="cmdRichFont" FontType="RichFont" />
      </Group>
    </Tab>
  </Ribbon.Tabs>
</Ribbon>
```

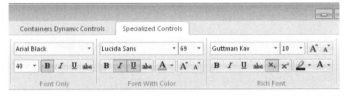

Like the color picker, the *Font* control also defines a set of attributes that help to shape its subcontrols. Using these attributes, you can show or hide the Underline, Highlight, and Strikethrough buttons. You can set the font size limits, and you can filter the font list to have only TrueType fonts or to filter out vertical fonts. Vertical fonts are shown with the @ sign at the beginning of their name. The following code demonstrates the use of those attributes:

```
<Ribbon>
  <Ribbon.Tabs>
    <Tab CommandName="cmdHome">
      <Group CommandName="cmdFontOnlyGroup">
          <FontControl CommandName="cmdFontOnly" FontType="FontOnly"
                       IsUnderlineButtonVisible="false"
                       MinimumFontSize="8" MaximumFontSize ="12"/>
      </Group>
      <Group CommandName="cmdFontWithColorGroup">
        <FontControl CommandName="cmdFontWithColor" FontType="FontWithColor"
                     IsHighlightButtonVisible="false"
                     IsStrikethroughButtonVisible="false"/>
      </Group>
      <Group CommandName="cmdRichFontGroup">
```

```
        <FontControl CommandName="cmdRichFont" FontType="RichFont"
                         ShowTrueTypeOnly="true" ShowVerticalFonts="false"/>
      </Group>
    </Tab>
  </Ribbon.Tabs>
</Ribbon>
```

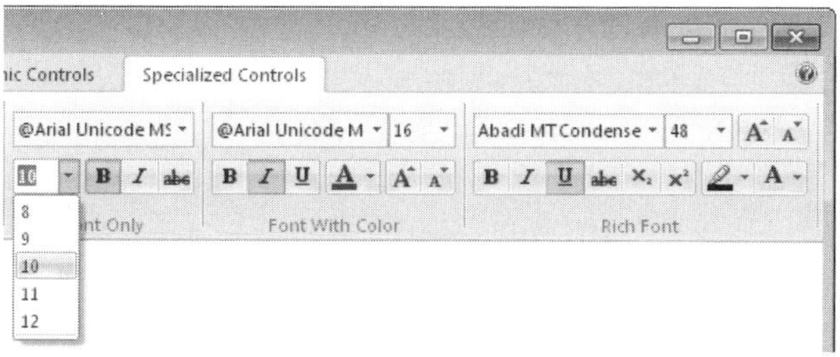

FontControl can also be used in a *ContextPopup* mini-toolbar; however, there is only one pre-defined type of font control that is used in the mini-toolbar, hence you can't set a template (*FontType*). The result is a toolbar that contains the common part of all three templates, as shown in the following screen shot:

You'll see how to manage the special controls from code in the next chapter.

Building the Ribbon

Now you've seen the various controls you can use to build your Ribbon. Building the Ribbon is a matter of creating container controls and populating them with basic controls. Figure 11-13 shows a summary of the Ribbon skeleton:

```xml
<?xml version="1.0" encoding="utf-8" ?>
- <Application xmlns="http://schemas.microsoft.com/windows/2009/Ribbon">
  + <Application.Commands>
  - <Application.Views>
    - <Ribbon>
      + <Ribbon.ApplicationMenu>
      + <Ribbon.QuickAccessToolbar>
      + <Ribbon.SizeDefinitions>
        <Ribbon.HelpButton />
      + <Ribbon.Tabs>
      + <Ribbon.ContextualTabs>
      </Ribbon>
    - <ContextPopup>
      + <ContextPopup.MiniToolbars>
      + <ContextPopup.ContextMenus>
      + <ContextPopup.ContextMaps>
      </ContextPopup>
  </Application.Views>
</Application>
```

Figure 11-17 The skeleton of the Ribbon.

What you see is that you are already familiar with everything in the tree. You know the building blocks of the Ribbon.

Setting the Group's Control Layout

There are more than 20 predefined layout templates, and you can also create a custom template if you don't find a predefined one that fulfills your needs. Each template can have one of three layouts: Large, Medium, or Small. The Popup layout is another pre-defined layout that always exists. According to the scaling policy, the Ribbon framework chooses the best layout. In the book source code folder, you can find the Ribbon Size-Definition markup, which demonstrates the various predefined templates. you can play with it using the RibbonExplorer tool. Figure 11-18 demonstrates the scaling behavior of the Ribbon.

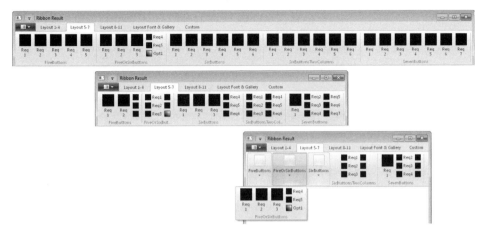

Figure 11-18 The scaling behavior of the Ribbon.

Size definition templates use the notion of a control family. For example, the *OneButton* size definition template takes one control that belongs to the button family. The button family members are *Button*, *ToggleButton*, *DropDownButton*, *SplitButton*, *DropDownGallery*, *SplitButtonGallery*, and *DropDownColorPicker*. The input family members are *ComboBox* and *Spinner*. Other controls do not belong to a family and they have predefined layout specific for them, for example the *InRibbonGalleryAndThreeButtons* or *OneFontControl* size definitions. The size definition template also defines whether a control is required or optional. Let's examine the *FiveOrSixButtons* predefined template:

```
<Group CommandName="cmdFiveOrSixButtons" SizeDefinition="FiveOrSixButtons">
    <Button CommandName="Req1"/>
    <Button CommandName="Req2"/>
    <Button CommandName="Req3"/>
    <Button CommandName="Req4"/>
    <Button CommandName="Req5"/>
    <Button CommandName="Opt1"/>
</Group>
```

This *FiveOrSixButtons* size definition template requires five controls from the button family and another optional control from the same family. This template defines three layouts. The additional popup layout shows the larger layout below the Ribbon when the user press the popup button. Figure 11-19 shows the three layouts of the *FiveOrSixButtons* size definition template. Black filled rectangle marks a required button while semi-black filled rectangle marks an optional button.

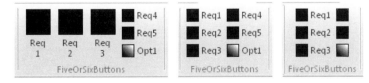

Figure 11-19 *FiveOrSixButtons* template: Large, Medium, and Small.

Not all size definition templates have all layouts. For example, the *OneButton* template has only the Large and Popup variations.

> **Note** According to the UICC.XSD schema, there are 27 predefined layout templates. However, three of them are used by the internal code of *FontControl* to manage the different font control layouts.

Controlling Scaling Behavior

By now, you know that each size definition template can have three custom layouts, the Large, Medium and Small, and one predefine layout, the Popup that always exist. The Large occupies the most space while the Popup occupies the least. You also know that the framework will try to do its best in choosing the right layout of each group in a Ribbon tab. It's your responsibility to instruct the framework about the size policy. You might want to use the large scale for the more important group of commands and the small or popup size for less important groups. Using the scaling policy of the Ribbon tab, you can tell the framework what the ideal size of each group is and how to arrange each group. In the following markup segment, you tell the framework to use the large scale whenever there is enough room in the Ribbon. If the user shrinks the window and makes the Ribbon narrower, the scaling policy tells the framework to move first to the medium scale, then to the small scale, and last to the popup size. The order of the scale elements defines the shrinking order of the groups.

```
<Tab CommandName="cmdLayout">
  <Tab.ScalingPolicy>
    <ScalingPolicy>
      <ScalingPolicy.IdealSizes>
        <Scale Group="cmdFiveButtons" Size="Large"/>
        <Scale Group="cmdFiveOrSixButtons" Size="Large"/>
      </ScalingPolicy.IdealSizes>

      <Scale Group="cmdFiveButtons" Size="Medium"/>
      <Scale Group="cmdFiveOrSixButtons" Size="Medium"/>

      <Scale Group="cmdFiveButtons" Size="Small"/>
      <Scale Group="cmdFiveOrSixButtons" Size="Small"/>

      <Scale Group="cmdFiveButtons" Size="Popup"/>
      <Scale Group="cmdFiveOrSixButtons" Size="Popup"/>
    </ScalingPolicy>
  </Tab.ScalingPolicy>
```

You can set up to maximum of 15 scale elements in *Tab.ScalingPolicy*.

Defining Custom Size Definition Templates

If the predefined size definition template is not suitable to your needs, you can define custom templates. The *Ribbon.SizeDefinition* section is used to define reusable custom templates, while the group *SizeDefinition* attribute has an inline form to define a single-time-use template. Suppose we need to have a layout of two buttons, by default one is big and the other one is small. Since we don't have a predefine template for such layout we can create one. The following markup demonstrates how to create the needed custom template in the *Ribbon.SizeDefinitions* :

```
…
<Ribbon>
  <Ribbon.SizeDefinitions>
    <SizeDefinition Name="TwoButtonsBigAndSmall">
      <ControlNameMap>
        <ControlNameDefinition Name="button1"/>
        <ControlNameDefinition Name="button2"/>
      </ControlNameMap>
      <GroupSizeDefinition Size="Large">
        <Row>
          <ControlSizeDefinition ControlName="button1" ImageSize="Large"
                                 IsLabelVisible="true" />
          <ControlSizeDefinition ControlName="button2" ImageSize="Small"
                                 IsLabelVisible="true" />
        </Row>
      </GroupSizeDefinition>
      <GroupSizeDefinition Size="Medium">
        <Row>
          <ControlSizeDefinition ControlName="button1" ImageSize="Large"
                                 IsLabelVisible="true" />
          <ControlSizeDefinition ControlName="button2" ImageSize="Small"
                                 IsLabelVisible="false" />
        </Row>
      </GroupSizeDefinition>
      <GroupSizeDefinition Size="Small">
        <ControlSizeDefinition ControlName="button1" ImageSize="Small"
                               IsLabelVisible="false" />
        <ControlSizeDefinition ControlName="button2" ImageSize="Small"
                               IsLabelVisible="false" />
      </GroupSizeDefinition>
    </SizeDefinition>
  </Ribbon.SizeDefinitions>
  …
  <Tab CommandName="CustomTemplate">
    <Tab.ScalingPolicy>
      <ScalingPolicy>
        <ScalingPolicy.IdealSizes>
          <Scale Group="cmdReuseSizeDefinitionGroup" Size="Large"/>
        </ScalingPolicy.IdealSizes>
        <Scale Group="cmdReuseSizeDefinitionGroup" Size="Medium"/>
        <Scale Group="cmdReuseSizeDefinitionGroup" Size="Small"/>
        <Scale Group="cmdReuseSizeDefinitionGroup" Size="Popup"/>
```

```
      </ScalingPolicy>
    </Tab.ScalingPolicy>
    <Group CommandName="cmdReuseSizeDefinitionGroup"
           SizeDefinition="TwoButtonsBigAndSmall">
      <Button CommandName="Req1"></Button>
      <Button CommandName="Req2"></Button>
    </Group>
      <!-- Extra controls to make the tab larger -->
    <Group>
      <FontControl/>
    </Group>
    <Group>
      <FontControl/>
    </Group>
    <Group>
      <FontControl/>
    </Group>
  </Tab>
  ...
```

When defining a new reusable custom template in *Ribbon.SizeDefinition*, the *Name* attribute of the *SizeDefinition* element defines the name of the template. In the previous code, the name is *"TwoButtonsBigAndSmall"*. In *ControlNameMap*, you declare the controls that the template manipulates. The *Row* element forces the control to be on one line. *ColumnBreak* adds a vertical line that separates the controls in a group. You cannot use *ColumnBreak* between elements inside *Row*.

The following markup demonstrates how to create the same custom template inside the group:

```
        <Group CommandName="cmdInLineSizeDefinitionGroup">
          <SizeDefinition>
            <ControlNameMap>
              <ControlNameDefinition Name="button1"/>
              <ControlNameDefinition Name="button2"/>
            </ControlNameMap>
            <GroupSizeDefinition Size="Large">
              <Row>
                <ControlSizeDefinition ControlName="button1"
                                       ImageSize="Large"
                                       IsLabelVisible="true" />
                <ControlSizeDefinition ControlName="button2"
                                       ImageSize="Small"
```

```
                                          IsLabelVisible="true" />
            </Row>
          </GroupSizeDefinition>
          <GroupSizeDefinition Size="Medium">
            <Row>
              <ControlSizeDefinition ControlName="button1"
                                     ImageSize="Large"
                                     IsLabelVisible="true" />
              <ControlSizeDefinition ControlName="button2"
                                     ImageSize="Small"
                                     IsLabelVisible="false" />
            </Row>
          </GroupSizeDefinition>
          <GroupSizeDefinition Size="Small">
            <ControlSizeDefinition ControlName="button1"
                                   ImageSize="Small"
                                   IsLabelVisible="false" />
            <ControlSizeDefinition ControlName="button2"
                                   ImageSize="Small"
                                   IsLabelVisible="false" />
          </GroupSizeDefinition>
        </SizeDefinition>
        <Button CommandName="Req1"></Button>
        <Button CommandName="Req2"></Button>
      </Group>
```

The inline custom definition is the same as the global definition, but you don't give a name to the template.

Summary

In this chapter, we looked at the building blocks of the Windows Ribbon. We started with the story of the Ribbon and the reasons for the change in users' perceptions of the UI. We continued with the concept of separating the UI and the logic. You learned about the UI side of the Ribbon framework. You also saw the tools needed to build and compile the markup file. Now you know how to define commands and how to associate them with controls. You're also familiar with the various Ribbon sections, such as the Quick Access Toolbar, Application menu, tabs, and groups. At the end of the chapter, you learned about the layout system. By now, you should have a solid understanding of the UI side of the Windows Ribbon framework. In the next chapter, you'll see how you can interact with the Ribbon from code.

Chapter 12
Develop with the Windows Ribbon, Part 2

By now, you know how to create a Ribbon markup file. You don't know yet how to load it and interact with it from code. Unlike the traditional Win32 UI system, which is based on the Microsoft Windows messages interface, the Ribbon framework defines its own way of interacting, using the Component Object Model (COM) as its interfacing mechanism. The interaction is a Ping-Pong game between the Ribbon framework and your application code.

You are responsible for creating an instance of the Ribbon framework, asking it to load the resource, and initiating the Ribbon. The Ribbon framework loads and builds the Ribbon. For each command in use, the framework asks your code for a known COM object that will be responsible for handling the command event. You can respond to events, invalidate the Ribbon or part of it, or call the Ribbon framework interface to change some of the Ribbon settings and properties. Many of the features you saw in the previous chapter come to life using code, from the *CheckBox* control that needs to be initiated and changed to reflect the application state to a *Gallery* that needs to be populated. Your code is responsible for handling Ribbon events and for changing the Ribbon state. In this chapter, you will see how to create an instance of the Ribbon, how to bind the Ribbon framework and your code so that they work together, and how to handle Ribbon events.

Programming the Ribbon

Because the Ribbon framework is based on the Component Object Model, you first need to choose your tool for using COM. To use the Ribbon framework, it is not enough to know how to consume COM objects; you also need to implement your own COM objects to let the framework call your code. You can use plain old C++ and implement all COM plumbing by hand, or you can use a framework such as Active Template Library (ATL), in which case you get the plumbing for free. In the book sample, we use ATL; however, many of the Windows SDK samples use only C++.

If you decide to use ATL, you can use the Microsoft Visual Studio Application Wizard to start an ATL project or create a Win32 project and add the ATL support by including the atlbase.h, atlcom.h, and initguid.h header files. You also need to have a global ATL object. The easy way to do this is to declare the *CComModule* object instance in one of your CPP files; however, as of ATL 7.0 this type is obsolete and you should use one of its new replacements, such as deriving from *CAtlDllModuleT* and declaring a global variable from this type.

There are many COM interfaces that involve programming with the Windows Ribbon framework, but three of them are especially important and are part of any Ribbon-based UI application: the *IUIFramework*, *IUIApplication*, and *IUICommandHandler*. These are the main interaction points of the Ribbon framework and the code behind. We'll start by introducing these interfaces and showing how to use them to initialize the Ribbon framework. Later, we'll see how to handle events and change the various Ribbon properties and state.

The Minimal Ribbon Revisited

Do you recall the minimal Ribbon application from the previous chapter? We'll begin with creating code that initiates the framework and loads the minimal Ribbon that is compiled into the resource markup. Our starting point is the Visual Studio new Win32 project template that creates the basic Windows application.

In the wizard, you can enable the Add Common Header Files For ATL option by selecting the ATL check box. This will add an `#include "atlbase.h"` line to the *stdafx.h* header file. If you don't select this check box, you will need to manually add this *include* line to your code. Let the Application Wizard finish creating the project files, compile the code, and then execute it. You get an application that shows an empty window. The first step is to add a Ribbon to the application.

Add the following code to the MinimalRibbon.h header file:

```
//MinimalRibbon.h

#pragma once

#include "resource.h"
#include <UIRibbon.h>
```

```
bool InitializeFramework(HWND hWnd);
void DestroyFramework();

extern IUIFramework *g_pFramework; // Reference to the Ribbon framework.
extern IUIApplication *g_pApplication;  // Reference to the application object.
```

InitializeFramework and *DestroyFramework* do exactly what their names suggest; you'll see their implementation shortly. The two other definitions are two interface pointers to the most important objects in the Ribbon game: the Ribbon framework object and your Application object. You need to implement a class that implements the *IUIApplication* interface. Then you need to create both the Ribbon framework and an instance of your application class, and then bind the application object to the Ribbon framework.

The following code demonstrates the minimal steps that are required to have a Ribbon using ATL for COM support. Since we have started the project with the Visual Studio "Win32 Application" project template and not an ATL project template we cannot use the Visual Studio template to add "ATL Simple Object". To use ATL you need to include the atlbase.h and atlcom.h header files and manually add the *CComObjectRootEx* derivation and COM interface map:

```
//Application.h

#pragma once
#include <propvarutil.h>
#include <initguid.h>
#include <UIRibbon.h>
#include <atlbase.h>
#include <atlcom.h>

class CApplication
    : public CComObjectRootEx<CComMultiThreadModel>
    , public IUIApplication // Applications must implement IUIApplication.
{
public:

    BEGIN_COM_MAP(CApplication)
        COM_INTERFACE_ENTRY(IUIApplication)
    END_COM_MAP()

    //
    //  FUNCTION: OnViewChanged(UINT, UI_VIEWTYPE, IUnknown*, UI_VIEWVERB, INT)
    //
    //  PURPOSE: Called when the state of a View (Ribbon is a view) changes;
    //           for example, when it is created, destroyed, or resized.
    //
    STDMETHOD(OnViewChanged)(UINT viewId,
    __in UI_VIEWTYPE typeId,
    __in IUnknown* pView,
    UI_VIEWVERB verb,
    INT uReasonCode);
```

```
//
// FUNCTION: OnCreateUICommand(UINT, UI_COMMANDTYPE, IUICommandHandler)
//
// PURPOSE: Called by the Ribbon framework for each command specified in
//          markup, to allow the host application to bind a command handler
//          to that command.
//
STDMETHOD(OnCreateUICommand)(UINT nCmdID,
    __in UI_COMMANDTYPE typeID,
    __deref_out IUICommandHandler** ppCommandHandler);


//
// FUNCTION: OnDestroyUICommand(UINT, UI_COMMANDTYPE, IUICommandHandler*)
//
// PURPOSE: Called by the Ribbon framework for each command at the time of
//          ribbon destruction.
//
STDMETHOD(OnDestroyUICommand)(UINT32 commandId,
    __in UI_COMMANDTYPE typeID,
    __in_opt IUICommandHandler* commandHandler);

private:
    CComPtr<IUICommandHandler> _spCommandHandler; // Generic Command Handler
    CComPtr<IUIRibbon> _spRibbon;                 // Ribbon
};
```

The following code shows the minimal implementation that is required to implement the application object and start the minimal Ribbon application:

```
//Application.cpp

#include "StdAfx.h"
#include "Application.h"
#include <UIRibbonPropertyHelpers.h>


CComModule _Module; //Needed by ATL

IUIFramework *g_pFramework = NULL;  // Reference to the Ribbon framework.
IUIApplication *g_pApplication = NULL;  // Reference to the application object.

//
// FUNCTION: InitializeFramework(HWND)
//
// PURPOSE:  Initialize the Ribbon framework and bind a Ribbon to the application.
//
// COMMENTS:
//
//    To get a Ribbon to display, the Ribbon framework must be initialized.
//    This involves three important steps:
//        1) Instantiating the Ribbon framework object (CLSID_UIRibbonFramework).
//        2) Passing the host HWND and IUIApplication object to the framework.
//        3) Loading the binary markup compiled by UICC.EXE.
//
```

```
bool InitializeFramework(HWND hWnd)
{
    // Instantiate the Ribbon framework object.
    HRESULT hr = CoCreateInstance(CLSID_UIRibbonFramework, NULL,
                            CLSCTX_INPROC_SERVER, IID_PPV_ARGS(&g_pFramework));
    if (FAILED(hr))
    {
        _cwprintf(L"CoCreateInstance on CLSID_UIRibbonFramework failed with"
                L"hr=0x%X\r\n", hr);
        return false;
    }

    // Create our application object (IUIApplication), and initialize the
    // framework, passing the application object and the host HWND.
    CComObject<CApplication> *pApplication = NULL;
    CComObject<CApplication>::CreateInstance(&pApplication);
    hr = pApplication->QueryInterface(&g_pApplication);
    if (FAILED(hr))
    {
        _cwprintf(L"IUIFramework::QueryInterface failed with hr=0x%X\r\n", hr);
        return false;
    }

    hr = g_pFramework->Initialize(hWnd, g_pApplication);
    if (FAILED(hr))
    {
        _cwprintf(L"IUIFramework::Initialize failed with hr=0x%X\r\n", hr);
        return false;
    }

    // Load the binary markup. This will initiate callbacks to the IUIApplication
    // object that was provided to the framework, allowing binding of command handlers
    hr = g_pFramework->LoadUI(GetModuleHandle(NULL), L"APPLICATION_RIBBON");
    if (FAILED(hr))
    {
        _cwprintf(L"IUIFramework::LoadUI failed with hr=0x%X\r\n", hr);
        return false;
    }

    _cwprintf(L"Ribbon has been loaded successfully.\r\n");
    return true;
}

//
// FUNCTION: DestroyFramework()
//
// PURPOSE:  Tears down the Ribbon framework.
//
//
void DestroyFramework()
{
    if (g_pFramework != NULL)
    {
        HRESULT hr = g_pFramework->Destroy();
```

```
            g_pFramework->Release();
            g_pFramework = NULL;
            if (FAILED(hr))
            {
                _cwprintf(L"IUIFramework::Destroy() failed with hr=0x%X\r\n", hr);
            }
        }

        if (g_pApplication != NULL)
        {
            g_pApplication->Release();
            g_pApplication = NULL;
        }

        _cwprintf(L"Ribbon has been torn down successfully.\r\n");
}


//
//   FUNCTION: OnCreateUICommand(UINT, UI_COMMANDTYPE, IUICommandHandler)
//
//   PURPOSE: Called by the Ribbon framework for each command specified in markup,
//            to allow the host application to bind a command handler to that
//            command.
//
STDMETHODIMP CApplication::OnCreateUICommand(
    UINT nCmdID,
    __in UI_COMMANDTYPE typeID,
    __deref_out IUICommandHandler** ppCommandHandler)
{
    return E_NOTIMPL;
}


//
//   FUNCTION: OnViewChanged(UINT, UI_VIEWTYPE, IUnknown*, UI_VIEWVERB, INT)
//
//   PURPOSE: Called when the state of a View (Ribbon is a view) changes;
//            for example, when it is created, destroyed, or resized.
//
STDMETHODIMP CApplication::OnViewChanged(
    UINT viewId,
    __in UI_VIEWTYPE typeId,
    __in IUnknown* pView,
    UI_VIEWVERB verb,
    INT uReasonCode)
{
    return E_NOTIMPL;
}



//
//   FUNCTION: OnDestroyUICommand(UINT, UI_COMMANDTYPE, IUICommandHandler*)
//
//   PURPOSE: Called by the Ribbon framework for each command at the time of
//            ribbon destruction.
```

```
//
STDMETHODIMP CApplication::OnDestroyUICommand(
    UINT32 nCmdID,
    __in UI_COMMANDTYPE typeID,
    __in_opt IUICommandHandler* commandHandler)
{

    return E_NOTIMPL;
}
```

For this application to successfully load the Ribbon, you need to complete a few more steps. First, add the following lines at the beginning of the _tWinMain_ function:

```
// Win32 application can have console window for logging messages.
AllocConsole(); //For debugging messages
//Initialize COM
HRESULT hr = CoInitialize(NULL);
if (FAILED(hr))
{
    _cwprintf(L"CoInitialize failed with hr=0x%X\r\n", hr);
    return FALSE;
}
```

When the application exits, for the sake of cleanup, add the following code just after the closing curly brace of the messages loop:

```
CoUninitialize();
// Sleep for a second before dismissing the console window.
Sleep(1000);
FreeConsole();
```

The last step is to initiate the Ribbon in the WM_CREATE message of the main window. Add the following code to the switch statement of the _WndProc_ function:

```
...
bool initSuccess;
switch (message)
{
    case WM_CREATE:
        // Initializes the Ribbon framework.
        initSuccess = InitializeFramework(hWnd);
        if (!initSuccess)
        {
            return -1;
        }
        break;
...
```

Of course, you have to add the Ribbon.xml file from the previous chapter as well as set the custom build to create the Ribbon resource and header file:

```
<?xml version="1.0" encoding="utf-8"?>
<Application xmlns='http://schemas.microsoft.com/windows/2009/Ribbon'>
```

```
<Application.Views>
  <Ribbon>
  </Ribbon>
</Application.Views>
</Application>
```

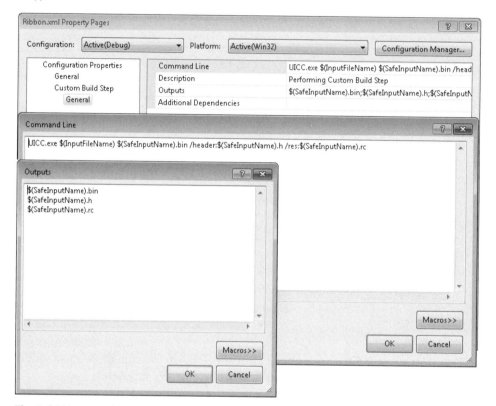

That's it! You are done. Compile and run the application. You can change the XML file to any of the Ribbon markup from the previous chapter and get the same result as when you used the *RibbonExplorer* tool.

Initialization Phase

You start by creating the Ribbon framework COM object and using its class ID definition: *CLSID_UIRibbonFramework*. Next you create the application object that, from the Ribbon framework point of view, has to implement the *IUIApplication* interface. You also set the two global interface pointers to point to these two instances for further use from your code. At this point, you must provide three important pieces of information to the Ribbon framework: the application object that will interact with the Ribbon framework, the handle to the Window that will own the Ribbon, and the resource that contains the Ribbon data. The first method of *IUIFramework* is *Initialize*. The method takes the *Application* object pointer and the main window handle. The second method is *LoadUI*. The method takes the handle to the module that contains the Ribbon resource and the name of the resource that the resource compiler gave to the Ribbon data. The default name is "APPLICATION_RIBBON".

Providing the Ribbon Resource

In the MinimalRibbon sample, the module that contains the Ribbon resource is the executable itself. To get the corresponding HMODULE, you can call *GetModuleHandle* with the NULL argument. However, sometimes the resource will be embedded in another dynamic-link library (DLL). For example, in the case of localization of the application, you can have more than one satellite DLL for each supported language. In this case, you can load the library as a resource library and get the HMODULE from the *LoadLibraryEx* API:

```
HMODULE hModule = LoadLibraryEx(szResourceDllName, NULL,
        DONT_RESOLVE_DLL_REFERENCES | LOAD_IGNORE_CODE_AUTHZ_LEVEL |
        LOAD_LIBRARY_AS_DATAFILE | LOAD_LIBRARY_AS_IMAGE_RESOURCE);
```

After calling the *LoadUI* method, the Ribbon framework creates the Ribbon. For each control that is bound to a command, the Ribbon framework calls back to the *CApplication::OnCreateUICommand* method . This is where the application provides an object that implements the *IUICommandHandler* interface. This object handles notifications from the Ribbon framework that are related to the specific command. You can design your application to provide the same object for all commands or a different object for each command. For example, the *CApplication* class can implement the *IUICommandHandler* interface, and it handles all callbacks in this one place. For a complex UI with many commands, you can choose to provide many objects; each one handles a set of related commands. The *OnCreateUICommand* method provides the command type, which could be vital information for choosing the code that will handle the command notifications. It's up to you to determine how the dispatching of callback invocations will be done in your code. You'll see shortly how to provide command handlers and how to respond to callbacks. First, look at Figure 12-1, which is a sequence diagram of the initialization phase.

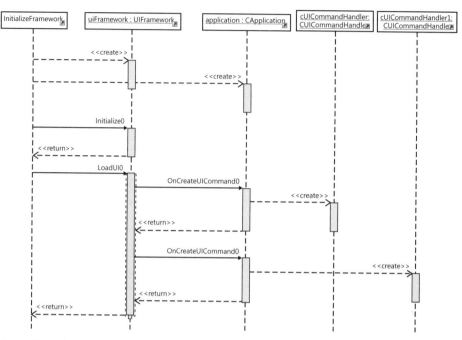

Figure 12-1 Initiating the Ribbon framework sequence diagram

Handling Ribbon Callbacks

During the initialization phase, you saw that for each command that is bound to a control, the Ribbon framework calls back to the object that implemented *IUIApplication::OnCreateUICommand* and asks it to provide an object that will handle the communication between the Ribbon framework and the application for this specific command. The application should return an object that implements the *IUICommandHandler* interface. This interface has two methods that we have to implement: *Execute* and *UpdateProperty*. The Ribbon framework calls *UpdateProperty* to request a new value of a command (control) property. We'll dive into the Ribbon Property system in the following sections. The *Execute* method is where you change the application state to reflect the user action:

```
HRESULT Execute(
    UINT32 commandId,
    UI_EXECUTIONVERB verb,
    const PROPERTYKEY *key,
    const PROPVARIANT *currentValue,
    IUISimplePropertySet *commandExecutionProperties
);
```

The *commandId* value is the one that you (using the command's *Id* attribute) or the UICC.EXE compiler gave to the command, and it's declared in the header file that was generated as part of the Ribbon markup compilation process. The *commandId* value is useful when the same object that implements the *IUICommandHandler* is responsible for more than one command, which is a common scenario. By checking the *commandId* value, you know which command originated the callback.

The verb tells you what to do in response to the user action. The Ribbon framework defines three possible actions: execute, preview, and cancel preview. For simple controls, the verb argument is always UI_EXECUTIONVERB_EXECUTE. It becomes much more interesting when working with Galleries. When the mouse cursor hovers over the gallery's controls, the *Execute* method is called with the verb value of UI_EXECUTIONVERB_PREVIEW. To support Live Preview, your application code should execute the command as if the user has chosen to press the control. The Preview verb never comes alone. If the user moves the mouse cursor to another control in the gallery, another call to *Execute* comes with another Preview verb. Whenever the user decides to either press the mouse button to make the change permanent or remove the mouse cursor from the control to cancel the change, UI_EXECUTIONVERB_EXECUTE and UI_EXECUTIONVERB_CANCELPREVIEW are the verb values that reflect the user's will.

The last three parameters provide extra information that comes from the control that invoked the command. For example, *ToggleButton* or *CheckBox* provides its Boolean state. This saves you the need to query the control state. We'll demonstrate how to use properties in the following section. For now let's see a simple sample of a handler that handles more than one command:

```
STDMETHODIMP Execute(UINT nCmdID,
        UI_EXECUTIONVERB verb,
        __in_opt const PROPERTYKEY* key,
        __in_opt const PROPVARIANT* ppropvarValue,
        __in_opt IUISimplePropertySet* pCommandExecutionProperties)
{
    switch(nCmdID)
    {
        case cmdButton1:
            DoSomething();
            break;

        case cmdButton2:
            DoSomethingElse();
            break;
    }
}
```

Avoid the Switch Statement

We don't like to use the switch statement in code. Using a switch statement contradicts the Open/Close Principle (OCP), which says that you should be able to extend the application without changing the application code. For example, if you add a new command to the Ribbon and use the same *IUICommandHandler*, you need to add another case to the previous switch statement. To support the OCP, the Windows Ribbon team provides you with the ability to register a different *IUICommandHandler* for each command. If you still don't want to implement a COM object to handle each command separately, you can make your own dispatching mechanism—for example, by using a Standard Template Library (STL) map, between command IDs and function pointers. In the book samples, for readability we use the switch statement.

The Property System

Like many other COM-based technologies, the Ribbon framework makes use of the COM property set. The property set is a key/value pair—or in COM terminology, a PROPERTYKEY and PROPVARIANT pair.

The key is a structure that ensures the uniqueness of each property. The UIRibbon.h header file contains the definitions of all the Ribbon control properties. Each command has one or more properties. The command "type" is defined by the control that is bound to the command. The Ribbon framework makes it possible to reuse the same command with different controls in different locations. For example, the same command can be bound to a button in a tab group or to a button in a menu group in the Application menu. But you cannot bind the same command to different control types or controls of the same type with different settings. If a command is bound to more than one control and they are not compatible, the UICC.EXE compiler issues a compilation error. After a command is bound to a control, it gets its command type and attributes; hence, it gets the set of properties that control the control state and behavior. For example, if a command is bound to a font control, more than a dozen properties can be used to query or set the font control state.

When the *IUIApplication::OnCreateUICommand* method calls back and asks for an object that implements *IUICommandHandler*, it also provides the UI_COMMANDTYPE, which is the command type associated with the control. Table 12-1 shows the correlation between controls and command types.

Table 12-1 Command Types and Their Related Controls

Command Type	Controls
UI_COMMANDTYPE_GROUP	*Group*
UI_COMMANDTYPE_ACTION	*Button, Ribbon.HelpButton*
UI_COMMANDTYPE_ANCHOR	*ApplicationMenu, DropDownButton, SplitButton, Tab*
UI_COMMANDTYPE_CONTEXT	*Ribbon.ContextualTabs*
UI_COMMANDTYPE_COLLECTION	*ComboBox, DropDownGallery, InRibbonGallery, SplitButtonGallery*
UI_COMMANDTYPE_COMMANDCOLLECTION	*DropDownGallery, InRibbonGallery, QuickAccessToolbar, SplitButtonGallery*
UI_COMMANDTYPE_DECIMAL	*Spinner*
UI_COMMANDTYPE_BOOLEAN	*ToggleButton, CheckBox*
UI_COMMANDTYPE_FONT	*FontControl*
UI_COMMANDTYPE_RECENTITEMS	*RecentItems*
UI_COMMANDTYPE_COLORANCHOR	*DropDownColorPicker*

Table 12-2 contains the most common properties, which are also all the properties of a command that is bound to the *Button* control.

Table 12-2 Common Properties

Property	Type	Description
UI_PKEY_Enabled	VT_BOOL	Enables or disables the control.
UI_PKEY_Keytip	VT_LPWSTR	The keyboard accelerator. Activated when the user presses the Alt key.
UI_PKEY_Label	VT_LPWSTR	The control label.
UI_PKEY_LabelDescription	VT_LPWSTR	Extended information. Shown when a control is displayed in the right pane of the Application menu.
UI_PKEY_LargeHighContrastImage	IUIImage	The high-contrast, large image of the control.
UI_PKEY_LargeImage	IUIImage	The large image of the control.
UI_PKEY_SmallHighContrastImage	IUIImage	The high-contrast, small image of the control.

UI_PKEY_SmallImage	IUIImage	The small image of the control.
UI_PKEY_TooltipDescription	VT_LPWSTR	Extended information for the ToolTip.
UI_PKEY_TooltipTitle	VT_LPWSTR	The ToolTip of the control, tab, or group.

Setting Properties Directly or Indirectly

Each ribbon control has a set of properties. The initial values of the properties come from the Ribbon XML file. Not every property value can be set in the XML file. You cannot set the current value of the *Spinner* control or its limits. You cannot set the initial state of the *ToggleButton* and *CheckBox* controls. You cannot set the state of the contextual tabs and so forth. During the initialization process of the Ribbon, the Ribbon framework creates a control and asks for its command handler. The *IUICommandHandler* interface declares two methods: *Execute*, which you saw before, and *UpdateProperty*. You should provide an object that implements this interface. Right after that, the framework calls back to the provided object's *UpdateProperty* method and asks for the commands' unknown property values. Here is a sample of this flow, taken from the RibbonExplorer trace window:

```
OnCreateUICommand -> ID:cmdContextualTabGrp    Type:Context
UpdateProperty -> ID:cmdContextualTabGrp    Key Name:UI_PKEY_ContextAvailable    Current
Value:UI_CONTEXTAVAILABILITY_NOTAVAILABLE
OnCreateUICommand -> ID:cmdContextualTabGrp2    Type:Context
UpdateProperty -> ID:cmdContextualTabGrp2    Key Name:UI_PKEY_ContextAvailable    Current
Value:UI_CONTEXTAVAILABILITY_NOTAVAILABLE
OnCreateUICommand -> ID:cmdPaste    Type:Action
UpdateProperty -> ID:cmdPaste    Key Name:UI_PKEY_Enabled    Current Value:True
OnCreateUICommand -> ID:cmdCut    Type:Action
```

For the Contextual tab group, the framework calls and asks for its UI availability. For a *Button*, it asks for its enabled state. Later in the lifetime of the Ribbon, the framework might call and ask again for these or other properties. For example, this might happen when the user is hovering the mouse pointer over the Ribbon and the framework needs to provide a ToolTip that does not exist in the XML, or the user opens the Application menu, which triggers a rendering of many new controls. These calls to *UpdateProperty* are done by the Ribbon framework when it needs additional data.

```
HRESULT UpdateProperty(UINT32 commandId,
                       REFPROPERTYKEY key,
                       const PROPVARIANT *currentValue,
                       PROPVARIANT *newValue
);
```

UpdateProperty receives four arguments; the first one is *commandId*. This is the same argument of the *Execute* method. The *commandId* argument is useful when the same object that implements *IUICommandHandler* is responsible for more than one command. The second argument is the property key that defines the unique property. The third argument is the current value of the property (which is NULL when no value is provided in the XML), and the last argument is the value that you should supply as the new value of the property.

Sometimes your application state changes and you need to reflect this change in the Ribbon. You have two ways to change a property value. The first way is to call the *IUIFramework::SetUICommandProperty* method and set the new property value:

```
HRESULT SetUICommandProperty(UINT32 commandId,
                             REFPROPERTYKEY key,
                             PROPVARIANT value
);
```

In many cases, when you use this method you get a failure result that informs you that the property you are trying to set is not suitable to direct property change, and you need to tell the framework to call you back and ask for that property value. Telling the framework to call back for a new property value is done by invalidating the command state, value, or property. You do that by using the *IUIFramework::InvalidateUICommand* method:

```
HRESULT InvalidateUICommand(UINT32 commandId,
                            UI_INVALIDATIONS flags,
                            const PROPERTYKEY *key
);
```

The only argument that needs an explanation is the *flags* argument. This argument tells the Ribbon framework what aspect of the command to invalidate. This can be the value, the state, the supplying property, or all the properties of the command. For example, the *Spinner* control numeric value is invalidated using UI_INVALIDATIONS_VALUE and a control enable/disable state is invalidated using UI_INVALIDATIONS_STATE. The *key* argument is used in conjunction with UI_INVALIDATIONS_PROPERTY. If you want the system to call you back for all of the properties of a command, use UI_INVALIDATIONS_ALLPROPERTIES. After invalidating a command, the framework calls *UpdateProperty* with the invalidated property. You need to supply the new value and to return S_OK to tell the framework to set that value.

The following code snippet shows how to change the button text when the user clicks the button:

```
Ribbon.xml:
<?xml version="1.0" encoding="utf-8"?>
<Application xmlns='http://schemas.microsoft.com/windows/2009/Ribbon'>
  <Application.Commands>
    <Command Name='cmdHome' Keytip='H' LabelTitle='Home'/>
    <Command Name='cmdGrp' Keytip='G' LabelTitle='Invalidate Commands'/>
      <Command Name='cmdButton' Keytip='B' LabelTitle='Change Me!'/>
  </Application.Commands>
  <Application.Views>
    <Ribbon>
      <Ribbon.Tabs>
```

```
            <Tab CommandName='cmdHome'>
              <Group CommandName='cmdGrp'>
                <Button CommandName='cmdButton'/>
              </Group>
            </Tab>
          </Ribbon.Tabs>
        </Ribbon>
      </Application.Views>
    </Application>


Application.cpp:
...
STDMETHODIMP CApplication::Execute(UINT nCmdID,
                    UI_EXECUTIONVERB verb,
                    __in_opt const PROPERTYKEY* key,
                    __in_opt const PROPVARIANT* ppropvarValue,
                    __in_opt IUISimplePropertySet* pCommandExecutionProperties)
{
    HRESULT hr = E_FAIL;
    if (nCmdID == cmdButton)
    {
        g_pFramework->InvalidateUICommand(nCmdID, UI_INVALIDATIONS_PROPERTY,
                                &UI_PKEY_Label);
        hr = S_OK;
    }
    return hr;
}


STDMETHODIMP CApplication::UpdateProperty(UINT nCmdID,
                        __in REFPROPERTYKEY key,
                        __in_opt const PROPVARIANT* ppropvarCurrentValue,
                        __out PROPVARIANT* ppropvarNewValue)
{
    HRESULT hr = E_FAIL;

    if (nCmdID == cmdButton && key == UI_PKEY_Label)
    {
        UIInitPropertyFromString(UI_PKEY_Label, L"Changed!", ppropvarNewValue);
        hr = S_OK;
    }
    return hr;
}
```

The *UIInitPropertyFromString* function is a helper function that initializes a Property Key value from a C++ Unicode string. In the preceding sample, the "Changed!" string is assigned to the ppropvalNewValue by this function. The *UIRibbonPropertyHelpers.h* header file contains this function and other similar helper functions that support initializing of the various property key types, such as the *UIInitPropertyFromBoolean* and *UIInitPropertyFromUInt32* functions. There is another family of helper functions in the *UIRibbonPropertyHelpers.h* header file that helps you to convert from property key values back to the C++ type representations such as the *UIPropertyToBoolean*, *UIPropertyToUInt32*, and *UIPropertyToStringAlloc* functions.

Controlling Controls

Now you know how to define the Ribbon using markup and the basics of communicating with the Ribbon framework from code. In the following sections, we'll get into some of the details related to each control.

Manipulating the *CheckBox* and *ToggleButtons* Boolean Values

CheckBox and *ToggleButton* share the same Boolean functionality. When the framework calls the *IUICommandHandler::Execute* method, the property key argument is of type *UI_PKEY_BooleanValue* and the Boolean value in the *ppropvarValue* argument reflects the control value: TRUE for a checked or toggled state. To read or change the control state, you can either call *IUIFramework::Get/SetUICommandProperty* or invalidate the control with UI_INVALIDATIONS_VALUE and get the checked or toggle state in the *IUICommandHandler::UpdateProperty* method.

Manipulating the *Spinner* Control

The *Spinner* control has a set of values that can be set at initialization. The following code snippet shows how to set the minimum, maximum, increment, and start values. The spinner starts with the value of 15, the increment/decrement amount is 0.5, and the limits are 10.0 to 20.0. You can find the complete sample under the SpinnerControl project.

```
STDMETHODIMP CApplication::UpdateProperty(UINT nCmdID,
                          __in REFPROPERTYKEY key,
                          __in_opt const PROPVARIANT* ppropvarCurrentValue,
                          __out PROPVARIANT* ppropvarNewValue)
{
    HRESULT hr = E_NOTIMPL;

    if (nCmdID != cmdSpinner)
        return hr;

    if (key == UI_PKEY_MinValue)
    {
        DECIMAL d;
        VarDecFromI4(10, &d);
        hr = UIInitPropertyFromDecimal(key, d, ppropvarNewValue);
    }

    if (key == UI_PKEY_MaxValue)
    {
        DECIMAL d;
        VarDecFromI4(20, &d);
        hr = UIInitPropertyFromDecimal(key, d, ppropvarNewValue);
    }

    if (key == UI_PKEY_Increment)
    {
        DECIMAL d;
```

```
        VarDecFromR8(0.5, &d);
        hr = UIInitPropertyFromDecimal(key, d, ppropvarNewValue);
    }

    if (key == UI_PKEY_DecimalValue)
    {
        DECIMAL d;
        VarDecFromI4(15, &d);
        hr = UIInitPropertyFromDecimal(key, d, ppropvarNewValue);
    }

    return hr;
}
```

Changing Image

You can set the image of the control at runtime. You can also change the image to reflect changes in the application state. Because Ribbon images are 32bpp (32 bits per pixel) .bmp images, the Ribbon framework provides a factory that knows how to convert the regular Win32 HBITMAP format into the Ribbon Image format. The COM object, which has a class ID of *CLSID_UIRibbonImageFromBitmapFactory*, exposes the *IUIImageFromBitmap* interface. This interface has only one method, *CreateImage*. The method gets the handle to the bitmap and returns an interface pointer to an object that implements the *IUIImage* interface. This object holds the new image. You initiate the *PROPVARIANT *newValue* argument of *IUICommandHandler::UpdateProperty* with the new image using the *UIInitPropertyFromImage* function.

To set an image at runtime from an embedded resource, you need to complete three steps. First, you need to load the embedded resource bitmap; then you need to use the Bitmap Factory to create the Ribbon image; and third, you need to invalidate the control Image to set the new image in the *IUICommandHandler::UpdateProperty* callback.

Note *IUIImageFromBitmap::CreateImage* takes another argument in addition to the Win32 HBITMAP and the expected *IUIImage* result. This argument defines the image ownership, which means the owner of the handle of the bitmap. It also defines whether you have the responsibility for destroying it or whether the system has. Passing UI_OWNERSHIP_TRANSFER means that the Ribbon framework has control over the lifetime of the bitmap, whereas using UI_OWNERSHIP_COPY enables the same bitmap to be used elsewhere in the UI of the application.

The following code snippet demonstrates how to convert a Win32-based resource bitmap to a Ribbon framework bitmap, and how to set this image as the large image of a *Button* control. (Screen shots of the conversion appear after the block of code.) Whenever the user clicks the button, the image is toggled. You can find the complete sample under the ChangeImage project.

```
//Ribbon.xml:

<?xml version="1.0" encoding="utf-8"?>
<Application xmlns='http://schemas.microsoft.com/windows/2009/Ribbon'>
  <Application.Commands>
    <Command Name='cmdHome' Keytip='H' LabelTitle='Home'/>
    <Command Name='cmdGrp' Keytip='G' LabelTitle='Image Sample'/>
    <Command Name='cmdImage'  Keytip='I' LabelTitle='Change Me!'
                                         TooltipTitle='Change image sample'/>
  </Application.Commands>
  <Application.Views>
    <Ribbon>
      <Ribbon.Tabs>
        <Tab CommandName='cmdHome'>
          <Group CommandName='cmdGrp' SizeDefinition='OneButton'>
            <Button CommandName='cmdImage'/>
          </Group>
        </Tab>
      </Ribbon.Tabs>
    </Ribbon>
  </Application.Views>
</Application>
Application.h:

class CApplication
    : public CComObjectRootEx<CComMultiThreadModel>
    , public IUIApplication, public IUICommandHandler
{
public:
    CApplication();
...

    STDMETHOD(OnCreateUICommand)(...);
    STDMETHOD(OnDestroyUICommand)(...);
    STDMETHOD(Execute)(...);
    STDMETHOD(UpdateProperty)(...)
    HRESULT CreateUIImageFromBitmapResource(...);
```

```
private:
    CComPtr<IUICommandHandler> _spCommandHandler;
    CComPtr<IUIRibbon> _spRibbon;
    IUIImage *_GreenOverRed, *_RedOverGreen;
    IUIImage *_current;
    IUIImageFromBitmap *_pifbFactory;
};

//Application.cpp

CApplication::CApplication() : _GreenOverRed(NULL), _RedOverGreen(NULL),
 _current(NULL), _pifbFactory(NULL)
{
    CreateUIImageFromBitmapResource(MAKEINTRESOURCE(IDB_GREEN), &_GreenOverRed);
    CreateUIImageFromBitmapResource(MAKEINTRESOURCE(IDB_RED), &_RedOverGreen);

    _current = _GreenOverRed;
}

CApplication::~CApplication()
{
    if (pifbFactory != NULL)
    {
        _pifbFactory->Release();
        _pifbFactory = NULL;
    }
}

STDMETHODIMP CApplication::OnCreateUICommand(
    UINT nCmdID,
    __in UI_COMMANDTYPE typeID,
    __deref_out IUICommandHandler** ppCommandHandler)
{

    return this->QueryInterface(IID_PPV_ARGS(ppCommandHandler));
}

STDMETHODIMP CApplication::Execute(UINT nCmdID,
                  UI_EXECUTIONVERB verb,
                  __in_opt const PROPERTYKEY* key,
                  __in_opt const PROPVARIANT* ppropvarValue,
                  __in_opt IUISimplePropertySet* pCommandExecutionProperties)
{
   if (nCmdID != cmdImage)
       return E_FAIL;

   return g_pFramework->InvalidateUICommand(cmdImage, UI_INVALIDATIONS_PROPERTY,
                                                &UI_PKEY_LargeImage);
}

HRESULT CApplication::CreateUIImageFromBitmapResource(LPCTSTR pszResource,
                                                __out IUIImage **ppimg)
{
    HRESULT hr = E_FAIL;
```

```
    *ppimg = NULL;

    if (_pifbFactory == NULL)
    {
        hr = CoCreateInstance(CLSID_UIRibbonImageFromBitmapFactory, NULL,
                                    CLSCTX_ALL, IID_PPV_ARGS(&_pifbFactory));
        if (FAILED(hr))
        {
            return hr;
        }
    }

    // Load the bitmap from the resource file.
    HBITMAP hbm = (HBITMAP) LoadImage(GetModuleHandle(NULL), pszResource,
                                    IMAGE_BITMAP, 0, 0, LR_CREATEDIBSECTION);
    if (hbm != NULL)
    {
        // Use the factory implemented by the framework to produce an IUIImage.
            hr = _pifbFactory->CreateImage(hbm, UI_OWNERSHIP_COPY, ppimg);
        if (FAILED(hr))
        {
            DeleteObject(hbm);
        }
    }
    return hr;
}


STDMETHODIMP CApplication::UpdateProperty(UINT nCmdID,
                            __in REFPROPERTYKEY key,
                            __in_opt const PROPVARIANT* ppropvarCurrentValue,
                            __out PROPVARIANT* ppropvarNewValue)
{
    HRESULT hr = E_NOTIMPL;

    if (nCmdID != cmdImage)
        return hr;

    if (key == UI_PKEY_LargeImage)
    {
        hr = UIInitPropertyFromImage(UI_PKEY_LargeImage, _current, ppropvarNewValue);
        _current = (_current == _GreenOverRed) ? _RedOverGreen : _GreenOverRed;
    }
    return hr;
}
```

Managing Galleries

Galleries are dynamic, rich list box–based controls. Each gallery owns an item list that can be populated and manipulated statically in the Ribbon markup or dynamically at runtime according to the gallery type. You can control many aspects of a gallery, such as the list box layout and item categories. Most of the gallery controls support Live Preview, a mechanism that provides better feedback to the user by previewing the outcome of an action before the user selects the gallery item. Galleries implement the *IUICollection* interface. *IUICollection* provides the ability to control the gallery item list. Table 12-3 shows the *IUICollection* methods.

Table 12-3 *IUICollection* Methods

Method Name	Description
Add(IUnknown *item);	Adds the item to the end of the collection
Insert(UINT32 index, IUnknown *item);	Inserts the item at the index location
Replace(UINT32 indexReplaced, *IUnknown *itemReplaceWith);*	Replaces the item at the *indexReplaced* location with the *itemReplaceWith* item
RemoveAt(UINT32 index);	Removes the item at the index location
Clear();	Deletes all items from the collection
GetCount(UINT32 *count);	Gets the number of items in the collection
GetItem(UINT32 index, IUnknown **item);	Gets the item at the specified index

As you can see, *IUICollection* methods take or return an *IUnknown*-based item. However, for galleries the value must be a COM type that implements *IUISimplePropertySet*. This interface is a simple interface that represents a read-only collection of properties. The only method that this interface has is *HRESULT GetValue(REFPROPERTYKEY key, PROPVARIANT *value)*.

Each type of gallery defines the set of valid properties. You should create a type that implements *IUISimplePropertySet::GetValue* and supplies a property value for each of the gallery items. Think of this type as a method of communication between the framework and your code for each of the gallery items. To get a better understanding of how to use *IUISimplePropertySet*, let's populate a *ComboBox* with a collection of numeric values and respond to a user selection. We'll start by defining a class that represents a *ComboBox* item entry and that implements *IUISimplePropertySet*. The class holds a numerical value and an image:

```
//ComboBoxItem.h

//#include section …
MIDL_INTERFACE("722b7d91-b3ae-45e4-95ec-033ebbe8222d")
IComboBoxItem : public IUnknown
{
 public:
   virtual HRESULT STDMETHODCALLTYPE Initialize(int value, CComPtr<IUIImage> image);
   virtual HRESULT STDMETHODCALLTYPE GetNumericValue(int *value);
};

class CComboBoxtItem : public CComObjectRootEx<CComMultiThreadModel>,
                       public IUISimplePropertySet, public IComboBoxItem
{
private:
    int _value;
    CComPtr<IUIImage> _image;

public:
    BEGIN_COM_MAP(CComboBoxtItem)
        COM_INTERFACE_ENTRY(IUISimplePropertySet)
        COM_INTERFACE_ENTRY(IComboBoxItem)
    END_COM_MAP()

    STDMETHOD(GetValue)(__in REFPROPERTYKEY key, __out PROPVARIANT *ppropvar);
    STDMETHOD(Initialize)(int _value, CComPtr<IUIImage> image);
    virtual HRESULT STDMETHODCALLTYPE GetNumericValue(int *value)
                                                { *value = _value; return S_OK;}
    CComboBoxItem(void) : _value(0), _image(0) {}
    virtual ~CComboBoxtItem(void) {}
};


//ComboBoxItem.cpp:

//#include section…

STDMETHODIMP CComboBoxtItem::GetValue(__in REFPROPERTYKEY key,
                                      __out PROPVARIANT *ppropvar)
{
    if (key == UI_PKEY_Label)
    {
        basic_stringstream<wchar_t> ts;
```

```
        ts << _value;

        return UIInitPropertyFromString(UI_PKEY_Label, ts.str().c_str(), ppropvar);
    }
    if (key == UI_PKEY_ItemImage)
    {
        return UIInitPropertyFromImage(UI_PKEY_ItemImage, _image, ppropvar);
    }
    return E_NOTIMPL;
}

STDMETHODIMP CComboBoxtItem::Initialize(int value, CComPtr<IUIImage> image)
{
    _value = value;
    _image = image;
    return S_OK;
}
```

The ComboBoxDemo sample uses the class shown in the preceding code. The Demo shows a
Ribbon with one *ComboBox* control populated with numbers. Each number has a round bullet
near it, colored red for even numbers and green for odd numbers.

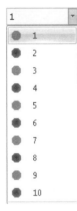

```
//Ribbon.xml

<?xml version="1.0" encoding="utf-8"?>
<Application xmlns='http://schemas.microsoft.com/windows/2009/Ribbon'>
  <Application.Commands>
    <Command Name='cmdHome' Keytip='H' LabelTitle='Home'/>
    <Command Name='cmdGrp' Keytip='G' LabelTitle='ComboBox Sample'/>
    <Command Name='cmdComboBox'  Keytip='C' LabelTitle='Select Item'
                 TooltipTitle='Select an Item from the ComboBox'/>
  </Application.Commands>
  <Application.Views>
    <Ribbon>
      <Ribbon.Tabs>
        <Tab CommandName='cmdHome'>
          <Group CommandName='cmdGrp'>
            <ComboBox CommandName='cmdComboBox' IsEditable='false'/>
```

```
        </Group>
      </Tab>
    </Ribbon.Tabs>
  </Ribbon>
 </Application.Views>
</Application>
```

When the user selects a number, this number is added to a total value presented in the middle of the client area. Previewing an item shows the future result if the user decides to select the number.

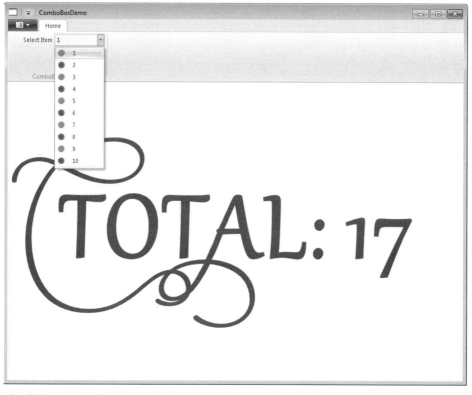

The following code is a snippet from the *CApplication* class that shows how to populate the *ComboBox* and how to interact with it:

```
//Application.h
...
MIDL_INTERFACE("b6f2f726-2576-4c2b-b44a-542f5e729a91")
    IApplicationDraw : public IUnknown
{
    public:
        virtual HRESULT STDMETHODCALLTYPE Initialize(HWND hWnd);
        virtual HRESULT STDMETHODCALLTYPE Draw();
        virtual HRESULT STDMETHODCALLTYPE Resize(UINT width, UINT height);
};
```

```
class CApplication
    : public CComObjectRootEx<CComMultiThreadModel>
    , public IUIApplication, public IUICommandHandler , public IApplicationDraw
{
public:
    CApplication() : _total(NULL), _lastValue(NULL), _hWnd(NULL) {}

    ...

    STDMETHOD(Execute)(...);
    STDMETHOD(UpdateProperty)(...);
    STDMETHOD(Initialize)(HWND hWnd) { _hWnd = hWnd; return S_OK; }

private:
    ...
    int _total;
    int _lastValue;
    HWND _hWnd;
    ...
};

//From Application.cpp
...

HRESULT STDMETHODCALLTYPE CApplication::Execute(UINT32 commandId,
    UI_EXECUTIONVERB verb, const PROPERTYKEY *key, const PROPVARIANT *currentValue,
    IUISimplePropertySet *commandExecutionProperties)
{
    if (commandId != cmdComboBox)
        return E_NOTIMPL;

    CComPtr<IComboBoxItem> comboBoxItem;
    HRESULT hr =
            commandExecutionProperties->QueryInterface(IID_PPV_ARGS(&comboBoxItem));
    if (FAILED(hr))
        return hr;

    int value;
    comboBoxItem->GetNumericValue(&value);

    switch (verb)
    {
        case UI_EXECUTIONVERB_PREVIEW:
        _total = _lastValue + value;
        break;

        case UI_EXECUTIONVERB_CANCELPREVIEW:
        _total = _lastValue;
        break;

        case UI_EXECUTIONVERB_EXECUTE:
        _total = _lastValue + value;
        _lastValue = _total;
        break;
```

```
    }
    InvalidateRect(_hWnd, NULL, TRUE);
    return S_OK;
}

HRESULT STDMETHODCALLTYPE CApplication::UpdateProperty(UINT32 nCmdID,
        REFPROPERTYKEY key, const PROPVARIANT *currentValue, PROPVARIANT *newValue)
{
    HRESULT hr;

    if (nCmdID == cmdComboBox)
    {
        if (key == UI_PKEY_Categories)
        {
            return S_FALSE;
        }
        //else
        if (key == UI_PKEY_ItemsSource)
        {
            IUICollection* pCollection;
            HRESULT hr = currentValue->punkVal->QueryInterface(
                                                IID_PPV_ARGS(&pCollection));
            if (FAILED(hr))
            {
                return hr;
            }

            CComPtr<IUIImage> redImage;
            hr = CreateUIImageFromBitmapResource(MAKEINTRESOURCE(IDB_REDBALL),
                                                                &redImage);
            if (FAILED(hr))
            {
                return hr;
            }

            CComPtr<IUIImage> greenImage;
            hr = CreateUIImageFromBitmapResource(MAKEINTRESOURCE(IDB_GREENBALL),
                                                                &greenImage);
            if (FAILED(hr))
            {
                return hr;
            }

            for (int i = 1; i <= 10; ++i)
            {
                CComObject<CComboBoxtItem> *pComboBoxItem;
                hr = CComObject<CComboBoxtItem>::CreateInstance(&pComboBoxItem);
                CComPtr<IComboBoxItem> comboBoxItem(pComboBoxItem);
                comboBoxItem->Initialize(i, i % 2 == 0 ? redImage : greenImage);
                hr = pCollection->Add(comboBoxItem);
            }
            pCollection->Release();
            return hr;
        }
```

```
            if (key == UI_PKEY_SelectedItem)
            {
                hr = UIInitPropertyFromUInt32(UI_PKEY_SelectedItem, 0, newValue);
                return hr;
            }
        }
        return E_FAIL;
    }
```

Notice that the *CComboBoxtItem* class holds the value as an integer but returns a string to the *IUISimplePropertySet::GetValue* method. This is the principle behind item galleries; you populate the gallery with your item types, and when the user selects an item you can interact with it by querying a custom interface that represents the item.

> **Note** It is not enough to handle the *UI_PKEY_ItemsSource* and *UI_PKEY_SelectedItem* properties;
> you must also handle the category-related properties, even in cases that there is no separation
> to categories.

```
if (key == UI_PKEY_Categories)
{
    return S_FALSE;
}
if (key == UI_PKEY_CategoryId)
{
    return UIInitPropertyFromUInt32(UI_PKEY_CategoryId,
            UI_COLLECTION_INVALIDINDEX, newValue);
}
//Failing to return S_FALSE will result in an empty gallery!
```

In the previous sample, the *ComboBox* contains odd and even numbers with red and green bullets that mark this characteristic. You could use categories to create two groups of numbers. To use categories, you need to create a category collection; in this case, the collection will have an "odd numbers" entry with a category ID of 0 (zero) and an "even numbers" entry with a category ID of 1. For each of the entries in the *ComboBox*, you need to return the correct category ID. The following sample does that:

```
//CategoryItem.h

//#include …
MIDL_INTERFACE("e577b8f4-cc30-47d3-b0f1-cd8d0ed93a5f")
ICategoryItem : public IUnknown
{
    public:
        virtual HRESULT STDMETHODCALLTYPE Initialize(UINT32 id, PWSTR name);
};

class CCategoryItem : public CComObjectRootEx<CComMultiThreadModel>,
                    public IUISimplePropertySet, public ICategoryItem
{
private:
```

```
        UINT32 _id;
        wstring _name;

public:
        BEGIN_COM_MAP(CCategoryItem)
            COM_INTERFACE_ENTRY(IUISimplePropertySet)
            COM_INTERFACE_ENTRY(ICategoryItem)
        END_COM_MAP()

        STDMETHOD(GetValue)(__in REFPROPERTYKEY key, __out PROPVARIANT *ppropvar);
        STDMETHOD(Initialize)(UINT32 id, PWSTR name);
        CCategoryItem(void) : _id(0) {}
        virtual ~CCategoryItem(void) {}
};
```

//CategoryItem.cpp

```
//#include …
STDMETHODIMP CCategoryItem::GetValue(REFPROPERTYKEY key, PROPVARIANT *ppropvar)
{
    if (key == UI_PKEY_Label)
    {
        return UIInitPropertyFromString(UI_PKEY_Label, _name.c_str(), ppropvar);
    }
    if (key == UI_PKEY_CategoryId)
    {
        return UIInitPropertyFromUInt32(UI_PKEY_CategoryId, _id, ppropvar);
    }
    return E_NOTIMPL;
}

STDMETHODIMP CCategoryItem::Initialize(UINT32 id, PWSTR name)
{
    _id = id;
    _name = name;
    return S_OK;
}

//Changes in ComboBoxItem.cpp
STDMETHODIMP CComboBoxtItem::GetValue(REFPROPERTYKEY key, PROPVARIANT *ppropvar)
{
    if (key == UI_PKEY_Label)
    {
        basic_stringstream<wchar_t> ts;
        ts << _value;
        return UIInitPropertyFromString(UI_PKEY_Label,  ts.str().c_str(), ppropvar);
    }
    if (key == UI_PKEY_ItemImage)
    {
        return UIInitPropertyFromImage(UI_PKEY_ItemImage, _image, ppropvar);
    }
    if (key == UI_PKEY_CategoryId)
```

```
        {
            return UIInitPropertyFromUInt32(UI_PKEY_CategoryId, _value % 2, ppropvar);
        }
        return E_NOTIMPL;
    }

    //Changes in Application.cpp
    HRESULT STDMETHODCALLTYPE CApplication::UpdateProperty(UINT32 nCmdID,
            REFPROPERTYKEY key, const PROPVARIANT *currentValue, PROPVARIANT *newValue)
    {
        HRESULT hr;

        if (nCmdID == cmdComboBox)
        {
            if (key == UI_PKEY_Categories)
            {
                IUICollection* pCollection;
                HRESULT hr = currentValue->punkVal->QueryInterface(
                                                IID_PPV_ARGS(&pCollection));
                if (FAILED(hr))
                {
                    return hr;
                }

                CComObject<CCategoryItem> *pCategoryItemEven;
                hr = CComObject<CCategoryItem>::CreateInstance(&pCategoryItemEven);
                CComPtr<ICategoryItem> categoryItemEven(pCategoryItemEven);
                categoryItemEven->Initialize(0, L"Even Numbers");
                hr = pCollection->Add(categoryItemEven);

                CComObject<CCategoryItem> *pCategoryItemOdd;
                hr = CComObject<CCategoryItem>::CreateInstance(&pCategoryItemOdd);
                CComPtr<ICategoryItem> categoryItemOdd(pCategoryItemOdd);
                categoryItemOdd->Initialize(1, L"Odd Numbers");
                hr = pCollection->Add(categoryItemOdd);

                pCollection->Release();

                return hr;
            }

            ...
            //The rest of the code has not been changed.
    }
```

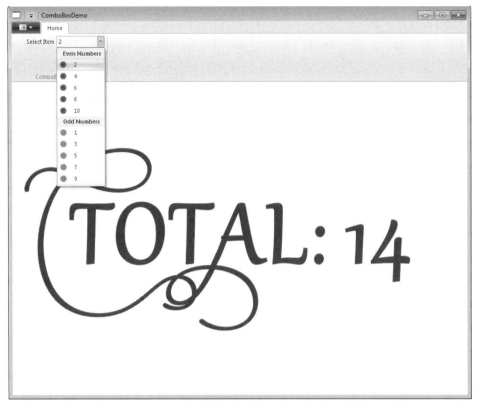

So far, you have seen how to work with galleries using the *ComboBox* gallery control. There are other gallery types, such as *DropDownGallery*, *InRibbonGallery*, and *SplitButtonGallery*. Each of these gallery controls support the two gallery types: the Command gallery and the Item gallery. *ComboBox* supports only the Item gallery.

As the name implies, the Command gallery contains a list with a set of unordered commands that are hooked to Ribbon commands. The Command gallery does not support Live Preview. The Command gallery can have a markup command space—a collection of commands that populate the gallery at compile time.

The Item gallery contains a list with a set of ordered items. Items can be represented by an image, a string, or a combination of the two. An Item gallery supports Live Preview. See the "Working with Live Preview" sidebar to understand how to handle Live Preview.

Working with Live Preview

When your gallery *IUICommandHandler::Execute* is called by the framework, you can extract the selected item index or get a custom interface that represents the selected item. No matter how you get this value, it comes along with an execution verb. The idea behind the execution verb is to support Live Preview.

The execution verb has three possible values that represent the user action: Preview, Cancel Preview, and Execute. When an item in the item list gets the focus or the mouse cursor hovers over it, the verb that you receive is UI_EXECUTIONVERB_PREVIEW. The application should respond by processing the action (or at least, reflect the result in the user interface) in the same way it does when the user clicks on that item. But the application should take all measures to ensure that an undo action can be taken if required. When the user moves the focus or the mouse pointer to another sibling element in the gallery, another callback with the UI_EXECUTIONVERB_PREVIEW verb is issued. The application should respond by undoing the last preview action and taking the new preview action. Only when the user selects an item does the framework call back with the UI_EXECUTIONVERB_EXECUTE verb. When the application receives this value, it should take the action. Or if a preview action with the same item was called before, it can make this last preview change permanent. If after browsing the gallery items list the user decides not to select an element, the framework issues a callback with the UI_EXECUTIONVERB_CANCELPREVIEW verb. This is when the application should undo all preview actions and go back to the beginning state.

By now, you should have a solid understanding of how to manage galleries. Managing galleries is one of the more complicated and powerful abilities of the Ribbon framework. There is more to learn about galleries, such as getting notification callbacks and manipulating other gallery controls. The Windows 7 SDK contains a very good gallery sample. (See the following screen shot.) On my machine, it installed at C:\Program Files\Microsoft SDKs\Windows\v7.0\Samples\winui\WindowsRibbon\Gallery. This sample shows many aspects of programming the gallery. For example, the sample defines a common *CPropertySet* class that implements the *IUISimplePropertySet* interface to support all property keys.

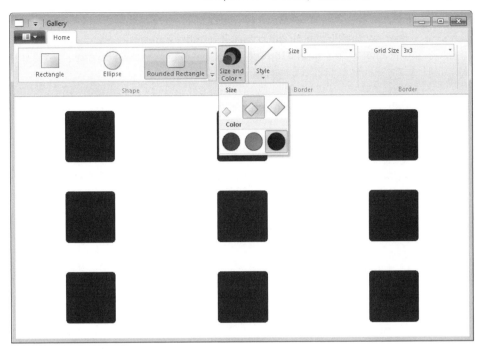

Using the Drop-Down Color Picker

The *DropDownColorPicker* control acts like a gallery of colors. When the user hovers his
mouse cursor over the color chips matrix, the control calls back to the
IUICommandHandler::Execute method with the UI_EXECUTIONVERB_PREVIEW execution verb.
If the user picks a color, you receive a call with the UI_EXECUTIONVERB_EXECUTE verb. If the
user decides not to pick a color, you get the UI_EXECUTIONVERB_CANCELPREVIEW verb.
Before you can read the color value, you need to find out whether the user pick a color or
choose one of the other options of the *DropDownColorPicker* control. If the *PROPVARIANT**
ppropvarValue argument has the value of UI_SWATCHCOLORTYPE_AUTOMATIC or
UI_SWATCHCOLORTYPE_NOCOLOR, you need to choose the color yourself.

The Automatic setting is mostly used to set a text color to the default Windows text color
returned by *GetSysColor(COLOR_WINDOWTEXT)*. Bear in mind that Automatic is available
only if the *ColorTemplate* control has a value of *ThemeColors* or *StandardColors*. The No Color
value is suitable for using the fill brush or applying a border color when the user might not
want to draw the element. If the value of *ppropvarValue* is UI_SWATCHCOLORTYPE_RGB, the
user has selected a color chip and you need to read the color value. To read the color value,
you use the last argument of the *IUICommandHandler::Execute* method, which is
IUISimplePropertySet* pCommandExecutionProperties. To get the value, simply call the
GetValue method with the *UI_PKEY_Color* property key. The following code is a snippet from
the RibbonColor code sample from the book code samples. (See the screen shot after the

code block for an illustration.) This sample shows how to use the *DropDownColorPicker* control to change the Ribbon global colors. It demonstrates preview, cancel, and execute, as well as how to change the global Ribbon color, a subject that will be discussed shortly.

Ribbon.xml

```xml
<?xml version="1.0" encoding="utf-8"?>
<Application xmlns='http://schemas.microsoft.com/windows/2009/Ribbon'>
  <Application.Commands>
    <Command Name='cmdHome' Keytip='H' LabelTitle='Home'/>
    <Command Name='cmdGrp' Keytip='G' LabelTitle='Ribbon Colors'/>
    <Command Name='cmdBackgroundColor'  Keytip='B' LabelTitle='Background Color'
                    TooltipTitle='Change the background color of the Ribbon'/>
    <Command Name='cmdHighlightColor'   Keytip='I' LabelTitle='Highlight Color'
                    TooltipTitle='Change the Ribbon Highlight Color'/>
    <Command Name='cmdTextColor' Keytip='T' LabelTitle='Text Color'
                    TooltipTitle='Change the Ribbon Text Color'/>
  </Application.Commands>
  <Application.Views>
    <Ribbon>
      <Ribbon.Tabs>
        <Tab CommandName='cmdHome'>
          <Group CommandName='cmdGrp' SizeDefinition='ThreeButtons'>
            <DropDownColorPicker CommandName='cmdBackgroundColor' ChipSize='Small'
                    ColorTemplate='ThemeColors' IsNoColorButtonVisible='false'/>
            <DropDownColorPicker CommandName='cmdHighlightColor' ChipSize='Small'
                    ColorTemplate='ThemeColors' IsNoColorButtonVisible='false'/>
            <DropDownColorPicker CommandName='cmdTextColor' ChipSize='Small'
                    ColorTemplate='ThemeColors' IsNoColorButtonVisible='false'/>
          </Group>
        </Tab>
      </Ribbon.Tabs>
    </Ribbon>
  </Application.Views>
</Application>


Application.h:

class CApplication
    : public CComObjectRootEx<CComMultiThreadModel>
    , public IUIApplication, // Applications must implement IUIApplication.
      public IUICommandHandler
{
public:
    CApplication();
    ~CApplication();

    BEGIN_COM_MAP(CApplication)
        COM_INTERFACE_ENTRY(IUIApplication)
        COM_INTERFACE_ENTRY(IUICommandHandler)
    END_COM_MAP()

    STDMETHOD(OnViewChanged)(…);
```

```
        STDMETHOD(OnCreateUICommand)(…);
        STDMETHOD(OnDestroyUICommand)(…);
        STDMETHOD(Execute)(…);
        STDMETHOD(UpdateProperty)(…);

private:
    class CRibbonColorSetter
    {
    private:
        UI_HSBCOLOR _originalColor;
        UI_HSBCOLOR _currentColor;
        const PROPERTYKEY _propertyKey;

        HRESULT SetRibbonColor(UI_HSBCOLOR color);
        UI_HSBCOLOR ConvertRGBToHSB(COLORREF color);

    public:
        CRibbonColorSetter(REFPROPERTYKEY propertyKey);
        HRESULT Execute(
                UI_EXECUTIONVERB verb,
                const PROPERTYKEY* key,
                const PROPVARIANT* ppropvarValue,
                IUISimplePropertySet* pCommandExecutionProperties);
    };

    CRibbonColorSetter *_pBackgroundColor;
    CRibbonColorSetter *_pHighlightColor;
    CRibbonColorSetter *_pTextColor;

};

From Application.cpp

CApplication::CApplication() : _pBackgroundColor(NULL), _pHighlightColor(NULL),
_pTextColor(NULL)
{
}

CApplication::~CApplication()
{
    delete _pBackgroundColor;
    delete _pHighlightColor;
    delete _pTextColor;
}

STDMETHODIMP CApplication::OnViewChanged(
    UINT viewId,
    __in UI_VIEWTYPE typeId,
    __in IUnknown* pView,
    UI_VIEWVERB verb,
    INT uReasonCode)
{
    if (verb != UI_VIEWVERB_CREATE && typeId != UI_VIEWTYPE_RIBBON)
        return E_NOTIMPL;
```

```
        _pBackgroundColor = new CRibbonColorSetter(UI_PKEY_GlobalBackgroundColor);
        _pHighlightColor = new CRibbonColorSetter(UI_PKEY_GlobalHighlightColor);
        _pTextColor = new CRibbonColorSetter(UI_PKEY_GlobalTextColor);

        return S_OK;
    }

    STDMETHODIMP CApplication::Execute(UINT nCmdID,
                        UI_EXECUTIONVERB verb,
                        __in_opt const PROPERTYKEY* key,
                        __in_opt const PROPVARIANT* ppropvarValue,
                        __in_opt IUISimplePropertySet* pCommandExecutionProperties)
    {
        if (*key != UI_PKEY_ColorType && nCmdID != cmdBackgroundColor &&
                            nCmdID != cmdHighlightColor && nCmdID != cmdTextColor)
            return E_NOTIMPL;

        switch (nCmdID)
        {
        case cmdBackgroundColor:
            return _pBackgroundColor->Execute(verb, key, ppropvarValue,
                                                pCommandExecutionProperties);
        case cmdHighlightColor:
            return _pHighlightColor->Execute(verb, key, ppropvarValue,
                                                pCommandExecutionProperties);
        case cmdTextColor:
            return _pTextColor->Execute(verb, key, ppropvarValue,
                                                pCommandExecutionProperties);
        }
        return S_OK;
    }


    CApplication::CRibbonColorSetter::CRibbonColorSetter(REFPROPERTYKEY propertyKey) :
                                                _propertyKey(propertyKey)
    {
        CComPtr<IPropertyStore> pPropertyStore;

        //Read the Ribbon original values and store them
        if (FAILED(g_pFramework->QueryInterface(&pPropertyStore)))
        {
            throw L"Error getting property store";
        }

        PROPVARIANT propvarColor;

        pPropertyStore->GetValue(_propertyKey, &propvarColor);
        UIPropertyToUInt32(_propertyKey, propvarColor, (UINT *)&_originalColor);
        _currentColor = _originalColor;
    }

    HRESULT CApplication::CRibbonColorSetter::SetRibbonColor(UI_HSBCOLOR color)
    {
```

```
    CComPtr<IPropertyStore> propertyStore;

    if (FAILED(g_pFramework->QueryInterface(&propertyStore)))
        return E_FAIL;

    PROPVARIANT propVariantColor;

    InitPropVariantFromUInt32(color, &propVariantColor) ;

    HRESULT hr = propertyStore->SetValue(_propertyKey, propVariantColor);
    if (FAILED(hr))
        return hr;

    return propertyStore->Commit();
}

HRESULT CApplication::CRibbonColorSetter::Execute(
        UI_EXECUTIONVERB verb,
        const PROPERTYKEY* key,
        const PROPVARIANT* ppropvarValue,
        IUISimplePropertySet* pCommandExecutionProperties)
{
    UI_SWATCHCOLORTYPE uType = (UI_SWATCHCOLORTYPE)PropVariantToUInt32WithDefault(
                                    *ppropvarValue, UI_SWATCHCOLORTYPE_NOCOLOR);
    COLORREF color = 0;;
    bool bUseOriginalColors = false;

    switch(uType)
    {
        case UI_SWATCHCOLORTYPE_RGB:
            PROPVARIANT var;
            pCommandExecutionProperties->GetValue(UI_PKEY_Color, &var);
            color = PropVariantToUInt32WithDefault(var, 0);
        break;
        case UI_SWATCHCOLORTYPE_AUTOMATIC:
            bUseOriginalColors = true;
        break;
        case UI_SWATCHCOLORTYPE_NOCOLOR: //Never gets called
            color = RGB(255,255,255);
        break;
    }

    UI_HSBCOLOR hsbColor = (verb == UI_EXECUTIONVERB_CANCELPREVIEW) ?
                        _currentColor : (bUseOriginalColors) ?
                        _originalColor : ConvertRGBToHSB(color);

    HRESULT hr = SetRibbonColor(hsbColor);
    if (FAILED(hr))
        return hr;

    if (verb == UI_EXECUTIONVERB_EXECUTE)
    {
        _currentColor = hsbColor;
    }
```

```
        return hr;
    }

    UI_HSBCOLOR CApplication::CRibbonColorSetter::ConvertRGBToHSB(COLORREF color)
    {
        WORD wHue, wLuminance, wSaturation;

        ColorRGBToHLS(color, &wHue, &wLuminance, &wSaturation);
        return UI_HSB( (BYTE)wHue, (BYTE)wSaturation, (BYTE)wLuminance);
    }
```

In addition to reading and setting color values, the *DropDownColorPicker* control has more properties: *invalidate*, *get*, and *set*. These properties control its appearance and some of its inner text titles. Consult the Ribbon documentation for more details about these properties.

Using the *FontControl*

The *FontControl* is a composite control that unifies the font selection user interface among all applications that use the Ribbon framework. Like any other control, *FontControl* has properties such as *UI_PKEY_Keytip* and *UI_PKEY_Enabled*. Unlike other controls, the *FontControl* has two properties that represent a collection of inner *FontControl* properties: *UI_PKEY_FontProperties* and *UI_PKEY_FontProperties_ChangedProperties*. These collections can contain the same properties, but the latter contains only properties that have been changed. The inner property collection contains properties such as font size, font family, bold, italic, color, and so forth. The *FontControl* supports Live Preview, which means that you should take care of the three execution verbs as you would with any other Live Preview controls. As with other controls, you can invalidate *FontControl* properties to set new values. A complete sample of a *FontControl* that sets the font properties of a Win32 *RichEdit* control can be found in the Windows 7 SDK samples. On my machine, it is installed here at C:\Program Files\Microsoft SDKs\Windows\v7.0\Samples\winui\WindowsRibbon\FontControl.

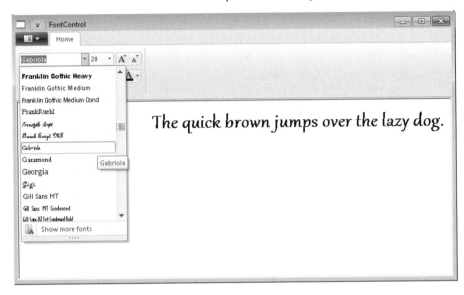

Setting Application Mode, and Showing Contextual Tabs and Pop-Ups

As you've already seen, the Ribbon framework replaces most of the user interface elements of a traditional Windows application. Before you start programming the user interface of your application, you have to go through the UX (User Experience) design phase. This means that you have to choose your ribbon tabs, groups, controls, application menu, and context pop-up menus. You can control the appearance and state of each control that builds the Ribbon, but this is not enough. Your application has many states that need to be reflected in the application user interface. Many operations of the user are related to specific context. Some good examples are Print Preview or changing the font of selected text. The Ribbon framework provides different methods that help focus the user's attention on the current state and task. You can set the application mode, show or hide contextual tabs, and present a context pop-up menu.

Application Mode is a state that is represented by a number from 0 (zero) through 31. This number is a bitmask, meaning that each bit in the bitmask represents an application mode. Using a bitmask provides a way to set several modes simultaneously—in other words, to be ORed between the modes. For example, number 5 represents mode 1 and mode 4. You can use the macro *UI_MAKEAPPMODE(x)* that is defined in the UIRibbon.h header file as *#define UI_MAKEAPPMODE(x) (1 << (x))* to get a mode number. To set the application modes 1 and 4, you need to use the following expression: *UI_MAKEAPPMODE(1) | UI_MAKEAPPMODE(4)*.

You can associate several modes to the same control. Zero is the default state. When the program sets a mode number that is not associated with the control, the control disappears.

Usually *ApplicationMode* is related to container controls such as *Tab* and *Group*. *Button*, *SplitButton*, and *DropDownButton* controls also have the *ApplicationMode* property, but it is relevant only when they are hosted in the left column of the Application menu. To set the current application mode, all you need to do is call the *IUIFramework::SetModes* method. *SetModes* accepts an INT32 argument that is the bitmask of the modes. Use the Application Mode technique to hide tabs, groups, and controls that are not valid in the current applica- tion state. Also, you can use the Application state to temporarily switch the Ribbon to a total new Ribbon, as in the case of Paint Print Preview.

The second mechanism to change the user interface of the Ribbon on the fly is to enable contextual tabs. A contextual tab has a command ID from the markup:

```
<Ribbon.ContextualTabs>
  <TabGroup CommandName='cmdContextualTabGroup'>
    <Tab CommandName='cmdContextualTab'>
      <Group CommandName='cmdGrpContextualTab'>
        <FontControl CommandName='cmdFontControl' FontType='FontOnly'/>
      </Group>
    </Tab>
  </TabGroup>
</Ribbon.ContextualTabs>
```

There are three states for the contextual tab group. The UI_CONTEXTAVAILABILITY enumeration defines them: UI_CONTEXTAVAILABILITY_NOTAVAILABLE, UI_CONTEXTAVAILABILITY_AVAILABLE, and UI_CONTEXTAVAILABILITY_ACTIVE. You change the state with the property key *UI_PKEY_ContextAvailable*. The following method gets the command ID that is bound to the contextual tab group and the needed availability state. The following code snippet and screen shot demonstrate how to change the activation state of a contextual tab:

```
HRESULT CRibbonResultView::ShowContextualTab(int nCmdID, UI_CONTEXTAVAILABILITY
UIContextAvailability)
{
    HRESULT hr = E_FAIL;
```

```
    PROPVARIANT ctxAvail;
    hr = UIInitPropertyFromUInt32(UI_PKEY_ContextAvailable, UIContextAvailability,
                                                             &ctxAvail);

    if (FAILED(hr))
        return hr;
    hr = m_pUIFramework->SetUICommandProperty(nCmdID, UI_PKEY_ContextAvailable,
                                                             ctxAvail);

    return hr;
}
```

The last contextual UI element is the context pop-up, a combination of a floating mini-toolbar with a menu that can be presented at any location on the screen. To show a context pop-up, you first need to get an *IUIContextualUI* interface from the framework object. Recall from the last chapter that a context pop-up is declared by a context map, which is bound to a command. You use this command as an input parameter to the *IUIFramework::GetView* method to get the *IUIContextualUI* instance. This interface has the *ShowAtLocation* method, which presents the context pop-up. The following code demonstrates how to do it:

```
HRESULT CRibbonResultView::ShowContextMenu(int nCmdID)
{
    CComPtr<IUIContextualUI> pUIContextualUI;
    HRESULT hr = m_pUIFramework->GetView(nCmdID , __uuidof(pUIContextualUI),
                                                      (void **)(&pUIContextualUI));

    if (FAILED(hr))
        return hr;

    RECT r;
    GetWindowRect(m_hWnd, &r);
    hr = pUIContextualUI->ShowAtLocation((r.left + r.right)/2,
                                              (r.bottom - r.top)/3 + r.top);

    return hr;
}
```

The coordination system is related to the screen and not to the client area. You can use the *ClientToScreen* API to convert a client location to the screen location—for example, if you want to show the context pop-up near a selected item.

Manipulating the Quick Access Toolbar from Code

You do not need to manipulate the Quick Access Toolbar (QAT) from code. By just adding the *QuickAccessToolbar* element to the markup, you get all the functionality of manipulating and executing commands from this toolbar. However, sometime you need more controls. For example, you can use the *CustomizeCommandName* element to enable the More Commands menu entry, and then create a custom dialog that provides an easier QAT manipulation. QAT resembles a command gallery; however, it does not support categories and you cannot replace the predefined *IUICollection* object. You can add and remove existing commands, but you cannot invent new commands. To add or remove commands from the QAT commands list dynamically, you need to get the QAT *IUICollection* collection interface. You can get the object that implement the QAT *IUICollection* interface in the *IUICommandHandler::UpdateProperty* method. The nCmdId argument has to be your assigned QAT command ID. The key argument should be *UI_PKEY_ItemsSource*, The *IUICollection* object is the value of the ppropvar*CurrentValue* argument. Use this interface to manipulate the list of commands. To get the framework's attention to do the QAT command list manipulation, you should call the *IUIFramework::InvalidateUICommand* with the QAT command ID.

Manipulating Most Recently Used Files from Code

Recent Items, also known as the Most Recently Used files, can be added to the Application menu by adding the Recent Item control to the Ribbon markup with the *ApplicationMenu.RecentItems* element:

```
xml:
...
<ApplicationMenu.RecentItems>
    <RecentItems CommandName="cmdMRU" MaxCount="10" EnablePinning="true"/>
</ApplicationMenu.RecentItems>
```

The list of files can be manually managed by your code—or better, it can be pulled from the Shell Taskbar Jump List recent or frequent file list by calling the *ApplicationDocumentLists::GetList*. If you are using Microsoft Foundation Classes (MFC), MFC has the *CRecentFileList* class, which manages recent files for your application. The recent list item type should implement the *IUISimplePropertySet* interface and respond to the property keys of *UI_PKEY_Label*, *UI_PKEY_LabelDescription*, and *UI_PKEY_Pinned*, as in the following code:

```
C++:
// IUISimplePropertySet methods.
```

```
STDMETHODIMP GetValue(__in REFPROPERTYKEY key, __out PROPVARIANT *value)
{
    if (key == UI_PKEY_Label)
    {
        return UIInitPropertyFromString(UI_PKEY_Label, m_fileName, value);
    }
    if (key == UI_PKEY_LabelDescription)
    {
        return UIInitPropertyFromString(UI_PKEY_LabelDescription, m_filePath,
                                                                    value);
    }
    if (key == UI_PKEY_Pinned)
    {
        return UIInitPropertyFromBoolean(UI_PKEY_Pinned, m_pinnedState, value);
    }
    return E_NOTIMPL;
}
```

The htmlEdit sample of the Windows 7 SDK shows how to migrate an MFC application UI to use the Ribbon and how to extract Recent File information from MFC to the Ribbon *RecentItems* control.

Playing with Ribbon Colors

Color cannot be set for individual controls or elements of the Ribbon. The Ribbon framework has three global properties that control the colors of all Ribbon elements and state: *UI_PKEY_GlobalBackgroundColor*, *UI_PKEY_GlobalHighlightColor*, and *UI_PKEY_GlobalTextColor*. To get and set these properties, query the *IPropertyStore* interface from the Ribbon framework object. *IPropertyStore* has *get* and *set* methods that accept two arguments: the property key and its corresponding value. The Ribbon framework uses a color system that is based on the HSB color space with the UI_HSBCOLOR as the type. UI_HSBCOLOR is a *typedef* of DWORD. Hue-saturation-brightness (HSB) differs from the known RGB value. *Hue* is the color itself, *saturation* is the purity of the color (0 for gray, with 255 for pure color), and *brightness* is the percentage brightness of the color (0 to 255, with 255 being 100 percent).

> **More Info** There are various ways to represent a color value in software. Traditionally, Windows uses the Red, Green, Blue (RGB) method. RGB is best when used by light-emitting devices, such as LCD or CRT monitors, because it represents the intensity value of each of the components that builds the color of the light. For humans, there are easier methods to represent a color. For example, the user can pick a color and then change the brightness or the saturation value. The Ribbon framework uses the HSB method. The shellwapi.dll exposes a utility method, *ColorRGBToHLS*, that converts RGB values to hue-lightness-saturation (HLS), which is similar to HSB. You can read more about color methods at *http://en.wikipedia.org/wiki/RGB_color_model* and *http://en.wikipedia.org/wiki/HSL_and_HSV*.

Recommended Ribbon Color Setting

Consider setting the global text color to be readable against the Ribbon background color. In some cases, the framework automatically adjusts the global text color value to provide sufficient contrast against any background shade or gradient derived from the Ribbon background color.

This code demonstrates how to set the Ribbon background color:

```
#include <UIRibbon.h>
...
CComPtr<IPropertyStore> pPropertyStore;

// _pFramework is a smart pointer to the IUIFramework interface
if (SUCCEEDED(_pFramework->QueryInterface(&pPropertyStore)))
{
    PROPVARIANT propvarBackground;
    UI_HSBCOLOR backgroundColor = UI_HSB(0x0F, 0x3A, 0x4D);

    InitPropVariantFromUInt32(backgroundColor, &propvarBackground);
    pPropertyStore->SetValue(UI_PKEY_GlobalBackgroundColor, propvarBackground);

    spPropertyStore->Commit();
}
```

The ChangeColor example in the book source code demonstrates how to use the *ColorPicker* control to set the Ribbon colors.

Persisting the Ribbon State

The user can change the state of the Ribbon during runtime to either the Ribbon Minimize state or the Quick Access Toolbar state. The user also can add or remove commands from the Quick Access Toolbar. To deliver a good experience to the user, your application should save its UI state. Whenever the user launches the application, she expects to have the same settings she did when she last used it. The Ribbon framework provides a method to store and load the Ribbon state. *IUIRibbon::SaveSettingsToStream* stores the ribbon status in a stream, whereas *IUIRibbon:: LoadSettingsFromStream* loads the stored settings from a COM stream. Use *SaveSettingsToStream* just before the application exits. Use *LoadSettingsFromStream* in *IUIApplication::OnViewChanged* when the verb parameter is UI_VIEWVERB_CREATE. There are two ways to get the *IUIRibbon* interface of the Ribbon. The first one involves- using the *IUIFramework::GetView* method. Passing 0 (zero) in the *viewId* parameter returns *IUIRibbon*. The second way is to cache the *IUIRibbon* that is provided by *IUIApplication::OnViewChange* when the Ribbon view is created:

```
//caching the IUIRibbon object in the IUIApplication::OnViewChange()
...
if (typeID == UI_VIEWTYPE_RIBBON && verb == UI_VIEWVERB_CREATE)
```

```
    pView->QueryInterface(__uuidof(IUIRibbon), (void **)&m_pRibbon);
...
}

HRESULT CRibbonView::LoadState()
{
    HRESULT hr = E_FAIL;
    if (m_stateStream != NULL)
    {
        LARGE_INTEGER liStart = {0, 0};
        ULARGE_INTEGER ulActual;
        hr = m_stateStream->Seek(liStart, STREAM_SEEK_SET, &ulActual);

        if (SUCCEEDED(hr))
        {
            hr = m_ribbon->LoadSettingsFromStream(m_stateStream);
        }
    }
    return hr;
}

HRESULT CRibbonView::SaveState()
{
    HRESULT hr = E_FAIL;

    if (m_stateStream != NULL) m_stateStream.Release();

    hr = CreateStreamOnHGlobal(NULL, TRUE, &m_stateStream);
    if (SUCCEEDED(hr))
    {
        if (SUCCEEDED(hr))
        {
            hr = m_ribbon->SaveSettingsToStream(m_stateStream);
        }
    }
    return hr;
}
```

Calling *SaveSettingsToStream* will fail (HRESULT 0x80070490) if the Ribbon does not contain the QAT element. The UICC.exe compiler issues a warning in that case. Bear in mind that the state of the Ribbon controls and the Ribbon colors are not saved. If you give the user a way to control these states and you want to save the altered state, you need to do it manually.

Summary

The Windows Ribbon framework is the Windows implementation of the Office Fluent User Interface. Although the Ribbon in Office 2007 is similar in concept to the one in Windows 7, it's a little bit different in appearance. Office 2010 has the same look and feel of the Windows 7 Ribbon. Keep in mind that there are many other Ribbon technologies for Native (C/C++) and Managed (.NET) code that are available, ranging from the free ones in the Windows

Presentation Foundation (WPF) toolkit to WinForm control libraries you can buy from controls vendors. If your application is built with MFC, you can use the Windows 7 Ribbon framework, or if you need to support the Windows XP/2003 operating systems you have the choice to use Visual Studio 2008 SP1 and Visual Studio 2010 MFC Ribbon. Pick your Ribbon technology according to the target operating system and the ease of use of the chosen toolkit. But no matter what technology you use, the Ribbon is here!

Chapter 13
Rediscover the Fundamentals: It's All About Performance

The single most important request customers have had about the next release of the Microsoft Windows operating system is flabbergasting from an engineering standpoint. Customers want Windows to run faster, on lesser hardware, using less system resources, while supporting all existing applications. Much less than they care about new features, Windows users—users of your software included—want the next version of the operating system to take better advantage of existing hardware and do everything increasingly faster.

Windows 7 on Netbooks

I, for one, expect Windows 7 to run smoothly on my 9-inch netbook, "featuring" a single low-end 900-MHz processor, 1 GB of physical memory, and an extremely slow solid-state hard drive (SSD). In fact, if Windows 7 ran any slower on it than Windows XP I would be utterly disappointed.

Fortunately, after installing the Windows 7 Release Candidate, I was positively surprised by every possible aspect of my machine—the system booted faster, applications launched faster, there was still some memory available after opening a few applications, and I could even install Microsoft Office and have some room left on the 16-GB SSD!

With full certainty, I can say that Windows 7 has turned a machine that I was using as a brick or a coffee coaster into a useful mobile PC that I often take with me when I have no specific client engagement during the day that requires a more powerful machine—and my back thanks me every day for its form and weight factors.

But that is not all. On a related note, users want to be able to use their mobile PC for an entire day without draining the battery or compromising for screen brightness or wireless connectivity. Users need the system to support larger screens, more connected hardware, and a variety of operating conditions—and still retain the same reliability characteristics. Finally, users want the system to let them focus on their tasks, and for any background processing to remain minimal, regardless of how many new features are added between releases of the operating system.

Reaching these goals is not a task for operating system developers alone. A typical consumer runs dozens of third-party applications that have nothing to do with Microsoft, and he has several hardware devices plugged into the system that have third-party drivers and background services. Every time a user downloads some software from the Web, every time a user plugs in his new $10 USB mouse, every time a user opens a game a friend sent in an e-mail message—every time one of these things happens, the particular version of Windows running on the system loses control over the performance and reliability of the machine. This is why it takes a joint effort from you, fellow developers, to maintain a stable, reliable, fast, and efficient system for years to come, across multiple releases of Windows.

This chapter deals with some ways to instrument your applications and the system as a whole and diagnose performance and correctness problems that prevent your users from performing their day-to-day tasks. Along with examining troubleshooting and diagnostics tools, we'll take a look at underlying improvements to background processing and power management on Windows, to see how our applications can cooperate with the system to deliver a better user experience.

Instrumentation and Diagnostics

Windows features a multitude of mechanisms that can assist you with the daunting task of diagnosing system-wide performance problems and troubleshoot hard-to-reproduce bugs. You already know that there's an amazing ecosystem for developers *on* Windows—but the reason there are so many troubleshooting tools and approaches is that the developers *of* Windows use them every day to ensure that the operating system we're all using is fast and reliable.

Even if you don't intend to use these tools right now to troubleshoot, monitor, or instrument your applications, you should plan your development accordingly so that maintenance programmers, system administrators, and support personnel can take advantage of the troubleshooting features Windows has to offer when your application is deployed in the field. The subsequent sections will show you how to accomplish some of these tasks. There are several topics that this chapter doesn't spell out, but don't despair—fortunately, there is a vast amount of documentation and online material that can guide you through these features of Windows.

> **Note** You might notice that some, if not most, of the features discussed in this section are not new to Windows 7. This might be surprising considering the title of the book and the fact that lots of interesting material was cut to leave room for this humble chapter. However, this reflects the authors' deep conviction that understanding of instrumentation, monitoring, diagnostics, and troubleshooting tools and techniques is vital for any Windows developer, and especially so on Windows 7.

Performance Counters

Performance counters are a simple yet very powerful mechanism that has been part of Windows for more than 15 years. They provide monitoring information that can give you insight about the system's performance as a whole, as well as the health of a particular component in a specific application. Performance counters, like many other diagnostic mechanisms in Windows, are exposed by system components but can be enhanced by individual frameworks or applications.

The architecture of the performance-counter mechanism is roughly the following. Objects that you categorize as classes or types are called *performance objects* or *performance counter categories*. Within each category you find *performance counters*—these are the properties or fields of a class. Finally, like every class, there might be more than one instance of a performance object—and that's a *performance counter instance*. Here are some examples of useful performance counters:

- **Processor**   % User Time, % Privileged Time (instances for each logical processor)

- **Physical Disk**   Avg. Disk Queue Length (instances for each physical disk)

- **.NET CLR Memory**   # Bytes in All Heaps (instances for each managed application)

- **TCPv4**   Connections Active (singleton)

Windows ships with dozens of performance counter categories, and external frameworks augment this set with their own diagnostic information. For example, ASP.NET features its own performance counters, Microsoft SQL Server has its own, and even individual applications might have performance counters for diagnostic and monitoring purposes.

The most obvious limitation of performance counters is that the information you can provide through this mechanism is restricted to numeric types only. For example, you can easily report the number of users logged on to your server, the percent of connections that were dropped, and even the rate of a physical event occurring. However, you can't render a report containing strings or other complex data types, and the maximum nesting of the report is limited to the category—instance—counter hierarchy.

Despite these limitations, performance counters are an extremely popular and useful mechanism, primarily because the means to consume performance information ships with Windows and doesn't require any additional installation—which is extremely useful when diagnosing problems in the field. The Performance Monitor utility (*perfmon*, also accessible from the Administrative Tools area of the Control Panel) is your primary tool to work with performance counters. By adding performance counters to the main view, you can use the Line, Histogram, or Report views to see the data flowing live onto the screen, and then you can configure the sampling time interval for the counters of interest.

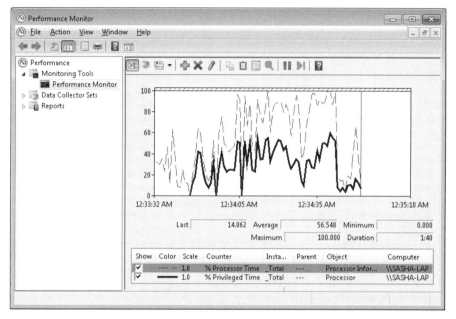

The best thing about performance counters is that you can access them remotely. If you have administrative privileges for a set of machines, you can use Performance Monitor to view performance counters from the comfort of your own desk and terminal. For example, you can overlay CPU utilization from multiple machines on the same performance graph and determine by a quick glance which machine is most loaded at any given instant.

> **Note** Unfortunately, the performance counters database can sometimes get corrupted, especially if you are experimenting with performance counter categories of your own. In this case, a useful command-line utility called *lodctr* can help you to restore your performance counters database to its initial state, or even to import the performance counter database from another, similarly configured machine. For more information on this utility's syntax, run *lodctr* with no arguments from a command line.

The performance counters infrastructure does not limit you to passive immediate observation of the data as it slides across your screen. Using Performance Monitors or using the built-in Windows APIs, you can log performance counter information in a variety of formats, including a compact, automatically rolling-over binary format as well as a CSV format or an SQL format. You can open the generated log files later at your convenience (from any machine) and view them in the Performance Monitor as if they were live.

Creating a Performance Counter Log

To create a performance counter log, follow these steps:

1. Open Performance Monitor, and navigate to the Data Collector Sets node in the tree on the left.

2. Right-click User Defined, and navigate the menu to create a new data collector set.

3. Give the new set a name, select the Create Manually option button, and click Next.

4. Choose the Create Data Logs radio button, select the Performance Counter check box, and then click Next.

5. Click Next again—it's not time yet to select the performance counters, but you can customize the sampling time interval for the performance counter log.

6. Specify a directory where you want the logs to be saved, and then click Next.

7. Click Finish.

8. Right-click the new entry under User Defined in the tree on the left, and navigate the menu to create a new data collector.

9. Give the new data collector a name, select the Performance Counter Data Collector radio button, and then click Next.

10. Choose the performance counters you want to log, specify the interval at which log samples should be taken, and then click Next.

11. Select the Open Properties For This Data Collector check box and then click Finish. In the Properties dialog box, you can customize the performance counters and sample intervals and log files for the selected data collector set.

You can now customize the data collector further by interacting with it from the main panel of the Performance Monitor, or you can start the entire data collector set by clicking the green Play button in the toolbar. When your logs are ready, go back to the main Performance Monitor window and press Ctrl+L to choose the log file you want to view instead of focusing on the system's current activity. Alternatively, you can use the Reports node of the Performance Monitor tree and find your data collector set there.

You can also use Performance Monitor to configure a performance counter alert, which executes a certain action whenever a threshold you set for a specific counter is met. When the alert occurs, you can choose to generate an event log entry, start a data collector set (a performance counter log), or even launch a custom task that will remedy the situation.

By now you are probably wondering how you can read performance counter information programmatically and how you can expose performance counters from your own code. Exposing performance counters from managed code is easy thanks to the *System.Diagnostics* namespace in the Microsoft .NET Framework. This namespace contains everything you need to provide diagnostic information from your application—or even to consume performance counters exposed by the operating system and other applications.

For example, assume that you want to provide a performance counter category related to your online gaming service. This type of counter is very useful for server administrators when game servers are deployed to production. Some performance counters that might make sense are the number of connected players, the number of ongoing games, and any other performance statistics you might find appropriate.

All you need to do to expose this information using the performance counter mechanism is create a new performance counter category (using the *PerformanceCounterCategory* class), create the performance counters that you want to belong to this category (using the *CounterCreationDataCollection* and *CounterCreationData* classes), and then update the performance counters whenever necessary (using the *PerformanceCounter* class).

> **Note** Unfortunately, creating a performance counter category is an operation that requires administrative privileges. To some extent, this makes sense because the diagnostic information that you can obtain using performance counters might have an effect on administrative decisions on a system, and thus modifying the performance counter catalog is an operation available only to administrators. This means that you will have to wrap category creation in a separate elevated process or create the category during your application installation.

The following code sample demonstrates how to initialize the performance counter category and the counters inside it (this will not work if you do not have administrative privileges), and how to update the performance counter information whenever a new event is generated in the system:

```
//Within the initialization procedure:
if (PerformanceCounterCategory.Exists("EmployeePresence"))
    PerformanceCounterCategory.Delete("EmployeePresence");

CounterCreationDataCollection coll = new CounterCreationDataCollection();
CounterCreationData counter = new CounterCreationData(
    "# employees", "The number of signed-in employees",
    PerformanceCounterType.NumberOfItems32);
coll.Add(counter);

PerformanceCounterCategory.Create("EmployeePresence",
    "Information about employee presence",
    PerformanceCounterCategoryType.SingleInstance,
    coll);

_signedInEmps = new PerformanceCounter("EmployeePresence",
    counter.CounterName, false);

//Elsewhere in the system when an employee signs in:
_signedInEmps.Increment();
```

Consuming performance counters from managed code is even easier, and it follows a symmetric path: if you have a *PerformanceCounter* object, you can read its value at any time by using the *RawValue* property (or other properties, which are suited for more advanced usage). The following code demonstrates how this property is used in a simple user interface (UI) application that is part of this book's sample code:

```
lblEmpCount.Text = _signedInEmps.RawValue.ToString();
pbarEmps.Value = (int)_signedInEmps.RawValue;
```

Exposing and consuming performance counters from native code is not quite as easy and is outside the scope of this book. You can find samples and documentation on the Microsoft Developer Network (MSDN) Web site at *http://msdn.microsoft.com/en-us/library/*aa373209.*aspx*.

> **Note** The Win32 performance counter API (also called Performance Data Helpers, or PDH) is complicated, and we have no room to cover it here. Among other things, you can use the PDH interfaces to read performance counter information, configure performance counter logs, parse and aggregate performance counter logs, and access lots of other functionality that is not available to managed code.

In closing, performance counters are a powerful monitoring mechanism that ships with Windows. Analyzing performance information, generating logs of monitoring activity, and distributing alerts whenever a threshold is breached are just some of the things performance counters can help you with.

Windows Management Instrumentation

Windows Management Instrumentation (WMI) is a built-in command and control (C&C) infrastructure for Windows. Using WMI, C&C providers can expose diagnostic information, run-time state, and events to C&C consumers, which can obtain this information in real time and invoke provider methods to modify the state of the system. Essentially, WMI is a full-blown distributed system infrastructure, geared toward command and control scenarios.

Unlike performance counters, which can be used to expose only read-only numeric information within a limited hierarchical form, WMI objects can use standard programming techniques such as inheritance, composition (aggregation), complex collections, events, and overridden methods. This richness is accessible from almost every programming language for Windows because WMI is COM-based and DCOM-based—even scripting languages can use WMI objects through late-bound COM invocations. Additionally, the emerging Windows PowerShell scripting platform for IT professionals (included with Windows 7) has special commands for interacting with WMI objects.

Here are some of the tasks made possible by WMI. Some tasks on this list are very difficult to perform without WMI, and other tasks are simply impossible without it.

- Determine which hot fixes are applied to a system.

- Create a network share, and set its security attributes.

- Receive a notification every time a new process is created.

- Enable and disable network firewall rules.

- Retrieve information about the system's BIOS, manufacturer, model, and make.

In addition to standard programming interfaces that allow you to create WMI objects, retrieve their properties, and invoke their methods, a specialized query language called WMI Query Language (WQL) is available that can be used to retrieve specific objects. For example, the following WQL statement retrieves all Notepad processes on the system:

```
SELECT * FROM Win32_Process WHERE ProcessName='Notepad.exe'
```

Writing a WMI consumer means interacting with the WMI COM interfaces to retrieve objects, register for events, handle event notifications, and invoke WMI provider methods. In unmanaged code, this interaction is done directly against the WMI interfaces, such as *IWbemServices*, and an explanation of how to do this is outside the scope of this book. (See *http://msdn.microsoft.com/en-us/library/aa389761.aspx* for more information.) In managed code, you use the *System.Management* namespace, specifically classes such as *ManagementObject*, *ManagementQuery*, and *ManagementEventWatcher*. Because of the sheer amount of WMI object types available, there are no ready-made, strongly typed wrappers for all WMI objects. Fortunately, however, the development environment steps in— Visual Studio Server Explorer is capable of generating on the fly the strongly typed managed wrapper needed for accessing any WMI object installed on the system, as depicted in the following screen shot:

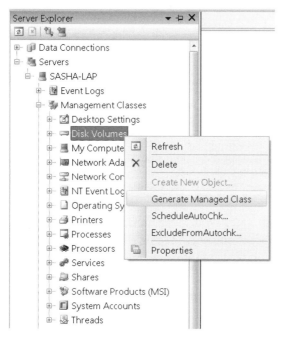

The following sample code shows how easy it is to write an application that waits for a new process to be created (by registering to a WMI event). It then uses the properties of the newly created WMI process object to output information about the process—in fact, because WMI objects are accessed just like any other managed object, you can use controls such as the Windows Forms *PropertyGrid* to display the properties of WMI objects. Note that it's very natural to use a LINQ to Objects syntax to interact with WMI collections, but it requires an ugly cast to the appropriate collection type. You can find on the Web third-party libraries that provide a true "LINQ to WMI" experience, such as *http://www.codeplex.com/linq2wmi*.

> **Note** The *only* user-mode API for receiving a notification when a process is created is the WMI notification interface. (Kernel-mode components can use the kernel interface *PsSetCreateProcessNotifyRoutine*.)

```
//Declaration for the Visual Studio Designer-generated class
using WMIProcess = Ch12.ManagedWMIConsumer.ROOT.CIMV2.Process;

//In the ManagementEventWatcher.EventArrived event handler:
newProcessesList.Items.Add(e.NewEvent["ProcessID"]);

//To zoom in on a specific process:
int procId;
if (!int.TryParse(selected.ToString(), out procId))
    return;
WMIProcess proc = WMIProcess.GetInstances(
    "ProcessId='" + procId + "'").Cast<WMIProcess>().FirstOrDefault();
processGrid.SelectedObject = proc;

//From the Visual Studio Designer-generated code:
this.eventWatcher.Query = new System.Management.EventQuery("SELECT * FROM
Win32_ProcessStartTrace");
this.eventWatcher.Scope = new System.Management.ManagementScope("\\\\Sasha-
PC\\root\\CIMV2");
this.eventWatcher.EventArrived += eventWatcher_EventArrived;
```

> **Note** As you can see, the generated managed wrapper is created in the ROOT.CIMV2 sub-namespace that corresponds to the WMI namespace of the original Process WMI class (root\cimv2). There are additional WMI namespaces that you can explore, and if you're creating a WMI class of your own, you might consider putting it in a separate namespace for organization and security purposes.

Writing a WMI provider is significantly more complicated than writing a WMI consumer. In unmanaged code, it means writing a COM server that implements several interfaces and is registered on the system as a WMI provider. In managed code (at least as of the release of .NET Framework 3.5), this has become significantly easier. You can now write a WMI provider that is nothing more than a .NET assembly decorated with a few attributes, which contains a managed class that serves as the WMI object. You can publish events, invoke methods of WMI objects, and dynamically change the set of objects exposed by the provider—the entire set of the WMI functionality is now at the fingertips of any managed developer. Still, the vast complexity of WMI makes it impossible to explore all its aspects in a short section of this book. For more information about writing WMI providers in managed code, see the following link: *http://www.codeproject.com/KB/system/WMIProviderExtensions.aspx*.

In closing, if you haven't had the chance to experiment with WMI yet, you should give it a try. By writing or using WMI consumers, you will be able to better understand the current state of the system, monitor it over time, modify its state, and receive notifications. By writing WMI providers, you will be able to extend the system's built-in C&C capabilities and naturally integrate them with dozens of third-party C&C solutions.

Event Tracing for Windows

Event Tracing for Windows (ETW) is an always-present, always-on infrastructure that performs selective logging of events in Windows. It provides a great level of detail and customization with regard to level, keywords, and filters, and it allows information to be defined by event templates in which only some parameters need to be filled in.

ETW information can be accessed from managed and native languages, scripting languages, PowerShell, the *tracerpt.exe* command-line utility, and the Windows Event Viewer. To export information, ETW providers register with the ETW infrastructure using event manifest files. These XML files define events that can be generated as well as log levels, filters, and templates. Usually, ETW manifest files are generated by the Manifest Generator (*ecmangen.exe*) utility, and then the CTRPP and MC preprocessors generate native code that can be used by providers to log events.

Events are categorized by tasks, in which multiple types of channels distinguish between their target audiences. ETW controllers can start and stop tracing sessions in which data is collected, and ETW consumers can subscribe to receive events as they occur or from a log file.

For more information about ETW, consult the MSDN documentation at *http://www.microsoft.com/whdc/devtools/tools/EventTracing.mspx*.

Windows Performance Toolkit

Performance counters, WMI, and ETW are specific ways to monitor system health and performance, but there's a definite need for a tool that can integrate information from all these various sources and present it in a comprehensible manner. The Windows Performance Toolkit (also known as Performance Analyzer, or *xperf*) does exactly that.

> **Note** You can download the Windows Performance Toolkit for free from the following URL: *http://msdn.microsoft.com/en-us/performance/cc752957.aspx*. It also ships with the Windows SDK for Windows 7 and Windows Server 2008 R2, where you can find the installers (for x86, x64, and ia64 architectures) under the SDK *bin* directory. At the time of this writing, if you're planning to

use the Windows Performance Toolkit to diagnose a Windows 7 machine, it's mandatory to use the SDK version.

The *xperf* utility is more than just a mechanism for integrating data from various sources. It's a system-wide kernel-sampling profiler that can also be used for profiling individual (unmanaged) applications. It's also a reporting and graphical analysis engine that can be used to overlay multiple sources of information to obtain a coherent picture of what the system was doing at any given time. In short, it's an extremely valuable and very powerful tool to add to your belt.

Profilers

Profilers are tools that dynamically inspect the performance behavior of a running program and record this information for later analysis. Typically, profilers record the frequency and duration of function calls, memory allocation and deallocation, and various other interesting performance metrics.

The profiler's accuracy, functionality, and applicability are determined by its underlying mechanism. Some profilers use instrumentation techniques to modify the source code or the binary image of the program that is being profiled; other profilers rely on the operating system or on hardware interrupts to sample information from a running program without requiring any interaction on its behalf.

Profilers often have an adverse effect on the profiled application's performance, which renders suspicious some of the results obtained in the process. Low-overhead profilers, such as the *xperf* utility, are extremely important for analyzing system-wide activity or the activity of individual applications over a long period of time.

Let's walk through an example of how *xperf* can be used to determine whether the work performed by an application is I/O-bound or CPU-bound.

> **Note** There are other ways to obtain the same information and to reach the same conclusion that we are going to reach through our analysis. However, the purpose of this section is to show you how the Windows Performance Toolkit can streamline this kind of analysis. Additionally, bear in mind that we could have modified the scenario to also look at network utilization, CPU-specific cache-related counters, and nearly anything else that the operating system kernel has access to.

First, open an administrative command prompt and navigate to the directory where the Windows Performance Toolkit is installed. Now you're ready to specify to the operating system which information you're interested in. The underlying engine collects this information (stemming primarily from ETW logging sources), buffers it, and waits for you to request a report. Multiple data collection profiles ship with Windows, and you can see them all by running the following command:

```
xperf -providers
```

You will notice that one of the provider groups is called *Base*, and it contains several useful flags for CPU utilization, page faults, memory usage, and disk I/O. This is the profile we'll use for this trace, so you can issue the following command:

```
xperf -on Base
```

The underlying data collection engine is now running. System activity is being monitored and buffered so that you can later generate a report and see exactly what was going on. After a few seconds, you can stop the profiling and request the engine to generate a report for you:

```
xperf -d my_result.etl
```

This command might take some time to complete—it mainly depends on the amount of information that was collected during the previous step. When everything is done, you have a report file you can freely transfer from system to system to analyze at your convenience. One of the ways to analyze the report is to generate a textual representation of it using predefined or custom actions:

```
xperf -i my_result.etl -o my_result.txt -a hardfault
```

Another way is to use the Performance Analyzer UI by issuing the following command:

```
xperf my_result.etl
```

And there we are, at last. The analysis UI shows you a summary of the collected data, and it has lots of options for filtering and sorting the information. It also has a master-detail view that allows you to focus on the important parts of the data by requesting a detailed graph or overlaying several graphs on top of each other to find correlations between different types of activity. (For example, could the disk I/O in one process be related to a flurry of CPU activity in another process?) One of my favorite graphs is a disk I/O graph that shows the physical seeks on the disk as they occur over time. The following screen shots depict some of the graphical representations of system activity that the Performance Analyzer UI can show you:

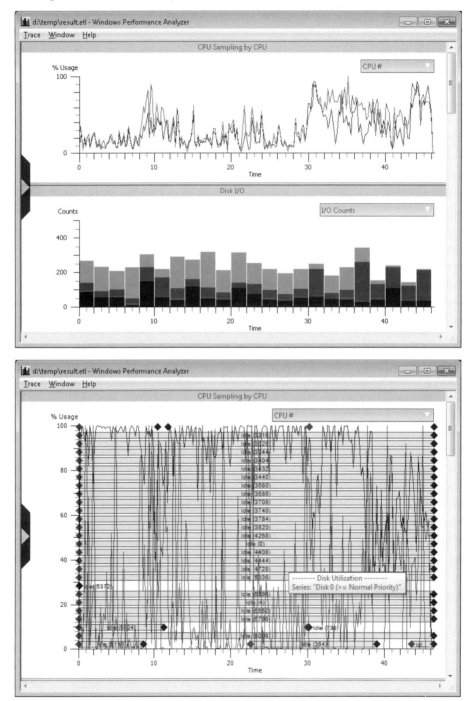

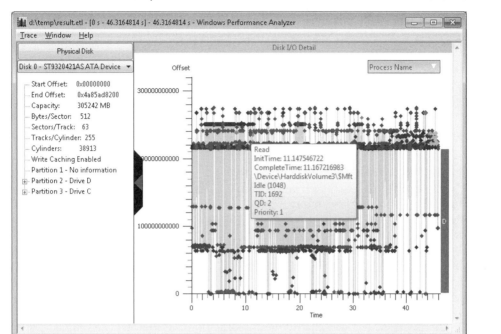

Note If you want to continue experimenting with the Windows Performance Toolkit profiling capabilities, consult the tutorials that ship with the toolset. Among other things, you'll learn how to profile actual applications and see symbols and call stacks, how to diagnose the system boot process, and many other fascinating performance disciplines.

Troubleshooting Platform

Even if you're not writing software for Windows, the fact that you're reading this book probably means you're the IT support person for your (possibly extended) family. Computer users upgrading to Windows 7 from Windows XP or Windows Vista might find some tasks more difficult to perform, resulting in more "support time" for you—after all, even something as trivial as muted speakers can take a few minutes to diagnose over the phone or in an instant messaging (IM) conversation.

Wouldn't it be wonderful if the operating system itself could troubleshoot common problems, suggest fixes, and even apply them if possible, verifying that the end result suits the user's expectations? This is precisely the purpose of the Windows Troubleshooting Platform, introduced in Windows 7. Under the Troubleshooting page accessed through Control Panel, users can find about a dozen troubleshooters aimed at fixing common problems and making specific tasks easier. Here are just a few that you'll see:

- Application compatibility troubleshooter, aptly named "Run programs made for previous versions of Windows"

- Audio playback and recording troubleshooters

- Printer configuration troubleshooter

- Shared folders and files troubleshooter

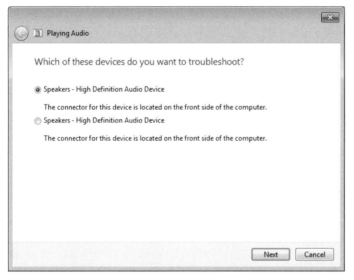

A troubleshooter is essentially a wizard that takes you through the diagnostic operations and remediation steps required to fix the problem. The troubleshooting packs that ship with Windows can already save a significant amount of time to an otherwise annoyed and frustrated user. However, the Windows Troubleshooting Platform is extensible, meaning that you can write your own troubleshooting packs and deliver them to the users of your software. The Windows Troubleshooting Pack Designer (part of the Windows 7 SDK) is a simple utility you can use to create a troubleshooting pack—you can create a troubleshooting wizard; specify detection, remediation, and verification steps; and package the result for redistribution.

Authoring Troubleshooting Packs

A troubleshooting pack contains the following parts, all bundled together in a single folder:

- **Troubleshooting manifest**   Indicates what root cause the troubleshooting pack was written to detect and what environmental requirements it has

- **Troubleshooting scripts**   PowerShell scripts used to detect whether the root cause exists

- **Resolver scripts**   PowerShell scripts used to resolve the root cause that the troubleshooter scripts found

- **Verifier scripts**   PowerShell scripts used to verify whether the resolver scripts were able to actually resolve the issue (The Troubleshooting scripts can be reused for this purpose.)

Troubleshooting wizards can interact with the user through a variety of built-in interactions. Among them you'll find list box–style single-choice and multiple-choice questions, text input boxes, and even the ability to launch a custom UI application that instructs the user what to do next. Troubleshooting packs don't have to be interactive, but if they are, they should adhere to the standard Windows UI guidelines and strive to be as simple and noninvasive as possible.

Although you can design troubleshooting packs manually by editing XML files, the Windows Troubleshooting Pack Designer is a useful utility you might want to consider using instead. For more information on authoring troubleshooting packs for Windows 7, consult the MSDN documentation at *http://msdn.microsoft.com/en-us/library/dd323712.aspx*.

Performance and Efficiency

Some of the things users had to say about the performance requirements of Windows 7 on the "Engineering Windows 7" blog were the following (with minor edits applied):

- "Boot very fast in all applications, especially many simultaneously."

- "I want to be able to run Windows 7 extremely fast and still look good graphically on a netbook with these specs: 1.5-GHz processor, 1 GB of RAM."

- "I do keep my fingers crossed for Windows 7 to be dramatically better in its performance than Windows Vista."

Since the outset of this chapter, we've already seen that building a high-performance operating system is not only a task for operating system developers—it's a task for the entire developer ecosystem, for you and me, for us fellow developers. One poorly written application or service is enough to bring a system to its knees, but a combination of multiple applications that are not so bad on their own but negatively interfere with each other's operation is also a deadly hit with regard to the user experience.

In the previous section, you saw how to monitor system and application performance and diagnose some of the prevalent issues. In this section, we'll discuss two ways to improve system performance and efficiency: writing unobtrusive background services, and maximizing the energy efficiency of your applications.

Background Services and Trigger Start Services

With almost every release of Windows, several new background services join the multitude of services and tasks that constitute most of the user-mode parts of the operating system. Background services in Windows perform various types of activity, ranging from critical services such as the remote procedure call (RPC) or Audio services through less critical services that are often turned off by default, such as the Font Cache service. Other functionality is offloaded to background tasks, such as disk defragmentation and power efficiency diagnostics. All in all, the microkernel design of Windows requires significant functionality to reside in background services and tasks.

Windows Services and Scheduled Tasks

Windows services (also known as NT services) are user-mode applications that usually do not interact with the user and do not require a user to be logged on in order to run. Most services run under the credentials of one of the system accounts: LocalSystem, LocalService, or NetworkService. Services are usually reactive programs that sit idly and wait for commands from the Service Control Manager, and they do not perform any user interaction.

Scheduled tasks are user-mode applications that usually do not interact with the user but require a user to be logged on in order to run. Scheduled tasks do not always run— they execute on a schedule or are triggered by system conditions, and they are managed by the Task Scheduler. In Windows Vista, the set of task triggers has been extended to include very useful conditions such as user logon, workstation lock, the system becoming idle, and even a custom entry being written into the system Event Log.

Almost every machine that comes with Windows preinstalled from an original equipment manufacturer (OEM) has multiple additional third-party services and tasks running on the system. Every service and every task represents an additional burden on the system's performance, reliability, stability, and robustness. Background services consume physical memory, use CPU resources, keep the system from entering power-saving states, increase the system's susceptibility to security breaches (attack surface), and introduce compatibility issues with each other. It is extremely important for developers to grasp the principles of designing background services that are both efficient and secure.

Design Goals for Windows Services

Some of the design goals for Windows services are actually quite simple:

- Immediate startup (under 500 milliseconds)
- Immediate shutdown (under 200 ms, and no interference with system shutdown)
- Less than 2% CPU activity when the system is idle
- No blocking calls in the service main thread
- Run with least privileges account
- Low-rights service account (not LocalSystem)

If all you learn from this section is that your services should adhere to these guidelines, it would be enough; if you want to learn *how* they can adhere to these guidelines, read on.

Until Windows Vista, services could have only two startup modes: manual and auto-start. Manual-start services required the user (or an administrative application on the user's behalf) to start the service. The usual alternative was the auto-start mode, when it was required for the service to be started during system boot, before the user even logs on. When the system starts, auto-start services significantly interfere with the system's startup performance because they perform their initialization while the user is trying to start using the machine immediately after booting it and logging on.

To address this issue, Windows Vista introduces delayed auto-start services, which are services designated to auto-start shortly (approximately two minutes) after the system boot sequence and initial logon have completed. This allows the user to start interacting with her favorite applications without background services getting in the way.

> **More Info** For more information about delayed auto-start services and other service-related features introduced in Windows Vista that are still relevant in Windows 7, see "Windows Services Enhancements" in the Launch 2008 issue of the MSDN Magazine, or online at *http://msdn.microsoft.com/en-us/magazine/cc164252.aspx*.

Marking a service as "delayed auto-start" is easy. One way to do so is through the built-in command-line utility, *sc.exe*. Its advanced service configuration interface allows you to mark a service as "delayed auto-start" (note the required space after the equal sign):

```
sc config MyService start= delayed-auto
```

Another alternative is using the explicit Win32 service control APIs, with the *ChangeServiceConfig2* method and the SERVICE_DELAYED_AUTO_START_INFO structure:

```
SC_HANDLE hSCManager = OpenSCManager(NULL, NULL, SC_MANAGER_ALL_ACCESS);
if (hSCManager == NULL)
{
    //...Handle error and return
}

SC_HANDLE hService = OpenService(hSCManager, serviceName, SERVICE_ALL_ACCESS);
if (hService == NULL)
{
    CloseServiceHandle(hSCManager);
    //...Handle error and return
}

SERVICE_DELAYED_AUTO_START_INFO delayedAutoStartInfo = {0};
delayedAutoStartInfo.fDelayedAutostart = TRUE;

if (!ChangeServiceConfig2(hService, SERVICE_CONFIG_DELAYED_AUTO_START_INFO,
&delayedAutoStartInfo))
{
    CloseServiceHandle(hService);
    CloseServiceHandle(hSCManager);
    //...Handle error and return
}
CloseServiceHandle(hService);
CloseServiceHandle(hSCManager);
```

Some built-in services already take advantage of this functionality to make sure the system boots faster and service activity doesn't interfere with the user's logon. Among them, you'll find Windows Update, Windows Media Player Network Sharing, Windows Defender, and other services.

Unfortunately, delayed auto-start services are not a panacea. They improve startup times and remove interference from a highly sensitive performance path, but as soon as the service is started it continues running unless someone explicitly stops it. Even if the service has absolutely nothing to do (for example, if it relies on Internet connectivity but you're working on a laptop in the middle of the desert), it still consumes significant system resources. As a service developer, you might be tempted to argue that the 5 MB of memory consumed by *your* service is not going to seriously affect the user's experience. However, the 50 other services on that user's system would beg to differ. If we want to provide our users with a high-performance experience on Windows 7, it takes more than delayed auto-start services.

One thing many services have in common is that they require some preconditions to exist on the system for their activity to have any meaning. For example, the Bluetooth Support service has nothing to do if there is no Bluetooth hardware device; the Tablet PC Input service shouldn't even start if there is no digitizer attached to the system. There are numerous other examples, and I'm sure that if you perform an inventory of your own services you'll have similar findings. Services of this type should have a more sensible startup mechanism: when I attach a digitizer, the Tablet PC Input service should start; when I disconnect it, the service should stop.

This is precisely the idea behind trigger-start services, a new kind of startup mechanism introduced in Windows 7 that allows services to indicate what trigger should cause the system to automatically transition them to the started state. The built-in service triggers include the following:

- Specific device arrived (for example, a USB storage device)

- Specific event logged by an ETW provider

- First IP address obtained

- Computer joined the domain

- Network port opened in the firewall

- Machine or user group policy changed

Some of these triggers also have stop semantics—for example, it's possible to configure a service so that it starts when the first IP address is acquired and stops when the last IP address is removed. The triggers that don't have stop semantics hint at a simple service design pattern:

> *The system will start the service when triggered; the service will shut itself down when it has nothing left to do.*

By using trigger-start services judiciously, you can significantly reduce the system's attack surface and permanent load. If services are started only when they are really needed, there is minimal waste of energy and resources.

Some Windows 7 services take advantage of this new functionality. Run the following command in a command prompt to see the triggers of the Tablet PC Input service, for example:

```
> sc qtriggerinfo TabletInputService
[SC] QueryServiceConfig2 SUCCESS

SERVICE_NAME: TabletInputService
```

```
        START SERVICE
          DEVICE INTERFACE ARRIVAL      : 4d1e55b2-f16f-11cf-88cb-001111000030 [INTERFACE
CLASS GUID]
             DATA                        : HID_DEVICE_UP:000D_U:0001
             DATA                        : HID_DEVICE_UP:000D_U:0002
             DATA                        : HID_DEVICE_UP:000D_U:0003
             DATA                        : HID_DEVICE_UP:000D_U:0004
```

Configuring your service to trigger-start is possible using the *sc.exe* utility. For example, the following command sets your service to start automatically when the first IP address is acquired:

```
sc triggerinfo MyService start/networkon
```

You can also do the same with the Win32 service control APIs. The *ChangeServiceConfig2* method can modify the trigger-start configuration of a service, through the use of elaborate data structures specific for each trigger type. (Some trigger types are simpler to configure than others.)

```
SC_HANDLE hSCManager = OpenSCManager(NULL, NULL, SC_MANAGER_ALL_ACCESS);
if (hSCManager == NULL)
{
    //...Handle error and return
}

SC_HANDLE hService = OpenService(hSCManager, serviceName, SERVICE_ALL_ACCESS);
if (hService == NULL)
{
    CloseServiceHandle(hSCManager);
    //...Handle error and return
}

SERVICE_TRIGGER serviceTrigger = {0};
serviceTrigger.dwTriggerType = SERVICE_TRIGGER_TYPE_IP_ADDRESS_AVAILABILITY;
serviceTrigger.dwAction = SERVICE_TRIGGER_ACTION_SERVICE_START;
serviceTrigger.pTriggerSubtype = (GUID*)&NETWORK_MANAGER_FIRST_IP_ADDRESS_ARRIVAL_GUID;

SERVICE_TRIGGER_INFO serviceTriggerInfo = {0};
serviceTriggerInfo.cTriggers = 1;
serviceTriggerInfo.pTriggers = &serviceTrigger;

if (!ChangeServiceConfig2(hService, SERVICE_CONFIG_TRIGGER_INFO, &serviceTriggerInfo))
{
    CloseServiceHandle(hService);
    CloseServiceHandle(hSCManager);
    //...Handle error and return
}

CloseServiceHandle(hService);
CloseServiceHandle(hSCManager);
```

Trigger-start services bring some very interesting scenarios to mind. The Windows 7 Training Kit (which you can download from *http://www.microsoft.com/downloads/details.aspx? FamilyID=12100526-ed26-476b-8e20-69662b8546c1&displaylang=en*) features two such services:

- A service that is trigger-started whenever a USB storage device is attached to the system. This service copies all files from the USB storage device to a designated directory on the local disk.

- A service that is trigger-started whenever an IP address is acquired. This service downloads weather information for consumption in offline scenarios.

Service Security Features

Windows Vista and Windows 7 also introduce service-hardening features, including session 0 isolation, meaning that services run in a separate Windows session that is not connected to the currently logged-on user's session; service SIDs, which provide services the ability to request precisely the access rights they need; and service privilege removal, which allows services to declare which privileges can be stripped from their access token. For example, the following C++ code sample shows how to configure a service so that its access token at runtime will have all privileged stripped off (except the *SeChangeNotifyPrivilege* which, for compatibility reasons, cannot be removed):

```
SC_HANDLE hSCManager = OpenSCManager(NULL, NULL, SC_MANAGER_ALL_ACCESS);
if (hSCManager == NULL)
{
    //...Handle error and return
}

SC_HANDLE hService = OpenService(hSCManager, serviceName, SERVICE_ALL_ACCESS);
if (hService == NULL)
{
    CloseServiceHandle(hSCManager);
    //...Handle error and return
}

//Here, specifying \0\0 doesn't work, so we're using SeChangeNotifyPrivilege,
//which is enabled (for compatibility reasons) anyway even if privileges are removed.
//This effectively strips out all other privileges.
SERVICE_REQUIRED_PRIVILEGES_INFO requiredPrivileges = {0};
requiredPrivileges.pmszRequiredPrivileges = SE_CHANGE_NOTIFY_NAME L"\0";

if (!ChangeServiceConfig2(hService, SERVICE_CONFIG_REQUIRED_PRIVILEGES_INFO,
&requiredPrivileges))
{
    CloseServiceHandle(hService);
    CloseServiceHandle(hSCManager);
    //...Handle error and return
}
```

```
CloseServiceHandle(hService);
CloseServiceHandle(hSCManager);
```

If you run this service and inspect its token with Process Explorer (available from
http://technet.microsoft.com/en-us/sysinternals/bb896653.aspx, or a similar utility), you'll
find all privileges removed, which significantly decreases this service's attack surface. If
an attacker were to take control of this service because of a security bug, he would not
be able to exploit this vulnerability as much as he would with a fully privileged service.

All in all, the combination of delayed auto-start for critical services (such that at least the
startup path is not adversely affected) and of trigger-start for services that do not always need
to run can improve the performance and stability of the system, as well as significantly reduce
its attack surface. If you add the service security improvements in Windows Vista and
Windows 7 to the mix, you'll find yourself equipped with all the tools necessary to develop
user-friendly background components that will co-exist with other third-party services and
tasks and have a minimal negative effect on the system's performance and energy efficiency.

Power Management

If you've been to any technology conference during the last 5 years, you must have seen at
least one presenter mention energy consumption, energy efficiency, or power savings. The
importance of power consumption increased over the past few years for two
objective reasons:

- Processor power consumption over the years has grown exponentially, from just under 20
  watts 10 years ago to over 100 watts today (on select models).

- Users expect mobile applications and operating systems (or, more precisely, "the
  computer") to provide them with ever-increasing battery life.

Unless something magical happens over the course of the next few years, we're likely to
witness a constant struggle of hardware manufacturers to pack more and more features into a
decreasing form factor, while still retaining the same level of energy consumption. As with
performance optimization, this dream cannot be obtained by the hardware manufactures and
operating system programmers alone; it needs to be a joint effort by every
Windows developer.

Windows 7 introduces significant improvements to energy efficiency—the operating system
itself has been restructured and optimized for battery life and environmental friendliness.
There are some simple tricks that Windows developers should know about to maximize the
energy efficiency of their applications.

The primary factor for reducing energy consumption is the system's CPU. The primary goal to strive for is minimizing CPU utilization when the application (or the system) is idle. Remember that an idle system is the most common user scenario, so any periodic work while the system is idle should be viewed with great suspicion. Generally speaking, applications should try to refrain from polling if possible, and they should use some kind of notification mechanism to wake up and perform their work.

If you must perform periodic activity when the system is idle, prefer to do so when the system is on AC power—this can be detected using standard Win32 APIs, and there's even a broadcast notification that you can register for. Here's a C++ sample and another sample using the Windows Vista Bridge Library *PowerManager* class:

```
//During application initialization:
RegisterPowerSettingNotification(
    hMainWnd,
    powerSettingGUID, //See SDK
    DEVICE_NOTIFY_WINDOW_HANDLE);

//In the window procedure:
case WM_POWERBROADCAST:
    if (lParam == PBT_POWERSETTINGCHANGE) {
        POWERBROADCAST_SETTING* setting = (POWERBROADCAST_SETTING*)lParam;
        //...Handle the notification
    }

//With the Vista Bridge Power Manager:
PowerManager.PowerSourceChanged += delegate {
    Console.WriteLine("Switched to " + PowerManager.PowerSource +
        ", remaining battery: " + PowerManager.BatteryLifePercent);
};
```

> **More Info**   For a similar example in C++, and for other samples of the Win32 power management APIs, see the CodeProject article "Vista Goodies in C++: Monitoring the Computer's Power Status" at *http://www.codeproject.com/KB/vista/VGPowerMonitor.aspx*.

To aid applications that need to poll the system regardless of these warnings, Windows 7 introduces a new timer mechanism called *coalescing timers*. Coalescing timers minimize the maximum-power consumption periods by combining adjacent timer invocations (by different applications) to a single time frame. For example, if an application requested a timer to be fired every 150 ms, and another application requested a timer to be fired every 100 ms, at least two invocations of these timers can coalesce. (Over a period of 300 ms there is no reason to wake the system up more than three times.)

Timers and Multimedia Timers

Timers in general are a fairly expensive mechanism with regard to energy consumption. Even more so are the high-resolution multimedia timers, which can affect the Windows scheduler timer's resolution (if the hardware supports it). Increasing timer resolution increases the timer's accuracy, but it might have dire effects on battery life and energy consumption and prevent the CPU from ever entering low-power states.

If you're using multimedia timers, turn them on when necessary, turn them off whenever you don't need them, and aim for a 10-ms resolution, not less. (If you require a sub-millisecond resolution, you might find it more convenient working with a full-blown interrupt service routine, or a true hard real-time operating system.)

To opt in to the coalescing timer mechanism, applications should use the new *SetWaitableTimerEx* API with the *TolerableDelay* parameter. This parameter specifies how far from the required interval the actual timer invocation is allowed to be. For example, if you provide a 10-ms delay and your timer is registered with a 100-ms interval, you might receive an invocation 90 ms or 110 ms after receiving the last invocation.

Other sources of potential power savings on Windows include these general rules:

- Avoid animations when idle, and avoid tray icon animations. (Several antivirus programs are particularly susceptible to this.)

- Avoid periodic disk and registry activity. (Registry activity is eventually translated to disk activity.)

- Defer work to background activities that will be scheduled only on AC power and stopped when the system goes on battery power.

- Do not block system power transitions (standby, hibernate, shutdown).

Although you can have your applications prevent the system from transitioning to a low-power state, it is a behavior we strongly advise you to avoid, unless there will be significant data loss if the transition occurs or the user experience demands that the transition does not occur. Some legitimate examples include downloading a file from the Internet, recording a TV show, burning a DVD, and displaying a presentation slideshow. The old API for interfering with power transitions was *SetThreadExecutionState*, which was replaced in Windows 7 by detailed power availability APIs.

The purpose of the new APIs is to provide the user with a detailed report of what application is blocking the power transition and why. For example, when I attempt to shut down the computer in my living room, Windows notifies me that the Media Center application is currently recording (or is scheduled to record) a TV show and will not be able to complete this task if the system shuts down. This gives the user more control and understanding over why the system is not transitioning to a low-power state.

The new power availability APIs include *PowerCreateRequest*, *PowerSetRequest*, and *PowerClearRequest*, as well as a command-line switch to the *powercfg.exe* tool. Try running the following command from your Windows 7 administrative command line:

```
powercfg /requests
```

The following code sample demonstrates how an application can register a power availability request so that the system does not transition to a low-power state while the request is active:

```
REASON_CONTEXT reason = {0};
reason.Flags = POWER_REQUEST_CONTEXT_SIMPLE_STRING;
reason.SimpleReasonString = L"You're downloading an important document.";

HANDLE hRequest = PowerCreateRequest(&reason);
PowerSetRequest(hRequest, PowerRequestSystemRequired);
```

Finally, if you're just interested in a power efficiency report on your system, you can use the *powercfg.exe* utility we saw earlier:

```
powercfg /energy
```

> **Note** A scheduled task executes this command when the system is idle (from time to time) and sends the anonymous report to the Microsoft Customer Experience Improvement Program (CEIP).

This command generates a power efficiency report for you to examine. Among other things, the report might point you in the direction of an application that is consuming too many idle CPU cycles, or a kernel-mode component (such as a driver) that is preventing a low-power state transition.

The following are some of the diagnostics produced by the *powercfg.exe* utility on my computer:

```
Power Policy:Display timeout disabled (Plugged In)
The display is not configured to turn off after a period of inactivity.

Power Policy:Sleep timeout is disabled (Plugged In)
The computer is not configured to automatically sleep after a period of inactivity.

Platform Timer Resolution:Platform Timer Resolution

The default platform timer resolution is 15.6ms (15625000ns) and should be used whenever the
system is idle. If the timer resolution is increased, processor power management
technologies may not be effective. The timer resolution may be increased due to multimedia
playback or graphical animations.
Current Timer Resolution (100ns units) 10000
Maximum Timer Period (100ns units) 156001
```

Power efficiency is too big a subject to cover in a single subsection, but it will become increasingly important as hardware manufacturers continue to pack more hardware features into a smaller form factor. It is not enough to take advantage of all the shiny new features; we, as developers, will have to learn to minimize our applications' energy footprint as well as improve their general performance characteristics if we want them to truly shine on Windows 7.

Summary

Throughout this chapter, we have seen multiple features and techniques that will assist us, as developers, to build applications that are faster, more reliable, and more power efficient on Windows 7. Remember that this is a joint effort—no single application, no single software or hardware vendor, and not even Microsoft itself can ensure that Windows 7 is a fast, stable, and power-efficient operating system. By using the instrumentation tools from this chapter, you will be able to diagnose problems in legacy applications, and by using this chapter's design guidance, you will ensure a better future for your Windows 7 applications

Index

A

AbortList method, 51
accelerometers, 202
access tokens, 93
accuracy values, 246, 257. *See also* error radius
Active Template Library (ATL), 309
Adaptive Brightness service, 230–231
addresses, street, 246
AddSensor, 210–211, 216, 226
AddStylusPoints method, 188, 190
Aero Peek, 103. *See also* live preview
alerts, performance counter, 359
altitude, 246, 250
ambient light sensors, 9–10, 208–218, 227–231
AmbientLightSensor type, 212, 217, 227–230
angles, rotation, 115, 118–119, 139
annotations, ink, 182–184, 191–192
APIs (application programming interfaces), 1, 170–171
    CFD (Common File Dialog) and, 86
    ink-based, 183–194
    managed in summary, 41
    sensor, 205
appearance
    controlling, 346, 347
    taskbar, 26, 35, 38, 103
AppID (application user model ID), 90
application ids (AppID)
    custom destinations and, 51
    determination process for, 33
    overview, 30–32
    setting specific window, 34–35
application menus
    adding, 285–286
    adding most recently used files to, 348
    creating, 293–295
    Quick Access Toolbar (QAT) and, 270–271
application modes
    contextual tabs and, 292–293
    defined, 289
    setting, 347–348
application user model ID (AppID), 90
APPLICATION_RIBBON, 313, 316–317
    (ribbon binary resource name), 277–279
Application.Commands, 282–285, 289, 323, 327, 332, 342
ApplicationDefaults, 289, 296
ApplicationDocumentLists, 350
ApplicationMenu
    command types for, 321
    commands in, 293

    compiling Ribbon markup file, 277–278, 285
    menu groups in, 294–295
ApplicationMenu.RecentItems, 294, 296, 297, 350–351
ApplicationMode, 289–290, 347–348
Application.Resources, 156
applications
    access to Windows Shell and, 89–90
    associating file type, 46–49
    associating taskbar buttons with, 30–32
    custom thumbnails for, 62–63
    deploying, to desktop, 179–182
    dual-touch, 160
    enumerating library contents, 92–93
    integrating, with libraries, 84–85
    light-aware, 230–231
    mapping, 124
    running, on taskbar, 21
    taskbar messages to, 57
    touch-aware, 104
    user mode, 372–373
Application.Views
    commands and, 282–283, 285–286, 323–324, 327, 332–333
    controls in, 289–291
    Ribbon markup XML file, 277–278, 315–316, 342
ApplyManipulationDelta function, 142
app.xaml files, 154, 156, 178
arrays, touch input, 130–133
ASP.NET Web Application Project type, 177–178
ATL (Active Template Library), 309
Automatic setting, for text color, 341
auto-start services, delayed, 373–374, 378

B

background services, 372–373
begin flags, 111, 114, 116, 118
BeginInvoke, 213, 229–230
binary files, 275, 278, 281
binding
    command handlers to commands, 312–314
    the Ribbon to applications, 312
bitmap images
    for controls, 326–329
    in Ribbon resource file, 278, 283
    thumbnail, 58, 63–65, 68
boundaries, 104, 110
    elastic, 147–150
    gutter, 123–124
    setting object behavior at, 163
BoundaryFeedback property, 163

brightness, 351
browsers, 173–176
button control, 289, 321–322, 327
buttons
  changing image size of, 327–329
  changing text on, 323–324
  taskbar, 22, 25, 30–34
  toggle, 290, 319, 322, 325
  toolbar, 57

C

C# programming, 166–167, 192–193
caching, the IURibbon, 352–353
callbacks, Ribbon, 316–320
CAmbientLightAwareSensorEvents class, 221, 223–227
CAmbientLightAwareSensorManagerEvents class, 208–211, 215–216, 226–227
cancel preview, 319, 340
Canvas, 188, 194, 195, 197
CApplication class
  background color, 343
  Execute, 324, 334, 344
  IUIApplication interface, 311, 313
  OnCreateUICommand method, 314, 315, 328
  OnViewChanged, 314
  populating a ComboBox, 333–336
  Ribbon color setter, 344–346
  UpdateProperty, 324, 325, 329, 338
categories
  constructing custom jump list, 51–52
  destination, 45–49
  performance counter, 357–358, 361
  pinned, 45
  of sensor types, 205
cbExtraArgs, 112
cbSize, 112
CComModule, 309, 312
center points
  in pan gestures, 115
  relative, in rectangles, 158–159
  in rotate gestures, 118–119
  in two-finger tap gestures, 120
  in zoom gestures, 105, 116–117
CFD (Common File Dialog), 84, 85–88
changes, detecting
  in data reports, 217, 229
  to library definition file, 100
  of sensor state, 213, 216–218, 225, 229–230
  of touch points, 139, 142
ChangeServiceConfig2, 374, 376, 377
ChangeWindowMessageFilter function, 58
changing
  button text, 321–322
  images for controls, 326–329
  Ribbon application state to reflect user action, 316–317

Win32-based bitmap to Ribbon framework bitmap, 325–328
checkbox controls, 289–290, 296, 309, 321, 322, 325
child windows
  compatibility with, 30
  creating thumbnails for, 66–70
Civic Address report, 244–248, 251
CivicAddressLocationProvider, 257–259
class extensions, sensor, 212–213, 227–228, 236
click events
  double, 119–121
  right, 102, 121
  thumbnail, 57, 59
ClientToScreen API, 350
CLocationEvents class, 251–253
Close button, 28
CloseGestureInfoHandle function, 112
CloseTouchInputHandle function, 130–131, 144
CLSID_ShellItem, 91
CLSID_TaskbarList COM object, 45
CLSID_UIRibbonFramework, 312–313
CLSID_UIRibbonFramework class, 316
CManipulationEventSink class
  implementing processor, 139–140
  initiating processor, 142–143
  setting elastic boundaries, 150
  setting up inertia, 147–149
CoCreateInstance method
  for choosing a library or folder, 87
  for creating a new library, 95
  for creating sensors, 208–209
  with ILocation interface, 241
  to initialize Ribbon framework object, 313
  initializing Com object, 86–87
  for shell links, 90–91
  using IPortableDeviceValues interface with, 221–222
code-behind files, 154, 166–167, 192, 275, 289
color, assigning, 132, 134, 272, 341, 343–346, 351–352
Color Hot-Tracking feature, 22
ColorRGBToHLS method, 346, 351
ColorTemplate control, 341
COM (Component Object Model). *See* Component Object Model (COM)
COM ITaskbarList3 interface, 45
ComboBox gallery control, 296, 303, 331–336
command and control providers, 362
Command gallery, 339
command prompt, 22
command types and controls, 320–321
commandid value, 312, 318–319, 322, 323
CommandName attribute, 283, 287, 289
commands, 277, 282–287
  property sets in Ribbon framework commands, 319–325
  Quick Access Toolbar (QAT) and, 271, 350
  in Ribbon Framework, 284–285, 289, 315–318
  tabs for, 271
Comment attributes, 284

Commit method, 96
CommitList method, 48, 51, 52, 55
Common File Dialog (CFD), 84, 85–88
compatibility
    application, 370
    backward, 29–30
    markup, 178, 179, 194
Component Object Model (COM), 307, 309–315, 320
consistency, 85, 99–100
console window, 315
Constant Special Item ID List (CSIDL), 73
consumers, writing WMI, 363–364
contact points, 134
container controls, 291–297, 348
content, library, 85, 91–94
ContextMenu, 294
ContextPopup, 293–294, 301
contextual tabs, 272, 291–293, 348–349
contrast, adjusting, 231, 352
control family, 303
controls
    basic, 290
    bitmap images for, 326–329
    container, 291–297, 348
    controlling Ribbon, 325–326
    gesture-enabled picture, 165–170
      Ribbon, 288, 289. See also galleries
    setting properties for Ribbon, 322–325
    specialized, 298–301
    table of command types for, 321
coordinates, touch point
    extracting, 133–134
    initial gesture, 112
    manipulation, 139, 144
    in pan gestures, 114–115
    raw data, 131
    in rotate gestures, 118–119
    starting points, 139
    transformation of, 136
    translation changes, 139, 142
    in zoom gestures, 105, 116–117
copying, file operation API, 40
Count property, 185, 186
CPU usage and idle systems, 379
CreateImage method, 326–327
CreateSensorUIElements helper function, 217–218
creating
    ContextPopup, 293–294
    performance counter logs, 359–362
    sensor manager instance, 208
    sensors, in Windows API Code Pack, 212
CRecentFileList class, 350
CSIDL (Constant Special Item ID List), 73
CStroke object, 133–134
ctrl property, 187
CurrentLuminousIntensity property, 212, 227, 229
custom build actions, 280–281, 315–316

CustomizeCommandName, 297
customizing
    live preview, 65–66
    Quick Access Toolbar (QAT), 296–297
    templates, 305–307
    thumbnail previews, 51–52, 63
CVTRES.EXE tool, 279

D

debugging, 365–369
    sensor, 218–219
deceleration
    curve, 145
    setting, 149, 163
definition files
    deleting, 98–99
    library, 80–83
DefWindowsProc, 109
DeleteList method, 52–53
Desktop Window Manager (DWM), 29, 60, 63–67
destinations
    categorized, 45
    custom, 49–53
    definition of, 22
    jump list, 23, 51
    recent and frequent, 45–49
DestroyFramework, 311, 313
device drivers, 204–205, 236
devices
    ink-based, 188
    location, 236–237
    sensor and location, 10, 204
DeviceType property, 188
diagnostics, 381–382
dialog templates, 205, 275
digitizers, 129, 184
Direct2D, 14
DirectWrite, 14–15
documents. See destinations
Documents library, 75–77, 97
DPI settings, 288
drag gestures, 102, 133, 184, 189, 195
DrawingAttributes, 185–186, 188–193
drivers, 204–205, 236
DropDownButton controls, 293, 303
DropDownColorPicker, 298–299, 303, 341–346, 352
DropDownGallery, 296, 303
dual-touch applications, 160
dwBlocks, 122
dwFlags, 111, 113, 114, 131
dwID, 111, 113, 122, 131, 133–135
dwInstanceID, 112
DWM (Desktop Window Manager), 29, 60, 63–67
dwMask, 131
DwmInvalidateIconicBitmaps function, 63, 65

DwmSetIconicThumbnail function, 63
DwmSetWindowAttribute function, 63
DWMWA_FORCE_ICONIC_REPRESENTATION attribute, 63, 65
DWMWA_HAS_ICONIC_BITMAP attribute, 63, 65
dwSequenceID, 112
dwSITFlags parameter, 66
dwTime, 131
dwWant, 122, 123
dynamic containers, 291, 296

E

eDLP (enhanced default location provider) tool, 259–260
efficiency, energy, 378–379
elastic boundaries, 147–150
ellipses, 194–195
EnableSingleContactManipulations, 171
encapsulation, of gesture controls, 165–170
end flags, 114
enhanced default location provider (eDLP) tool, 259–260
environmental information and sensors, 202
error radius, 238, 240
    location accuracy and, 237, 257
    printing, 250
    values, 245–246
ETW (Event Tracing for Windows), 365
event handlers
    adding definition for FrameReported event, 194
    for moving objects using touch, 157
    for rotating objects, 161
    for scaling objects, using touch, 159
    for Silverlight applications, 189
event notifications
    location, 250–252
    sensor, 224–225, 226–227
event sink class, 138, 147, 151
event sinking objects, 210, 216, 226–227
Event Tracing for Windows (ETW), 365
Execute method, 318, 319, 325, 341
execution verbs, 319, 339–340, 346
expansionDelta, 139
explorer.exe, 57
Extensible Application Markup Language (XAML). See XAML (Extensible Application Markup Language)
Extensible Markup Language (XML). See XML (Extensible Markup Language)

F

file types, 46–49
FileName property, 88
FileSystemWatcher, 100
Filter property, 88
FindStrokeByID function, 133–134
First Touch project, 178–182

flags
    begin, 111, 114, 116, 118
    clearing inertia, in manipulations, 147
    end, 114
    for gesture configuration, 122–123
    inertia, 114, 115
    for operating system touch behavior, 128
    in Ribbon framework, 321
    for two-finger taps, 120
flick gestures, 101, 104, 105
Flip-3D, 27–28
Fluent user interface. See Office Fluent user interface
FOLDERID_Libraries, 75, 80, 96
folders, 75–80, 86–87, 89, 95
font size, 231
FontControl, 298, 300–301, 321, 346–347
FOS_FORCEFILESYSTEM flag, 87
FrameReported event, 194–197
free-style mode, pan gestures, 124
frequent destination categories, 45–49

G

galleries, 273, 296, 319, 330–340
GC_AllGESTURES flag, 122
gesture messages
    configuring, 121–124
    decoding, 111–113
    generating, 110
    sending, 107–108
    terminating, 127–128
    in Win32 applications, 111
GESTURECONFIG structure, 121–122, 124
gestures
    basic, 104–105
    complex, 135–136
    compound, 113
    configuring, 121–124
    defined, 8–9
    determing state of, 114
    disabling all, 122
    enabling all, 122
    limitations on default, 127
    Silverlight and, 198
    types of, 110
    using inertia with, 162
get function (getter), 167
GetBounds, 185, 186
GetDeltaManipulation function, 157
GetFolders method, 94
GetGestureInfo function, 111, 112
GetInitialVelocities method, 162
GetItem(index), 185
GetMessageExtraInfo function, 105
GetModuleHandle, 317, 329
GetOpenFileName, 86

GetPosition method, 187
GetReport function, 247–249, 256, 257, 258
GetReportStatus method, 247–248, 256
GetSaveFileName, 86
GetSensorByID method, 208
GetSensorData helper function, 209–210, 223, 225–226
GetSensorID method, 241, 245, 249
Get/SetUICommandProperty, 325
GetStylusInfo method, 188
GetStylusPoints method, 188
GetSystemMetrics function, 129
GetTimeStamp method, 245, 249
GetTouchColor helper function, 133–134
GetTouchInputInfo function, 130–132, 143, 144
GetTouchPoint helper function, 133–134
GetTouchPoints method, 195, 197
GetValue, 245
GF_BEGIN flags, 114, 116, 118
GF_END flags, 114
GF_INERTIA flags, 114, 115
GID_PAN switch, 112, 114, 115, 124
GID_PRESS_AND_TAP value, 121
GID_ROTATE value, 112, 118–119, 122
GID_TWOFINGERTAP, 112, 120, 121
GID_ZOOM, 112, 116, 122, 124
graphics platform, enhanced, 13–15
grid control, 154–155
group containers, 272, 291, 293
grouping
   related tasks son jump lists, 44–45
   windows on single taskbar button, 31
gutters, 123–124

H

handleLoad function, 189
handwriting recognition, 128, 131, 182
hardware
   Sensor and Location platform, 204
   touch-sensitive, 107, 129
   Windows 7, 16
   Windows Media Center, 1
HelpButton control, 290
hit surface areas, on taskbars, 103
hit testing, 137
HitTest method, 185, 186
HKEY_CLASSES_ROOT registry hive, 46–47
Home tab, 271, 292
horizontal pan gestures, 110, 123–124
HRESULT GetValue method, 330
HSB (hue, saturation, brightness) method, 351
hue, 351
HWND handle, 128, 147, 274

I

ICivicAddressReport interface, 244, 246, 251–253
iconReference element, 81–82, 98
icons
   controlling library, 98
   Internet Explorer, 22
   taskbar overlay, 4, 25–26, 29, 32, 35–36
ICustomDestinationList interface, 48–56
ID parameters, 144, 208
IDefaultLocation interface, 243–244
idle systems and CPU usage, 379
IFileDialog, 86–87
IFileOperation interface, 26, 39–40
ILatLongReport interface, 244–246, 249
ILocation interface, 239–242, 247, 256
ILocationEvents interface, 251–253, 258
ILocationReport interface, 244–245, 248–249, 252–253, 258
image size and DPI setting, 288
images
   changing control, 326–327
   gesture-enabled, 166, 167–170
   ownership of, 327
   in Ribbon framework, 273, 278–284, 286
   thumbnail, 58, 63–65, 68
IManipulationEvents interface, 137–140, 146–148
indexing, folder, 74
inertia, 111, 115, 123
   processors, 106, 136, 144–151
   timer, 148–149
   using, with gestures, 161–163
InertiaProcessor interface, 151
InitializeFramework, 311, 312–313, 315, 318
initializing
   inertia, 151
   manipulation, 142–143, 151
   performance counters, 359
   Ribbon framework, 311–313
   sensors, 208–209
Ink
   annotations, 182–184, 191–192
   classes, 184–188
   programming, 189–194
InkPresenter, 182–185, 188–190
input messages, 105–108
InRibbonGallery, 296
instrumentation tools, 362–369
Intent UI, 282
Internet Explorer, 6, 22, 26
Internet Explorer 8, 66–70
InvalidateRect, 114–115, 117–121, 135, 144, 148
InvalidateUICommand, 323–324, 328, 350
IObjectCollection, 51–54
IPortableDeviceValues interface, 221
IPropertyStorage interface, 90
IPropertyStore interface, 34–35, 53–54, 90, 344–345, 351–352

ISensor interface, 218–219, 222
ISensorCollection, 208, 209–210
ISensorDataReport interface, 222–224, 225, 227
ISensorEvents interface, 211, 222, 224–225, 226–227
ISensorManager interface, 207–211, 214–215
ISensorManagerEvents interface, 208, 210
IShellFolder interface, 90, 92–93
IShellItem interface, 49–52, 90, 91–93, 96
IShellItemArray, 94
IShellLibrary, 85, 91–97
IShellLink, 49, 51–54, 91
IsInverted property, 188
isLibraryPinned element, 81
IsManipulationEnabled attribute, 155, 162, 164, 166
ITaskbarList3 interface, 45, 57, 60–62, 67–68, 91
Item gallery, 339
item ID lists, 73, 89, 90
IUIApplication interface, 310–313, 316–318, 320–321, 342–343, 352
IUICollection interface, 330–331, 335, 338, 350
IUICommandHandler interface, 314–315, 317–322, 325–328, 334, 339–343, 350
IUIContextualUI interface, 349
IUIFramework, 311–314, 316–317, 323, 325, 348–350, 352
IUIImage, 321–322, 327, 328–329, 331–332, 335
IUIImageFromBitmap interface, 326, 327
IUIRibbon, 312, 328, 352–353
IUISimplePropertySet, 324, 328, 330–337, 340–345, 350–351

J

JavaScript, 185–194
jump lists, 5, 22–24, 43–45
  clearing, 52–53
  components of, 44
  constructing custom categories for, 51–52
  creating, 48–49
  destinations, 23, 51
  most recently used files on, 45–49, 350–351
  retrieving items removed by users, 50–51
  tasks, 23
  thumbnail toolbars versus, 26–27
  Window Live Messenger, 23

K

Kernel Transaction Manager, 3
keys, property, 321–332, 336–340, 343–345
Keytip, 284–285, 287, 290, 321
Known Folders, 73–74, 77, 90
KNOWNFOLDERID, 73, 74–75, 94

L

LabelDescription, 284, 286, 287

LabelTitle, 287, 297
latitude, 238, 245, 249
Lat-Long report, 244–245, 248–249
launch surfaces, single, 20, 21
layout templates, 302–304
LayoutRoot, 178–179, 197–198
legacy applications, 18, 104–106, 108–110, 113, 117
libraries
  applications and, 80–88
  creating new, 95–98
  definition files for, 80–83
  deleting, 98–99
  FOLDERID for, 75
  managed code API for, 97–98
  management dialog, 100
  managing, 99–100
  overview, 6–7, 77–79
  shell programming model and, 88–97
license agreements and Ribbon framework, 266–267
light sensors, ambient, 9–10, 208–218, 227–231
lines, drawing, 132–135
LINK.EXE command, 278–279
LINQ to Objects syntax, 364
list-building transactions, 51, 53
live preview. See also Aero Peek
  for child windows, 65–70
  commands and, 319
  customizing, 65–66
  FontControl in, 346
  gallery support for, 273, 330, 339–340
  invalidating, 65
  thumbnails for, 27–28, 59
loading binary markup, 313
LoadSettingsFromStream, 352–353
LoadUI method, 313, 316–318
localizing, the Ribbon, 289
location
  accuracy, 237, 257
  awareness, 233–234
  default, 243–244, 254, 259–260
  event handling, 252–254, 258–259
  platform architecture for, 235–236
  reports, 241, 244–253, 257, 258
Location IDispatch Interface, 236
location information
  getting, 241–242
  printing, 253–254
LocationChanged event, 256–257, 259
LocationChangedEventHandler, 258–259
locationListener class, 257
LocationProvider class, 256–257
LocationReport class, 256, 258
lodctr utility, 358
LODWORD macro, 116–117, 118
longitude, 238, 245, 249
lParam parameter, 111
LUX values, 210, 218, 223–230

M

m_bIsInertiaActive, 141, 147–148
m_pcDrawingObject, 141–142, 148
MainPage.xaml, 178, 194, 196
MainWindow.xaml.cs, 154
manifests, troubleshooting, 371
manipulation
    initializing, 142–143, 151
    moving an object using, 155–158
    of multiple objects, 164–165
    processors, 106, 135–138, 146–147
    rotating an object, 160–161
    scaling an object using, 158–160
    setting up, 138–148
ManipulationCompleted function, 139, 141, 146–148, 171
ManipulationDelta event, 156–159, 161, 164, 166–167, 171
ManipulationDelta function, 139
ManipulationInertiaStarting event, 162, 171
ManipulationMode property, 166, 171
ManipulationPivot property, 171
ManipulationProcessor, 138, 142
ManipulationStarted event, 139–140, 147, 171
ManipulationVelocities, 162–163
maps, 259–260, 347
margins, setting, 150
MatrixTransform, 156–157, 159, 161, 164–167. *See also*
    transformation matrix
menu groups, 294–295
messages
    gesture, 110, 111–113, 121–124, 127–128
    input, 105–108
    raw touch, 107–108, 127–135, 137, 143–144
    taskbar, 57
Microsoft Foundation Class (MFC), 109, 267, 350–351
Microsoft IntelliSense, 276
Microsoft .NET Framework, 5, 86–88, 153–154, 360
Microsoft Office
    Fluent User Interface, 263, 265, 266–267, 274
    history of, 263–265
    Outlook taskbar button, 20, 22
    Word, 264–265
Microsoft Paint, 267–268, 271–272, 288, 291–293, 296, 348
Microsoft Professional Developer Conference (PDC) 2005, 265
Microsoft Silverlight, 173–179, 189, 198
Microsoft Visual Studio 2008
    event handler code, 194
    resource files in, 82–83
Microsoft Visual Studio 2008 Service Pack (SP1), 267
Microsoft WindowsAPICodePack.Sensors, 211–212, 227, 229
Microsoft WordPad, 267, 269
MinimalRibbon.h header file, 308–309
MinimalRibbon.res, 279
MiniToolbar, 294
modal tabs, 292
mode, application. *See* ApplicationMode

most recently used files, 294, 296, 297, 350–351
    jump lists and, 45–49
    manipulating, from code, 350–351
mouse events, 187–189
mouse inputs, 119–121, 184
MouseEventArgs, 188
multitouch platform
    architecture, 136–137, 145–146
    configuring, without gutters, 124
    legacy applications and, 104–106
Music library, 75, 78–80, 97
My Pictures, 75, 79–80, 97

N

Name property, 187
native programming model, 108
.NET CLR Memory, performance counter, 357
.NET Framework, 193
    obtaining sensors using, 211–212
    touch messages and, 108
.NET Location API, 255–260
Netbooks, 355
network folders, 79
no color value, 341
"No Touch Left Behind" concept, 104
Non-Uniform Memory Access (NUMA) paradigm, 16

O

objects
    global ATL, 307
    implementing application, 310–313
    moving, with pan gesture, 113–114
    moving , using touch, 155–157
    scaling, with zoom gesture, 115–117
    target, 136–138
OCP (Open/Close Principle), 319–320
Office Fluent User Interface. *See* Microsoft Office. Fluent User Interface
offset parameter, 66
OnCreateUICommand, 312, 317–318, 320, 322, 327–328, 343
OnDataUpdated method, 225
OnEvent method, 224
OnLeave method, 225
OnLocationChanged, 252, 254–255
OnSensorEnter method, 210–211, 212–213
OnStateChange method, 225
OnStatusChanged method, 252, 255
OnTouchDownHandler helper function, 131, 132, 133
OnTouchMoveHandler helper function, 132, 134
OnTouchUpHandler helper function, 133, 135
OpenWithProgId subkey, 46
Outlook taskbar button, 20, 22
out-of-browser applications, 179–182

overlay icons, 4, 25–26, 29, 32, 35–36
ownership, image, 327
ownerSID element, 81

P

packs, troubleshooting, 370–371
page-turning applications, 184–185
Paint, 267–268, 271–272, 288, 291–293, 296, 348
paint program, creating a. *See* Scratch Pad application
pan gestures, 104–105, 110, 113–114, 123–124
Paste command, 275–276, 283–286, 293, 322
PDC (Microsoft Professional Developer Conference) 2005, 265
PDH (Performance Data Helpers), 362
perfmon (Performance Monitor) utility, 357–358
performance
    analyzing application, 365–366
    improving system, 372–376
    monitoring system, 355–359
Performance Analyzer (xperf) utility, 365–369
performance counters
    creating logs, 359–362
    overview, 357–359
Performance Data Helpers (PDH), 362
Performance Monitor (perfmon) utility, 357–358
permissions
    enabling location, 239
    requesting location, 242–243
    requesting sensor, 213–218
    for sensors, 203, 207, 220–222
physical disk, performance counter, 357
picture controls, gesture-enabled, 165–170
Pictures library, 75–80, 97
pinching movements, 115–116, 158
pinned categories, 45
PixelFormer, 288
pixel/msec^2 (velocity), 149
POINTS structure, 112, 114–115
PopulatePanel method, 213, 216–217
pop-ups, context, 293–294, 301, 345, 349–350
power management, 378–382
powercfg.exe utility, 381
Powershell, 362, 365, 371
presentation models, 175
press-and-tap gestures, 102, 119–121
PressureFactor property, 187
preview verbs, 319, 334, 340, 341, 345
previews
    live. See live preview
    print, 292
    thumbnails, 63–65, 68–69
primary touch points, 132
print preview, 292
PrintCivicAddress, 252–253, 258
PrintLatLongReport, 249, 253

privacy, 203, 214–216
privileges
    removal of service, 377
    standard user and administrative, 57–58
Problem Steps Recorder, 17
Process functions
    inertia, 148
    manipulation, 144
Process WMI class, 364
ProcessDown helper function, 143, 144
ProcessMove helper function, 114, 115, 143, 144
processors
    inertia, 106, 136, 144–151
    manipulation, 106, 135–138, 146–147
ProcessPressAndTap function, 121
ProcessRotate helper function, 119
ProcessTime function, 147
ProcessTwoFingerTap function, 120
ProcessUp helper function, 143, 144, 146
ProcessZoom helper function, 117
profilers, 366–369
profiles. *See* user profiles
programming
    declarative, 275
    models, 104–107
progress bars, 26, 35–40
properties
    for gallery types, 331–332
    of, the Ribbon, 318–324
    of sensors, 206, 219–220
property element syntax, 275–276
property sets, 318
property store, 90
Propvariant structure, 90, 224, 245
providers, writing WMI, 364–365
proxy windows, 59, 66–70
pTIArray, 132
ptsLocation, 112, 114–119

Q

QAT (Quick Access Toolbar), 270–271, 296–297, 350, 352
Qualibyte Software, 288
QueryInterface method, 248–249, 253
Quick Access Toolbar (QAT), 270–271, 296–297, 350, 352
Quick Launch toolbar, 20–21, 29

R

radians/msec^2 (angular velocity), 149
raw touch messages, 127–135, 143–144
    handling, using manipulation and inertia processors, 137
    registering windows for, 129
    sending and receiving, 107–108
    unpacking, 129–132
RC.EXE tool, 278

readability, 10, 230–231
ready state, of sensors, 214, 225–226
recent items, 45–49, 294, 350–351
RecordedTV library, 75
Red, Green, Blue (RGB) method, 351
RegisterForReport method, 251–252
RegisterTouchWindow function, 128, 129
RegisterWindowMessage messages, 58
Reliability Monitor, 17
remote control functionality, 56–59
RemovedDestinations property, 51
Render Transform, 156, 157
report time interval, 220–222
REPORT_ACCESS_DENIED, 247
REPORT_ERROR, 247
REPORT_INITIALIZING, 247
REPORT_NOT_SUPPORTED, 247
REPORT_RUNNING, 247, 248–249
REPORT_TYPES, 242
ReportInterval property, 256, 257
reports, location, 241, 244–253, 257, 258
ReportStatus property, 256–258
ReportStatus.Running, 257, 258
RequestPermission method, 214–217, 242–243
RequestPermission property, 256
resident tabs, 271–272
Resource Compiler, 278–279
resource files, 82, 278, 288, 313, 315
Restart and Recovery, 3
results-oriented design, 266
RGB (Red, Greeen, Blue) method, 351
Ribbon
    background color, 350
    building the, 301–307
    minimal, 279–282, 308–313
Ribbon framework, 10–13, 266
    components of, 270–272
    controlling scaling behavior in, 304
    creating Ribbon, 315
    flags argument, 321
    initiating sequence diagram, 316
    resource files, 278
    storing and loading Ribbon state, 350–351
Ribbon Image Resource Format, 288
RibbonExplorer, 282, 289
Ribbon.QuickAccessToolbar, 296–297
Ribbon.SizeDefinition, 305–306
ROOT.CIMV2 sub-namespace, 364
rotate gestures, 113, 117–119, 160–161
rotation angles, 115, 118–119, 139

S

saturation, 346, 351
save locations, default, 79, 87–88, 97–98
SaveSettingsToStream method, 352–353

ScaleAt function, 159, 161, 165, 167
scaleDelta, 139, 140, 142
scaling
    gestures, 158–160
    objects, 115–117
    objects, using touch, 158–160
    readability and, 231
sc.exe utility, 374, 376
schema files, Windows Ribbon markup, 276
Scratch Pad application, 132–135
screens, 50
ScreenToClient function, 114, 116–117, 119
scripting model, 236
scripts, Powershell, 371
scrolling, 106, 110, 113
SDK (Windows 7 Software Development Kit). See Windows 7
    Software Development Kit (SDK)
Search, Windows, 77, 79, 89
search filters, 76
search function, 6, 74–77, 88
searchConnectorDescription element, 81–82
searchConnectorDescriptionList element, 81–82
security, 203, 216
    of location information, 238–239
    services, 377–378
sender, 156
Sensor and Location platform, 9–10, 202
    architecture, 204–205
sensor h files, 205, 212, 245
sensorapi.h files, 205, 218
SensorCategories class, 212
Sensor.DataReportChangedEventHandler, 229
SensorManager class, 211–213, 227
SensorManager_SensorsChanged function, 213
SensorManager.RequestPermission method, 217
SensorPropertyKeys class, 212, 219–220, 228
sensors, 201–202, 205, 218–230
    ambient light, 9–10, 208–218, 227–231
    class extensions, 212–213, 227–228, 236
    integrating, into applications, 207–230
    location-based, 202–203, 235–236
    obtaining, 207–213
    virtual, 204, 236
sensorsapi.h files, 205, 218
SensorsChanged event, 213
sensors.h files, 205, 212, 220, 245
SensorState event, 216
separators, 44, 53–56
serialized element, 82
Server Explorer, 363
servers, names of, in title bars, 182
service privilege removal, 377
service SIDs, 377
session 0 isolation, 377
set function (setter), 167
SetColor method, 134
SetCurrentProcessExplicitAppUserModelID function, 33

SetElasticBoundaries function, 141, 148, 150
SetEventSink method, 209–210, 215, 226
SetFolderType method, 97
SetGestureConfig, 121–122, 124
SetIcon method, 96
SetImage method, 64, 69
SetInertia function, 148–149
SetModes method, 348
SetOption method, 96–97
SetThumbnailClip method, 61
SetThumbnailTooltip method, 60
SetTimer helper function, 149
setting
    Ribbon background color, 350
    Ribbon property values, 321
    sensor event sinking, 226–227
    sensor property values, 220–222
SetUICommandProperty method, 325, 349
SHAddFolderPathToLibrary, 94, 95–96
SHAddToRecentDocs Win32 API, 48
SHChangeNotifyRegister function, 100
SHCONTF_FOLDERS flags, 93
SHCONTF_NAVIGATION_ENUM flags, 93
SHCONTF_NONFOLDERS flags, 93
SHCreateItemFromIDList function, 90–91
SHCreateItemFromParsingName function, 90–91
SHCreateLibrary function, 91, 94, 95–96
Shell, Windows, 45–49, 78–79, 88–97
ShellLibrary.DefaultSaveFolder property, 97–98
SHFileOperation function, 26, 39
SHGetDesktopFolder function, 90
SHGetKnownFolderItem function, 90, 92, 93
SHGetPropertyStoreForWindow function, 34, 35
shift property, 187
SHLoadLibraryFromItem function, 91, 94
SHLoadLibraryFromKnownFolder function, 91, 93–94
SHLoadLibraryFromParsingName function, 91, 94
Shobjidl.h header file, 91, 95
ShowAtLocation method, 349
ShowManageLibraryUI function, 99
SHRemoveFolderPathFromLibrary function, 94
SHResolveFolderPathInLibrary function, 94–95
SHSaveLibraryInFolderPath function, 95
Silverlight, 173–179, 189, 198
size definition, 293, 303–304
sizing, thumbnail, 64–65
SM_DIGITIZER, 129
spinner controls, 289, 290–291, 303, 322, 325–326
SplitButton controls, 285, 293, 295, 321, 348
SplitButtonGallery, 296, 303, 321, 339
Spy++ utility, 273–274
StandardColors, 341
Start menu, 4, 22–24, 43–44, 179, 182. *See also* jump lists
static containers, 291
status
    conveying, 35
    location updates, 240

    report, 256–258
StatusChanged property, 257
Sticky Notes, 5
stopping thumbnail previews, 64
string tables, 278–279, 289
Stroke, 184, 185–186, 188
StrokeCollection, 184, 185, 188
strokes, 184, 185–186
    creating, 132–134, 188–193
    finding individual, 134
    removing, 134–135
StylusPoint, 184, 186–187
StylusPointCollection, 184–186, 188, 190
StylusPoints property, 186
surface platforms, 8, 20, 21, 103
switch statements, 109–112, 114, 116, 118, 120, 315–316
Symbol attributes, 284, 287
synchronizing library files, 99–100
system notification area (system tray), 21, 25, 29
System.Diagnostic namespace, 360
System.Management namespace, 363, 364
System.Windows, 195

T

tabbed-document interface (TDI) applications, 28
TabbedThumbnail, 62, 64, 69
TabbedThumbnailPreview, 64, 69
TabbedThumbnail.SetImage method, 64
TabbedThumbnail.TabbedThumbnailBitmapRequested
    event, 64
TabGroup, 292
Tablet PCs, 107–108, 109, 184, 194
tabs, contextual, 272, 291–293, 348–349
Tab.ScalingPolicy, 290, 304, 306
tap gestures, 119–121
task lists, 53–56
Task Scheduler, 372–373
task triggers, 372–376
taskbar
    buttons, 22, 41
    design goals of, 21
    destination categories and, 48
    organizing, 6
    overlay icons, 4, 25–26, 29, 32, 35–36
    overview, 4–6
    progress control values and, 36–40
    redesign considerations, 19–20
    tasks, 44
TaskbarManager class, 45
TaskbarManager.Instance.ApplicationID property, 51
TaskbarManager.Instance.TabbedThumbnail property, 64–
    65, 69
TaskbarManager.Instance.ThumbnailToolbars property, 59
tasks
    jump list, 23

scheduled, 372–373
taskbar, 44
user, 44–45
TCPv4, performance counter, 357
TDI (tabbed-document interface) applications, 28
templateInfo element, 82
templates, layout, 302–303
testing
commands in Ribbon Framework, 283
enhanced default location provider, 259–260
hit, 137
location-aware console application, 254–255
for multitouch capabilities, 129
text
custom, 65
tab, 272
ThemeColors, 341
ThumbBarAddButtons method, 57, 59
ThumbBarUpdateButtons method, 58
THUMBBUTTON structure, 57
thumbnail toolbars, 26–27, 56–59
thumbnails, live window
clipping, 61–62
customizing, 59–66
overview, 27–28
sizing, 64–65
switching in child windows, 66–70
ToolTips, 60
timers, setting
for inertia, 148–149
for two-finger taps, 120
timestamps, 144
ToggleButton controls, 290, 325
toolbars
ContextPopup mini, 293–294, 301
quick access, 270–271, 296–297, 348
quick launch, 20–21
thumbnail, 26–27, 56–59
TooltipDescription, 284, 287
tooltips, 60, 272
TooltipTitle, 284, 287
Toub, Stephen, 39
touch, 8–9, 101
applications, 194–198
feedback for all, 104
messages. See raw touch messages
screens, 184
touch points
coordinates. See coordinates, touch point
ending, 134–135
hit testing, 137–138
number of simultaneous, 129
removal of, 134–135
in single-touch system, 195
tracking, 132
tracking IDs, 132–135
TouchFrameEventArgs, 194–195, 197

TOUCHINPUT structures, 130–131
tracking fingers on multitouch screen, 196–198
trajectory, 146–148, 162
tranform objects, 156
transformation, 113
transformation matrix, 106, 136, 138. See also
MatrixTransform
Translate method, 157
translation property, 157
translationDeltaX and translationDeltaY parameters, 139,
140, 142
translations, 139–140, 142, 159
trigger start services, 372–376
Troubleshooting platform (TSP), 1, 17, 369–371
TSP (Troubleshooting platform), 1
two-finger taps, 119–121

U
UI Command Compiler (UICC). See UICC (UI Command
Center).exe; UICC (UI Command Center).xsd schema
UI_COMMANDTYPE, 312, 314–315, 320–321, 328
UI_CONTEXTAVAILABILITY, 322, 348–349
UI_EXECUTIONVERB_CANCELPREVIEW, 319, 334, 340, 341,
345
UI_EXECUTIONVERB_EXECUTE, 319, 334, 340, 341, 345
UI_EXECUTIONVERB_PREVIEW, 319, 334, 340, 341
UI_HSBCOLOR, 346, 351
UI_INVALIDATIONS, 323–324, 325, 328
UI_MAKEAPPMODE(x) macro, 347
UI_OWNERSHIP, 327, 329
UI_PKEY properties, table of, 321–322
UI_PKEY_ContextAvailable, 348–349
UI_PKEY_FontProperties, 346
UI_PKEY_ItemsSource properties, 336
UI_PKEY_SelectedItem properties, 336
UI_SWATCHCOLORTYPE, 341, 345
UICC (UI Command Center).exe, 277–278, 281, 284, 287,
289
UICC (UI Command Center).xsd schema, 276, 304
UIElement, 171, 217–218
UIInitPropertyFromString function, 324
UIPI (User Interface Privilege Isolation), 57
UIRibbon.h header file, 320
UIRibbonPropertyHelpers.h header file, 324
ullArguments
defined, 112
in pan gestures, 115
in press-and-tap gestures, 121
in rotate gestures, 118
in two-finger taps, 120
in zoom switch, 116–117
UMDF (User Mode Driver Framework), 204
UpdateProperty method, 318, 322, 324–329, 334–335, 338,
350
url element, 81–82

user expectations, 75–76, 104, 174, 355, 369
User Experience (UX), 174–175, 182, 347
User Interface Privilege Isolation (UIPI), 57
user interfaces
  intent, 282
  light-aware, 202
  Microsoft Office Fluent, 263, 265, 266–267, 274
  separation from code, in Windows Ribbon framework, 275
  Silverlight, 173, 178–179
  taskbar, 4
  Windows Vista, 20, 267–269
  XML (Extensible Markup Language) and, 12, 275
user manipulations, 164
User Mode Driver Framework (UMDF), 204
user profiles, 74, 75, 79
user tasks, 44–45, 53–56
user32 controls, 273–274
UX (User Experience), 174–175, 182, 347

V

velocity, 146–149, 163
verbs, execution, 319, 339–340, 346
version element, 81
vertical pan gestures, 110, 123–124
Videos library, 75, 78, 80, 97
View tab, 271, 292
Virtual Earth maps, 259–260
virtual folders, 89
Virtual Light Sensor application, 218, 231
virtual sensors, 204, 236
Visual Studio 2008, 194–195
  schema file, Windows Ribbon markup, 276
  Silverlight tools in, 176–178
Visual Studio 2008 Service Pack (SP1), 267
Visual Studio 2010, 153–155, 165–166
  MFC Ribbon

W

Web applications, 173–174, 177–179
Wi-Fi triangulation, 236
WIM (Windows Integrity Mechanism), 57
Win32 functions, 5, 40, 109, 111, 376
window application ID, 48
window handles, 35–36
window messages, 5
window switching, 28
windows
  proxy top-level, 66–70
  setting application ids for, 34–35
Windows 7
  new features of, 1
  setting up for touch messaging, 127–129
Windows 7 Ribbon framework, ch11

Windows 7 Software Development Kit (SDK), 113, 266
  integrating into Visual Studio, 279–280
  Windows Performance Toolkit, 365–367
Windows 7 Training Kit for Developers, 70, 377
Windows API Code Pack, 5, 45
  JumpList.RemovedDestinations property, 51
  location sensor in, 255
  obtaining sensors using, 211–212
  reading sensor data using, 227–228
  removed items and Jump List applications, 51
  TaskbarManager.Instance.ThumbnailToolbars property, 59
  Windows Presentation Foundation (WPF) UIElement objects, 64
Windows Explorer, 22, 73–79, 82
Windows Forms applications, 36, 64
Windows Ink Services Platform Table Input Subsystem (WISPTIS), 107–108, 127, 137
Windows Integrity Mechanism (WIM), 57
Windows Live Messenger, 5, 23
Windows Management Instrumentation (WMI), 362–365
Windows Media Center, 1
Windows Media Player, 22, 78–79
Windows Performance Analyzer, 365–369
Windows Performance Toolkit, 16, 365–369
Windows Photo Viewer, 105, 124
Windows Powershell, 362, 365, 371
Windows Presentation Foundation (WPF) applications
  creating, in Microsoft Visual studio, 153–154
  obtaining window handles, 36
  Ribbon license agreement, 266–267
  UIElement objects, 64, 170–171
  User Control library, 165
Windows Ribbon framework, ch11
  layout of, 277
  markup language, 275–276
  programming, 274–306
Windows Search, 77, 79, 89
Windows services, 5, 372–377
Windows Shell, 45–49, 78–79, 88–97
Windows Troubleshooting Pack Designer utility, 370
Windows Troubleshooting Platform, 369–370
Windows Vista, 101
  auto-start services, 373–374Bridge Power Manager, 379
  changes since, 1–2
  common file dialog and libraries, 85–86
  file storage in, 73–74
  service security features, 377–378
  Start menu, 43–44
  task triggers in, 372–376
  thumbnails, 28
  user interfaces, 20, 267–269
  Windows Explorer in, 76
Windows7.Location, 256
WinMain entry point, 142, 151
WISPTIS (Windows Ink Services Platform Table Input Subsystem) process, 107–108, 127, 137

wizards, troubleshooting, 371
WM_ACTIVATE, 68–69
WM_ACTIVATE messages, 58
WM_CLOSE, 68
WM_COMMAND, 57
WM_COMMAND messages, 58
WM_CREATE, 63, 67, 68, 313
WM_DWMSENDICONICLIVEPREVIEWBITMAP messages, 58, 65
WM_DWMSENDICONICTHUMBNAIL, 63, 68
WM_DWMSENDICONICTHUMBNAIL messages, 58
WM_DWMSENDICONLIVEPREVIEWBITMAP, 68
WM_DWMSETICONICTHUMBNAIL, 64
WM_GESTURE messages, 108–111, 127–128
WM_GESTURENOTIFY messages, 122
WM_SYSCOMMAND messages, 58
WM_TIMER messages, 148
WM_TOUCH messages, 106, 108, 128, 129–132, 143–144
WMI (Windows Management Instrumentation), 362–365
WMI Query Language (WQL), 363
WndProc function, 108–109, 111, 129
WordPad, 267, 269
WPF (Windows Presentation Foundation) applications
   creating, in Microsoft Visual studio, 153–154
   obtaining window handles, 36
   Ribbon license agreement, 266–267

UIElement objects, 64, 170–171
User Control library, 165
WQL (WMI Query Language), 363

X

XAML (Extensible Application Markup Language), 173
   adding ellipses, 194
   adding InkPresenter, 188
   basic window code, 154
   changing grid to canvas, 194
   for gesture-enabled picture control, 165–168
   matrix transformation, 156
   multiple object manipulation, 164
   Silverlight and, 173, 178–179
   window manipulation, 162
XML (Extensible Markup Language)
   library definition files, 80–83, 95, 99
   user interfaces and, 12, 275
xperf (Performance Analyzer) utility, 365–369

Z

zoom factor, 117
zoom gestures, 105, 108, 113, 115–117, 124

About the Authors

Yochay Kiriaty is a technical evangelist at Microsoft, focusing on Windows. He has more than a decade of experience in software development and management and has written and taught academic computer science courses. He is also the main contributor to the official Windows 7 Developers blog (*http://windowsteamblog.com*) and has written several articles in various media.

Sasha Goldshtein is a Microsoft Visual C# MVP, senior consultant and instructor for Sela Group, and leader of the Performance and Debugging team in the Sela Technology Center. He consults on various topics—including production debugging, application and system troubleshooting, performance optimizations, distributed architecture and others—and likes to speak about these subjects at various Microsoft conferences. Sasha's experience revolves around managed and native application development in C#, C++, and C++/CLI; designing interoperability solutions; architecting multitier high-performance and high-scalability systems; and finding the solutions to "impossible" problems in the field. Sasha has authored multiple Sela training courses, including courses for Windows Internals, .NET Performance and Debugging, and Windows 7.

You can find Sasha's blog at *http://blogs.microsoft.co.il/blogs/sasha*.

Laurence Moroney is a senior product manager at Microsoft, focusing on the Microsoft Web Platform, Silverlight, and the user experience. He has more than a decade of experience in software development, architecture, and implementation and has written more books than he can count on subjects as diverse as Silverlight, ASP.NET, security, and Java interoperability.

Alon Fliess is a Microsoft Visual C++ MVP, and the CTO of Sela Group. He works as a technological leader for various projects and is an expert in Microsoft technologies. Alon speaks at conferences about Windows development, the internals of Windows, C++, and software architecture. He also has co-authored Sela training courses on these subjects. He led the team that developed the Windows 7 training materials for Microsoft DP&E and participated in the writing of the Windows 7 Training Kit and application-compatibility materials for Windows 7. Alon has a Computer Engineering B.Sc. degree from Technion, the Israeli Institute for Technology.

Alon's blog can be found at *http://blogs.microsoft.co.il/blogs/alon*.

What do you think of this book?

We want to hear from you!

To participate in a brief online survey, please visit:

microsoft.com/learning/booksurvey

Tell us how well this book meets your needs—what works effectively, and what we can do better. Your feedback will help us continually improve our books and learning resources for you.

Thank you in advance for your input!

Stay in touch!

To subscribe to the *Microsoft Press® Book Connection Newsletter*—for news on upcoming books, events, and special offers—please visit:

microsoft.com/learning/books/newsletter